Texts and Studies in Medieval and Early Modern Judaism

Edited by

Ivan G. Marcus · Peter Schäfer

28

Rachel S. Mikva

Midrash vaYosha

A Medieval Midrash on the Song at the Sea

Mohr Siebeck

RACHEL S. MIKVA, born 1960; 1982 graduated from Stanford University (BA); 1990 ordained by Hebrew Union College/Jewish Institute of Religion; 2003 doctoral studies at Jewish Theological Seminary, 2005–09 teaching at Jewish Theological Seminary; 2008 doctorate awarded; 2009 appointed Rabbi Herman A. Schaalman Chair in Jewish Studies at Chicago Theological Seminary.

ISBN 978-3-16-151009-0
ISSN 0179-7891 (Texts and Studies in Medieval and Early Modern Judaism)

Die Deutsche Nationalbibliothek lists this publication in the Deutsche Nationalbibliographie; detailed bibliographic data are available on the Internet at *http://dnb.d-nb.de.*

The book was printed by Gulde-Druck in Tübingen on non-aging paper and bound by Buchbinderei Spinner in Ottersweier.

Printed in Germany.

Acknowledgements

This volume is an outgrowth of my doctoral research at the Jewish Theological Seminary (JTS). I am deeply grateful to the Graduate School of JTS and the Charles H. Revson Foundation for supporting me academically and financially during my studies, and to the staff of the Library and Rare Book Room for their generous assistance. Thanks are also due to the Institute for Microfilmed Hebrew Manuscripts at Hebrew University and to the libraries that hold the manuscripts of *Midrash vaYosha*, for facilitating access to microfilm copies. Their foresight in collecting and grace in sharing such treasures from the past make scholarship possible.

My teachers and colleagues, Alan Cooper, David Kraemer, Marjorie Lehman and Avigdor Shinan read the work as a dissertation and their insights provided valuable direction for its ultimate revision. The small circle of scholars who have devoted attention to this midrash, including Günter Stemberger and Elisabeth Wies-Campagner, have been most generous in sharing their expertise.

I can scarcely articulate the tremendous debt of gratitude I owe to my doctoral advisor, Burton Visotzky. His patient wisdom, prodigious scholarship and remarkable kindness have been blessings in my life from the day I met him. He has become a treasured colleague and friend.

Drs. Stemberger and Visotzky graciously lent their careful eyes and inspiring breadth of knowledge in reading through this work, and the volume is better for it. Any errors that remain, of course, are my own responsibility.

Chicago Theological Seminary has been my community for the last two years, providing a home in which to share my love of rabbinic literature. I am inspired by its commitment to the notion that religious leaders and teachers in our multifaith context must know something about a religious tradition other than their own. I am grateful for the supportive environment and for the abiding challenge to draw the past into critical conversation with contemporary issues.

For my teachers and my students,
with deep appreciation for the fact that they are often one and the same.

Table of Contents

Chapter 1

Introduction

A. *Midrash vaYosha* and the Genre of Minor Midrash

Relatively short midrashim focusing on a brief biblical narrative or section were composed in large numbers during the medieval period, and their extant manuscripts are sufficient in number to demonstrate the great popularity of the genre. Thanks to the collections of nineteenth- and early twentieth-century scholars such as Adolph Jellinek, Solomon Wertheimer, and J.D. Eisenstein, numerous texts are available in print.[1] The midrashim have not, however, garnered as much attention as the anthologies of the Middle Ages, e.g. *Tanḥuma, Yalkut Shimoni, Midrash haGadol*. Many of the shorter works lack any in-depth critical treatment, and there is much still to learn about the nature of this genre, its shaping forces and purposes.

Generally identified as "minor midrashim" (describing their length, not their significance), these works frequently have a tenuous connection to exegesis. They may involve a biblical character, motif, or smattering of verses, but present texts that appear to be narrative more than interpretive. Thus, scholars classify them with other late midrashim that share this narrative quality. In truth, however, there is a range of material. There are frame-stories and unitary tales, emulations of biblical Hebrew style and hints of Arabic influence, compilations of classical midrash and reworkings of folk traditions, single manuscripts and multiple recensions. They may contain a great deal of exegesis or very little. Some are lemmatic[2] and others are not; some focus on a single book of the Bible or an individual story, while others are organized thematically (odd spellings, teachings grouped by number, letters of the alphabet, tales of the ten tribes, contrasts in the world, etc.). They may be mystical, homiletical, "historical," apocalyptic or theological. Composed over more than 500 years in different regions, it is difficult to generalize about these varied midrashim.

This study undertakes a close examination of *Midrash vaYosha* (MV), a medieval rabbinic text which explicates the Song at the Sea (Ex 15:1–18) and the events of the exodus from Egypt leading up to that climactic moment. Linked to the special recitation of the song on the seventh day of Passover, the exegesis begins with the last two verses of Exodus 14 (30–31). *Vayosha*, the first word of verse 30, reflects both a medieval name for the holy day and the title of the midrash: ויושע יי' ביום ההוא את-ישראל מיד מצרים – *Thus the Lord delivered Israel that day from the hand of Egypt.*

Organized in lemmatic form, the midrash exists in at least two early recensions. One appears to be a rather conventional adaptation of exegetical traditions (Recension A), and the other is significantly longer with elaborate narratives and additional literary characteristics (Recension B). Both were first published in Constantinople in 1519, but the latter is the one that has continued to circulate in print.

Midrash vaYosha is of special interest for several reasons. The rich textual record (34 extant Hebrew manuscripts and fragments)[3] reaches across cultures and continents, allowing for a detailed analysis of its geographical and chronological journey. Multiple manuscript families reveal an ongoing evolution that may trace several significant stages of midrash in the Middle Ages. Copied into *maḥzorim* as well as collections of midrash and miscellanies, the text indicates a connection with the synagogue at a certain point in its development. Its balance of exegetical and narrative purposes illuminates the integration of these modes of discourse – and it offers creative, compelling interpretations of biblical text.

Many of MV's motifs can be found in earlier rabbinic literature, including *Mekhilta, Targum, Pirqe Rabbi Eliezer* and *Tanḥuma*, but they are collected and expanded in unique ways. As Daniel Boyarin states regarding all midrashic texts, it is a "mosaic of conscious and unconscious citations of earlier discourse."[4] The manner in which MV continually reshapes this discourse is key to understanding its character, purposes, and evolution.

Recently, scholars have begun to "rediscover" previously neglected medieval midrashim, and two valuable treatments of *Midrash vaYosha* have been published.[5] Günter Stemberger offers a detailed summary of the content and structure of the text, utilizing Recension B (*editio princeps*). He includes some of the rabbinic sources and later parallels, along with brief discussion of the language, style, mythological elements, character portrayal and emphasis on narrative evident in the midrash.[6] His student, Elisabeth Wies-Campagner, contributes a dissertation-*cum*-book that addresses the need for critical analysis of the manuscripts. She presents seventeen manuscripts copied before the first printed editions, compiles critical sections in synoptic form for comparison, and provides German translation of the two recensions with major textual variants.[7] Each work offers some degree of literary and historical analysis.

My own study advances the project, training the tools of textual, historical and literary criticism on *Midrash vaYosha* to mine it for all it can tell us about itself and about medieval Jewish exegesis. Beginning with textual and historical criticism, there is a comprehensive review of extant manuscripts and genizah fragments. The consequent stemmatic analysis pays particular attention to narrative variation, geographical and chronological distribution, and literary setting of the text within the manuscripts. Combined with insights gleaned from linguistic and folklore studies, texts describing *halakha* and *minhag*, and other Jewish literature, these details can reveal a lot about the evolution of the text and its *Sitz im Leben*. They also provide enticing hints regarding the directions of exegesis in diverse Jewish cultures. By tracing the journey of *Midrash vaYosha*, this volume explores the relationship of midrash to synagogue homily and Targum, the evolution of a text through its written transmission and re-oralization, and the changing dimensions of narrative within midrash.

Much of what we can learn comes from a close reading of the text itself. The earliest quality manuscript of each recension serves as the basis for translation and comparison. Within the annotation and commentary, there are biblical citations, textual parallels (Jewish and non-Jewish), noteworthy variants and other comments – especially the exegetical logic of the interpretation when it can be discovered. As James Kugel points out, texts framed as midrash are at least "formally" exegesis.

> However they may come into existence... they do not come into existence as mere stories, floating around the biblical text, or only subsequently come to be attached, more or less at random, to this or that biblical verse. From the start they are presented as illuminating, bringing out the hidden implications of, something that *is* in the biblical text.[8]

Sometimes their interpretive character must be ferreted out, hunting through the intertextual imagination to discover how the path of hermeneutics leads to such a creative reading. In the end, the puzzle frequently delights as much as the exegesis itself.

But they are also stories. Analysis of the narrative component, especially in Recension B, is critical to an appreciation of the literary artistry of this midrash. Exploration of character, language, imagery, tone and narrative structures throughout the annotation and commentary enhances our understanding of the text. Of special interest is the "synergy of narrative and exegesis"[9] that typifies this stage of midrash.

Because the text is part of an ongoing engagement with the Bible and rabbinic literature, certain themes must be fleshed out in order to discern their significance. These and other elements that require more extended discussion comprise the sections of commentary. Each topic is set in proximity to the pericope that most embodies the theme, although it frequently arises in more than one place. With this combination of critical lenses, *Midrash vaYosha* reveals the richness of its story.

B. Two Primary Recensions: Differences, Provenance and Dating

In the commonly printed version of the text, one finds a wonderful collection of expanded biblical narratives and imaginative exegesis. While it is still structured in lemmatic form, it appears to say very little about the Song at the Sea. Story comes to dominate the text with the addition of a lengthy narrative on the binding of Isaac (*akeidah*), a vast expansion of Moses' first-person recounting of Divine salvation at work in his own life, a digressive yet somehow cohesive tale of Pharaoh's complete repentance, and a dramatic, detailed unfolding of events at the End of Days.[10] This printed edition represents a significantly different text than the early redaction that took shape in Ashkenaz[11] in the eleventh to twelfth century (Recension A, 11–12th c.).

The provenance of the earlier redaction is established most clearly by the manuscript record. Fifteen of the thirty-four extant Hebrew manuscripts and fragments contain Recension A, twelve of which are specifically copied in an Ashkenazi hand. One Italian and one Byzantine manuscript indicate that the text begins to travel, but these records do not call into question the regional base of the midrash. Only one copy of Recension A is written in the Arabic milieu (N. Africa), and it dates to the seventeenth or eighteenth century, over one hundred years after both redactions were available in print.

Recension A is significantly shorter than the standard printed edition, and its exegesis stays more closely trained on the verses of the Song. A number of clues, including numerous parallels with the expansive Palestinian Aramaic translations, suggest it is likely an outgrowth of the special Targumic-exegetical practice attached to the Torah reading for the seventh day of Passover. MV is included in at least two manuscript *maḥzorim* (one French and one Italian rite), and other manuscripts attach Torah reading notes as found for Targum. Relevant halakhic discussion confirms that expanded explication continues in Ashkenaz with *toseftot* (lit: additions) in poetry and prose, and that Aramaic is sometimes supplanted by Hebrew or vernacular so that everyone can understand and appreciate the miracle. With several manuscript families in Recension A, including one containing large amounts of different narrative and exegetical material, the fluid manuscript record reinforces the notion of synagogue performance, either as supplementary explication to the Targum or its replacement. These substantial variants serve as witness to a continuing relationship between written transmission and re-oralization (see Section D for further discussion).

The later recension, however (Recension B, 12–13th c.), manifests the qualities of a literary redaction. These manuscripts demonstrate remarkable development of narrative, character, emotion, dialogue, irony, and drama – a revolution of literary aesthetics. In addition, the text stabilizes, becomes more regularly titled, has several verbatim parallels in Tanhuma, and is on occasion excerpted with the introduction, "I found in *Midrash vaYosha....*" It also ceases to be found in prayerbooks (see Section E for further discussion).

Stemberger manages, even without access to the manuscripts, to discern that the beginning and ending of Recension B are not original to the midrash. Reasoning from the seams which are evident in the longer text, and from the fact that the oldest extant manuscript does not include the expansions, Stemberger rightly concludes that what is here called Recension B is the later version of *Midrash vaYosha*. He also claims that the notion of martyrdom, central to medieval Jewish identity in Europe, offers a precise historical context for the addition of the *akeidah* near the beginning, with its origin in Ashkenaz after the First Crusade (1095):

> Como es bien conocido, se trata de un motivo que después de la primera cruzada fue de gran importancia para reforzar el sentido religioso de la historia reciente, sobre todo en lo que se refiere a los martirios cuando, ante la alternativa del bautismo o de la muerte, muchos judíos no sólo preferían el suicidio para no caer en manos de los cristianos, sino que incluso mataban a sus propios hijos, que muchas veces consentían de buena voluntad con esta decisión de sus padres (Midráš Wa-yoša‘ y sus paralelos insisten en que Isaac obedecía no sólo a Dios, sino a su padre). Pienso que este contexto histórico es precisamente el de la primera parte del *midráš Wa-yoša‘* y que, en consecuencia, no puede ser anterior al s. XII; su país de origen podría ser Francia o más probablemente Alemania.[12]

Relying on this historical-thematic linkage of the Crusades with Abraham's readiness to sacrifice his son for his faith, Stemberger argues the likelihood of a twelfth-century redaction for all of Recension B, most likely in Germany.[13] Wies-Campagner supports Stemberger's hypothesis and gathers additional historical information. Association with the Crusades has suggestive power; Jewish liturgical poets of Ashkenaz repeatedly use motifs from the tale of Abraham and Isaac as they wrestle with martyrdom, including several that echo the motifs of MV.[14] Although Jewish persecution and martyrdom are not unknown under the aegis of

Islam, it is a far more prevalent theme for medieval Jews living in Christian Europe.

In addition to the credible historical context sketched by Stemberger and Wies-Campagner, I found a piece of tantalizing textual evidence regarding the binding of Isaac narrative. Two of the Ashkenazi manuscripts of MV (Recension A: MSS Drm 25, 14th c.; War 258, 15th c.) contain a separate midrash called *Akeidat Yitzḥak* (The Binding of Isaac), with a very similar tale. The textual witnesses certainly suggest that the midrashic narrative itself developed in Ashkenaz, although there is also a close parallel in the Near Eastern recension of *Tanḥuma* which precedes all these manuscripts, and it is not found in its European counterpart.[15] Motifs or passages found in proximity in one place often become integrated in another,[16] but the presence of *Akeidat Yitzḥak* in Ashkenazi manuscripts cannot prove that it became attached to MV in that context.

A second textual anomaly also relates to this question. A fifteenth-century Byzantine manuscript (Ox 104) contains what the scribe calls a תשלום, a supplement to *Midrash vaYosha*. It transcribes only one portion of MV: Recension B from the beginning up to the exegesis that stands as the start of Recension A, i.e. the story related to the *akeidah* and its introductory frame. Either the scribe did not recognize or care about the multitude of differences further on in Recension B, or they were not in evidence. Since there is no extant complete manuscript that adds the Binding of Isaac narrative but none of the other expansions, the evidence is not sufficient to argue for a distinct stage of development that adds only the *akeidah*.[17] Nonetheless, it is possible given the continuous evolution of the text evident through its multiple manuscript families.

Admitting a degree of uncertainty about the process by which the *akeidah* becomes incorporated in MV, I assert that Recension B is redacted in an Arabic milieu, based on a number of factors, including: the geographical distribution of manuscripts, parallel motifs in Islamic "Lives of the Prophets" (*qiṣaṣ al-anbiya*) literature, minor linguistic changes, early genizah fragments, an increase of supernatural elements and a thematic confluence of apocalyptic imagery.

As with Recension A, the geographic distribution of manuscripts is pronounced. There is not a single Ashkenazi manuscript of MV that contains Recension B until a century after both recensions were published in 1519. In fact, of the nineteen extant manuscripts and fragments containing Recension B or a hybrid, only one is of Ashkenazi origin, from the seventeenth century. The rest are from Sepharad, the Eastern Mediterranean and the Near East.[18]

In addition to the manuscript testimony, there is also literary and linguistic evidence that the transition took place in an Arabic milieu. Reflecting the rich exchange between Hebrew and Arabic legends,[19] many of the themes of MV are found in Islamic tales of biblical figures, including dozens of elements only in Recension B. The motif of Moses and the staff *ad* 15:2, for example, may sound like the romantic theme of King Arthur and Excalibur. It has more similar parallels, however – about Moses – in the history of al-Tabari from tenth-century Persia, as well as *qiṣaṣ al-anbiya* (Tales of the Prophets) by al-Thalabi and al-Kisai in eleventh- to twelfth-century Iraq.[20] Jethro has possession of the staff, which comes to Moses' hand through semi-miraculous means and demonstrates that he is the intended owner. Al-Kisai has the chain of ownership, while the others include a version of the "trial" by which Moses is the one who can raise it from the ground.

The closest parallel (and possible source) is found in *Pirqe Rabbi Eliezer 40*, a link which reinforces the likelihood that this tradition circulated within the Islamic empire. *Pirqe R. El.* has certain references to Islam and other clues that it takes shape in a Muslim milieu, including evidence that retold Bible or exegetical narrative as a genre first reappears in this sphere.[21] Scholars frequently point to midrashic collections such as *Pirqe Rabbi Eliezer* and *Seder Eliahu Rabbah* as evidence that the increased interest in Hebrew narrative emerged out of Islamic culture.[22]

Several Arabisms sneak into the text: e.g., the transformation of פ to ב-phoneme in the term for naphtha: נפט –> נבט (and, later, נבז).[23] Themes of magic, angels and Satan are believed to be more prevalent within the aegis of Islam, and they are certainly more prevalent within Recension B.[24] In addition, there is a good deal of evidence that the eschatological vision incorporated in Recension B was composed in the Near East or North Africa, outside the Northern European origins of *Midrash vaYosha.*

> *Near Eastern* [emphasis added] Jewish, Christian, and Muslim apocalypses of late antiquity and the early medieval era exhibit a series of remarkable structural correspondences that reach across the permeable boundaries of ethnic and religious affiliation. Despite the inevitable individual doctrinal variations, these apocalypses reveal a number of common motifs, dramatis personae, and discursive sequences.[25]

The physical description of the arch-enemy Armilos resembles the figure of the false messiah in Arabic folklore, *al-Dajjal.*[26] Since Recension A does not mention Armilos at all, the integration of this legend is helpful in identifying the place of the new redaction. The *piyyut* and Targumim which mention Armilos are Palestinian in origin, and the geonim who are among the first to cite the tradition are Egyptian/Babylonian. Also, the two identified genizah fragments of *Midrash vaYosha* (from two different manuscripts), providing the earliest textual evidence available from Cairo and its environs, include the Armilos passage.

The text which "seeded" the popularity of these apocalyptic traditions, *Sefer Zerubbabel*, also emerged from the Near East, "rooted within the bitter wars of the 620's [610–630] between Heraclius and the final Sasanian rulers for possession of Syria, Palestine and Egypt."[27] According to Martha Himmelfarb,

> These wars touched Palestine and seem to have stirred some messianic hopes among Jews, including the author of *Sefer Zerubbabel*, for whom the wars appear to be eschatological events leading to the appearance of the Messiah. The work mentions the defeat of the king of Persia and the subsequent victory of the Antichrist, Armilos, who represents Christendom.[28]

The Arab conquest likely further fueled messianic speculation, with the appearance of a kingdom to crush Edom/Christianity.[29] Evidence of Hebrew apocalyptic texts can be found in Ashkenaz around the time of Recension B's appearance.[30] Yet these narratives permeate the Levant to an entirely different degree, spanning the religious spectrum as part of a written discourse with formulaic conventions, tropes and figures.[31]

Apocalyptic themes are not the only narrative traditions to sweep the Near East; collections of short stories like "1001 Nights" and "Kalila waDimna" influence literatures as well. As Hebrew narrative flourishes in this environment, the setting is ripe for a more literary redaction of MV (especially as there is no place for it within synagogue ritual in Sephardi tradition; see Section D). Scholars of medieval folklore and narrative have long tried to confirm a theoretical path of story traditions from the Far East, through Persia, then into the imperial languages of Arabic and eventually Latin.[32] According to Eli Yassif, the crystallization of Hebrew narrative takes place among Jews in the East and then moves into Europe.[33] Narrative developments are unfolding throughout the Jewish world by the time of Recension B. There are shared literary developments bridging the different cultures (not impassable chasms) between East and West, Israel and Babylon, Sephard and Ashkenaz.[34] The cumulative evidence, however, supports a conclusion that Recension B is redacted in an Arab milieu.

Stemberger cites the eleventh-century estimate for redaction found in his update of the classic reference work, *Introduction to the Talmud and Midrash*; the brief description there notes the dependency of MV on *Tanḥuma* and *Chronicles of Moses*, along with the assumption that *Yalkut Shimoni* is familiar with *Midrash vaYosha*.[35] Having recognized different recensions of the midrash in his article, he works to establish a pair of dates. The only early explicit mention of MV is in the Torah commentary (*ad.* Ex 14:10) of Baḥya ben Asher, who states that he saw there the name "Uza" for the angelic prince of Egypt. Since this is a reference found in both recensions, it would yield a late *terminus post quem* for Recension A: the end of the thirteenth century. Stemberger proposes to move it earlier by asserting that Rashi did not seem to know the name, but R. Eleazar of Worms (*c.*1176–1238) did.[36]

According to Wies-Campagner, Recension A is redacted in the eleventh century. She points out that it appears to borrow material from *The Alphabet of Rabbi Akiva*, which she dates to the tenth century, but does not draw from the eleventh-century *Chronicles of Moses* until the later redaction, even though the earliest form of the midrash certainly expresses interest in episodes of Moses' young life. At the same time, she admits that it is risky to argue from the absence of parallels.[37] A conservative reading of the evidence would have to leave open a range between the first part of the eleventh century to the beginning of the thirteenth, when the earliest manuscript is found, although late eleventh–early twelfth century seems most plausible. According to Israel Ta-Shma, "[t]he multifaceted literary creation of Ashkenazi Jewry... had its origins at the turn of the eleventh century," reflecting a broad curriculum that included a great deal of midrash and its explication.[38] MV's composition is likely aligned within the period of this flowering.

Both Stemberger and Wies-Campagner posit the redaction of Recension B in the twelfth century, in large part due to their identification of it as a response to the First Crusade in 1095. Stemberger also mentions various parallels, especially for the eschatological climax (e.g., in *Pesiq. Rab.*, *Secrets of R. Shimon b. Yoḥai*), and struggles to determine clear influences among the midrashim and their direction. Ultimately, he simply deems Recension B to come not much later than the earlier redaction;[39] Wies-Campagner depends more heavily on the historical context she outlines for the twelfth century.

Having challenged their conclusions regarding the geographical origin of the expanded version, I rely on different evidence for dating and expect a slightly longer lag between A and B as it traverses regions. The primary evidence for dating Recension B is based on the manuscript record. There are two ENA genizah fragments of the eschatological conclusion of *Midrash vaYosha*. Due to the limited material, the manuscripts are impossible to date, but they appear to be relatively early, perhaps twelfth-thirteenth century. Since the earliest complete manuscript of Recension B is a fourteenth-century Sephardi text, the conservative estimate of its redaction is the twelfth-fourteenth centuries, but I lean toward the earlier portion of this range.

C. Manuscripts and Stemmatic Analysis

Manuscripts are classified according to their textual similarities, with family names that begin by identifying their recension (A or B). Texts that blend aspects of each recension carry the hybrid marker AB.

Within each recension, there are manuscript families that have varying degrees of distinction from other families and resemblance to kin. Major families simply add a number to the recension identification (e.g. A1, B2), while other groups carry a letter that stands for its identifying difference, detailed below.

The earliest representative of each family serves as the primary model for translation of unique narrative motifs and describing distinctions among families; where that model is seriously lacking and the annotation relies on later members of the family, it is so noted.

Family A1

The early examples of Family A1 establish the basic form of the midrash, also found in one *editio princeps* (Constantinople 1519-A), and as the seed that remains visible within Recension B.

There are a total of seven manuscripts in the base family; each has an interesting piece of the historical puzzle contained within it. The earliest full manuscript of MV on record is MS Oxford – Bodleian Library Or. 135 (Ox 135), written between 1215–1260 in an Ashkenazi hand, most likely from the northern Champagne region of France. It is a generally reliable and legible copy of Recension A, even though the scribe acknowledges he does not have the interpretation for one of the verses. The manuscript serves as the Recension A base-text for this study, with the missing pericope supplied by MS Wolfenbüttel 36.25. As would be expected, it does not contain the narrative expansions or extended eschatological ending found in Recension B; in many regards, the exegesis of this manuscript and its family is most closely linked to the biblical text.

MS Cambridge University Library Add. 667.1 (Cam 667.1, 13–14c. Ashkenazi) is a *mahzor* according to the French rite, which indicates that *Midrash vaYosha* was most likely set there as a homiletical collection for the seventh day of Passover, when the special Torah reading is the Song at the Sea. The manuscript also contains additional Passover material, with numerous midrashic expansions and *piyyutim*.

Although MS Universitäts- und Landesbibliothek Darmstadt Cod. Or. 25 (Drm 25, 14c. Ashkenazi) is a clear example of Recension A, the MV text immediately follows *Akeidat Yitzḥak* (fol. 30v–31r), the brief midrash that recounts many elements of the *akeidah* narrative found in Recension B.[40]

MS Munich Bayerische Staatsbibliothek Cod. Heb. 232 (Mun 232, 14c. Italian) and MS Vatican – Biblioteca Apostolica Ebr. 303 (Vat 303, 13–14c. Ashkenazi-Byzantine) set a mythology of creation via Torah just before MV; the latter links it explicitly to the midrash.[41] It was customary to offer special praise for Torah on the festivals according to the liturgical instructions of MS Parma 2736 (fol. 80v). Paeans to Scripture like this one may have been composed for such a purpose, and thus attached to Torah reading and explication for the holy day.

MS Jewish Theological Seminary 5000 (JTS 5000, 15c. Ashkenazi) is a genre-aware collection of brief midrashim.

All the families of Recension A have a representative from the sixteenth-century or later. MS Cambridge University Library Add. 1505 (Cam 1505, 17–18c. N. African) is interesting because it is the sole example of this recension from the non-European world.

Family A1-ד (ד for דבר אחר; it includes an alternative interpretation)

Late medieval scribes and collectors were aware of the two recensions, as evidenced by MS Wolfenbüttel Cod. Guelf. 36.25 Aug. 2^0 (Wolf 36.25, 13–14c. Ashkenazi). It provides a clear and early example of Family A1, but has several interpretations from Recension B recorded as ד"א (דבר אחר, another interpretation) in the margin in a different hand which cannot be dated with precision. These alternative explications are integrated within the text of a direct descendant manuscript, namely MS Oxford – Bodleian Library Or. 27 (Ox 27, 16c. Ashkenazi), also marked with ד"א. Because the additions of Recension B are separated as a distinct tradition, these manuscripts are still classified as Recension A.

Family A1-ק (ק for הבדלים קטנים, *small* differences).

There is a family of Ashkenazi manuscripts with numerous small differences from Family A1, but still very clearly within the same recension: MS Warsaw Uniwersytet Instytut Orientalistyczny 258 (War 258: 1430), MS Parma – Biblioteca Palatina 2269 (Prm 2269, 15c. Ashkenazi), and MS Oxford – Bodleian Library Opp. 225 (Ox 225, 16c. Ashkenazi).

Family A2

MS Oxford – Bodleian Library Opp. 614 (Ox 614, 13–14c. Ashkenazi) is the earliest representative of a family of manuscripts that adds significant midrashic material which belongs to neither major recension of MV. The other two manuscripts of this family, MS Paris – Bibliothèque nationale de France 335 (Par 335, 16c. Ashkenazi) and Real Biblioteca del Monasterio de El Escorial MS hebreo G-III-11 (Esc G3, 16c. Ashkenazi), each end with a note to the Torah reader in the synagogue: "The reading should continue up to רֹפְאֶךָ" (Ex 15:26). Since this is the end of the Torah reading for the seventh day of Passover, the comment reinforces the link between the midrash and customs related to the conclusion of the holiday. Unfortunately, MS Ox 614 is cut off shortly before the end.[42] Nonetheless, the presence of additional midrashic material alongside synagogue reading notes in this manuscript family conjures the image of a text that is reshaped multiple times by homiletical creativity before it is firmly established as a redacted midrash.

Family AB1

Most interesting of all the manuscripts that likely predate the earliest extant text of Recension B is MS Parma Biblioteca Palatina 2736 (Prm 2736, 14c. Italian), a *maḥzo*r according to the Italian rite. Its context again suggests a synagogue role for MV (to be discussed in Section D). There is a variety of material collected in connection to seventh-day Passover, as there was in the French prayerbook. Following the liturgy for Passover, there are midrashim on the beginning of Exodus (called מילי דפסח – *Milei d'Fesaḥ*) and then מילי דויושע – *Milei d'vaYosha*, which begins with exegetical comments on *Parashat Beshallaḥ* and segues (marked only by enlarged lemmas) to *Midrash vaYosha*. Both MV and the material that precedes it contain numerous elements of Recensions A and B.

Although MS Prm 2736 is classified as a mixed recension, one should not presume that the scribe selected his favorite elements of two established recensions; the parallels with Recension B are approximate and partial. More likely, the midrash continued to be substantially reshaped in oral and written presentation, and the additional material demonstrates that numerous other traditions which eventually were included in MV first circulated in casual collections associated with Passover. Italy, that eclectic, dynamic meeting-place of east and west in the Jewish Middle Ages, seems to draw from numerous traditions.

Family B1

As the first complete extant text of Recension B, MS Paris – Bibliothèque nationale de France 716 (Par 716, 14–15c. Sephardi) was chosen as the base-text for this study, despite a few minor errors. MS Warsaw Zydowski Instytut Historyczny 374 (War 374, 14–15c. Italian) copies MS Par 716 in its entirety, incorporating marginal corrections and repairing some of the scribal errors, but otherwise remarkably similar. For the next two centuries, Recension B is found only in manuscripts that are described by experts as written in Byzantine, Mizraḥi (Eastern),

Sephardic, Babylonian, Italian or Farsi script, strongly indicating that Recension B takes shape outside of the Ashkenazi world.

Family B1-ג (ג for גניזה, genizah)

Corroborating this conclusion is the fact that there are at least two Cairo Genizah fragments containing parts of the expanded eschatological ending. As artifacts of non-European rabbinic textual traditions, these fragments, Jewish Theological Seminary ENA 2934.4–6 (JTS ENA1) and Jewish Theological Seminary ENA 3142.1 (JTS ENA2), represent the earliest textual evidence of Recension B.

Family B2, Family B2-ח (ח for חסר, incomplete)

The other major family of Recension B has numerous but relatively minor differences from the base family; most of the variations are found in passages that are *not* parallel to Recension A, suggesting that the form of the earlier material was relatively well-established. Family B2 presents the text most closely related to the *editio princeps* (Constantinople 1519-B) and several later printed editions.

Although most of the nine extant manuscript copies of this family are *later* than the *editio princeps*, there is one large fragment from the fifteenth century: MS Jewish Theological Seminary 4920 (JTS 4920, Family B2-ח Mizraḥi). It contains material on Ex 15:1–15:15. MS Cambridge University Library Add. 854 (Cam 854, 16–17c. Mizraḥi) might also predate the printed edition, or at least precede its wide circulation. If the cataloguers' analysis of the paleography in MS Budapest Magyar tudomanyos akademia MS Kaufman A167 (Bud A167, 17c. Ashkenazi) is correct, Recension B makes its way back to Askhenaz by the seventeenth century, or at least to the hand of a refugee from Ashkenaz.[43]

One of the most historically significant distinctions of this family is the additional evidence of influence by the Arab milieu. For instance, they transform the deal struck between Jethro and Moses regarding offspring; half are to be יהודי (Jewish) and half ישמאלי (Ishmaelite, i.e. Arab). The shift from בדאי to the synonym with an Arabic cognate (כוזב) may be attributable to the linguistic impact of Arabic. Also, several of the manuscripts contain texts in Judeo-Arabic as well as Hebrew.

Family B-ע (ע for עוד מצאתי, I further found [in *Midrash vaYosha*])
Family B-ת (ת for תשלום, supplement)

Three manuscripts appear to contain aspects of Family B1 and Family B2. They are only fragmentary examples of the midrash, so there is not sufficient material to determine the dominant influence. Two of them, MS

Vatican – Biblioteca Apostolica Ebr. 285 (Vat 285, 14–15c. Byzantine) and MS Montefiore Library 279 (Mon 279, 16c. Italian), contain three segments explicitly cited from *Midrash vaYosha*. Their appearance is intriguing because they are placed in the midst of a shared story anthology, suggesting that the collector was interested in the narrative dimensions of the work.

The third of these manuscripts that blend Family B1 and Family B2 has no peer; it is Oxford – Bodleian Library MS Selden Superius 104 (Ox 104, 15c. Byzantine), specifically described as a תשלום, a supplement to *Midrash vaYosha*. Containing only the interpretations found at the beginning of Recension B before Recension A starts, it indicates that the scribe did not see or did not care about other differences between them, or they were not in evidence.

Family AB2

Moscow – Russian State Library MS Guenzburg 111 (Mos 111, 1462 Sephardi) and Zurich – Zentralbibliothek Zuerich MS Heid. 192 (Zur 192, 1682 Italian) intertwine the recensions of MV. They contain more elements of Recension A than B, but they jump back and forth between recensions without notice (e.g., including the *akeidah* passage but not the expanded version of Moses' tale), and add significant narrative material of their own. Unlike MS Prm 2736, it seems possible that the original scribe of this family had both recensions at his disposal, selecting and improvising as he saw fit. Since both recensions are published in Constantinople in 1519, they could be circulating in the Sephardic world by the time of MS Mos 111. Alternatively, the manuscripts may descend from an intermediate stage of textual development.

The following chart illustrates manuscript family groupings.

Manuscript Families

Family A1

Oxford 135	(13c, France)
Cambridge 667.1	(13-14c, Ashkenazi)
Darmstadt 25	(14c, Ashkenazi)
Munich 232	(14c, Italian)
Vatican 303	(13-14c, Ashk/Byz.)
JTS 5000	(15c, Ashkenazi)
Cambridge 1505	(17-18c, N. Afr.)

Family A1-ד (דבר אחר)

Wolfenbüttel 36.25	(13-14c, Ashkenzi)
Oxford 27	(16c, Ashkenazi)

Family A1-ק (הבדלים קטנים)

Warsaw 258	(1430, Ashkenazi)
Parma 2269	(15c, Ashkenazi)
Oxford 225	(16c, Ashkenazi)

Recension A

Editio princeps (1519, Constantinople)

Family A2

Oxford 614	(13-14c, Ashkenazi)
Paris 335	(1543, Ashkenazi)
Escorial G3	(16c, Ashkenazi)

Family AB1

Parma 2736	(14c, Italian)

Family AB2

Moscow 111	(1462, Sephardi)
Zurich 192	(1682, Italian)

Family B1-ג (geniza fragments)

JTS ENA1
JTS ENA2

Family B1

Paris 716	(14-15c, Sephardi)
Warsaw 374	(14-15c, Italian)

Family B2-ח (חסר)

JTS 4920	(15c, Mizrahi)

Family B-ע (עוד מצאתי)

Vatican 285	(14-15c, Byzantine)
Montefiore 279	(16c, Italian)

Family B-ת (תשלום)

Oxford 104	(15c, Byzantine)

Recension B

Editio princeps (1519, Constantinople)

Family B2

Cambridge 854	(16-17c, Mizrahi)
London 10851	(1652, Bab/Greek)
Budapest A167	(17c, Ashkenazi)
Jerusalem 6234	(1740, Persian)
Jerusalem 3833	(1808, Tunisian)
JTS 4998	(1809-16, Tripoli)
JTS 4966	(1819, Persian)
Jerusalem 7706	(1889-1902, Persian)

D. Recension A: Midrash in the Synagogue[44]

Scholars generally acknowledge that several of the minor midrashim are related to the festivals on which their designated Torah passage is read. In addition to *Midrash vaYosha*'s connection to the seventh day of Passover, it is likely that *Midrash on the Ten Commandments* has some connection with the reading of the Ten Commandments on Shavuot, even though the printed recensions appear to be more similar to short story collections than to standard rabbinic exegesis.[45]

Investigation of the manuscript evidence for these texts, however, reveals more than a thematic association with the festivals. It argues for the presence and likely performance of midrash in the synagogue as explication of the assigned Torah readings, a hypothesis supported by related literature. As a continuing outgrowth of targumic-exegetical practice, these midrashim took shape within the synagogue, developing in a literary and oral performance interface. They became part of live interpretation of Torah on specific holy days in Ashkenaz and Italy for several centuries (*c.*1250–*c.*1500), after Aramaic Targum ceased to be a useful tool for the general Jewish population.

Evidence for the integration of MV in synagogue reading and teaching of Torah is compiled from a variety of sources:

1. Medieval discussions of liturgical customs found in prayer books and *minhag* manuals.
2. Manuscripts establishing the presence of this midrash in the synagogue and its extraordinarily close relationship to Targum.
3. An assortment of textual clues that hint at oral performance, not merely copying into *mahzorim*.
4. Complementary manuscript evidence showing strikingly different development of the midrash outside the synagogue.

I. The Development and Decline of Targum

In order to substantiate the claim for *Midrash vaYosha* in the synagogue as a consequence of the attenuation of Targum, it is important to examine first the history of live Targum in Europe.[46] Printed recensions of Palestinian Targums (e.g., Neofiti, Pseudo-Jonathan) include varying degrees of imaginative exegesis in their rendering of the biblical text (in contrast to the relatively literal translation of the Babylonian *Targum Onkelos*), but live Targum was frequently more extensive. References to Targum in this discussion indicate the varied matrix of Aramaic biblical traditions, most often relying upon passages found in prayerbook manuscripts – the best textual evidence available for Targum in the synagogue. Several scholars working in Aramaic *piyyut*, including

Michael Sokoloff, Joseph Yahalom and Menachem Schmelzer, mention an expansive targumic tradition associated with synagogue observance of the holiday cycle, dating back to late antiquity in Palestine.[47] The majority of extant material relates to the seventh day of Passover and Shavuot, most likely because the practice of live Targum was preserved for these occasions until a rather late date.[48] *Mahzor Vitry* instructs,

וקטן מתרגם כל פסוק ופסוק מן *ויהי בשלח*, ומשירה כולה, שהיום עברו ישראל את הים. ומתרגם הפרשה לפרסם הנס. וכיון שנהגו לתרגם בתורה נהגו לתרגם אף בנביא. וכן בעצרת, ולא בשאר מועדים.

A young person translates [to Aramaic] verse by verse from *When [Pharaoh] let [the people] go* (Ex 13:17), and the entire song, for it is the day on which Israel crossed the sea. One translates the portion to publicize the miracle. Since it is customary to translate the Torah reading, it is also customary to translate the prophetic portion. Similarly with Atzeret (Shavuot), but not the remainder of the festivals.[49]

This eleventh or twelfth-century prayerbook (French rite) then proceeds to record Aramaic Targum with broad midrashic expansions, including the following prose and poetic themes. (The significance of midrashic parallels will be addressed further on.)

1. God did not lead Israel by way of the Philistines, although it was shorter, lest the people see the bones of the 200,000 Ephraimites who died when they left Egypt thirty years before the Exodus. (The tradition of the Ephraimites leaving Egypt early is referenced in a different fashion in MV *ad* Ex 15:15.)
2. Trapped at the sea, the Israelites split into four groups, with differing opinions: Some want to drown themselves; others to return to Egypt; some to fight; and others to confound the Egyptians with noise, perhaps hoping to escape in the confusion. Moses's charge to the people in Ex 14:13–14 then is parsed so that each phrase addresses one of these groups (similar to MV *ad* Ex 15:9).
3. The *piyyut Ezel Moshe* records the sea's objections to parting at the command of Moses, a mere human being who was created three days later than the sea and therefore has no authority to boss the mighty waters around. (The motif is reflected in MV's explication of Ex 14:15.)

Numerous other prayerbook manuscripts contain targumic "*toseftot*," midrashic elaborations in prose.[50] Moses Ginsburger and Michael Klein, for instance, each discuss a variation on the miraculous birth of Israelite children who were sustained by angels with milk and honey suckled from two stones (rendered in *Midrash vaYosha* at Ex 15:1). Ginsburger draws from a thirteenth-century Ashkenazi *mahzor,* and Klein locates his text in a manuscript of the Roman rite copied in 1403.[51]

Apparently, "publicizing the miracle" meant to elaborate a good deal as well *during the course of the Torah reading* with both well-established and innovative midrashic motifs. The ancient custom of reading one verse of Hebrew from the Torah scroll, followed by a recitation of Targum, was preserved – with room to elaborate on ethical, narrative, poetic, and homiletical possibilities. In addition to many *maḥzorim* that reflect this practice, it is confirmed by the Tosafot on *b. Meg. 24a*, as well as the *Sefer haMinhagim* of R. Isaac Tirna who mentions specific *toseftot* for several verses of the Shavuot reading.[52] Thus the inclusion of orally performed expanded explication (real prose, not brief additions, and not merely *piyyut*) as part of the Torah reading for certain holy days was a targumic phenomenon, establishing a verse-by-verse exegesis and elaboration. Shavuot and seventh-day Passover Targum of this sort is commonly found in French, Ashkenazi, and Italian manuscripts at least into the fifteenth century.[53]

It may be somewhat surprising to find live Targum still performed in the synagogue long after it ceased to serve as the vernacular of the Jewish community. Once Aramaic faded as a language suitable for explication, communities responded in various ways. The rise of Islam and adoption of Arabic as a Jewish vernacular appear to have spurred the rapid disappearance of Targum in Spain, North Africa and the Near East. Geonic literature indicates that some congregations merely abandoned the practice of live targumic performance. Natronai b. Hilai in the mid-ninth century reproved congregations that dispensed with the Aramaic translation of Torah in favor of the more common vernacular (in this case, Arabic). Scholars of the tenth and eleventh centuries similarly reproached communities that neglected reading the Aramaic text.[54]

In parts of Europe, however, cultural elements played a role in preserving targumic custom for a longer period. Israel Ta-Shma describes Jewish communities of northern France and Germany as profoundly committed to ancestral tradition, explaining their retention of Palestinian and other customs even as they formally embraced Babylonian halakhah. "In many areas,... primarily that of ritual, the old practices continued to persist as in the past, acquiring the force of *minhag* and, in the process, gaining authority superior to that of the theoretical halakhah: a position not open to doubt or debate." What he calls the gradual "Babylonization" of Europe unfolded even more slowly in Italy.[55]

Continuation of synagogue targumic performance in these regions long after its explanatory function diminished seems consistent with this perspective, but sustaining the practice required various adaptations. Reciters were allowed to work from a written text – a practice that had once been proscribed[56] – and children learned to perform it, as recorded in prayerbooks beginning in the eleventh century.[57] In addition, Targum was accompanied by interpretation that people *could* understand.

One finds Hebrew *peirushim* (explications) supplementing the expanded Targum in prayerbooks.[58] While Hebrew was not the native speech of medieval Jewish communities, it served as a universal Jewish liturgical and literary language, especially beyond the borders of the Arabic-speaking world. Written supplements, however, could not uphold Targum's role in bringing the Torah to life in its public recitation. The *meturgeman* theoretically used to sing, yell and do other things to draw the people's attention, going to great lengths to ensure that Scripture remained a vibrant and eternally relevant text.[59] *Sefer Kolbo 52* (*c.*14th century, most likely in France) explains that the purpose of the Aramaic translation was originally so that women and the unlearned would be drawn to listen and understand. Acknowledging that Aramaic was no longer the *lingua franca* of the common folk, the author states,

ונהגו בשביעי של פסח ובראשון של עצרת לתרגם הפרשה כלה כדי להבין לנשים ולעמי הארץ הנסים והנפלאות ולשכך אזנם ויתנו לשם שבח והודאה על הדבר כי באותו הזמן שנקבע המנהג היו מדברים הכל בלשון ארמית, ובזמן הזה לא זז המנהג ממקומו אבל הוסיפו עליו לדרוש עשרת הדברות בלע"ז וכן בשביעי של פסח מויושע עד סוף השירה ומספרים נפלאות שעשה לנו השם ולאבותינו בלשון שיבינו הכל, וגם דורשין מה שעתיד הקב"ה לעשות כשיוציאנו מן הגלות.

It was customary on the seventh day of Passover and the first day of Shavuot to translate the entire portion in order to make women and the unlearned understand the miracles and wonders, and to make [it] intelligible for them so they might give praise and thanksgiving to God (*haShem*) for the matter. Because when the custom was fixed, everyone spoke Aramaic. Currently, the custom has not budged from its place, but they have added to it, expounding the Ten Commandments in the vernacular. And likewise on the seventh day of Passover, from *vaYosha* to the end of the song. They relate the wonders that God has done for us and for our ancestors in language that everyone will understand, and they also expound what the Blessed Holy One will do in the future when He takes us out of exile.

This book of Jewish customs articulates the path by which midrash may have been incorporated into live Torah explication as a result of Targum's declining relevance. Although it provides evidence of additional orally performed exegesis on the seventh day of Passover, it does not mention *Midrash vaYosha* explicitly. It is worth noting, however, that the content it describes matches the midrash quite nicely. *Midrash vaYosha* elaborates on God's miraculous gifts, including the salvation of Israelite infants under Pharaoh's decree, manipulation of events to save Moses multiple times so he could fulfill his destiny, transformation of the sea into twelve channels with potable water and windows between the walls so the Israelite tribes could see one another, etc. In describing the ten plagues in Egypt, it also suggests comparable wonders to be wrought against Edom in the future "when Israel goes forth from exile," and it offers messianic musings in explicating the last few verses of the Song. On the other hand, these are not particularly unusual qualities for midrashic literature.

The author's specific mention of the vernacular (לע"ז)[60] also mitigates against reading *Sefer Kolbo* as sufficient evidence that *Midrash vaYosha* is a base-text for such additional recitation. It is rendered in Hebrew, not vernacular, so it can at best represent literary translation of the described exegetical performances. We will return to this question after presenting the remainder of the evidence.

II. Midrash in the Synagogue

The numerous manuscripts of *Midrash vaYosha* provide the most comprehensive support for the theory that the midrash filled this need to "publicize the miracle" of crossing the Reed Sea in ways that inspired the congregation to give thanks and praise.

1. Parallels

Manifold parallels between our midrash and Targum reveal only a textual relationship, but these are still worth reviewing briefly. Almost all the motifs found in the seventh-day Passover Targum, including those described above from *Maḥzor Vitry*, are found in some form – in Hebrew – in *Midrash vaYosha*. A review of parallels across exegetical literature reveals that the most frequent textual relationship of MV is to Targum.

Shared motifs include the following: Abraham's servants are identified as Eliezer and Ishmael; Isaac asks to be bound tightly lest he kick; Abraham's trial is called to mind when the people are in trouble; the sea refuses to part because Moses is born of woman and three days younger; the four hundred years of exile for Abraham's descendants begin with the birth of Isaac; angels suckle infants with milk and honey from the rock; Egyptians divine the birth of an Israelite redeemer; Moses is sustained by Zipporah in the pit and then retrieves the staff; only one son is circumcised due to a pact with Jethro; Dathan and Abiram are identified as the Hebrews who were fighting; the loud cry of Ex 12:30 is Pharaoh's; Armilos is mentioned, albeit in a different context; the sea splits into twelve channels; Israelite opinion divides into different camps at the sea; land and sea argue about accepting the bodies; the nations' immobilizing fear should last until Israel crosses the Arnon and the Jabbok; and the dead bodies of the Ephraimites who left Egypt too early may terrify the children of Israel. These themes are not exclusive to the Targum, since its expansive traditions are themselves based primarily on pre-existing midrash. Nonetheless, the frequency of parallels between Targum and *Midrash vaYosha* is striking.[61]

By comparing manuscripts of *Midrash vaYosha* not only with the printed Palestinian Targums, but also with the Aramaic *toseftot* found in various *mahzor* manuscripts, one discovers additional shared traditions.[62] These correlations suggest that the textual relationship may have grown within the shared "space" of fluid, changing synagogue performance.

2. Inclusion in Maḥzorim

At least two of the manuscripts that contain *Midrash vaYosha* are prayerbooks: Cambridge 667.1, a thirteenth- to fourteenth-century example of the Northern French liturgical rite; and Parma 2736, a late fourteenth-century Roman *maḥzor*.[63]

Of course, works of various genres were copied into prayerbooks: halakhic treatises, midrash, calendars, responsa, etc. Surely most of these were for reference and study, not public performance. Indeed, MS Cam 667.1 collects our festival midrash together with a miscellany of additional material, separated from the holiday liturgy. MS Parma 2736, on the other hand, incorporates it in a section entitled *Seder Inyan Pesah* – the liturgical order for the holy day. The unit is comprised of a few halakhot, then liturgy, *piyyut*, expanded Targum, and midrashim.[64] This last category has the sections subtitled *Milei d'Fesah* and *Milei d'vaYosha* – potentially "words of explication" for the first and last days of Passover.[65]

3. Notes to the Reader/Reciter

While these texts clearly link the midrash to the festival, they do not necessarily evince oral performance. There is additional evidence that points in this direction, however, including two manuscripts which attach a note regarding the Torah reading as is frequently done for Targum. At the end of *Midrash vaYosha*, MS Paris 335 has: להקורא מסיים הקריאה כמשפטו עד רפאיך – To the reader: One concludes the reading according to the rule, up to *your healer* (Ex 15:26, the end of the passage for seventh-day Passover). Addressing the reader, or even alluding to the reader as appears to be the case in MS Escorial G3, strengthens the link with recitation.[66]

Unfortunately, the language is not conclusive regarding enactment; it could simply indicate a text to peruse while a child was honoring the ancient Aramaic custom and reading aloud in a language no longer understood. Still, there are additional clues of oral performance.

4. Rhetoric of Orality

The text contains many of the markers of orality identical to those enumerated by Avigdor Shinan in association with Targum: a preference for dialogue and direct speech rather than narration, direct address to the audience and to God, repetitions and recurrent formulas, rhetorical questions, brief doxologies, etc.[67]

5. Multiple Recensions

Also arguing for public performance is the fact that there are multiple recensions, with synagogue-related manuscripts representing a variety of stemmatic branches. The three different ways in which *Midrash vaYosha* manuscripts "mark" their connection with the synagogue: 1) added instructions for the Torah reader, 2) copied into a *maḥzor* among miscellaneous rabbinic material, and 3) copied into a *maḥzor* fully integrated into the liturgical framework for the festival, correspond to three different manuscript families with significant textual variation.[68]

Philip Alexander notes that festival collections of Targum differ from each other in content and degree of expansion, reflecting different synagogue presentations.[69] MV provides evidence of the same phenomenon in relation to a Hebrew text, supporting the likelihood of public recitation.

Surely the fact that books in the Middle Ages were not generally considered closed affairs contributed to the ongoing evolution of the midrash.[70] Its likely birth and development in connection with synagogue observance of seventh-day Passover, however, make orality a critical component in its composition and transmission. The tremendous fluidity of the text is in large part attributable to its synagogue performance.

III. From Synagogue to Literature

One last argument for establishing the *Sitz im Leben* of MV in the synagogue is a comparison of the manuscripts of Ashkenaz and Italy with those that were copied in an Arabic milieu. Recension A, the redaction with more direct exegetical focus and shorter pericopes, is best suited for synagogue performance. As discussed earlier, these manuscripts are overwhelmingly from Ashkenaz.

The geographic dichotomy returns us to the history of synagogue Targum. Given the earlier demise of live Aramaic translation in the Arabic-speaking world, interruptions in the Torah reading quickly became halakhically suspect altogether in Sephardi tradition.[71] Recension B is not found in a single prayerbook. There seems to be little place in the synagogue for a text like *Midrash vaYosha*. Instead, it develops a more literary style.[72]

Eventually the practice of expanded explication as part of the Torah reading became suspect in Ashkenazi and Italian ritual as well. The vestige of exegesis and poetry delivered during the Torah recitation, reciting the *Akdamut* after the first verse of the Shavuot Torah reading, was questioned by a group of Jews who lived in the mixed Ashkenazi-Sephardi community of Venice in the seventeenth century. The community requested a legal ruling from Ephraim Cohen of Vilna on the placement of this lengthy *piyyut* which elaborates on the revelation at Sinai. In his responsum, he declares that the sages who instituted the practice surely understood the issues related to interrupting the Torah reading and argues that it should be preserved as an ancient tradition (*Sha'ar Ephraim 10*). His great-grandson Rabbi Jacob Emden, however (d. 1776), notes in his *siddur* that the early Ashkenazi Jews interrupted the Torah reading in numerous instances, but it simply is not done any more.[73]

IV. Orality and the Written Text

Based on the manuscript evidence and halakhic discourse, along with comments scattered among medieval prayerbooks and *minhag* manuals, the hypothesis takes hold: *Midrash vaYosha* emerged in close relationship with synagogue observance of seventh-day Passover, as a continuing outgrowth of the Targumic-exegetical practice attached to the prescribed Torah reading. The translation of Torah and haftarah into Aramaic within the service gradually became limited to a few holy days because it no longer served the function of engaging the congregation and making the biblical passages comprehensible. To make Torah live again in the imagination of the community, congregations enhanced the teaching in various creative ways. In France, Germany and Italy *c.*1250–*c.*1500, it appears they fashioned midrashim to accompany the Targum which became integrated into oral Torah explication. The texts born of this endeavor (or adapted to it) eventually departed the synagogue and became works of literature, but traces of their origins remain in the matrix of manuscript traditions.

Scholars have begun to articulate an increasingly sophisticated sense of what "orality" means in our context.[74] It was not a linear progression from oral traditions to written ones, but a literary and oral performance interface: texts were composed so as to be orally enacted – recited, paraphrased, elaborated, or discussed. Rabbinic culture long fostered concurrent oral and written forms of transmission, with the *beit midrash* and the *beit knesset* as primary venues for re-oralizing the texts. Scribes, teachers, translators, and performers all had recourse to a mixed oral-written inheritance from which they drew when they re-created the "text" with their quill or their voice. Every performance of the text reshaped it. Texts like MV were meant to be publicly performed, brought to life again and again, recreated each time in the process. Extant manuscripts represent *one* vehicle for transmission, not only to be copied, but potentially to be studied like a script or "speaking notes" as well.[75] Yet there are many questions about the nature of the oral performance that we cannot answer.

It is possible that the interpretations were delivered in the vernacular but written in Hebrew, like some early medieval sermons.[76] In discussing transmission of folktales, Dan Ben-Amos notes the choice available to medieval authors and scribes, and asserts that rendering the texts in literary Hebrew demonstrates that "they wished to ascribe to popular tales a cultural and ethical function similar to that of the traditional canonical tales."[77] In a liturgical setting, such a desire to make the exegeses authoritative is surely compounded, potentially rendering Hebrew as the preferred language of written transmission (if not oral performance as well). If translated into the vernacular when performed, however, even the most persuasively integrated midrashic-targumic text can represent only a sort of aide-mémoire for the contemporary *meturgeman*, not a verbatim record of traditions taught on a series of occasions.

We lack clues regarding the length of the presentation as well. It seems unlikely that every verse would be fully explicated even during a holiday service, and a number of the *mahzor* manuscripts contain only parts of the midrashim. There is no way to know, however, whether the interpretive material was excerpted or sometimes presented in its entirety. Was the exegesis presented simply as a creative interpretation of the text, or was it woven into a homily? The close relationship to Targum and its attenuation argues for the former, but we cannot be certain.

One of the most interesting variables is *when* during the service these teachings were shared. If, as some of the textual evidence suggests, they were offered like Targum in the midst of the Torah reading, it conjures an image of dramatic and dynamic performance that might indeed have brought to life the historical miracles conveyed by Scripture. This is a striking difference from modern custom in many synagogues, where the Torah reading is still central but many congregants become distracted during the long recitation and ritual. The current lack of interruption and elaboration inside the boundary of the blessings, intended to preserve the honor and clarity of Torah, may have had an inverse effect.

Among the questions that have drawn midrashists ever since Leopold Zunz put pen to paper is the *Sitz im Leben* of midrash: Are these *derashot* performed for the general public in the *beit knesset*, or are they anthologies of exegesis collected for rabbinic studies in the *beit midrash*?[78] Although it is still enticing to imagine Joseph Heinemann's Amoraic *darshan* stand up in the synagogue and open his discourse with some verse from afar while the congregation is on the edge of their seats, knowing that he must eventually arrive at the first verse of their *sidra* but not knowing how he will manage to get there, scholars have challenged the premise that Amoraic midrash represents oral homilies in any measure.[79] The period remains an enigma in this regard, with insufficient evidence to substantiate a direct link between the synagogue and our redacted texts of midrash.

By the medieval period, however, a plethora of manuscripts in a variety of interrelated genres yields numerous clues, tantalizing pieces of a complex puzzle. Many of the relevant texts remain unpublished or lacking a critical edition, so one must hunt through prayerbook, midrash and *minhag* manuscripts to reconstruct the history. Traditions vary among communities and over time. Nonetheless, there is compelling evidence for association of midrashic works with synagogue worship, performed for and perhaps shaped by liturgical use. The surprise may be that it is not the *darshan* we see, but a new-fangled *meturgeman*.

Whether MV was formally presented as sermonic homily or within the Torah reading as a new "targum," its purpose was to actualize the possibilities of meaning found within the Scriptural reading and sacred story of the Exodus.

> The texts under consideration here are not dramatic in the modern sense of the theatrical. But to a medieval audience, performance must have made them alive, immediate, animated. The combination of preaching, storytelling and performance makes short pious stories, united by the catalyst of eminently performable raw material, an intriguing body of narratives in performance. There is a wide range of possibilities for vocal modulation given that the texts include combinations of themes which are earthly and divine, boorish and inspirational, comic and serious.[80]

Like storytelling and preaching within the contemporaneous Christian church, the performance medium was part of the message of Scripture's eternal relevance.

E. Recension B and the Development of Narrative

Indications that Recension B reflects a transition from the synagogue to "literature," meaning a work intended to be transmitted and received in written form, were briefly discussed above. At this juncture it is worth exploring further the historical context for its remarkable development of narrative. The midrash not only integrates elaborate exegetical tales; it also devotes significantly increased attention to character, emotion, dialogue, irony and drama. This later redaction was selected as the base text for this volume precisely on account of these qualities that make for such a "good read."

The development of MV may partake of a broader trend in the evolution of the short story within and outside of Jewish literature. Within midrash, there is an explosion of brief narrative works in the Middle Ages. Some of the more well known among them include *Maaseh Avraham Avinu, Chronicles of Moses,* and *Petirat Moshe*, but there are scores of texts collected in the work of Jellinek, Eisenstein and Wertheimer alone.[81] While the brief narrative form includes material with no biblical basis, many of the stories found in these collections are expansions on scriptural tales and characters. The diversity of texts and manifold manuscripts testify to the genre's popularity and importance in the evolution of exegesis and Hebrew literature.[82]

Joseph Dan has speculated that the short, focused midrash genre develops in part because there is too much material accumulated to be comprehensive, especially with the apocryphal and non-Jewish sources that are included in expanded biblical narratives of the medieval period.[83] The contemporaneous anthological enterprise would seem to challenge his theory. It appears instead that the minor midrashim are shaped by the growing prevalence of the short story form. Deliberately filtering the body of inherited traditions, they generally select a single interpretative line in order to link exegeses together in a continuous narrative.

Recension B of *Midrash vaYosha* is neither a short story per se, nor a single continuous narrative, but rather a belletristic rendering of a lemmatic midrash. Consequently, the intermediate stages of development of and influences on the short story in Hebrew literature are especially relevant. As Dan discusses in his history of the Hebrew story in the Middle Ages, narrative was for centuries one of many vehicles for aggadah, midrash, historiography, exempla and sage stories, functioning within rabbinic literature as illustration, example and digression. With the specialization of literature that began in Hebrew works in the geonic period, the story emerged as an independent literary force. Beginning primarily with loose collections or adaptations of aggadic tales, they demonstrated continuity with earlier literature as well as the growing independence of story. This autonomy enabled the development of new themes and forms along with increasingly complex narrative composition.[84] Recognizing multiple influences in the emergence of medieval Hebrew stories, Tova Rosen and Eli Yassif note,

> The main causes for the evolution of the Hebrew prose literature of the period may be related to factors other than the literary autonomy of this form – the influence of European and Arabic literatures, changes in the leisure culture of the Jews, their search for new expressions for their everyday life, and other socio-historical factors.[85]

Within transitional works, Eli Yassif identifies three major chronological stages of development: 1) continuity with Jewish textual sources but increased interest in the story; 2) absorption and Judaization of foreign material, especially via the influence of Islam; 3) original Jewish stories.[86] Although *Midrash vaYosha*'s Recension B is a late contribution to the intermediate stage of literary development, the history of this one text parallels the general trend. Recension A demonstrates both continuity with Jewish textual sources and interest in story; the later Recension B involves significant development of narration and the assimilation of foreign elements.

Again, MV is not a short story. Rather, it represents the impact of the rise of the short story on existing midrashic traditions. One should not be surprised that Jewish texts did not simply invent new fictional narratives, but rather Judaized the new genre with familiar religious themes. It calls to mind C. S. Lewis' imaginary interview with Chaucer: Why didn't Chaucer bother to think up his own plots? The reply, indicative of medieval attitudes toward innovation, was, "Surely we are not yet reduced to that."[87]

The other major trend in medieval Jewish exegesis, of course, is the rise of *peshat* commentary, emphasizing the contextual meaning of the Hebrew Bible. Although MV has a somewhat different "take" on contextual interpretation, creatively expanding and reshaping the connections within or between biblical tales, its history and composition amidst these diverse trends draws a critical question to the fore: Does the developing conception of narrative change how exegetes perceive the biblical text, contributing to the marked shift toward contextual interpretation in all its forms? The introduction of grammatical studies and comparative semitics is a well-established factor in the emergence of *peshat* exegesis, but it does not appear to be a comprehensive explanation.[88] Linguistic sensitivity is only one aspect of the radical shift from midrash to commentary as the primary exegetical form, especially as it develops in the twelfth and thirteenth centuries. Like the later redaction of *Midrash vaYosha*, medieval *peshat* commentary generally addresses whole verses or larger contexts in determining the meaning of a passage. They both explore principles of causality and character motivation. They frequently choose a single interpretation.

It may at first seem counterintuitive, that the same catalyst for vast and fanciful expansion of biblical narrative could also shape and intensify the focus on more "straightforward" interpretation. Yet Jewish medieval commentators like Joseph Bekhor Shor, David Kimḥi, and Naḥmanides – from Ashkenazi and Sephardi backgrounds – do not focus merely on grammar in their contextual readings. They bring to their interpretation a more nuanced sense of literary technique, character insight, and internal motivation.

Admittedly, the evidence is circumstantial and coincidence cannot prove causality. It is worth mentioning, however, two previous scholars who have broached this tentative possibility without marking it as such. In Beryl Smalley's foundational study, *The Bible in the Middle Ages*, she concludes that the "physics" of narrative, e.g., character motivation and causation, compelled the imagination of Christian exegetes. She describes the shift as a rise in the power of the story to shape interpretation: "The actual narrative of Scripture, the story of the nativity, infancy, ministry and passion is perceived more intensely. The scene itself becomes too absorbing in its human pathos to need the aid of symbol in transmuting it into something different."[89] Smalley attaches this analysis to the advance of nature study. From the time of the Victorines and their interest in the natural beauty of "literal" interpretation in the twelfth century to the thirteenth-century homilies that applied the biblical text to this-worldly questions, she seems to view the workings of story as one of those natural processes – affirming that developing conceptions of narrative reshape interpretation to become more contextual.

An insight by Meir Sternberg similarly suggests larger ramifications of narrative development within Jewish exegesis: "Narrative master forces also narrativize everything else in the text by assimilating it willy-nilly to their dynamics of life-like development and/or artful disclosure."[90] Such a principle arguably operates on a macroscopic level as well. The impact of narrative master forces on biblical exegesis as a whole is tremendous. As consciousness of plot, character, drama, dialogue and other aspects of story take hold on the collective imagination, the priority of contextual interpretation should become inevitable. It assimilates questions and interpretations to its "dynamics of life-like development and/or artful disclosure."

Context in MV is not the same as *peshat*; it includes a background of long-standing rabbinic traditions and newer folk elements that can be woven into the terse biblical text, to clarify its sense and enrich its meaning. In the attack on Moses en route to Egypt (*ad* 15:2), for instance, MV inserts an untenable deal with Jethro, the appearance of Satan, and an encounter with Dathan and Abiram – none of which can be found in the simple reading of the biblical narrative. Yet it is the elegance of a tale which resolves over half a dozen textual problems that persuades. In many cases, such as God's question, "*Why do you cry out to Me*?" (Ex 14:15), reading it as part of the larger context of covenant and salvation violates the plain sense of the text. And still, narrative master forces are at work in both *peshat* and expanded exegetical narrative, manifested differently. Changes in the literary aesthetic of the medieval milieu appear to stimulate both sorts of exegesis. In terms of a narrow focus trained solely on grammar and comparative linguistics, the *peshat* revolution was short-lived. As part of a larger contextual approach to biblical interpretation, however, the lens fashioned by medieval Jewish exegesis continues to reveal new understandings of sacred Scripture to this day.

F. Exegesis and Narrative: The Poetics of *Midrash vaYosha*

A literary analysis of MV is, first and foremost, an effort to understand the text itself more completely, by applying the rabbinic methodology of close reading and insights from modern literary theory. These tools help to uncover the full range of possible meanings, both intended and unintended by the author(s), that the text may contain within its pages. Exposing dialogue structures, revealing exegetical cruxes, exploring subtle ironies, etc. all contribute to our appreciation of the literary art of *Midrash vaYosha* and our comprehension of its message. Thus most of the discussion is set within the annotation and commentary, within the context that gives it full-bodied voice and clearest sense. There are several aspects of the midrash, however, that are of general importance and application.

One of the most striking features of *Midrash vaYosha* is the integration of lengthy narratives involving biblical characters and events within the exegetical format.[91] As mentioned above, it is most prevalent in Recension B, but it is evident to some extent in the earlier redaction as well. Ofra Meir suggests calling such passages "darshanic stories" rather than expanded biblical narratives or re-told Bible, because

> most stories of this sort were fashioned via one (or more) methods of *derash*, and their source is in the exegesis of a verse or verses. The *derashah* never comes primarily to tell a story. The *darshan* explicates in order to draw out from the Bible ethical, religious, educational and other ideas, although one of his literary means is to fashion a story by way of *derashah*.[92]

Joshua Levinson similarly calls them *exegetical narratives*, and offers significant insight into the reading of this genre. Since the story "simultaneously represents and interprets its biblical counterpart," the reader is expected to navigate between the biblical and the midrashic stories, recognizing the third story that is narrated between them. It is comprised of questions raised by the biblical text but frequently left unspoken, omitted details and roads not taken. Invoking Mikhail Bakhtin, he defines such reading as dialogical, in which the reader must discern the biblical and the rabbinic voice talking to each other, as it were, within the singular telling of the story. Suspense is created precisely in the ways that the text challenges or develops what the reader knows about the characters and events.

As exegesis, it is subservient to the biblical narrative, but as a story in its own right, it creates a narrated world which is different from its biblical shadow. It is obvious that the combination of these two elements creates a certain dissonance. Narrative and exegesis are two very different methods of persuasion, based upon divergent, if not opposing, presuppositions of "author-ity." It is specifically this tension between sameness and difference, subservience and creativity, which establishes the genre's identity.[93]

In MV, familiar markers of exegesis (שנאמר, ככתוב, etc.) are frequently missing in the flow of the most elaborate narratives, and numerous details are detached from the verses on which they comment. Consequently, the exegesis is at times covert, but the dialogical engagement between scripture and interpretation is clear. An outstanding example is discussed in the commentary *ad* 15:2, illuminating the powerful dynamism it creates in the midrash. By re-opening the canon, by showing how old meanings become sources for new ones, "...[t]he exegetical narrative performs what Dolezel has called 'the most magic of all transformations that fiction can accomplish: past made present.'"[94]

The embedded interpreter, with its ability to give voice to the figures of silence in the biblical text, is an essential component in this exegetical-narrative synergy. While the phenomenon can be identified in earlier rabbinic literature and even within the Bible itself, its prominence and sophistication within MV is notable. One of the best examples is the character of Uza, who interprets the complex tale of slavery and Exodus, forcing critical questions and new possibilities of interpretation; it is discussed in the commentary *ad* 14:31.

Significant literary elements discussed solely within the commentary include: compositional units (14:30), metaphor (15:3), mythology (15:5), single interpretive thread, mashal (15:6), irony (15:9), character development (15:11), context (15:15) – along with prominent themes and imagery. Several more minor aspects of MV's style can be treated briefly here:

Language – The text is written in a clear and simple medieval Hebrew, with a few Greek loan words (especially as related to siege tactics in 15:3) and infrequent emulation of biblical style.

Orality – Scholars who address orality within rabbinic literature have identified certain traits that are suggestive of oral origins and/or performance, such as rhetorical questions, recurrent phrases and mnemonic structural patterns.[95] In addition to the historical significance discussed in Section D, the *rhetoric* of orality has a literary impact.[96] The frequent use of rhetorical questions about the identity, actions or motivations of figures in the text, has the power to draw in the listener or the reader as an active participant in the unfolding of the story: "Who were these young men?" "What did they [the angels] say?" (14:30) "What did he do?" (Satan in 14:30, Pharaoh in 14:31, the sea in 15:5). Why did the sea and land refuse to swallow the Egyptians? (15:12). Why did God bring each of the plagues? (15:7). In addition, there are occasional examples of invoking the first person plural, as an author or preacher speaking "with" the reader/congregant: "How do we know that judgment will be on the third day?" (15:18), and the petitionary close of the text speaking in the collective voice ("...May He gather us from the four corners of the earth and lead us to Jerusalem so that we may rejoice in it. Let us say Amen, Amen. Selah."), are two instances. This voice draws participation to the next level: Events in the narrative somehow touch those who encounter it.

Repetitions – Another frequently-invoked indicator of oral performance or oral origins is a repetitive pattern within the interpretation. A simple structure, like the three camps of Israelites and then Egyptians who debate how to proceed at the Sea of Reeds, provides a mnemonic for unfolding the exegesis (15:9). These patterns have a rhetorical value aside from any hints they provide regarding historical context. Elijah's sequential pronouncements, for instance, enable the messianic drama to build suspense and momentum (15:14). Repeated evocation of Ezekiel 16 in MV 15:17 (I clothed you, will wash you, gave you sandals) emphasizes the homiletical point: God is the exceptional ruler who puts the welfare of subjects first. Rhythmic comparison of a human king laying siege and God sending the plagues (15:3) is so repetitive that most manuscripts take shortcuts somewhere in the middle. MS Paris 716 is typical, writing out the refrain, "If they reconsider, good; if not..." a few times, but then just listing the stages of attack. As rhetoric, they serve to make the textual structure so predictable that the reader (or preacher) can fill it in, and the listener can anticipate it. Anticipation is a powerful tool within midrash; dramatic tension compounds as the reader/listener knows the next piece but still cannot complete the puzzle.

Key words – Another aspect of repetition, the use of key words, accentuates themes and binds elements together, as with the motif of crying in the first story. The launching point for the narrative of the *akeidah* is the lament and weeping by Moses and Israel at the sea, prompting God to respond, *"Why do you cry out to Me?"* (Ex 14:15). Then, after enduring Satan's temptations with great courage, nearly every character in the ensuing narrative weeps. This theme highlights the emotional tension of the scene that is underdeveloped in the biblical tale of Abraham's faithfulness to the Divine command, and it connects the patriarchal narrative with the people's distress at the sea.

Rhetorical strategies – One finds certain strategies of rhetorical control in the narration, such as delayed exposition and anticipatory caution.[97] The odd placement of Jethro's imprisonment of Moses at first mention of his flight to Midian, even though it does not transpire for several "scenes," is (if not a mistake) a model of both elements (15:2). The reader is engaged to discover the cause of the imprisonment and is warned not to see Jethro as a hero for saving Moses' life in Egypt. From a more global perspective, the perception of Pharaoh also seems deliberately determined. The first impression is framed by his overbearing manner in refusing Moses' request and denying his god (14:31). It appears in contrast with the grateful praises of Moses and Israel (15:1–2). Only after the plagues (15:3) and the confirmation of God's love for Israel (15:4) and power over the whole universe (15:5) does the reader see Pharaoh begin to change. These techniques of rhetorical control powerfully influence reader response to the text.

Rabbinic attributions and formulaic language – There are almost no citations of individual rabbis (15:6 is the exception), and most sections (in most manuscripts) begin with the introduction, "The Sages said" – even if the interpretation is not found in earlier extant rabbinic literature. The text adheres to the lemmatic form whether or not it actually focuses on explicating the Song at the Sea. As commonly found in medieval Hebrew texts, the terms מיד and באותה שעה (literally, "immediately" and "at the same time," respectively) are used to connect threads of a narrative or thoughts within a lemma, generally without actual time reference. Also, the characters all use rabbinic epithets for God, e.g. רבונו של עולם (Master of the world).

Rabbinization – The rabbinization of biblical figures, evident in narrative choices like Moses' concern about impure breast milk, can also be seen in the prayer language set into the stories. Isaac, for instance, offers upon his resurrection an approximation of the *hatimah* to the Amidah's second prayer: "Blessed are You, [O Lord], who revives the dead" (14:30).[98] Uza requests a *beit din* (rabbinic court procedure), and all the characters are exegetes. Typical of biblical interpretation through the ages, the authors imagine the characters as versions of themselves.

These and other elements of MV's artful use of language and conventions will become clear as we turn to the text itself.

G. Notes on Texts and Translations

1. The primary Hebrew text follows the fourteenth- to fifteenth-century manuscript of Recension B, Paris – Bibliothèque nationale de France 716; folio pages are indicated in the transcription. For purposes of comparison, the earlier recension (A) is also transcribed and translated, based on one of the oldest extant manuscripts (13c.), Oxford – Bodleian Library Or. 135, with its missing pericope supplied by MS Wolfenbüttel Cod. Guelf. 36.25 Aug. 2^0. Both redactions are presented for each lemma, with Recension B first – B/A/B/A, etc.

For ease of reading, the Hebrew text in this chapter has been altered in the following ways:

– Most abbreviated words are spelled out, without any special notation. The primary exception is the regular epithet for God, הקדוש ברוך הוא, translated "the Blessed Holy One" or simply "the Holy One." This abbreviation is preserved as the scribes rendered it: הב"ה or הקב"ה. Although it is possible the shorter acronym stands for a different rabbinic epithet for God: המקום ברוך הוא=the Blessed Place (of all being), the translation opts for the former.

– The manuscripts frequently begin a word at the end of a line without sufficient room to complete it; the entire word is then written at the beginning of the next line. Less often, the entire word is found on both lines. These *custodes* are not reflected here.

– Marginal and interlinear notes are included as part of the text, framed by < > if it appears to be in the scribe's own hand, and by { } if it appears to be in a different hand. Words in the English translation are similarly marked, or there will be an endnote explaining the irregularity.

– Biblical citations that do not match the Masoretic Text add the MT version in brackets.

– Punctuation and paragraphing are added, reflecting my understanding of the text, to make reading the Hebrew easier. Enlarged letters marking the beginning of pericopes are indicated by bold font.

– Biblical verses and partial citations are noted in italics, including instances in which dialogue or narration simply makes use of the precise wording of the Bible as an integral part of the story rather than an explicit quotation. The textual reference can be found in the English translation.

– Instances in which the scribe seemed to accidentally omit significant words or phrases display the missing text [in brackets]. Similarly, if the manuscript appears to contain an error that affects the translation or interpretation, the corrected form appears alongside, marked with brackets. The corrected form is generally corroborated by other manuscripts, as indicated in the notes. The presumed error is highlighted with a grey box. On occasion, there are phrases written out of place (and then repeated in the proper one); these are also highlighted with a grey box. The English translation reflects the preferred reading, with notes explaining the irregularities.

– There are numerous marks within the Paris manuscript that indicate a word or phrase is to be deleted. When a word is clearly crossed out, it appears with a ~~strike-through~~ in the Hebrew. If the word or phrase is merely marked with a single or double slash above, it appears with a strike through (as a suggested edit by the scribe or a later hand), and it is highlighted with a grey box as an error.

– Grammatical errors are corrected in the text only if neglecting to do so might lead to misunderstanding of the text. When a correction is offered, the original text is noted in a grey box, and the suggested correction in brackets.

2. On occasion, words are added or biblical citations are extended in the English translation for the sake of clarity; the additions are indicated with brackets.

3. The translation is designed to render the Hebrew as accurately as possible while employing an English idiom. Examples of liberties taken for this purpose include: active verbs made passive, change of tense/aspect, and repetitive use of "he said" replaced by English dialogue markers.

4. Within the translation, God is described with masculine pronouns. Although such gendered language is problematic for contemporary theology, it is consistent with rabbinic discourse.

5. The English translation of biblical verses follows the New Jewish Publication Society (NJPS) *Tanakh* (2000) unless it does not fit the syntax or exegesis of the midrash.

6. Citations of other primary literature rely on the Bar-Ilan Responsa Project, Version 17 CD, unless a specific edition is indicated in the bibliography. Two frequently cited texts that have long undifferentiated sections include page numbers from a printed edition indicated in parentheses. The key for these references is as follows:

HR = H.S. Horovitz and I.A. Rabin, *Mekhilta d'Rabbi Ishmael* Critical Edition (Jerusalem: Wahrmann Books, 1970)

Eis = J.D. Eisenstein, *Otzar midrashim*

Chapter 2

Midrash vaYosha
with Translation and Commentary

יד:ל וַיּ֨וֹשַׁע יְהוָ֜ה בַּיּ֥וֹם הַה֛וּא אֶת־יִשְׂרָאֵ֖ל מִיַּ֣ד מִצְרָ֑יִם
וַיַּ֤רְא יִשְׂרָאֵל֙ אֶת־מִצְרַ֔יִם מֵ֖ת עַל־שְׂפַ֥ת הַיָּֽם׃
לא וַיַּ֨רְא יִשְׂרָאֵ֜ל אֶת־הַיָּ֣ד הַגְּדֹלָ֗ה אֲשֶׁ֨ר עָשָׂ֤ה יְהוָה֙ בְּמִצְרַ֔יִם וַיִּֽירְא֥וּ הָעָ֖ם
אֶת־יְהוָ֑ה וַיַּֽאֲמִ֙ינוּ֙ בַּֽיהוָ֔ה וּבְמֹשֶׁ֖ה עַבְדּֽוֹ׃
טו:א אָ֣ז יָשִֽׁיר־מֹשֶׁה֩ וּבְנֵ֨י יִשְׂרָאֵ֜ל אֶת־הַשִּׁירָ֤ה הַזֹּאת֙ לַֽיהוָ֔ה וַיֹּאמְר֖וּ לֵאמֹ֑ר
אָשִׁ֤ירָה לַּֽיהוָה֙ כִּֽי־גָאֹ֣ה גָּאָ֔ה ס֥וּס וְרֹכְב֖וֹ רָמָ֥ה בַיָּֽם׃
ב עָזִּ֤י וְזִמְרָת֙ יָ֔הּ וַֽיְהִי־לִ֖י לִֽישׁוּעָ֑ה זֶ֤ה אֵלִי֙ וְאַנְוֵ֔הוּ אֱלֹהֵ֥י אָבִ֖י וַאֲרֹמְמֶֽנְהוּ׃
ג יְהוָ֖ה אִ֣ישׁ מִלְחָמָ֑ה יְהוָ֖ה שְׁמֽוֹ׃
ד מַרְכְּבֹ֥ת פַּרְעֹ֛ה וְחֵיל֖וֹ יָרָ֣ה בַיָּ֑ם וּמִבְחַ֣ר שָֽׁלִשָׁ֔יו טֻבְּע֖וּ בְיַם־סֽוּף׃
ה תְּהֹמֹ֖ת יְכַסְיֻ֑מוּ יָרְד֥וּ בִמְצוֹלֹ֖ת כְּמוֹ־אָֽבֶן׃
ו יְמִֽינְךָ֣ יְהוָ֔ה נֶאְדָּרִ֖י בַּכֹּ֑חַ יְמִֽינְךָ֥ יְהוָ֖ה תִּרְעַ֥ץ אוֹיֵֽב׃
ז וּבְרֹ֥ב גְּאוֹנְךָ֖ תַּהֲרֹ֣ס קָמֶ֑יךָ תְּשַׁלַּח֙ חֲרֹ֣נְךָ֔ יֹאכְלֵ֖מוֹ כַּקַּֽשׁ׃
ח וּבְר֤וּחַ אַפֶּ֙יךָ֙ נֶ֣עֶרְמוּ מַ֔יִם נִצְּב֥וּ כְמוֹ־נֵ֖ד נֹזְלִ֑ים קָֽפְא֥וּ תְהֹמֹ֖ת בְּלֶב־יָֽם׃
ט אָמַ֥ר אוֹיֵ֛ב אֶרְדֹּ֥ף אַשִּׂ֖יג אֲחַלֵּ֣ק שָׁלָ֑ל
תִּמְלָאֵ֣מוֹ נַפְשִׁ֔י אָרִ֣יק חַרְבִּ֔י תּוֹרִישֵׁ֖מוֹ יָדִֽי׃
י נָשַׁ֥פְתָּ בְרוּחֲךָ֖ כִּסָּ֣מוֹ יָ֑ם צָֽלְלוּ֙ כַּֽעוֹפֶ֔רֶת בְּמַ֖יִם אַדִּירִֽים׃
יא מִֽי־כָמֹ֤כָה בָּֽאֵלִם֙ יְהוָ֔ה מִ֥י כָּמֹ֖כָה נֶאְדָּ֣ר בַּקֹּ֑דֶשׁ
נוֹרָ֥א תְהִלֹּ֖ת עֹ֥שֵׂה פֶֽלֶא׃
יב נָטִ֙יתָ֙ יְמִ֣ינְךָ֔ תִּבְלָעֵ֖מוֹ אָֽרֶץ׃
יג נָחִ֥יתָ בְחַסְדְּךָ֖ עַם־ז֣וּ גָּאָ֑לְתָּ נֵהַ֥לְתָּ בְעָזְּךָ֖ אֶל־נְוֵ֥ה קָדְשֶֽׁךָ׃
יד שָֽׁמְע֥וּ עַמִּ֖ים יִרְגָּז֑וּן חִ֣יל אָחַ֔ז יֹשְׁבֵ֖י פְּלָֽשֶׁת׃
טו אָ֤ז נִבְהֲלוּ֙ אַלּוּפֵ֣י אֱד֔וֹם אֵילֵ֣י מוֹאָ֔ב יֹֽאחֲזֵ֖מוֹ רָ֑עַד נָמֹ֕גוּ כֹּ֖ל יֹשְׁבֵ֥י כְנָֽעַן׃
טז תִּפֹּ֨ל עֲלֵיהֶ֤ם אֵימָ֙תָה֙ וָפַ֔חַד בִּגְדֹ֥ל זְרוֹעֲךָ֖ יִדְּמ֣וּ כָּאָ֑בֶן
עַד־יַעֲבֹ֤ר עַמְּךָ֙ יְהוָ֔ה עַד־יַעֲבֹ֖ר עַם־ז֥וּ קָנִֽיתָ׃
יז תְּבִאֵ֗מוֹ וְתִטָּעֵ֙מוֹ֙ בְּהַ֣ר נַחֲלָֽתְךָ֔ מָכ֥וֹן לְשִׁבְתְּךָ֛ פָּעַ֖לְתָּ יְהוָ֑ה
מִקְּדָ֕שׁ אֲדֹנָ֖י כּוֹנְנ֥וּ יָדֶֽיךָ׃
יח יְהוָ֥ה ׀ יִמְלֹ֖ךְ לְעֹלָ֥ם וָעֶֽד׃

14:30 Thus the LORD delivered Israel that day from the hand of Egypt.
Israel saw the Egyptians dead on the shore of the sea.
31 And when Israel saw the wondrous power which the LORD had wielded
against the Egyptians, the people feared the LORD;
They had faith in the LORD and His servant Moses.
15:1 Then Moses and the Israelites sang this song to the LORD. They said:
I will sing to the LORD, for He has triumphed gloriously;
Horse and driver He has hurled into the sea.
2 The LORD is my strength and might; He is become my deliverance.
This is my God and I will enshrine Him;
The God of my father, and I will exalt Him.
3 The LORD, the Warrior – LORD is His name!
4 Pharaoh's chariots and his army He has cast into the sea;
And the pick of his officers are drowned in the Sea of Reeds.
5 The deeps covered them; they went down into the depths like a stone.
6 Your right hand, O LORD, glorious in power,
Your right hand, O LORD, shatters the foe!
7 In Your great triumph You break Your opponents;
You send forth Your fury, it consumes them like straw.
8 At the blast of Your nostrils the waters piled up, the floods stood straight
like a wall; the deeps froze in the heart of the sea.
9 The foe said, "I will pursue, I will overtake, I will divide the spoil;
My desire shall have its fill of them.
I will bare my sword, My hand shall subdue them."
10 You made Your wind blow, the sea covered them;
They sank like lead in the majestic waters.
11 Who is like You, O LORD, among the celestials; Who is like You,
majestic in holiness, awesome in splendor, working wonders!
12 You put out Your right hand, the earth swallowed them.
13 In Your love You lead the people You redeemed;
In Your strength You guide them to Your holy abode.
14 The peoples hear, they tremble; agony grips the dwellers in Philistia.
15 Now are the clans of Edom dismayed; the tribes of Moab – trembling grips
them; all the dwellers in Canaan are aghast.
16 Terror and dread descend upon them; through the might of Your arm they
are still as stone, till Your people cross over, O LORD,
Till Your people cross whom You have ransomed.
17 You will bring them and plant them in Your own mountain,
The place You made to dwell in, O LORD,
The sanctuary, O LORD, which Your hands established.
18 The LORD will reign for ever and ever!

Exodus 14:30

וַיּוֹשַׁע יְהוָה בַּיּוֹם הַהוּא אֶת־יִשְׂרָאֵל מִיַּד מִצְרָיִם
וַיַּרְא יִשְׂרָאֵל אֶת־מִצְרַיִם מֵת עַל־שְׂפַת הַיָּם׃

Thus the Lord delivered Israel that day from the hand of Egypt.
Israel saw the Egyptians dead on the shore of the sea.

ויושע יי'

אמרו חכמים: בשעה שרדפו המצרים את ישראל וראו אותן ישראל אחזם אימה ורעדה. אז נמשלו ישראל ליונה שהיתה בורחת מפני הנץ וכשבאה לקנה מצאת שם נחש. כך ישראל בשעה שראו ישראל את המצרים אמרו למשה: משה רבנו אנה נלך – הרי המצרים לאחרינו והים לפנינו! אז נשאו קולם בבכיה ואף משה בכה עמהם.

מיד נתגלגלו רחמיו של הב"ה ואמר למשה: *מה תזעק אלי*? כבר זכור אני התפלה שהתפלל אברהם אוהבי בשעה (fol. 232r) שאמרתי לו, לך ושחוט את בנך לפני. מיד קבל באהבה ולמחר השכים לעשות רצוני, שנאמר *וישכם אברהם בבקר ויחבוש את חמורו ויקח את שתי [שני] נעריו אתו ואת יצחק בנו.*

ומי היו הנערים האלה? אליעזר עבד אברהם וישמעאל.

אמר יצחק לאביו: אבא לאן אנו הולכים לבדנו?

אמר לו: בני *עד כה*, עד מקום ~~רחוק~~ קרוב.

וכתיב *ויקח אברהם את עצי העולה וישם על יצחק בנו ויקח בידו את האש ואת המאכלת וילכו שניהם יחדיו.*

אמר יצחק לאביו: אבא לאנה נלך יחידים?

אמר לו: בני להקריב קרבן.

אמר לו: וכי כהן אתה להקריב קרבן?

אמר לו: הרי שם שהוא כהן גדול והוא יקריב את העולה.

מיד נפלה אימה גדולה על יצחק מפני שלא ראה כלום ביד אביו להקריב. וכתיב *ויאמר יצחק אל [אברהם] אביו ויאמר אבי ויאמר הנני בני [ויאמר] הנה האש והעצים ואיה השה לעולה?* מיד נזדעזע יצחק וירגזו אבריו שהכיר מחשבת אביו ולא היה יכול לדבר. ואף על פי כן נתחזק ואמר לאביו: אבי אם אמת שבחר בי הב"ה הרי נפשי נתונה לו. ונתפייס יצחק במותו בעבור לקיים מצות יוצרו.

אמר אברהם: אני יודע בני בך שאינך מעכב צווי יוצרך וצוויי.

The Lord delivered *[Israel that day from the hand of Egypt]* (Exodus 14:30 – Recension B)

The Sages said: When Israel saw the Egyptians pursuing them, fear and trembling seized them. In that moment, Israel was comparable to a dove fleeing to her nest in order to escape from a hawk, only to find a serpent once she got there.[1] Similarly, when Israel caught sight of the Egyptians, they said to Moses, "Moses our teacher, where will we go – the Egyptians are behind us and the sea is in front of us?!" Then they lifted up their voice in lament, and even Moses wept with them.

The mercy of the Blessed Holy One was stirred,[2] and He said to Moses, "*Why do you cry out to Me?* (Ex 14:15). I have already called to mind the prayer which my beloved Abraham asked of Me when I told him, 'Go and slaughter your son before Me.' He willingly agreed,[3] and the next day he rose early to do My will." As it is said, *So early next morning, Abraham saddled his ass and took with him two of his servants and his son Isaac* (Gen 22:3).

And who were these young men? Eliezer, the servant of Abraham, and Ishmael.[4]

Isaac said to his father, "Abba, where are we going by ourselves?"

"*Up to there* (Gen 22:5), my son, to a place nearby."[5]

It is written, *Abraham took the wood for the burnt offering and put it on his son Isaac. He himself took the firestone and the knife; and the two walked off together* (Gen 22:6).

Isaac said to his father, "Abba, where are we heading off together?"[6]

"To offer a sacrifice, my son."

"Are you a priest that you can offer a sacrifice?"

"Shem is high priest, and he will sacrifice the burnt offering."[7]

Just then, a great terror fell upon Isaac because he did not see anything in his father's hand to sacrifice. It is written, *Then Isaac said to his father [Abraham,] "Father!" And he answered, "I am here, my son." [And he said,] "Here are the firestone and the wood, but where is the sheep for the burnt offering?"* (Gen 22:7). Then Isaac shook, and his limbs shuddered, for he realized his father's intention. He was unable to speak.[8] Nonetheless, he fortified himself and said to his father, "Father, if the Blessed Holy One has truly chosen me, behold my soul is given unto Him." Isaac was reconciled to his death in order to fulfill the command of his Creator.[9]

Abraham said, "I know you, my son; you would not impede your Creator's command or my own."

השיב יצחק לאביו: אבי מהר ועשה רצון קונך והוא יעשה רצונך.

בעוד שהיו מהלכין בדרך קדמו שטן לאברהם בדרך ונדמה לו לזקן. אמר לו: לאנה תלך?

אמר לו: להתפלל.

אמר לו: ומי שהלך להתפלל מה צריך לו לישא עצים על כתפיו ואש ומאכלת בידו?

אמר לו: הן שמא נשהא יום או יומים ונשחט ונאפה ונאכל.

אמר לו: עני לא שם הייתי כשאמר לך [המשטין], *קח נא את ברכתי בנך את יחידך אשר אהבת* והעלהו לי לעולה?! וזקן כמותך יאבד בן חמוד כזה ובחור שנתן לך הב"ה למאה שנה!

אמר לו אברהם: הב"ה בעצמו אמר לי, *קח נא את בנך את יחידך אשר אהבת את יצחק* ועשה לפני עולה.

אמר לו השטן: *הלא יראתך כסלתך תקותך ותם דרכיך?*

אמר לו אברהם: (fol. 232v) מי הוא יאבד נקי איפה רשעים נכחדו?!

כיון שראה השטן שלא <קבל> אברהם דבריו אמר לו: תדע אברהם אומר לך בשורה, משה תעשה עולה ולא מן יצחק.

אמר אברהם: כך עונשו של בדאי שאפילו אומר אמת אין שומעין לו. ואיני מאמינך אלא הב"ה הטוב בעיניו יעשה.

בא שטן ועמד לפני יצחק ונדמה לו לנער כמותו. אמר לו: להיכן אתה הולך?

אמר לו: ללמוד תורה.

אמר לו: בחייך או במותך?

אמר לו: וכי יש אדם שילמוד תורה אחר מותו?!

אמר לו: אי בן עלובה, היאך יקהו שניך. ואי אתה יודע כי לזבוח מוליכך אביך בזו הדרך.

אמר לו: אני בעצמי יודע, והרי נפשי מסורה ביד הב"ה וביד אבי, כל מה שירצה לעשות יעשה.

ושוב הלך שטן לשרה ונדמה לה לאיש זקן. אמר לה: אברהם בעליך היאך הלך?

אמרה: למלאכתו הלך.

ובנך יצחק להיכן הלך?

Isaac answered his father, “Father, hurry and do the will of your Owner, so that He may do your will.”[10]

While they were still walking along, Satan, looking like an old man, intercepted Abraham on the path. He said, “Where are you going?”

“To pray.”

“What need is there for one going to pray to carry wood on his shoulders and a firestone and knife in his hand?”

“They are in case we tarry for a day or two; then we can slaughter, cook and eat.”

[Satan] said, “Poor soul, wasn’t I there when [the Deceiver][11] said to you, ‘*Please take*[12] *your son, your only one, whom you love* (Gen 22:2), and raise him up to Me as a burnt offering.’ An old man like you, losing a darling son like this, a young man whom the Blessed Holy One gave to you at age one hundred!”

Abraham said to him, “The Blessed Holy One Himself told me, ‘*Take your son, your only one, whom you love, Isaac* and make a burnt offering before Me.’”[13]

Satan said to him, “*Should not your piety be your confidence, your integrity your hope?*” (Job 4:6).[14]

Abraham retorted, “Who is it causing the innocent to perish; where have the wicked been destroyed?”[15]

When Satan saw that Abraham would not [accept][16] his words, he said, “You know, Abraham, I will tell you some good news: You will make a lamb the burnt offering and not Isaac.”

Abraham replied, “Such is the punishment of a liar:[17] Even when he speaks the truth, people do not listen to him. I do not believe you. The Blessed Holy One will simply do what is good in His eyes.”

Satan came and stood before Isaac, with the appearance of a young man like him. He said to him, “Where are you going?”

“To study Torah.”

“During your lifetime or after your death?”

“Is there anyone who can study Torah after his death?”

“Such an unfortunate son! How they set your teeth on edge.[18] You don’t even know that your father is leading you to sacrifice along this path.”

He said to him, “I *do* know and, look, my soul is delivered into the hand of the Blessed Holy One and into the hand of my father. Whatever he desires to do, he may do.”[19]

So Satan went off again, appearing to Sarah as an old man. He said to her, “Abraham, your husband – where did he go?”

“He went to work.”

“And your son, Isaac? Where did he go?”

אמרה לו: עמו הלך ללמוד תורה.

אמר לו [לה]: זקנה עלובה איך יקהו שניך על בנך, שאת יודעת שלזבח הוליכו בדרך.

באותה שעה נזדעזעו מתניה ונתחלחלו כל איבריה ולא היתה בעולם. ואף על פי כן נתחזקה וענתה: כל מה שאמר לו הב"ה יעשה לחיים ולשלום.

וכיון שראה אותו שטן לא עלתה בידו מחשבתו ותאות לבו לקבל [לבטל] קרבנו של אברהם אבינו מה עשה? הלך לעשות עצמו כנהר גדול. וכיון שהגיעו לאותו נהר אמר אברהם ליצחק: המתן לי מעט, ואכנס תחלה אני ואראה אם הוא עמוק. וכן עשה, ירד עד חצי הנהר ואין מגיעין המים עד ברכיו. אמר ליצחק: רד אחרי, אל תירא שהמים אינן מגיעין עד ברכי.

וירד יצחק אחריו. ולא הספיקו לרדת עד חצי הנהר עד שגברו המים והגביהו עד צואריהם. באותה שעה נשא אברהם את עיניו לשמים ואמר: רבונו של עולם גלוי וידוע לפני כסא כבודך שאתה הוא העליונים והתחתונים, ונגלית עלי ואמרת לי, אני יחיד שאין כמותי ואתה יחיד שאין צדיק בעולם כמותך, הודע שמי בעולם ועלה יצחק בנך לפני לעולה. ואני מהרתי לעשות רצונך (fol. 233r) ולא הרהרתי לומר: אתמול אמרת לי, *כי ביצחק יקרא לך זרע* ועכשו אתה אומר לי שאעלהו עולה?! ואם עכשו אנו טובעים מי מתיחד שמך בעולם הזה?

אמר לו הב"ה: בחייך אל תירא, על ידך יתיחד שמי בעולם. מיד גער הב"ה בשטן וחרבו המים על הארץ, ומצאו עצמם עומדים ביבשה.

בעוד שהיו מהלכים בדרך אברהם ויצחק נכנס תגרות בין ישמעאל ובין אליעזר שהיו שומרים את הכלים ואת בהמתם. אמר ישמעאל: עכשו יקריב אבא את יצחק ואני אירש כל הנכסים שנשארו מאבא.

אמר לו אליעזר: אתה כבר גרשך כאשה גרושה מבעלה ושילחך במדבר, אבל אני עבדו נאמן ביתו ביום ובלילה. ורוח הקדש משיבה ואומרת: לא זה יורשו ולא זה יורשו.

וכתיב *ויבואו אל המקום אשר אמר לו האלהים ויבן שם אברהם [את ה]מזבח <ויערוך את העצים> ויעקוד את יצחק בנו וישם [אותו על] אל המזבח ממעל לעצים.*

"He went with him to study Torah."[20]

He said to [her], "Unfortunate old woman, how they set your teeth on edge regarding your son! You know, he is leading him along a path to sacrifice."

At that moment, her loins convulsed and all her limbs trembled; she was no longer in this world. Nonetheless, she fortified herself and answered, "All that the Blessed Holy One told him, he will do for life and peace."[21]

When Satan saw that his scheme had not succeeded, and he desperately wanted to [prevent][22] the sacrifice of Abraham our father, what did he do? He went and turned himself into a large river. When they arrived at the river, Abraham said to Isaac, "Wait for me a little bit; I will go in first and see if it is deep." So he did; he went down into the middle of the river but the water did not even reach his knees. He said to Isaac, "Come in after me. Don't be afraid; the water doesn't even reach my knees."

So Isaac went in after him. Before he managed to reach the middle of the river, the waters swelled and rose up to their necks. At that moment, Abraham raised his eyes to heaven and said, "Master of the world, it is revealed and known before the throne of Your glory that You are the One among celestials and terrestrials. You were revealed to me, saying, 'I am unique, for there is no one like Me; and you are unique, for there is no one in the world righteous as you are. Make My name known in the world by presenting Isaac your son to Me as a burnt offering.' And I hastened to do Your will. I did not consider saying, 'Yesterday You told me, *It is through Isaac that offspring shall be continued for you* (Gen 21:12), and now You tell me that I should offer him up as a sacrifice?!'[23] If we drown now, who will unify Your name in this world?"

The Blessed Holy One said to him, "By your life, do not be afraid. It is through you that My name will be unified in the world."[24] Then the Blessed Holy One rebuked Satan and the waters dried up on the earth; they found themselves standing on dry land.[25]

While Abraham and Isaac were still en route, haggling commenced between Ishmael and Eliezer, who were guarding their animals and the utensils. Ishmael said, "Now Abba will sacrifice Isaac and I will inherit all that remains of my father's property."

Eliezer said to him, "You have already been kicked out, like a wife divorced from her husband; he sent you into the wilderness. But I am his faithful household servant, day and night." The Holy Spirit responded, saying, "Neither this one nor that one will inherit."[26]

It is written, *They arrived at the place of which God had told him. Abraham built [the] altar there; <he laid out the wood>; he bound his son Isaac; he laid [him] on the altar, on top of the wood* (Gen 22:9).

אברהם היה בונה את המזבח ויצחק מושיט לו את העצים ואת האבנים. אברהם היה דומה לאדם שהיה בונה בית חתנות לבנו ויצחק היה דומה לאדם שהיה מכין עצמו לחופה שעושה בשמחה.

ואמר יצחק: אבא זרז עצמך וחשוף זרועך ואסור ידי ורגלי יפה יפה שאני בחור בן שלשים ושבע שנה ואתה זקן, וכשאראה את הסכין בידך אבעת מפחד הסכין ואבע<ט> בך, שהנפש חצופה, ושמא אעשה בי מום הבעיטה ואפסל מהקרבן. אלא בבקשה ממך אבא מהר עשה רצון קונך ואל תעכב וגלול בגדיך וחגור מתניך. ושרפני יפה יפה וטול אפר שלי והוליכה אצל שרה אמי, ותניחה בתיבה בחדר שלה, תזכור לה מן יצחק בנה בבכי.

ועוד אמר לו יצחק: יותר מזה כשתשחטני ותבדל ממני ותלך לשרה אמי ותשאל אותך, היאך יצחק בני? מה תאמר לה ומה תעשו לזקנתכם?

אמר לו: יודעים אנו שאחריך מעט יהיו ימינו. הוא שנחמנו עד שלא נולדת הוא ינחמנו מיום זה ואילך. מיד ערך את העצים ועקד אותו על גבי המזבח ממעל לעצים, אמץ את זרועותיו (fol. 233v) וגלגל את בגדיו ונתן שתי ארכבותיו עליו בכח גדול. והב"ה יתברך שמו יושב על כסא רם ונשא ראה היאך לבם שוה משניהם, והיה דמעות נושרות מאברהם ונופלות על יצחק ומיצחק נופלות על העצים והיתה נטבלת בדמעות.

מיד *וישלח אברהם את ידו ויקח את המאכלת לשחוט את בנו.* אמר הב"ה למלאכי השרת: ראיתם אברהם אוהבי היאך מתיחד שמי בעולם? אם הייתי שומע לכם בשעה שאמרתם בבריאת עולם, *מה אנוש כי תזכרנו ובן אדם כי תפקדנו*, מי היה מיחדני שמי בעולם הזה כאברהם?

באותה שעה בכו מלאכי השרת במר נפש. ומה היו אומרים? *נשמו מסלות שבת עובר אורח הפר ברית.* היכן הוא מתן שכרן של מכניסי אורחים? שכל האורחין שהיו באין מכל מקום מכניס אברהם בתוך ביתו ומאכילן ומשקן ומלוון לדרכים. היכן השכר שנטל אברהם? *הפר ברית*, הופר אותו ברית שאמרת לו, *כי ביצחק יקרא לך זרע*, *ואת ברית[י] אקים את יצחק* – והרי המאכלת על צוארו!

Abraham was building the altar while Isaac handed him the wood and the stones.[27] Abraham was like a man building a bridal chamber for his son, and Isaac was like a man getting ready for the huppah, which one does joyfully.[28]

Isaac said, "Abba, hasten to bare your arm and bind my hands and feet very well, since I am a young man, thirty-seven years old,[29] and you are elderly. When I see the knife in your hand, I could startle from fear of the knife and kick you, for the spirit is rash – lest I make a blemish on myself with the kick and be rendered unfit for the sacrifice.[30] Please Abba, just quickly do the will of your Owner and do not delay; roll up your garments and gird your loins. Burn me very well and take my ashes to Sarah, my mother. Let her set them in a chest in her room so she may tearfully be reminded of her son Isaac."

Isaac went on, "Further, once you have slaughtered me and are separated from me, what will you say when you go to Sarah, my mother, and she asks, 'How is Isaac, my son?' And what will the two of you do in your old age?"

He said to him, "We know that after you, our days will be few. He who comforted us before you were born, will comfort us again after today."[31] Then he arranged the wood and bound him on top of the altar, on top of the wood. He flexed his arms, rolled up his garments, and set his two knees on top of him with great strength. The Blessed Holy One, may His name be praised, sitting on a throne high and exalted, saw how their two hearts were the same. Abraham shed tears that fell upon Isaac, and from Isaac they fell on to the wood, immersing it in tears.[32]

And Abraham picked up the knife to slay his son (Gen 22:10). The Blessed Holy One said to the ministering angels, "Have you seen how My beloved Abraham unifies My name in the world? If I had listened to you when you said during creation, '*What is man that You are mindful of him, mortal man that you take note of him?*' (Ps 8:5) – who would unify My name in this world like Abraham?"[33]

At that moment, the ministering angels wept bitterly. And what did they say? "*Highways are desolate, wayfarers have ceased; a covenant has been renounced* (Isa 33:8).[34] Where is the reward of those who welcome guests? For Abraham would bring inside his home all the guests that came from every place, give them food and drink, and accompany them on their way.[35] What reward has Abraham taken? *A covenant has been renounced* – the covenant has been renounced which you declared to him: *It is through Isaac that offspring shall be continued for you* (Gen 21:12), and *My covenant I will maintain with Isaac* (Gen 17:21)[36] – and here the knife is at his throat!"

ובכו מלאכי השרת ונפלו דמעותיהם על הסכין עד שעמד ולא שלט בצוארו של יצחק. מיד פרחה נשמתו. אמר לו הב"ה למיכאל: מפני מה אתה עומד? אל תניחנו לשוחטו!

מיד קרא מיכאל לאברהם ואמר: [אברהם אברהם! ויאמר אליו הנני. ומפני מה קראו שני פעמים?] לפי שאברהם אבינו ממהר, והמלאך צווח כאדם מצרה ואומר: פלוני פלוני מה אתה עושה? *אל תשלח ידך אל הנער ואל תעש לו מאומה*.

אמר לו אברהם למלאך: הב"ה אמור לי ואתה אומר לי לא תשחטנו. דברי הרב ודברי תלמיד, דברי מי שומעין?

מיד *ויקרא מלאך יי' אל אברהם שנית מן השמים ויאמר בי נשבעתי נאם יי' יען אשר עשית את הדבר הזה ולא חשכת את בנך את יחידך כי ברך אברכך והרבה ארבה את זרעך ככוכבי השמים וכחול אשר על שפת הים ויירש זרעך את שער אויביו*.

מיד הניחו וחזרה נשמתו בו ועמד על רגליו ובירך: ברוך אתה מחיה המתים.

ובאותה שעה נשא עיניו לשמים ואמר: רבונו של עולם (fol. 234r) בשעה שיעמדו בני בצער תזכור להם זו השעה שאני עומד לפניך.

ועתה *דבר אל בני ישראל ויסעו*. ויען משה לפני הב"ה: רבונו של עולם ואני מה אעשה?

טול המטה אשר נתתי לך ולך לים בשליחותי, ואמור לו, אני שלוחו של יוצר בראשית, גלה דרכיך לבני שיעברו בך.

מיד הלך משה אל הים ואמר לו דברי הב"ה. ויען הים למשה: לא אעשה כדבריך לפי שאתה ילוד אשה, ולא זו בלבד אלא שאני גדול ממך שלשה ימים שאני נבראתי ביום השלישי ואתה לא נבראתי [נבראת] עד יום הששי.

מיד השיב ~~משה~~ משה דברי הים להקב"ה, ואמר לו הב"ה למשה: עבד מסרב לרבו, מה עושין לו?

אמר לו משה: מלקין אותו במטה.

אמר לו הב"ה: אף *אתה הרם את מטך ונטה את ידך על הים ובקעהו*. מיד *ויט משה את ידו על הים* ויבקעהו.

The ministering angels wept, and their tears fell upon the knife so that it no longer had any power over Isaac's neck.[37] But then his soul took flight. The Blessed Holy One said to Michael, "Why are you just standing there? Don't let him slaughter him!"

Then Michael called out to Abraham, saying, [*"Abraham, Abraham!" And he answered, "Here I am."* Why did he call him twice?][38] Because Abraham was rushing so the angel yelled out like a man in distress who says, "Hey you... hey you! What are you doing?! *Do not raise your hand against the boy, or do anything to him*" (Gen 22:12).[39]

Abraham said to the angel, "The Blessed Holy One, told me [to do it], and you are telling me, 'Don't slaughter him.' To whose words do we listen, to the words of the teacher or the words of a student?"[40]

Just then, *The angel of the Lord called to Abraham a second time from heaven, and said, "By Myself I swear, the Lord declares: Because you have done this and not withheld your son, your only one, I will bestow My blessing upon you and make your descendants as numerous as the stars of heaven and the sands on the seashore; and your descendants shall seize the gates of their foes"* (Gen 22:15–17).[41]

Then he let him be and [Isaac's] soul returned to him; he stood up and recited a blessing: "Praised are You, who revives the dead."[42]

At that point, [Abraham][43] lifted up his eyes to heaven and said, "Master of the world, when my children face difficulty, remember for them this moment that I stand before You."

And now *[Then the Lord said to Moses, "Why do you cry out to Me?] Tell the Israelites to go forward"* (Ex 14:15).[44] Moses responded to the Blessed Holy One, "Master of the world, what am I to do?"[45]

"Take the staff which I gave you and go to the sea in My commission. Tell him, 'I am the emissary of the Fashioner of creation. Reveal your paths to My children so they may cross over you.'"

So Moses went to the sea and declared the words of the Blessed Holy One. The sea answered Moses, "I will not do as you say, for you are born of woman. Not only that, but I am three days older than you, for I was created on the third day and [you] were not created until the sixth day."[46]

Moses[47] then reported the sea's words to the Blessed Holy One. The Holy One said to Moses, "If a servant refuses his master, what do they do to him?"

Moses said to him, "They strike him with a staff."

The Blessed Holy One said to him, "You, too – *Lift up your staff, extend your hand over the sea and split it*" (Ex 14:16). Then *Moses held out his arm over the sea* (Ex 14:27) and split it.[48]

והיו יראין ישראל לבא בים עד שקפץ נחשון בן עמינדב וירד תחלה בים, ואחריו באו כל ישראל ביבשה *והמים להם חומה מימינם ומשמאלם*.

אמרו חכמים ז"ל: וכי ישראל היו מסורין ביד המצריים, שהוא אומר *ויושע יי׳ ביום ההוא את ישראל מ[יד] מצרים*? עמד עוזא שר של מצרים לפני הב"ה ואמר לפניו: רבונו של עולם אומה זו שאתה מוציא ממצרים יש לי דין עליהם, אם רצונך יבוא מיכאל שר שלהם וידון עמי לפניך.

מיד קרא הב"ה למיכאל שר של ישראל: בא לדין עם עוזא לפני.

מיד התחיל עוזא ואמר לפניו: רבון העולמים אתה גזרת על אומה זו שיהיו משועבדים תחת יד אומתי ארבע מאות שנה. ועדין לא עבדו בהם אלא שמונים שנה ושש שנים מיום שנולדה מרים. ולפיכך נקראת שמה מרים על שם שמררו המצרים חייהם. וכאתה קיים כך וכך תהא גזרתך קיימת.

כששמע כך מיכאל נשתתק ולא היה לו מענה לעשות לעוזא שר של מצרים. כיון שראה הב"ה שהיה רוצה עוזא להחזיק את ישראל במצרים אמר לעוזא: מפני מה אתה רוצה להחזיר את בני לשעבודך? כלום נתחייבו בני לעבור[ד] לאומתך אלא בעבור דבר אחד שדבר אברהם בשעה שאמרתי לו *אני יי׳* (fol. 234v) *אשר הוצאתיך מאור כשדים לתת לך את הארץ הזאת לרשתה*. אמר לפני, רבון העולמים *במה אדע כי אירשנה*? ועל דבר זה אמרתי לו גרים יהיו, במצרים לא אמרתי אלא *בארץ לא להם*. גלוי וידוע מיום שנולד יצחק היו גרים. וכבר עבדו אותם ארבע מאות שנה ואין לך רשות לשעבד את בני.

וזה שאמר הכתוב *ויושע יי׳ ביום ההוא את ישראל מיד מצרים, וירא ישראל את מצרים מת על שפת הים*.

But Israel was afraid to come into the sea until Naḥshon b. Aminadav jumped in and went down first into the sea.[49] After him all the Israelites came into the dry seabed, *and the water was a wall for them, on their right and on their left* (Ex 14:29).

[50]The Sages, may their memory be for a blessing, said: But was Israel delivered into the hand of the Egyptians[51] that the text should say, *Thus the Lord delivered Israel that day from [the hand of] Egypt* (Ex 14:30)? Uza, guardian angel of Egypt,[52] stood before the Blessed Holy One and said to him, "Master of the world, I have a legal claim against this nation that You are bringing out of Egypt. If You please, let Michael their guardian angel come and dispute with me before You."[53]

Then the Blessed Holy One called Michael, the guardian angel of Israel, "Come with Uza to a court case before Me."[54]

Uza then began[55] speaking before Him, "Master of all worlds, You decreed that this nation should be enslaved under the authority of my nation for four hundred years.[56] But they have enslaved them only eighty-six years, since the day Miriam was born.[57] That is why she was named Miriam, because the Egyptians embittered their lives.[58] And just as You endure, so too Your decree should endure."[59]

When Michael heard this, he was silenced and had no answer for Uza, guardian angel of Egypt.[60] Once the Blessed Holy One saw that Uza wanted to hold[61] Israel in Egypt, He said to him, "On what account do you want to return My children to your servitude? Nothing obligated My children to serve your nation, except for one thing that Abraham said when I told him, '*I am the Lord who brought you out from Ur of the Chaldeans to assign this land to you as a possession*' (Gen 15:7). He said to Me, 'Master of all worlds, *how shall I know that I am to possess it*?' (15:8). For this, I told him that they would be strangers;[62] I did not say 'in Egypt,' but only *in a land not their own* (15:13). It is well-known that from the day Isaac was born, they were strangers. They have already served the four hundred years, and you have no authority to enslave My children."[63]

This is what the text means, *The Lord delivered Israel that day from the hand of Egypt, and Israel saw Egypt dead on the shore of the sea* (Ex 14:30–31).

וזו היא אגדות של ויושע

***ויושע** יי' ביום ההוא את ישראל מיד מצרים*

אמרו חכמים: וכי ישראל מסורין היו ביום ההוא ביד מצרים, שהוא אומר ***ויושע** יי' ביום ההוא את ישראל מיד מצרים*? אמרו חכמים: בשעה שיצאו ישראל ממצרים עמד עוזא שר של מצרים לפני הקב"ה ואמר לפניו: רבונו של עולם אומה זו שאתה מוציא ממצרים יש לי עליהם דין. יבא מיכאל שר שלהם וידון עמי בפניך.

באותה שעה אמר הקב"ה למיכאל: בא לדון עמו בפני.

פתח שר של מצרים לפני הקב"ה ואמר לפניו: רבונו של עולם אתה גזרת על אומה זו שיהיו משועבדים תחת אומה שלי ארבע מאות שנה שנאמר *ועבדום וענו אותם ארבע מאות שנה.* ועדיין לא שעבדו אלא שמונים שנה מיום שנולדה מרים. לכך נקרא מרים על שם שמררו אותם שנאמר *וימררו את חייהם בעבודה קשה.* ועדיין לא הגיע זמן יציאת מצרים אלא תן לי רשות ואחזירם למצרים ויהיו משועבדים תחת יד אומה שלי שלש מאות וארבע עשרה שנה. כשם שאתה קיים כך שבועתך קיימת.

באותה שעה אמר הקב"ה למיכאל שר של ישראל: החזר תשובה לשר של מצרים שהוא רוצה להחזירם לשיעבודם. באותה שעה שתק מיכאל ולא היה בידו להחזירו.

באותה שעה ענה הקב"ה לשר של מצרים: שמא יש בידך זכות לך או לאומה שלך שאני אמסור בניי לשעבד בשעבוד קשה שבעולם, או שמא <לא> באתם אלא מכחו של (fol. 352v) כוש שבמעשיו הרעים שניתי אותו מכל ברייא ועשיתי אותו שחור?

ואומר: שמא נתחייבו בניי בשבילו לשעבוד זו? אלא בשביל דיבור אחד שדיבר אברהם אוהבי לפני בשעה שאמר *במה אדע כי אירשנה?* על כן אמרתי יהיו גרים במצרים *בארץ לא להם.* וגלוי וידוע לפני כי מיום שנולד יצחק זרעו של אברהם נעשו כולם גרים. כבר יש להם ארבע מאות שנה אין לך שעבוד עליהם כלל.

This is "Tales of vaYosha."[64]
The Lord delivered *Israel that day from the hand of Egypt* (Exodus 14:30 – Recension A).

The Sages said: But was Israel delivered on that day into the hand of Egypt, that the text should say, *The Lord delivered Israel that day from the hand of Egypt*? The Sages said: When Israel left Egypt, Uza guardian angel of Egypt stood before the Blessed Holy One and said, "Master of the world, I have a legal claim against this nation whom you are bringing out from Egypt. Let Michael their guardian angel come and dispute with me before You."

Then the Blessed Holy One said to Michael, "Come to dispute with him before Me."

The guardian angel of Egypt opened, "Master of the world, You decreed that this nation should be enslaved under the authority of my nation for four hundred years, as it is said: *They shall enslave and oppress them four hundred years* (Gen 15:13). But they have been enslaved only eighty years since the day Miriam was born. That is why she was named Miriam, because they embittered their [lives], as it is said, *They embittered their lives with harsh labor* (Ex 1:14). The time has not yet arrived for the exodus from Egypt. So give me permission to return them to Egypt and let them be enslaved under the authority of my nation three hundred fourteen years [more]. Just as you endure, so too your oath endures."

Then the Blessed Holy One said to Michael, guardian angel of Israel, "Give an answer to the guardian angel of Egypt, for he wants to return them to their servitude." But Michael was silent and had no response for him.[65]

Then the Blessed Holy One answered the guardian angel of Egypt, "What merit do you or your nation possess that I should deliver My children to the harshest servitude in the world? Didn't you come from the line (lit: strength) of Cush whom I turned black on account of his evil deeds, making him different than other creatures?!"[66]

He went on, "Did My children do anything that made them liable for this servitude? It is only on account of one thing that My beloved Abraham said to Me: *How shall I know that I am to possess it?* (Gen 15:8). For this I said they would be strangers in Egypt, *in a land not their own* (v. 13). It is revealed before Me that from the day of Isaac's birth, all of Abraham's descendants have been strangers. They already have four hundred years. You have no claim of servitude over them at all."

באותה שעה הציל הקב"ה את ישראל מיד מצרים לכך נאמר *ויושע יי׳ ביום ההוא את ישראל מיד מצרים.*

It was then the Blessed Holy One saved Israel from the hand of Egypt; thus it is said, *The Lord delivered Israel that day from the hand of Egypt* (Ex 14:30).

Exodus 14:30 Commentary

I. Abraham and the Song at the Sea

Akeidat Yitzḥak, the Binding of Isaac, is often invoked in rabbinic literature as bearing salvific power for later generations. Within the biblical narrative itself, Abraham's exceptional faith in following the Divine charge earns abiding blessing for his descendants (Gen 22:16–18). In later imagination, the trial becomes key to God's remembrance and forgiveness. During Rosh haShanah, for instance, a number of *seliḥot* (penitential prayers) dramatize the passage; it stands as a prescribed Torah reading; the shofar becomes a symbolic remembrance of the ram; and the middle movement of the symphonic shofar service (*zikhronot*) specifically recalls the near sacrifice for the vicarious merit it may bestow.

Many Talmudic and midrashic texts entreat God to bear in mind Abraham's trial when the people are in trouble or are accused of wrongdoing, without a context that makes it specific to salvation at the sea.[67] Among passages that connect the *akeidah* to the miracle at the Sea of Reeds, several offer an exegetical correlation: Abraham splits wood for the sacrifice (יבקע, Gen 22:3), just as the waters are split during the Exodus (ויבקעו המים, Ex 14:21).[68]

Midrash vaYosha presents an alternative logic for the association, prompted by the textual difficulty of God's incongruous reply to Moses regarding the frightened Israelites: *"Why do you cry out to Me?"* (Ex 14:15). Trapped at the sea, there is good reason to cry out for help and no way Moses should expect he has the power to save the people. Rather than read God's question as rebuke, the midrashist transforms it into reassurance: You do not even need to ask for help; it has been ready for you ever since Abraham offered his prayer before Me. Indeed, at the end of the trial, the midrash sets a prayer into the mouth of Abraham, creating a narrative frame for the passage.

The other connective tissue between the two biblical tales is comprised of tears. In the midrash, the Israelites, Moses, Abraham, and the angels all weep. It is presumed that Sarah will cry, and perhaps Isaac sheds tears as well. Together, they shape the flow of the narrative. Traveling barely long enough to dream of freedom, Moses and the Israelites see the Egyptian troops in pursuit and weep at the shore of the sea. Their cry stirs Divine mercy and leads to remembrance of the *akeidah*. When Abraham weeps, then, he not only manifests the emotional bond with Isaac sorely lacking in the biblical narrative; he similarly advances discourse between heaven and earth and builds a bridge to the nation's plight at the Sea of Reeds.[69]

II. The Bridal Canopy

One of the moments that gives body to the relationship of father and son is their shared labor in building the altar, undertaken with the joy of preparing a bridal canopy (*ḥuppah*). If Isaac is the young man about to marry, who is his bride? It is the Blessed Holy One, to whom Isaac will be forever wed in his sacrifice.

Tragically, many such marriages did take place in the Jewish community during the Middle Ages, granting the metaphor historical reality and transformative power. Jewish communities that were attacked during the Crusades and other medieval assaults found the image of the *ḥuppah* compelling, as countless martyrs gave their lives to God in order to avoid sin and apostasy. Rabbi Hillel ben Jacob, for instance, portrays the courageous martyrs of Blois who were killed in reaction to a blood libel (1171) with the metaphor:

And when it was said, "Bring them out to the fire,"
They rejoiced together as a bride at the bridal canopy.
"It is for us to praise," they recited, their souls filled with longing.[70]

Rabbi David bar Meshullam of Speyer similarly invokes the incongruous image of wedding joy in describing Jewish victims of the First Crusade. Like Abraham in MV, the poet expects the Jews' unfathomable faithfulness to draw down Divine salvation:

Has it ever been heard or ever been seen,
Who can believe so astounding a thing?
They lead their children to slaughter
as to a beautiful bridal canopy,
About *this* can You be silent, O Exalted Divinity?![71]

In another stanza, he employs subtle allusion to the *akeidah* in his language, which portrays women and children preparing for death with images of binding. Other liturgical poems (*piyyutim*) are more explicit:

O Lord, Mighty One, dwelling on high!
Once, over one *akeidah*, Ariels cried out before You.
But now how many are butchered and burned!
Why over the blood of children did they not raise a cry?[72]

Of course, it is only an exegetical tradition that the angels protest,[73] but it is real enough to medieval Jewry to make the celestial silence they experience unbearable. As a fundamental principle, God is expected to answer the cries of the faithful.

III. Compositional Units

None of the above interpretation is found in Recension A, which begins with Uza's complaint. In the explication of *Thus Moses sang* (15:1), it does make a brief connection between Abraham's obedience and God's salvation at the sea (not found there in Recension B). A separate midrash titled עקידת יצחק (*Akeidat Yitzḥak – The Binding of Isaac*) that includes many elements of this narrative did circulate in Ashkenaz and is found in two manuscripts (Drm 25 and War 258) next to MV.[74] In the evolution of the midrash, it is possible that a juxtaposition of texts later became an integration of texts, but the precise catalyst is not clear.[75]

As it stands, the passage reflects nicely the more literary quality of Recension B, with a lengthy narrative and carefully developed dialogue structure. While the plot elements are very similar to the separate midrash on the *akeidah*, our redactor seems to have reshaped the text with more deliberate construction of compositional units. The section leading up to Mt. Moriah is composed of a series of dialogue scenes: Isaac and Abraham, Satan and Abraham, Satan and Isaac, Satan and Sarah, Abraham and God, Ishmael and Eliezer. In turn, these scenes appear to align as a series of pairs. This chart reveals the profound symmetry of the first pair:

Isaac and Abraham:	*Satan and Abraham:*
A1: Where are we going? (place)	B1: Where are you going? (purpose)
A2: Where are we going? (for what purpose)	B2: Why carry these things if that is your purpose?
A3: Can you do this? (offer sacrifice like a priest)	B3: Will you really do this? (sacrifice son God gave you)
A4: Isaac speaks Gen 22:7.	B4: Abraham speaks Gen 22:2.
A5: Isaac embraces God's command.	B5: Satan impugns God's command.
A6: Abraham expresses his faith in Isaac.	B6: Abraham expresses his faith in God.
A7: Isaac: Hurry to do it (God's will), so God may do yours.	B7: Satan: You won't really do it. Abr: God will do His will.

Isaac and Satan both pepper Abraham with questions, trying to get him to reveal the nature of this journey. While the first two queries are logistical (where/why), Abraham's honest but deliberately ambiguous answers force a third question that cuts to the heart of the matter: Can you really do this? Such powerful comparisons usually point to a powerful contrast: When Isaac asks his father if he can offer this sacrifice, he has no idea of the true theological dilemma, one that has nothing to do with priestly status. In fact, all of his first three questions are spoken in ignorance. Satan, on the other hand, knows precisely what he is asking, especially when he questions whether Abraham will really go through with this misguided mission.

In both scenes, Part 4 is the center and climax of the scene in which the hero is confronted with the Divine command, and it is encapsulated in an actual verse from the biblical narrative. Isaac's question takes on new meaning in light of the midrash. Transformed into a moment of realization, he is not asking about the location of the sheep for the burnt offering, but its identity. Abraham, too, is focused on identity in his verse: It is God who spoke those fateful words (B4).[76]

The denouement in both dialogues also presents a parallel structure, highlighting critical differences between Abraham's interlocutors. While Isaac is reconciled to God's will, Satan challenges the justice of it (5). Isaac urges his father to fulfill the command, but Satan argues that it is not going to happen (7). The last, rather poignant contrast between the scenes is that Isaac suggests faithful obedience will ultimately enable Abraham to accomplish his own goals as well, while Abraham concludes the second scene by affirming that the only issue of substance is what God wills.

Parallels between the third and fourth dialogue scenes (Satan with Isaac, Satan with Sarah) are simpler to recognize: Satan asks a question, then a more pointed question, and then explains to each of them that Isaac is being led to his death. The phrase, "how they set your teeth on edge" is an interesting one, suggesting that "they" are Abraham and God, inflicting vicarious suffering on Isaac and Sarah, just as in Jeremiah 31:28: *The fathers have eaten sour grapes, and the children's teeth are set on edge*. The tension between the two dialogues is drawn in the disparity of knowledge; Isaac knows his fate at this point, but Sarah does not. Still, each is resolved at the end to submit to the Divine will.

The last pair of scenes before arriving at Mt. Moriah is not quite as tidy; there are additional actors or voices, and they seem distinct from each other in substance and tone. Still, the connection between them enhances the narrative:

E1:	Hoping to protect Isaac, Abraham seeks safe passage across the river.	F1:	Hoping to outlive Isaac, Ishmael seeks inheritance.
E2:	Presenting himself as worthy based on service, Abraham claims uniqueness.	F2:	Presenting himself as worthy based on service, Eliezer claims inheritance.
E3:	God: (Do not be afraid); you are the one.	F3:	Heavenly voice: You are *not* the ones.

Again, contrast between them magnifies the message. Because Abraham recognizes here, as he does in the first pair of scenes (and as Isaac and Sarah do in the second), that *God* is the actor of consequence, he is the one to unify the Divine name. Some of the background differences are also significant: 1) In E, the speakers try to calm each other's fears, while the actors in F try to stoke them; 2) Abraham is wrestling with the spiritual inheritance, while Ishmael and Eliezer are arguing about material goods.

In addition to the *form* of the dialogue scenes, three thematic elements tie the chain together. One is fear: In Scene A, Isaac is afraid when he learns of the Divine command (even though he ultimately is reconciled to it). In Scene E, Abraham is afraid that he will not live long enough to fulfill it. The second theme is challenging God. Both Satan and Abraham question God's actions with a rabbinically sanctioned method for *ḥutzpa klapei shamaya* (audacity toward Heaven): They quote the Bible or God's previous statements against Him.[77] Satan challenges God by claiming a dialectical tension between Divine justice, which should reward the righteous, and the command to sacrifice Isaac. Abraham is willing to accept the inscrutability of God's justice, but he offers two challenges to God. Sneaking the first in "through the back door," Abraham claims that he did not question the command to sacrifice Isaac even though it contradicts the promise to perpetuate Abraham's seed through him. Now that Plan B is also threatened, Abraham articulates the second challenge: You said I was *the* person for this job; if you let me die, Your will will not be done and Your name will not be unified.

Satan as the antihero is the strongest of the unifying factors, advancing the drama with his increasingly desperate actions. First he attempts to drive a wedge between the hero(es) and God, then between Abraham and his family, then – physically – between Abraham, Isaac and the place of sacrifice. An objective reader might sympathize with Satan's position at the beginning, expressing an average person's doubts about the propriety of such a mission. By the time he threatens the lives of the heroes, however, Satan's failure is absolute. He prevents nothing and proves nothing; Abraham and Isaac emerge as knights of faith, and the covenant is affirmed.

After the altar is built at Mt. Moriah, the unfolding drama is also composed of dialogue scenes: Abraham and Isaac, God and the angels, Abraham and Michael. Here the structure forces a series of ironies to the fore. It is ironic that the scene describes preparations for a wedding, a scene of joy, but all the characters (both present and merely mentioned) end up distressed or in tears. It is ironic that the earthly actors are both resolved while the doubt moves on high, and this tension becomes so acute that Abraham resists the angel who comes to prevent Isaac's slaughter. It is ironic that Isaac dies anyway, and that the scene which begins with him laying dead is the one that is most full of blessing: The angel delivers Divine blessing, Isaac is revived and utters blessing, and Abraham invokes blessing for his descendants in a future time of trouble.

IV. The Seams

Even though Recension B manuscripts distinguish, "**And now** *Tell the Israelites to go forward*" (Ex 14:15) with enlarged letters for the first word(s), it is best not to consider the passage a separate pericope. "And now" suggests a self-consciousness about the lengthy excursus involving Abraham: "and now" we return to our previous discussion. The midrash picks up the thread of biblical narrative after God asks Moses why they cry out at the shore of the sea. In fact, the dialogue begins with "he responded" and gives the distinct impression of resuming a conversation interrupted in the middle. Bracketing the *akeidah* of the previous section, the text flows smoothly into Divine instruction to split the sea, and the challenges Moses faces in fulfilling this charge. It then culminates in repetition of the original lemmatic verse (Ex 14:30), as do most of the pericopes. Integration of the passages also obviates the textual difficulty of improperly sequenced lemmas (Ex 14:15 between Ex 14:30 and 14:31).

Another seam appears where the midrash conveys material that stands at the beginning of Recension A: Uza's suit before the Most High. The text repeats both the lemmatic verse and the introductory formula, "The Sages say...," revealing a trace of the original opening of the midrash.[78]

V. Uza and Egypt

Assigning angels to the nations is pervasive in rabbinic literature. The fact that the verse speaks of Egypt as a collective entity elicits this exegesis which imagines a corporate representative who tries to take Israel in its power again. Here, both "hand" and "dead" are written in the singular form (Ex 14:30).[79]

Uza figures in numerous midrashim, frequently as an advocate for the Egyptians against Israel, but at times identified as one of the angels who mated with human women and taught magical arts, a fallen angel, or an angel who opposed the creation of humanity.[80] Linkage between these roles is possible. For example, rabbinic tradition considers Egypt to have been rife with magical practices, and the angel's reputation as a a teacher of magic could suggest his patronage of the nation.[81] Alternatively, the lust of the fallen angels in Genesis (Gen 6) could have become associated with rabbinic stereotyping of Egypt as a place of fornication, again insinuating that Uza is its most appropriate angelic patron.[82] Al-'Uzzà is also identified as one of three chief goddesses in pre-Islamic Arabia, mentioned in inscriptions at Petra and Dedan.

Recension A manuscripts develop the negative character of Egypt more explicitly here, including disturbingly racist remarks that trace the ancestry of Egyptians to Cush and assert that he was "turned black" for his evil deeds. The biblical record (e.g., Jer 13:23, which asks if a Cushite can change his skin) suggests the descendants were distinguished by skin color and the Septuagint uniformly translates Cush as Ethiopia, but these are not derogatory references.[83] It is possible that Recension B manuscripts omit the offensive material because they are created by Jews with dark skin, given that these texts were copied in Sepharad, North Africa and the Near East.

The lineage is problematized as early as Noah, when Ham (the father of Cush) saw his father's nakedness and did not modestly cover him as did his brothers (Gen 9:22–10:7). It is another of Ham's sons, Canaan, who is cursed at that point as part of the biblical polemic against Canaanites, but Cush's line is condemned in rabbinic literature as the ancestor of Nimrod and the Babylonians. Portrayed as creators of weaponry and empires (see Gen 10:8–10), they were easy to demonize, especially in light of the fact that the Babylonian empire destroyed the First Temple and exiled the Judeans.

Exodus 14:31

וַיַּרְא יִשְׂרָאֵל אֶת־הַיָּד הַגְּדֹלָה אֲשֶׁר עָשָׂה יְהוָה בְּמִצְרַיִם
וַיִּירְאוּ הָעָם אֶת־יְהוָה וַיַּאֲמִינוּ בַּיהוָה
וּבְמֹשֶׁה עַבְדּוֹ׃

And when Israel saw the wondrous power which the LORD
had wielded against the Egyptians,
the people feared the LORD; they had faith in the LORD
and His servant Moses.

ויַּרא ישראל

אמרו חכמים: בשעה שבקש הב"ה להטביע [המצריים בים עמד עוזא שר של מצרים לפני הב"ה ואמר לפניו: רבונו של עולם מפני מה אתה רוצה להטביע] את בני בים? כלום טבעו בני מבניך או הרגו אפילו אחד מבניך? ואם בשביל שעבדו בהם שעבוד גדול אתה רוצה להטביעם, כבר ב[נ]טלו בניך את שכרם של כסף וזהב שהיו להם נטלו.

מיד כנס הב"ה כל פלמיא [פמליא] של מעלה ואמר להם: שפטו ביני ובין עוזא שר של מצריים. באמת ב{מ}תחלה הבאתי עליהם רעב ו{ה}עמדתי להם יוסף אוהבי שהצילם בחכמתו, ואחר כך באו בני לשם כגרים מפני הרעב, והם שעבדו בהם בכל עבודה קשה שבעולם, והם צעקו מרוב העבודה. ותעל שועתם לפני ושלחתי להם לפרעה שלוחי נאמן משה ואהרן. ובאו לפני פרעה ואמרו, *כה אמר יי' שלח עמי ויעבדוני*.

ולפני אותו רשע היו יושבים מלכי מזרח ומערב והתחיל להתגאות ואמר, *מי יי' אשר אשמע בקולו*? איך לא בא לפני כמו שבאין כל מלכי העולם, ולמה לא הביא לי דורון כמו שמביאין לי כל המלכים? אבל אלוה זה שאתם אומרים אינ[י]ו מכירו. מה עשה? חזר ופשפש בנקביו [בפנקסיו] ולא מצא כתב משליחות.

השיב ואמר לעבדיו [אלוה זה מעולם שמעתם? השיבו לו חכמיו ואמרו] שמענו *שבן חכמים הוא ובן מלכי צדק קדם*.

ואמר לשלוחי, מה מעשיו של אלוה זה? השיבו לו ואמרו לו, הוא אלהי האלים ואדני האדנים, הוא ברא את השמים ואת הארץ, והוא ממית ומחיה ונפש כל חי בידו.

השיב ואמר לשלוחי, לא יש אלוה בכל העולם שיעשה אלו המעשים אלא אני לבדי, שאני בראתי עצמי ונילוס נהר. ועל דבר זה שכפר בו [בי] שלחתי בו עשר מכות עד ששלח בני בעל כרחו. ועל כל זאת (fol. 235r) לא מנע עצמו מרשעו וחוזר ורודף אחריהם להחזירם לשעבודו. לפי שנעשה בו כל זאת ולא הכיר אותי ואנו רוצים לטבעו בים הוא וכל חילו.

מיד ענו כל מפליא [פמליא] של מעלה ואמרו: דין גדול יש לך להטביעם בים.

And Israel saw *[the wondrous power which the Lord had wielded]* (Ex 14:31 – Recension B)

The Sages said: When the Blessed Holy One sought to drown [the Egyptians in the sea, Uza, guardian angel of Egypt, stood before the Blessed Holy One and said, "Master of the world, why do You want to drown][84] my children in the sea? Did my children drown any of Your children, or kill a single one? If it is because they worked them with slave labor that You wish to drown them, Your children already took[85] their reward with all the silver and gold that they procured."

The Blessed Holy One then convened all the heavenly retinue[86] and said, "Judge[87] between Me and Uza, guardian angel of Egypt. It is true that at first,[88] I brought famine upon them and elevated My beloved Joseph over them, who saved them with his wisdom. Later, My children came there as strangers on account of the famine. They subjugated them with every sort of hard labor that exists, and they cried out due to the crushing labor. Their cry rose up before Me, so I sent my faithful messenger Moses and Aaron to Pharaoh on their behalf. They came before Pharaoh and said, '*Thus said the Lord: Let My people go that they may serve Me* (Ex 8:16).'

"Kings of the east and west sat before this wicked man, and he began to boast,[89] '*Who is the Lord that I should listen to his voice* (Ex 5:2)? How is it that he has not come before me like all the kings of the world, and why has he not brought me tribute as do all the kings? [I] do not recognize this God of whom you speak.'[90] What did he do? He went back and searched in his [tablets][91] and found no written record of embassy.[92]

"He turned and said to his servants, ['Have you ever heard of this god?' His sages answered him,][93] 'We have heard that he is a *scion of sages*, and *a scion of Kedemite kings*.'[94]

"He said to My messengers, 'What are the deeds of this god?' They answered him, 'He is the God of gods, the Lord of lords; He created the heavens and the earth, grants life and death, and the spirit of all that lives is in His hand.'

"He responded to My messengers, 'There is no god in all the world who does these deeds except me alone, for I created myself and the Nile river.'[95] On the grounds that he denied Me,[96] I sent ten plagues[97] against him until he sent forth My children against his will. Nevertheless, he did not cease from his wickedness and went on to pursue them in order to return them to his servitude. Since all this was done to him and still he did not recognize Me, we want[98] to drown him in the sea, him and all his army."

Then the entire heavenly retinue[99] answered, "You have a strong claim to drown them in the sea."

כשראה עוזא פתח ואמר: רבון העולמים יודע אני שחייבין הם לך אלא יהי רצון מלפניך שתתנהג עליהם במדת רחמים ורחם על מעשה ידיך, כמו שכתוב *ורחמיו על כל מעשיו*.

ובקש הב"ה לרחם עליהם, עד שבא גבריאל שר של ישראל ונטל דפוס של לבנים שהיו עושין ישראל במצרים והראה אותם לפני הב"ה ואמר לפניו: רבון העולמים אומה ארורה שבזו העבודה הקשה שיעבדו את בניך, תרחם עליהם? וחזר הב"ה מן מדת רחמים וישב עליהם בכסא הדין וטיבען בים.

לכך נאמר *וירא ישראל את היד הגדולה אשר עשה יי' במצרים ויראו העם את יי' ויאמינו ביי' ובמשה עבדו*.

When Uza saw this, he opened by saying, "Master of the worlds, I know that they are culpable to You, but let it be Your will to behave toward them with the aspect of mercy, and have compassion on the work of Your hands, as it is written: *His mercy is upon all His works*" (Ps 145:9).

The Blessed Holy One sought to show mercy on them until Gabriel, guardian angel of Israel, came with a mold for bricks that Israel made in Egypt and showed them to the Blessed Holy One, saying, "Master of the worlds, You would have mercy on a cursed nation that enslaved Your children with this hard labor?!" The Blessed Holy One moved back from the aspect of mercy, and sat upon the throne of judgment – and drowned them in the sea.

Thus it is said, *When Israel saw the mighty hand which the Lord had wielded against Egypt, they were in awe of the Lord; they had faith in the Lord and his servant Moses* (Ex 14:31).[100]

וירא *ישראל את היד הגדולה*

בשעה שביקש הקב"ה להטביע את מצרים בים עמד עוז~~ה~~<א> שר של מצרים לפני הקב"ה: רבונו של עולם נקראת צדיק וישר אין לפניך לא שכחה ולא עוולה ולא משוא פנים ולא מקח שוחד, ולמ<ה> אתה רוצה להטביע את בניי בים? אם טבעו בניי מבניך או הרגו מהם כלום? ואף בשביל שעבוד קשה ששיעבדו בהם כבר נטלו מהם שכרם של כסף וזהב שלהם.

באותה שעה כינס הקב"ה כל פמליא של מעלה ואמר להם: הוו דיינין ביני ובין ישר של מצרים ודונו אותי באמת. בתחלה הבאתי עליהם רעב והעמדתי עליהם יוסף והציל אותם בחוכמתו ונעשו כולם עבדיו. ולבסוף באו בניי כגרים ושעבדו בהם שעבוד קשה מאד, עד שעלתה צעקתם לפני ושלחתי להם ולפרעה ~~לה~~ מלך שלהם משה ואהרן עבדיי ונאמניי. ואמרו לו: *כה אמר יי' אלהי העברים שלח עמי ויעבדוני.*

והיו לפניו כל מלכי מזרח ומערב והתחיל להתגאות לפניהם ומתרעם על שמי ואמר להם: *מי יי' אשר אשמע בקולו?* ומי אלוה זה שלא בא לפני כשם שבאו לפני כל אלהות שבעולם הם ומלכיהם ועבדיהם ומביאין לי מנחה? אלא אלוה זה מעולם לא ידעתי אותו, אלא המתינו לי ואשלח להביא לי ספרי ואראה שמא שמו כתוב אצלי או שיגר לי מנחה מעולם. שלח והביאו לו ספרים שלו ובדק ולא מצא.

ואמרו לו משה ואהרן: הוא שברא שמים וארץ, הוא צר וזן העובר במעי אמו, והוא משיב רוחות ומוריד גשמים וטללים, והוא מצמיח עשבים ואילנות, והוא ממית ומחיה, ונפש כל חי בידו.

השיב ואמר לשלוחיי: אין אלוה בעולם מי יעשה הללו אלא אני הוא בלבד. ואני הוא שבראתי עצמי ואת נילוס נהר שלי שנאמר אשר *אמר לי יאורי ואני עשיתיני.* השיב ואמר להם: השמעתם אלוה זה מעולם? ואמרו לו: שמענו שהוא בן חכם ו*בן מלכי קדם.*

And Israel saw *the wondrous power which the Lord had wielded* (Ex 14:31 – Recension A)

The Sages said: When the Blessed Holy One sought to drown the Egyptians in the sea, Uza, guardian angel of Egypt, stood before the Blessed Holy One, "Master of the world – called righteous and upright, before whom there is no forgetfulness or injustice, no favoritism or bribery – why do You want to drown my children in the sea? Did my children drown any of Your children, or kill a single one? Even if it is because they enslaved them with oppressive servitude, they already took from them their reward of their silver and gold."

The Blessed Holy One then convened all the heavenly retinue and said, "Judge between Me and the guardian angel of Egypt – and judge Me honestly.[101] In the beginning, I brought famine upon them and elevated Joseph over them, who saved them with his wisdom and everyone became his servants.[102] In the end, My children came as strangers on account of the famine. They subjugated them with such exceedingly difficult servitude, their cry arose before Me and I sent my faithful servants Moses and Aaron to them and to Pharaoh their king. They said to him, '*Thus said the Lord, God of the Hebrews: Let My people go that they may serve Me'* (Ex 9:13).

"All the kings of east and west sat before him, and he began to boast in front of them, thundering against My name, '*Who is the Lord that I should listen to his voice* (Ex 5:2)? And who is this god who has not come before me as have all the gods in the world, they and their kings and their servants, bringing me a gift? No, I have never known this god. But wait and I will direct that my books be brought to me, and I will see if perhaps his name is written in my records (lit: in my possession), or whether he has ever sent me a gift.' He sent [word] and they brought him his books. He checked but did not find anything.

"Moses and Aaron said to him, 'It is He who created heaven and earth, He formed and sustained the fetus in his mother's womb. He drives the winds and causes rain and dew to fall. He makes the grasses and trees grow. He grants death and life, and the spirit of all that lives is in His hand.'[103]

"He answered My messengers, 'There is no god in the world who does these [deeds] except me alone. I am the one who created myself and the Nile, my river.' As it is said, *...who said 'My Nile is my own; I made it for myself'* (Ezek 29:3). He turned to [his servants] saying, 'Have you ever heard of this god?' They said to him, 'We heard he is the scion of a sage, the *scion of Kedemite kings*.'[104]

השיב ואמר לשלוחיי: *לא ידעתי את יי' ואת ישראל לא אשלח.* וכיון שכפר בי שלחתי בו עשר מכות ולא הועיל לי. וכל כך היה כופר בי ומוסיף שיעבוד על בניי ולאחר שהודעתי לו כחי וגבורתי שלח אותם בעל כרחו. ועכשיו חוזר ורודף אחריהם להחזירם לשעבודם. ולמי עשה (fol. 353r) כל זאת אינו ראוי אלא לטובעו כי אם בים הוא וכל חילו.

השיבו פמליא של מעלה ואמרו: הדין עמך עשה מה שאתה חפץ.

באותה שעה ענה {שר} של מצרים לפני הקב"ה: רבונו של עולם יודע אני שהם חייבים לך אלא השב עליהם מדת רחמים.

באותה שעה עמד גבריאל ולקח מלבן של טיט ועמד לפני הקב"ה ואמר לפניו: רבונו של עולם אילו ששיעבדו {בשיעבוד זה} בניך תרחם עליהם? מיד שב עליהם הקב"ה במדת הדין וטבעם בים.

לכך נאמר *וירא ישראל את היד הגדולה אשר עשה יי' במצרים ויראו העם את יי' ויאמינו ביי' ובמשה עבדו.*

"He turned and said to My messengers, '*I do not know the Lord... nor will I let Israel go* (Ex 5:2)' Because he denied Me, I sent ten plagues against him to no avail; still he denied Me and increased the subjugation of My children. After I made known to him My power and might, he sent them forth against his will. And now he goes back and pursues them in order to return them to their servitude. To one who has done all this, is not drowning him and all his army in the sea the only fit thing to do?"

The heavenly retinue answered, "Judgment is with You. Do as You desire."

Then the {guardian angel} of Egypt responded before the Blessed Holy One, "Master of the world, I know that they are culpable to You, but respond to them with the attribute of mercy."

At that moment Gabriel arose and took a clay brickmold and stood before the Blessed Holy One and said to Him, "Master of the world, You would have mercy on these who subjugated Your children?!" Then the Blessed Holy One responded to them with the attribute of judgment and drowned them in the sea.[105]

Thus it is said, *When Israel saw the mighty hand which the Lord had wielded against Egypt, they were in awe of the Lord; they had faith in the Lord and his servant Moses* (Ex 14:31).

Exodus 14:31 Commentary

I. Embedded Interpreters

One of the essential narrative-exegetical synergies of *Midrash vaYosha* is the frequent embedding of interpreters within the tale. Characters are transformed into exegetes, frequently citing verses and setting biblical phrases within a narrative context that shapes their meaning.[106] Without interrupting the flow of the story, the text can address multiple cruxes, old and new, and even offer several readings in a single narrative through its collection of voices. Satan challenges Abraham's blind faith, Uza questions Divine justice, the sea dares to resist the grand scheme, etc. Classical midrash frequently conveys the multivocal quality of its interpretation by bringing alternative explanations (דבר אחר). *Midrash vaYosha* reveals the more subtle and compelling multiplicity that can be discovered within a single interpretation, although the designated voices frequently determine a preferred reading and the exchange transforms exegesis into drama.

Uza presents one of the best examples of this rhetorical strategy as he interprets the complex tale of slavery and Exodus. His initial charge, that the Israelites are violating a contractual obligation to four hundred years of slavery, reflects a long tradition of wrestling with conflicting chronologies in the biblical account. Uza references the vision presented to Abraham and spells out the theological ramifications if God should have a change of heart. He plays with Hebrew roots and quotes verses to determine the onset of servitude.

Unfortunately for him, his debate opponent turns out to be not Michael but God, a capable reader of text and the most reliable interpreter of Divine speech. "Stranger" does not mean slave, and "a land not their own" does not designate Egypt, God informs him; the clever dodge enables a different calculation that resolves the inconsistency and refutes the charge. In the process, another thread is woven into the fabric binding Abraham and the Exodus. Not only does Abraham's prayer help get the people out of their predicament, as seen in MV's treatment of the *akeidah*; Abraham's brief display of doubt also gets them into it in the first place. The symmetry has a certain elegance.

Setting the scene as a heavenly tribunal allows the midrash to entertain diverse perspectives on events at the Sea of Reeds. As Galit Hasan-Rokem points out, focusing on narrative dialogue can highlight the presence of orality in the written, and the possibility of plurality in the canonical.[107] Uza challenges the justice of requiring both payment and capital punishment for the sins of slavery; he is correct that compensation and execution are generally considered mutually exclusive avenues of justice. In response, God presents a litany of Pharaoh's unrelenting arrogance and failure to acknowledge the sovereignty of God, collecting evidence from Exodus, Isaiah and Ezekiel – a list so offensive it proves sufficient to condemn his entire army to death.[108]

When Uza admits culpability but makes a plea for Divine mercy, he articulates the problems some readers have (probably more frequent in modern times) with the severity of God's wrath. In Recension B, he even cites a verse from Psalms to make his case for clemency, and the midrash presents God moving onto the seat of mercy as a result. It displays the constant dialectic in God's stewardship of history and portrays a kinder, gentler face of the Divine. Gabriel sweeps in, however, to argue a different perspective. His evidence with the brickmold indicts the whole nation of Egypt for inflicting cruel oppression on Israel in construction of their garrison cities; justice must be done.

The most interesting question Uza raises, however, is the surprising defense: Did my children drown any of Your children, or kill a single one? At first it appears to be dripping with irony or patently absurd; of course the Egyptians drowned *and* killed the Israelites, the reader instinctively responds. What about Pharaoh's decree to drown all the male infants in the Nile? What about the beatings by the overseers? A careful review of the biblical narrative reveals that the only record of a baby actually being deposited in the river is Moses – by his mother – and the only documented murder during these years was at the hand of Moses! Their desperate actions *imply* that many Israelite lives were lost during Egyptian slavery, but there is no mention of it and Uza's creative exegesis forces an alternative possibility. He challenges what the reader "knows" about the terribly familiar narrative of the Exodus. Nonetheless, cast as the Egyptian angel he is doomed to failure; neither the reader nor the text is inclined to let his voice prevail.

In these first few passages, God, Abraham, Satan, Isaac, the angels on high, Uza, Gabriel – all are portrayed as interpreters of text as well as characters within it. The remainder of the midrash reveals many more examples of the embedded interpreter. Naomi Schor, in her analyses of modern fiction, identifies protagonists who explicate the meaning of events in the narrative as "interpretants." Although midrash is different in that the characters are also explicating an exterior text (the Bible), in both genres the technique shapes the reader's understanding, advances the narrative and tells the reader something about the necessary act of interpretation.[109]

Exodus 15:1

אָז יָשִׁיר־מֹשֶׁה וּבְנֵי יִשְׂרָאֵל אֶת־הַשִּׁירָה הַזֹּאת לַיהוָה וַיֹּאמְרוּ לֵאמֹר
אָשִׁירָה לַיהוָה כִּי־גָאֹה גָּאָה
סוּס וְרֹכְבוֹ רָמָה בַיָּם׃

Then Moses and the Israelites sang this song to the Lord:
I will sing to the Lord, for He has triumphed gloriously;
Horse and rider He has hurled into the sea.

אז ישיר משה

אמרו חכמים בשעה שבאו ישראל ליתן שירה להב"ה אמרו למשה: משה רבנו, אמור אתה תחלה ואחר כך נאמר אנחנו. מיד ענה משה לישראל: אמרו אתם תחלה ואחר כך אומר, שאני יחיד וכבוד רבים גדולה משל יחיד.

מיד פתחו ישראל: *נשיר ליי'* עד שעשה לנו נסים ונפלאות. בשעה שגזרו עלינו המצרים ואמרו, *כל הבן הילוד היאורה תשליכוהו*, היו אמותנו יוצאות לשדה ואתה מפיל עליהן תרדימה והיו יולדות אותנו בלא שום צער. ומשימין בידיהם שתי חתיכות והיו מלאכים ~~יוצאין~~ יורדים מן השמים ורוחצין וסכין אותנו והיו ומלבישין אותנו צבעונין, ומסימין בידיהם שתי חתיכות אחת של חמאה ואחת של דבש. ושנערות אמותינו, רואות אותנו רחוצים וסוכים ומלובשים ממשי, והיו נותנות שבח לשמך הגדול והיו אומרות, ברוך המקום שלא הניח חסדו ואמתו מזרעו של אברהם אבינו. ואומרות הרי הם בידך, עשה מה שאתה חפץ, והולכות להם.

וכשהיו המצריים רואין אותנו, באים להרגנו, ואתה ברחמיך הרבים הי[י]תה מצוה את האדמה ובולעת אותנו (fol. 235v) ופולטת אותנו במקום אחר, והיית מציל אותנו מידם. וכשהיינו גדולים היינו נכנסין למצרים חבורות חבורות וכל אחד ואחד היה מכיר אביו ואמו ומשפחתו. וכל זאת עשית לנו, לפיכך נשיר לפניך. לכן נאמר *אז ישיר משה ובני ישראל את השירה הזאת ליי'.*

Then Moses sang
(Exodus 15:1 – Recension B)[110]

The Sages said: When Israel came to offer song to the Blessed Holy One, they said to Moses, "Moses, our teacher, you recite first and then we will recite." Moses answered Israel, "You recite first, and then I will recite. For I am a single individual, and the honor of the multitude is greater than that of an individual."[111]

So Israel opened, "We will sing unto the Lord for[112] He performed miracles and marvels for us. When the Egyptians decreed against us: *Every boy that is born you shall throw into the river* (Ex 1:22), our mothers would go out into the field and You cast upon them a deep sleep so they would give birth to us without any pain. Angels came down from the heavens and bathed us, rubbed us with oil and swaddled us in colorful cloth. They set two portions in their hands, one of cream and one of honey.[113] And when our mothers awoke, seeing us bathed, anointed, and dressed in silk, they would give praise to Your great name, saying, 'Blessed is the Omnipresent who did not withhold His lovingkindness and His truth from the seed of Abraham our father.' Then they would say, 'Behold they are in Your hand; do as You wish,' and depart.

"When the Egyptians would see us, they would come to kill us, and You in Your great mercy commanded the earth to swallow us and deliver us to another place. Thus You saved us from their hand. When we were grown, we entered Egypt in groups,[114] and each one recognized his father, his mother and his family. All this You did for us, and therefore we sing unto You. Thus it is said, *Then Moses and the children of Israel sang this song to the Lord* (Ex 15:1)."[115]

אז ישיר משה

בשעה שאמר הקב"ה על הים נראה להם לישראל בעצמו ואין עמו לא מלאך ולא כרוב ולא שרף אלא הוא בעצמו ובכבודו לבדו כבתחלה. אמרו מלאכי השרת לפני הקב"ה: רבונו של עולם הנח לנו ונעשה נקמתך ורצונך בפרעה במצרים.

אמר להם הקב"ה: אני בעצמי ארד ואעשה נקמת בניי ואוהבי. שכך עשה אברהם אביהם כשאמרתי לו *קח נא את בנך את יחידך* את יצחק אשר אהבת. הוא בעצמו עמד בהשכמה לילך לעשות רצוני. וחבש החמור הוא בעצמו ועבדים היו לו הרבה, ולא נתקררה דעתו עד שעשה הוא בעצמו. אף אני לא נתקררה דעתי עד שארד אני בעצמי לעשות נקמה במצרים.

באותה שעה פתח הקב"ה עובר עיני עוברין במעי אמן ונתן להם רשות להסתכל בו. ופתחו כולם בשירה לפני הקב"ה ואמרו: אתה הוא שהצלתנו מיד מצרים בשעה שגזר *כל הבן הילוד היאורה תשליכוהו.* והיו אמותינו יוצאות לשדה ואתה ברחמיך הרבים הייתה מטיל עליהם שינה ויולדות בשינה שלא בצער ושלא בעצב. ויהיו מלאכי השרת יורדין ומרחיצין וסכין ומלפפין אותנו ונותנים בידי<נו> שני אבנים אחת של חמאה ואחת של דבש ואנו יונקין אותם. ואחר כך היו אמותינו מתעוררת ורואות את בניהן מרוחצין וסכין ומלופפין ושבעים חמאה ודבש. והן עומדות ונותנות שבח והודאה לשמו הגדול והנורא ואומר<ות>: ברוך שלא הניח זרעו של אברהם אביהם וחוזרות ואומרות ריבונו של עולם הרי הם בניך עשה מה שאתה חפץ לעשות והולכות לעצמן.

זכרות [וכיון] שמצרים רואים {ורוצים} אותנו מיד להורגינו ואתה ברחמיך הרבים צויתה לארץ והוא בולעת {אותנו} ומוציאה אותנו למקום אחר. והם מביאין שוורים וחורשים על גבינו שנאמר *על גבי חורשו חורשים.* ואתה מציל אותנו וכשנעשינו גדולים היינו מתאספים עדרים עדרים ונכנסנו במצרים וכל אחד היה מכיר אבותיו ומשפחתו. כל זאת עשה לנו הקב"ה במצרים ואף כאן טבע אותם בים. ולכך אנו משוררים שירה *כי גאה גאה סוס ורכבו רמה בים.*

***Then** Moses sang*
(Exodus 15:1 – Recension A)

When the Blessed Holy One spoke at the sea, He appeared to Israel by Himself; there was no angel or cherub or seraph with him – only God Himself in His glory as at the beginning.[116] The ministering angels said to the Blessed Holy One, "Master of the world, let us execute Your desired retribution on Pharaoh in Egypt."

The Blessed Holy One said to them, "I Myself will go down and execute retribution for My beloved children. For thus their father Abraham did when I said to him, '*Take your son, your only one* (Gen 22:2), Isaac whom you love.' He himself rose early to go and do My will. He saddled the ass himself, even though he had numerous servants, and he was not satisfied until he took care of it himself. Similarly, I am not satisfied until I go down Myself to execute retribution against Egypt."[117]

Then the Blessed Holy One opened the eyes of the fetuses in their mothers' wombs and gave them permission to look upon Him. They all launched into song before the Blessed Holy One,[118] saying, "You are the One who saved us from the hand of Egypt when it was decreed: *Every boy that is born you shall throw [into the river]* (Ex 1:22). Our mothers would go out into the field and, in Your great mercy, You cast sleep upon them so they would give birth while asleep, without pain or distress. Ministering angels came down and bathed us, rubbed us with oil and swaddled us. They set two stones in our hands, one of cream and one of honey, and we suckled from them. Afterwards, our mothers would wake up and see their children bathed, anointed, swaddled and sated with cream and honey; they would rise and give praise and thanksgiving to His great and awesome name, saying, 'Blessed is the One who did not abandon the seed of Abraham their father.' They would continue, 'Master of the world, behold they are Your children; do as You wish,' and then go off on their own.

"[When][119] the Egyptians would see us, they wanted to kill us, but You in Your great mercy commanded the earth to swallow us and take us away to another place. They would bring oxen to plow upon our backs as it is said, *Plowmen plowed across my back* (Ps 129:3).[120] But You saved us. When we were grown, we gathered in groups and entered Egypt;[121] everyone recognized his ancestors and family. All this the Blessed Holy One did for us in Egypt – and here He drowned them in the sea. Therefore we sing a song: *He has triumphed gloriously; horse and driver He has hurled into the sea* (Ex 15:1)."[122]

Exodus 15:1 Commentary

I. Miraculous Births in Egypt: Evolution of an Exegetical Narrative

Avigdor Shinan traces the motif of miraculous births in Egypt in order to illustrate the evolution of a narrative, with clear exegetical anchoring found in the *Babylonian Talmud* but a more independent aggadah in medieval midrash. Analyzing parallels in *b.Sotah 11b, Deut. Rab.* (only Lieberman, 14–15), *Midrash vaYosha* and *Chronicles of Moses,* he persuasively demonstrates that many of the motifs within the narrative trace back to an extended metaphor in Ezekiel 16. Upon reading the passage, it becomes clear how profoundly the biblical imagery shapes the story, in which the midrashist actualizes the figures within the narrative-historical context of slavery in Egypt:

> [4] *As for your birth, when you were born your navel cord was not cut, and you were not bathed in water to cleanse you; you were not rubbed with salt, nor were you swaddled.* [5] *No one pitied you to do any of these for you, to have compassion upon you; on the day you were born, you were left lying, rejected out in the open field....*
> [7] *I have caused you to grow like the plants of the field, and you continued to grow up until you attained to womanhood; your breasts became firm and your hair sprouted. Yet you were naked and bare....*[9] *Then I bathed you with water, and washed the blood off you, and anointed you with oil.* [10] *I clothed you also with embroidered garments, and gave you leather sandals to wear, and I wound fine linen around your head, and dressed you in silks.* [11] *I decked you out in finery and put bracelets on your arms, and a chain on your neck.* [12] *I put a ring in your nose, and earrings in your ears, and a splendid crown upon your head.* [13] *Thus were you adorned with gold and silver, and your apparel was of fine linen, silk, and embroidered cloth. Your food was choice flour, honey, and oil. You grew more and more beautiful, and became fit for royalty.*

The image of the abandoned infant, which the prophet uses as a symbol for the people Israel, becomes far more concretely the Israelite infants born in Egypt. The newborn was not *bathed* or *swaddled* (v. 4); God *bathes and anoints* the babe, dressing him in *fine silk* (vv. 9–10);[123] God causes him to grow like a plant *in the field* (v. 7), and sustains him with fine flour, *oil and honey* (v. 13).[124] Some of the traditions change (e.g. oil and honey as in Ezekiel and Deut 32 become cream and honey as in 2 Sam 17 and Job 20); other connections would not be evident at all were it not for the more directly exegetical approach of the parallel in the *Babylonian Talmud.* For instance, there is a word play on the “groups” that return to Egypt, based on Ezekiel 16:7: *You continued to grow up until you <u>attained to womanhood</u>* (בעדי עדים, an unusual phrase). The Talmudic passage states: “Don’t read בעדי עדים, but rather בעדרי עדרים (in groups).” Recension A preserves this word play in calling the groups עדרים עדרים but drops the overt exegesis; thus obscured, the link to the Ezekiel verse is completely lost at some point in manuscript transmission, yielding the alternative phrase, חבורות חבורות, in Recension B.

Another exegetical component leaves a visibly diminishing trace in MV. The Talmudic passage states that when the Egyptians come hunting for the newborns, they plow the earth where mothers and children disappeared; it cites Ps 129:3 to establish this detail: *Plowmen plowed upon my back*. After they are gone, the infants and mothers sprout up, *increasing like a plant in the field* (Ezek 16:7). What the prophet intended as a metaphor to express the amazing speed of Israelite population growth, the Talmudic narrative actualizes as women and children sprouting out of the ground. This reading is preserved in Recension A; in MS Family AB2, the plowing remains but without the verse, and the rest of the manuscripts of *Midrash vaYosha* have only the motif of the earth swallowing the Israelites to keep them safe from the Egyptians. Instead of imagining the earth as a fertile womb, it becomes a conduit to whisk the Israelites away from danger. In general, one finds a lessened exegetical connection to Ezekiel and more minimal prooftexting in MV than in the Talmudic passage.

Shinan asserts that this change exemplifies an evolution from exegetical narratives in the classical rabbinic period to free-standing stories that become more common in later collections of midrash. (He describes the passage in *Deuteronomy Rabbah*, which is part of the *Tanhuma-Yelammedenu* literature, as something in between.) Although Shinan is primarily focused on demonstrating that midrashic traditions are more dependent on exegesis in their formation than we may recognize, and that our appreciation of those foundations enhances our understanding, he also asserts that classical rabbinic exegesis (homiletical, exegetical and occasionally historical) is primarily didactic, while in medieval texts like *Midrash vaYosha* the story is key. "In medieval literature, the desire of a scribe sitting at his table to describe and to narrate has become primary; the epic impulse prevails over the other motivations."[125]

While the observation is compelling, it is important to note that the distinctions are neither consistent nor absolute. Each stratum of rabbinic literature both reveals and obscures exegetical strands based on its didactic requirements and textual sources. The Talmudic passage concludes with the children at the sea recognizing their Divine benefactor and exclaiming a verse from the Song, "*This is my God and I will enshrine Him, the God of my father, and I will exalt Him*" (Ex 15:2), but it is missing a piece for the sake of its story. *Ex. Rab. 23:8* and *Deut. Rab.* (Lieberman, 14–15) – medieval collections – record the missing exegetical connection; it could be "new," except that it makes sense of the signature verse. These texts emphasize that it was God Himself, not an angel, who tended the newborns in the wilderness. The mothers give birth, tell the Most High to do His part, and leave without knowing the fate of the infants. Thus, when the children return home, their parents ask how they survived, and they are told about a fair and ruddy young man with beautiful curls – the lover in Song of Songs 5:10–11, allegorically understood to be God.[126] When they get to the Sea of Reeds, the children recognize this same manifestation of God and point Him out to their parents, "*This is my God....*"[127]

Why is this absent in the Talmudic rendering of the motif? The *Sotah* passage is part of a sequence about righteous women and the blessings bestowed on their account; the omission might be because it does not suit the didactic purpose of the text to include child abandonment. Also, once God is removed as the nursemaid and replaced by an angel, the exegetical-narrative link to Song of Songs does not really work.

In *Midrash vaYosha*, the tradition travels to find new exegetical grounding. It abandons linkage to Ex 15:2 and the physical identification of God at the sea, but is not presented as an independent narrative. Instead, the passage explicates the confusion of plural and singular words in Ex 15:1 (Recension B) and the glorious aspects of Divine redemption, with God acting personally on behalf of Israel in Egypt and at the sea (Recension A). A story of miraculous births gains rhetorical power if "recalled" by the Israelites when it is their turn to praise; they recognize that God's salvation is comprised not simply of devastating plagues and marvels at the sea – but in having preserved the people through generations of oppression as well. Divine triumph over the arrogant, as Rashbam renders the doubled verb in Ex 15:1 (גאה גאה, triumphed gloriously), becomes vividly concrete when infants whom the Egyptians tried to kill stand as adults on the far shore of the sea and watch the imperial soldiers drown.

II. Alternative Interpretations

The numerous manuscripts and dynamic evolution of *Midrash vaYosha* leave a profoundly varied record. Many differences are minor, but rich alternative interpretations are also preserved in various manuscript families. In this instance, two variants are worth transmitting verbatim. In place of the miraculous tale about angels tending to the newborn Israelites in Egypt, MS Family A2 collects several different traditions:[128]

They opened their mouths in song saying, *"I will sing unto the Lord for He has triumphed gloriously. Horse [and driver He has hurled into the sea]"* (Ex 15:1). The Sages said: All songs and praises that a man recites to praise the Holy One in this world, he merits reciting (lit: praising with them) in the next world, as it is said: *Then Moses and the children of Israel will sing...* (Ex 15:1). It does not say "sang" (שר) but "will sing" (ישיר), teaching that just as one sang it [the song] in this world, so too will he merit singing it in the next world.[129]

It is written: *I will sing unto the Lord for He has triumphed gloriously* (Ex 15:1). The Sages said: Just as Israel rejoiced in the Egyptians' fall, so too the angels rejoiced when the Holy One called to the ministering angels and said to them, "Take care regarding My children and help them."

Then they rejoiced greatly and, amidst all the celebration, they went and stood on the shore of the sea and cried out to the waters on Israel's right, "Take care regarding Israel, for they are destined to receive Torah from the right hand of the Holy One, as it is said: *From His right hand went a fiery law for them* (Deut 33:2)."[130] Turning to the waters on their left, they said, "Take care regarding Israel, for they are destined to lay tefillin on the left [hand], as it is said: *You shall bind them as a sign upon your hand (ידכה).* יד כהה, the weak hand, is the left."[131] Turning to the waters behind them, they said, "Take care regarding Israel, for they are careful to cast the *tzitzit* (fringes) on the corners [of their garments] behind them, as it is said: *Instruct them to make fringes on the corners of their garments throughout their ages* (Num 15:38)." Turning to the waters in front of them, they said: "Take care regarding Israel, for they are careful about the commandment of circumcision."[132]

When the waters heard this, they guarded Israel. What did the ministering angels do? They stood behind the Egyptians and brought them down to throw them into the sea, but they couldn't do it. When the Blessed Holy One saw this, He sent an angel in front of them that looked like a mare, and the horses ran after her into the sea against their will, as it is said: *I have likened you, my darling to a mare in Pharaoh's chariots* (Song 1:9). Thus it is written: *Horse and driver He has hurled into the sea.*[133]

MS Prm 2736 prefaces the newborn narrative with four brief explications of אז ("then," the first word of the verse) at the beginning:

What did Moses see to recite a hymn here? א, One – ז, seven. He praised the Blessed Holy One, for He is One and sits above seven firmaments. Another interpretation: אז for the merit of circumcision that was given for the eighth day [1+7]. The Sages said: For the merit of circumcision He split the sea for us and sunk our foes in it, and He gave us the Torah and brought down manna for us. Another interpretation: Moses said, "Here He restored my life, as it is said, *Then (אז) she said, 'You are a bridegroom of blood on account of the circumcision'*" (Ex 4:26). Here I will praise Him. Another interpretation: א, One – this is Israel who is one nation in the land; ז, seven nations whom they will conquer.

Exodus 15:2

עָזִּי וְזִמְרָת יָהּ וַיְהִי־לִי לִישׁוּעָה
זֶה אֵלִי וְאַנְוֵהוּ
אֱלֹהֵי אָבִי וַאֲרֹמְמֶנְהוּ׃

Yah is my strength and my song, He is become my salvation.
This is my God and I will enshrine Him,
the God of my father and I will exalt Him.

עזי וזמרת יה

אמרו חכמים ז"ל: אמר משה לישראל: אתם נתתם הודאה להב"ה, אף אני אתן הודאה לשמו שעשה עמי נסים ונפלאות. בשעה שבאה מרים אחותי ואמרה לאבי, אבי בא אלי בנביאות שיצא ממך בן שיגאול את ישראל מעבודה זאת. וכשנולדתי הצפינה אותי אמי ג' ירחים. ולא יכלה עוד להצפיני ותקח תבת גמא ותשם אותה על שפת היאור, ותתצב אחותי מרחוק לדעה מה תהא בנבואתה.

והב"ה, יתעלה שמו לעדי עד, הוריד חום גדול במצרים עד שירדה *בת פרעה לרחוץ על היאור. ותרא את התיבה[...] ותשלח את אמתה ותקחה* ותפתח ותראני ותחמול עלי, שהב"ה נתן חן בעיניה לבלתי המיתני. ולקחה אותי לינק את שדיה, והב"ה נתן בי דעת שלא רציתי לינק בחלב טמא. והחזירה אותי לחיק אמי ונתן לה בשבילי שכר גדול.

וכשהייתי גדול בן שלש שנים בת פרעה הלבישה אותי בגדי צבעונין ושגרה אותי לאביה. וכשראה אותי שהייתי נאה לקח אותי בחיקו, ונטלתי הכתר מראשו ושמתי אותו בראשי. והיו יושבין לפניו כל חרטומי מצרים וחכמיה ואמרו לו, תינוק זה שנטל הכתר מעל ראשך ונתנו בראשו מתייראין אנו שלא יהיה אותו שעתיד להוציא מלכות זה מידך.

מהם אומרים להרגני בחרב ומהם אומרים לשרפני, עד שענה אחד מהם יתרו שמו ואמר, תינוק זה אין לו דעת. אלא רצונך אומר לפניך דבר אחד, ישימו לפני ילד זה דינר זהב וגחלת אש. אם ישלח ידו ויקח הדינר תדע שיש בו דעת ותעשה ממנו משפט. ואם ישלח ידו ויקח הגחלת תדע שהוא נער ואולת קשורה בלבו והניחוהו. כששמע פרעה ועבדיו דבר זה כשר הדבר בעיניו ועשו כן. וישימו הדינר והגחלת במזרק אחד, ואני (fol. 236r) רציתי ליטול הדינר ובא גבריאל ודחף ידי בתוך הגחלת. ונטלתיה והכנסתיה לתוך פי, בשביל כן אני ערל שפתים.

וכשגדלתי נשאתי [יצאתי] לראות דוחק אחי וראיתי *איש מצרי מכה איש עברי מאחי*, והכתיו

Yah is my strength and my song[134] (Exodus 15:2 – Recension B)

The Sages, may their memory be for a blessing, said: Moses told Israel, "You gave thanks to the Blessed Holy One. I, too, will give thanks to His name, for He did miracles and marvels for me, as when my sister Miriam came to my father and said, 'Father, it came to me via prophecy that a son will come forth from you who will redeem Israel from this servitude.'[135] When I was born, my mother hid me for three months. When she could no longer hide me, she took a reed basket and set it on the shore of the river. My sister stationed herself at a distance to find out what would become of her prophecy.[136]

"The Blessed Holy One, may His name be exalted forever, made a tremendous heat descend on Egypt, so intense that the *daughter of Pharaoh* went down to *bathe in the river.*[137] *She spied the basket... and sent her slave girl to fetch it* (Ex 2:5). She opened it and saw me, and took pity on me, for the Holy One made her take kindly to me so that she did not kill me.[138] She took me to nurse from her breast, but the Blessed Holy One gave me understanding, so that I did not want to suckle impure milk. She returned me to my mother's bosom and paid her handsomely [to take care] of me.[139]

"When I grew to be three years old, Pharaoh's daughter dressed me in colorful clothes and presented me to her father. When he saw that I was attractive, he took me in his lap; I took the crown off his head and put it on my own. Sitting before him were all the magicians and sages of Egypt, and they said, 'We are afraid that this child who took the crown off your head and set it on his own might be the same one who is destined to extract this kingdom from your grasp.'[140]

"Some of them said to kill me with a sword and others said to burn me – until one of them, whose name is Jethro,[141] responded, 'This child has no discernment. But if you wish, I will suggest something: Let them set in front of this boy a gold dinar and a burning ember. If he reaches out to take the dinar, your will know that he has discernment, and you will execute judgment upon him. But if he reaches out to take the ember, you will know that he is merely a child acting foolishly (lit: "folly bound to his heart" = mind), and you will let him be.' When Pharaoh and his servants heard this, it seemed appropriate in his view and that is what they did. They placed the dinar and the ember in a single firepan, and I wanted to take the dinar, but Gabriel came and pushed my hand to the ember. I took it and put it[142] in my mouth, which is why I am of uncircumcised lips.[143]

"When I grew up, I went out[144] to see the oppression of my brothers and I saw an Egyptian man beating one of my Hebrew brethren.[145] I struck him

וטמנתי[ו] בחול. וכששמע פרעה הדבר בקש להרוג אותי. והביא חרב שנונה שבכל העולם לא היתה כמותה והכני בה עשר פעמים. ועשה לי הב"ה נס ונדמה צוארי כעמוד של שיש ולא שלטה בי החרב.

וברחתי אצל יתרו, אף הוא חבשני בבור שבע שנים. שכשיצאתי ממצרים בן ארבעים שנה הייתי. ועמדתי על הבאר ומצאתי צפורה בת יתרו, וראיתי אותה שהיא צנועה ביותר. אמרתי לה שאשאנה לאשה, ואמר צפורה לי מנהג אביה ואמרה לי: כל אדם שבקש לישא מבנותיו של אביו מנסה אותו באילן אחד שיש לו בגנתו, וכשמגיע לאילן מיד בולעו.

אמרתי לה: אילן זה מאין היה לו?

אמרה לי: מקל הוא שברא הב"ה אותו בערב שבת כשברא הב"ה את עולמו. והב"ה הפקידו לאדם הראשון, ואדם הראשון הפקידו לחנוך, וחנוך הפקידו לנח, ונח הפקידו לשם, ושם הפקידו לאברהם, ואברהם הפקידו ליצחק, ויצחק הפקידו ליעקב, ויעקב הורידו למצרים והפקידו ליוסף בנו. וכשמת יוסף שללו המצריים את ביתו והביאו אותו המטה בפלטרין של פרעה. ויתרו אבי היה אחד מגדול[י] חרטומי פרעה, וראה אותו מטה וחמדו בלבו וגנבו והביאו בביתו. ובאותו מטה חקוק עליו שם המפורש ואותן עשר מכות שעתיד הב"ה להביא על המצרים במצרים, והיה כתוב בו דצ"ך עד"ש באח"ב.

ועוד כמה ימים וכמה שנים היה מונח המטה בבית אבי, עד שאבא פעם אחת ולקחו בידו ונכנס לגנה ונועצו לקרקע, ושב בגנה ללקחו מצאו שהוא פרח ויצץ ציץ. ובו היה בודק כל מי שמבקש לישא מבנותיו.

וכששמעתי דבריה הטובים וראיתי שהרועים גרשום, הצלתי צפורה ואחיותיה מיד הרועים וגם דלה דליתי להן והשקיתי את צאנן. *ותבאנה אל רעואל אביהן* ואני באתי עמהן ונכנסו (fol. 236v) הן תחלה ואני מבחוץ. כשראה אותן יתרו אמר להן, *מדוע מהרתן בא היום! ותאמרנה, איש מצרי הצילנו מיד הרועים*. ואני שמעתי מבחוץ כי הן מעידות עלי שאני איש מצרי, ובשביל שלא נכנסתי ולא אמרתי, איש עברי אני, לא אזכה ולא אכנס לארץ ישראל.

וכיון שאמרו בנות יתרו, איש מצרי הצילנו, אמר להם: אדם שנעשה עמה[כ]ן טובות אתון גמלתון לו גמול זה?

down and hid [him] in the sand. When Pharaoh heard about it, he sought to kill me. He brought the sharpest sword in the world, without compare, and struck me ten times. But the Blessed Holy One performed a miracle for me, so that my neck seemed like a pillar of marble and the sword had no effect on me.[146]

"I fled to Jethro, but even he imprisoned me in a pit for seven years.[147] When I left Egypt, I was forty years old. I stood by the well and found Zipporah, the daughter of Jethro, and I saw that she was exceedingly modest. I told her I would take her as a wife, and Zipporah told me about her father's custom. She said to me, 'Any man who wants to marry one of [my][148] father's daughters, he tests with a tree that he has in his garden. When he gets to the tree, it immediately swallows him.'

"I said to her, 'This tree – where did he get it?'

"She told me, 'It is the staff that the Blessed Holy One created in the twilight of the Sabbath, when the Holy One was creating the world. The Holy One entrusted it to Adam, who entrusted it to Enoch, who entrusted it to Noah, who entrusted it to Shem, who entrusted it to Abraham, who entrusted it to Isaac, who entrusted it to Jacob. Jacob brought it down to Egypt and entrusted it to his son Joseph. When Joseph died, the Egyptians plundered his house and brought this very staff to Pharaoh's palace. Jethro, my father, was one of Pharaoh's great magicians; he saw the staff and coveted it. He stole it and brought it home. On this staff is inscribed the Explicit Name, and the ten plagues that the Blessed Holy One is going to bring against the Egyptians in Egypt. Written on it is [the acronym]: DTZ"CH ADa"SH BAKHa"V.[149]

"'For some number of days and years afterward, the staff lay in my father's house – until daddy once took it in his hand and went into the garden. He stuck it in the ground; when he went back into the garden to get it, he found that it had sprouted and blossomed.[150] With it, he tests any one who seeks to marry one of his daughters.'

"When I heard her good words and saw that the shepherds were driving them out, I rescued Zipporah and her sisters from the hand of the shepherds, and I even drew water for them and watered their flocks.[151] *They came to Reuel their father* (Ex 2:18) and I came with them; they went inside first and I remained outside. When Jethro saw them, he said, *'Why were you so quick in coming back today?' They said, 'An Egyptian man rescued us from the hand of the shepherds'* (Ex 2:19). I heard this from outside, that they described me as an Egyptian man. Because I did not then enter and say 'I am a Hebrew,' I will not merit entering the Land of Israel.[152]

"When Jethro's daughters said, 'An Egyptian man saved us,' he responded, 'A man who has done [you] such favors, you repay like this?

קראן לו ויאכל לחם. כיון שנכנסתי לבית אכלתי ושתיתי ודברתי ליתרו שיתן לי צפורה בתו לאשה.

וענה בי: אם תוכל להביא לי את המטה העומד בגנתי אני אתננה לך. הלכתי ופשפשתי את הגן ומצאתיו והבאתיו בידי. מיד הרהר יתרו ואמר: בודאי זהו האיש הנביא שכל חכמי ישראל מקסמין עליו שעתיד נביא לצאת מישראל, שעל ידו תחרב מצרים וכל המצרים שבתוכה. מיד כעס עלי יתרו ותפשני והכניסני לבור שהיה בתוך ביתו.

באותה שעה אמרה צפורה: היאך אני יכולה להציל את הצדיק ממיתה משונה? אמרה לאביה: אבי אם רצונך לשמוע לעצתי, אתה אדם שאין לך אשה ויש לך שבעה בנות. אם רצונך תעמודנה שש אחיותי בבית ואני אלך עם הצאן, ואם לאו תלכנה שש אחיותי עם הצאן ואני אתקן הבית.

אמר לה אביה: יפה אמרת, תלכנה אחיותיך עם הצאן ואת שבי בבית ושמרי את ביתי וכל מה שיש לי. ובכל היתה צפורה מפרנסת אותי מכל מעדני יתרו אביה, עד שהשלימו שבע שנים בבור.

לאחר שבע שנים אמרה לאביה: אבי, זוכרת אני פעם אחת שלקחת איש אחד שהביא לך את המקל והשליכתו בבור, ועשית עון גדול בדבר. אם רצונך פתח הבור וראה שהוא מת הוציאו משם והשלך את נבלתו בחוץ כדי שלא יהא גופו מוסרח בביתיך. אם הוא חי תדע שהוא צדיק גמור.

אמר לה: בתי יפה אמרת, כלום את זוכרת מה שמו?

אמרה לו: זוכרת אני ששמו משה בן עמרם. מיד הלך יתרו ופתח את הבור וקראני: משה! מיד עניתי ואמרתי: הנני. והוציאני משם, ונשקני על ראשי ואמר: ברוך המקום ששמרך בבור שבע שנים, מעיד (fol. 237r) אני עליו שהוא ממית ומחיה ומעיד אני בך שאתה צדיק גמור, ועל ידך עתידה מצרים שתחרב ועל ידך עתיד הב"ה להוציא את ישראל ממצרים, ועל ידך עתידים המצרים להטביעם בים, לפרעה ולכל חילו.

ונתן לי ממון הרבה ונתן לי את צפורה בתו לאשה, והתנה עמו [עמי] זה התנאי: כל מה שתוליד בביתי יהיה מחצה על מחצה, מחצה יהודי ומחצה מצרי.

לאחר זמן נתעברה צפורה ונולד גרשום בחלקי ונמלתיו והנקתיו אמו שתי

Call to him that he may eat bread' (Ex 2:20). When I entered the house, I ate and drank, and I spoke to Jethro about giving his daughter Zipporah to me as a wife.

"He answered me, 'If you can bring me the staff that stands in my garden, I will give her to you.' I went and searched the garden, found it, and brought it in my hand.[153] Jethro was immediately suspicious and said, 'This man is surely the prophet that all the sages of Israel[154] divine will emerge among Israel, by whose hand Egypt and all the Egyptians within it will be destroyed.' Jethro was then angry with me; he grabbed me and put me in a pit that was in his home.[155]

"At that moment, Zipporah said, 'How can I save this righteous man from an unnatural death?' She said to her father, 'My father, if you please, listen to my advice: You are a man without a wife, but with seven daughters. If you please, let my six sisters stay at home and I will go with the flock or, if not, my six sisters can go with the flock and I will take care of the house.'

"Her father answered, 'You have spoken well. Your sisters will go with the flock and you stay at home and tend my house and all my things.' Zipporah completely[156] sustained me with all the delicacies of her father Jethro, until seven full years had passed in the pit.

"After seven years, she said to her father, 'Father, I remember once you took a man that brought you the staff and cast him in the pit. You have committed a grave sin in this matter. If you wish, open the pit and see; [if] he is dead, take him out of there and discard his corpse so that his body will not stink up your house. If he is alive, you will know that he is completely righteous.'

"He replied, 'My daughter, you have spoken well. Do you remember his name?'

"'I remember that his name is Moses ben Amram.' Immediately, Jethro went and opened the pit; he called me, 'Moses!' and I answered, 'Here I am!' He took me out of there, kissed me on the head[157] and said, 'Blessed is the Omnipresent who guarded you for seven years in the pit. I bear witness that he is the One who gives death and life, and I bear witness that you are completely righteous. By your hand Egypt will be destroyed, and by your hand the Blessed Holy One will bring Israel out of Egypt. By your hand, He will drown the Egyptians in the sea, Pharaoh and all his army.'

"He gave me a great deal of money and he gave me his daughter Zipporah as a wife. He established this condition with [me]: 'Of all those you father in my house, let us divide equally; half will be Jewish and half will be Egyptian.'[158]

"After a while, Zipporah became pregnant and Gershom was born in my portion; I had him circumcised and had his mother nurse him for two

שנים. לשנה השלישית נולד אליעזר. אמרתי: איך אעשה? עכשו לא יניח אותי למולו. מיד לקחתי אשתי ושתי בני לשוב ארץ מצרים.

באותה שעה בא שטן בדמות נחש ופגע בי, ובלעני מראשי ועד המלה, ומעולם לא היה יכול ליגע בברית מילה. הרהר צפורה ואמרה: יודעת אני שאין דבר זה אלא בשביל עון שלא מלנו אליעזר בננו. מיד לקחה צפורה צור ותכרות את ערלת בנה, ונטלה מן הדם וזרקה על רגלי.

באותה שעה יצתה בת קול ואמרה לנחש: הקא אותו, וכן עשה. זה שאמר הכתוב: *וירף ממנו אז אמרה חתן דמים למולות*. הרי הצילני אשתי משתי מיתות.

כיון שבאתי למצרים פגעו בו [בי] דתן ואבירם שהן היו ראשי ישראל ואמרו לי: להרוג אותנו באת, או שמא אתה רוצה לעשות לנו כדרך שעשית למצרי.

מיד חזרתי למדין ועמדתי שם שתי שנים עד שנגלה עלי הב"ה בחורב ואמר לי: לך והוציא את בני ממצרים. וכל זאת עשה לי הב"ה, ולכך אני חייב לשורר לפניו, ולכך נאמר: *עזי וזמרת יה ויהי לי לישועה זה אלי ואנוהו אלהי אבי וארוממנהו*.

years. In the third year, Eliezer was born. I said, 'What do I do now? He will not let me circumcise him.' I immediately took my wife and two sons to return to the land of Egypt.[159]

"Then Satan came in the form of a snake, and assaulted me;[160] he swallowed me from my head down to my circumcision – he could never touch the covenantal circumcision. Zipporah thought, 'I know that this is happening solely because of the sin that we did not circumcise our son Eliezer.' Zipporah then took a stone and cut off her son's foreskin. She took some of the blood and threw it on my 'leg.'[161]

"Just then, a heavenly voice emerged and said to the snake, 'Vomit him out,' and he did. This is what the text conveys, *And when he let him alone, she said, 'A bridegroom of bloods on account of the circumcisions'* (Ex 4:26). Behold, my wife saved me twice from death.[162]

"When I came to Egypt, Dathan and Abiram confronted [me]; they were two leaders of Israel. They said to me, 'Have you come to kill us, or perhaps you want to do to us what you did to the Egyptian?!'[163]

"I immediately returned to Midian and stayed there for two years, until the Blessed Holy One was revealed to me at Ḥoreb and said, 'Go and bring My children out of Egypt.' All this the Holy One did for me, and so I am obliged to sing before Him. Thus it is said, *Yah is my strength and my song, He is become my salvation. This is my God and I will glorify Him, the God of my father and I will exalt Him* (Ex 15:2)."[164]

***עזי** וזמרת יה ויהי לי לישועה*

בשעה שבאו ישראל ליתן שירה (fol. 353v) לפני הקב"ה אמרו למשה רבינו: אמור תחילה ואחר כך נאמר אנו. אמר להם משה: אמרו תחלה ואחר כך נאמר אני, שאני יחיד ואתם רבים וכבוד של רבים גדול משל יחיד. אמרו לו: משה רבינו אמור אתה עמנו. באותה שעה פתחו משה וישראל ואמרו שירה זו: *אשירה לי' כי גאה גאה.*

פתח משה ואמר לישראל: הניחו לי ואני אתן שירה להקב"ה שהצילני ממצרים ועשה עמי נסים. בשעת שעשתה אמי לי תבת גומא והניחה לי בסוף על שפת היאר, והוריד הקב"ה חורב גדול עד שירדה ביתיה בת פרעה להצטנן ביאר. ונתן לי הקב"ה חן וחסד בעיניה ולא הרגתני. ונתן לי הקב"ה דיעה כדי שלא טמאתי בחלב טמא עד שבאתה אמי וינקתני מחלבה. ולא דיי לי שהחזירני הקב"ה לאמי אלא שנטל עלי שכרה וגידלתי בחיקה.

וכשגידלתי הכניסני אמי אצל בתיה בת פרעה והיתה מלבשת אותי צבעונים ונתנה רביד זהב על צווארי והייתה משגרת אותי אצל פרעה. והיה פרעה נוטל אותי בחיקו והייתי עולה על צווארו ונוטל עטרה שלו מעל ראשו והייתי נותן אותה על ראשי. והיו המצריים אומרים לפרעה: תינוק זה נטל עטרה מראשך ונתנה בראשו. סבורין אנו שהוא זה שאנו בודקין אחריו והוא בן עברי והוא יש בו דיעה.

באותה שעה הביאו גחלת ודינר זהב לפני לידע אם יש בי דעת אם לא. ורציתי ליטול דינר של זהב ולקחתי הגחלת והכנסתי אותה לתוך פי. ומשם נעשיתי *כבד פה וכבד לשון.*

וכשגדלתי ויצאתי לראות בסבלות אחי וראיתי *איש מצרי מכה איש עברי.* והכיתי אותו וטמנתיו בחול. ורצה פרעה להרוג אותי והביא חרב שנונה בכל העולם אין כמותה. והכה אותי עשר פעמים ועשה לי הקב"ה נס ועשה צווארי כעמוד דשייש ולא שלטה בי חרב.

והניח אותי וברחתי אצל יתרו ואף הוא אסר אותי שבע שנים הייתי בבור. ונתן לי הקב"ה חן בלבה של ציפורה וסיפק לי מזונות. ולאחר שבע שנים הוציאני

*Yah is **my strength** and my song, He is become my salvation* (Exodus 15:2 – Recension A)

When Israel came to offer song before the Blessed Holy One, they said to Moses our teacher, "You recite first, and then we will recite." Moses said to them, "You recite first, and then I will recite. For I am a single individual, and the honor of the multitude is greater than that of an individual." They told him, "Moses our teacher, you recite with us." Then Moses and Israel began to recite this song, "*I will sing unto the Lord for He has triumphed gloriously* (Ex 15:1)."[165]

Moses began [a discourse], saying to Israel, "Let me give song to the Blessed Holy One who saved me from Egypt and did miracles for me. When my mother made a reed basket for me and set me in the reeds on the shore of the river, the Blessed Holy One made a heat descend, so intense that Bityah, the daughter of Pharaoh, came down to cool off in the river. The Blessed Holy One made her extend grace and lovingkindness toward me so that she did not kill me. The Blessed Holy One gave me understanding so that I did not [suckle], making myself unclean with impure milk, until my mother came and nursed me with her milk. Not only did the Blessed Holy One return me to my mother, but also provided her payment for me, and I grew up in her care.

"When I was older, my mother brought me into the home of Bityah, daughter of Pharaoh, who dressed me in colorful clothes, set a golden choker around my neck, and sent me to Pharaoh.[166] Pharaoh took me in his lap; I climbed on his neck and took his crown from off his head and set it on my own. The Egyptians said to Pharaoh, 'We think that this toddler who took the crown off your head and set it on his own is the one for whom we have been watching. He is the son of a Hebrew and he has understanding.'[167]

"Then they brought an ember and a gold dinar before me, to learn whether I had understanding or not. I wanted to take the gold dinar but I took the ember and put it in my mouth. I became *slow of speech and slow of tongue* (Ex 4:10) from this [experience].

"When I grew older, I went out to see the suffering of my brethren, and I saw an *Egyptian man beating a Hebrew man* (Gen 2:11). I struck him down and hid him in the sand. Pharaoh wanted to kill me; he brought the sharpest sword in the world, without compare, and struck me ten times. But the Blessed Holy One performed a miracle for me, making my neck like a marble pillar so that the sword had no effect on me.

"[Pharaoh] let me be and I fled to Jethro, but even he imprisoned me for seven years in a pit. The Blessed Holy One set grace into Zipporah's heart, so she provided sufficient food for me. After seven years, he took

מן הבור וזיוג לי צפורה בתו ונתן לי צאנו לרעות במדבר, עד שנגלה עלי הקב"ה ואמר: הוצא את עמי בני ישראל ממצרים. כל זאת עשה לי הקב"ה. לפיכך חייב אני לשבחו, *עזי וזמרת יה ויהי לי לישועה זה אלי ואנוהו אלהי אבי וארוממנהו.*

me out of the pit and paired me with his daughter Zipporah. He gave me sheep to pasture in the wilderness, until the Blessed Holy One was revealed to me saying, 'Bring My people, the children of Israel, out of Egypt.' All this the Holy One did for me, and so I am obliged to render praise to Him: *He is my strength and my song, He is become my salvation. This is my God and I will glorify Him, the God of my father and I will exalt Him* (Ex 15:2)."

Exodus 15:2 Commentary

I. The Exegetical Narrative: Reading Dialogically

As discussed in the introduction, MV relies on a sophisticated synergy between narrative and exegesis for much of its rhetorical power. The lengthy narrative in Recension B, in which Moses recounts the miraculous deeds God performed on his behalf, constitutes the richest example in the text. Its foundational premise, that Moses recites this litany of Divine marvels in response to the Israelites' song of thanksgiving, is itself exegesis. Although Ex 15:1 states, *Moses and Israel sang this song to the Lord*, the verb is singular and the next two statements present the subject as a singular "I." Thus, it appears that the midrash translates each statement (Ex 15:1 and 15:2) into a song of praise by one of the parties.

Integration of narrative and exegesis, of dialogical and didactic composition, is sustained throughout the passage. By the Middle Ages, Jewish readers[168] could be expected to be familiar with many of the questions rabbinic exegetes had posed regarding Moses in the Bible, and would discern this dialogue even though *Midrash vaYosha* frequently omits the formal markers of exegesis found in classical rabbinic texts.

1. Miriam's prophecy

The idea that Miriam has to convince her father to sire the child who turns out to be Moses is a motif that appears in several forms within rabbinic literature. What is there in the biblical text that prompts, or at least allows, such a reading? A passage in the Talmud, *b.Sotah 12a*, relates exegesis of the verse: *A certain man of the house of Levi went and married* [literally, "took"] *a Levite woman* (Ex 2:1). He "went" in the counsel of his daughter and "took" back his wife whom (according to the tradition) he had divorced. The crux is that there are two older children, Aaron and Miriam, but their births are not mentioned. Instead, this description of "taking" leads directly to the narrative of Moses' birth. In the rabbis' reading, this is not a mcre matter of biblical style omitting unnecessary details, but rather a reference to the fact that Israelite husbands separated from their wives in the wake of Pharaoh's murderous decree.[169] The Talmudic passage makes no mention here of Miriam's prophecy, instead citing a tradition in which Miriam argues with her father that his decree is harsher than Pharaoh's. Because all the other Israelite men followed Amram's example and divorced their wives, there could be no male or female children, and they would be denied life in this world and the next. Pharaoh's order to kill the boys would at least leave girls alive, and allow both life in the world to come.[170]

MV's rendering of the tradition, rooting Miriam's intervention in a prophetic experience, gives it the requisite miraculous overtones to be included in Moses' discourse of praise. But it has exegetical grounding as well: Ex 15:20 gives Miriam the title "prophetess" without indicating any specific communication from God. MV fills in the missing information at the same time that it resolves the obscured crux of Ex 2:1; the impending birth of a redeemer is revealed to her and, after she shares this prophecy with her father, Amram *takes* his wife again.

This tradition serves the larger theme of the lemma, since it is miraculous not only that Moses survived, but also that he was born in the first place, that Israelites would continue to have children when threatened with infanticide. The courage or audacity required to procreate under these circumstances is the figure of silence that speaks between the lines of the biblical text, hinted at in the Bible only by the juxtaposition of Pharaoh's decree and the act of conception by these "anonymous" Levites. "The midrash transforms biblical reticence into narrative."[171]

2. Moses' rescue from the river

Reading dialogically transforms the dramatic arc of the story. Theoretically, the reader of the biblical narrative does not know what is at stake in the survival of this infant set adrift in the reeds along the shore. By framing Miriam's careful watch "to see what would happen to her prophecy," the midrash recognizes in the Hebrew reader someone who knows that it is not merely a question of one infant's survival, but the redemption of a people. Moses as narrator of the tale, after the exodus from Egypt and salvation at the sea, further empowers the dialogical reader. Unlike Miriam, the reader knows from the outset that the prophecy will be fulfilled.

What the biblical reader may attribute to coincidence, the dialogical reader is forced to recognize as miraculous. How did it come to pass that Pharaoh's daughter happened to be at the river precisely at the right time, and why did she take Moses in? These are marvels that the biblical story neglects in its rapid exposition of the narrative. The fate of an infant set afloat on the water should be death from exposure, drowning or animal attack, and the king's daughter would be an unlikely candidate to show mercy to a Hebrew infant. This latter presumption is expanded in some of the partial parallels to MV. In *Pirqe R. El. 48*, for example, she is leprous when she comes down to bathe in the river and is healed at Moses' touch – thus inspiring her to rescue him. The Talmudic passage alternatively establishes the tension by placing the logical argument in the mouths of her attendants: The king's daughter, of all people, should obey Pharaoh's decree.

One should also wonder why Pharaoh's daughter would give the infant to a random Hebrew girl to find a nursemaid. If a recent mother, she could try herself; if not, she must surely have Egyptian staff to handle such arrangements. Again, the midrash answers the exegetical query through narrative. The story of Moses nursing from his own mother's breast is a result of Miriam's cleverness according to Exodus; in the midrash, it becomes additional evidence of Divine providence. Incorporating a common folk motif of the hero as a preternaturally wise infant, the story suggests Moses knew his ethnic identity from birth (with God's help); it also manages to incorporate later rabbinic concerns about the ritual purity of non-Jewish breast milk.

3. The missing years of Moses' life

There is then an enormous gap in Moses' biblical biography. Numerous long-standing traditions fill it in, including the famous legend of taking Pharaoh's crown. It has been used to explain Moses' speech impediment – an exegetical element that establishes dialogue with the Bible. In intertextual fashion, the midrashic reader should also hear echoes of Isaiah's call, when an angel touched his lips with a burning ember as a purifying measure.

The dismay of the wise men who warn of a Hebrew savior originally served as explication for Pharaoh's decree to drown the Hebrew male infants at birth (e.g., Josephus *Antiquities II:205–7*); the prediction shifts exegetical context in MV and becomes justification for assessing the threat presented by Moses. Again due to the fact that Moses is telling the story, the reader of *this* midrash knows something that no character can (although they suspect): Moses will indeed survive this ordeal, free the Israelites and effectively strip Pharaoh of his crown.[172] In the context of MV, the motif's larger purpose is to demonstrate yet again the saving power of God, which it does by emphasizing the angel's guiding hand.[173]

The narrative also establishes Jethro's presence in Pharaoh's court, essential to his possession of the powerful staff that is destined to become Moses'. Thus, *Midrash vaYosha* weaves the strands of the legend together in a way that reveals its exegetical and theological intent as well as its rather sophisticated sense of literary continuity. Redactors rework earlier narrative sources to serve their own theological, ideational and literary purposes.[174]

Avivah Zornberg offers a splendid exposition of the legend which demonstrates how it considerably deepens the narrative power of the biblical text:

Moses' "speech-defect" thus can be understood as the "scar" left by a failed infanticidal attack, like Oedipus's wounded feet. He has survived his "father's" fatal attack; later he will kill this father at the Red Sea. In the interim, Pharaoh will again seek to kill him, in punishment for killing the Egyptian taskmaster (2:15). Two "paternal" attacks on his life provide the filicidal justification for his own ultimate act of "patricide."[175]

Again parallel to the Oedipal myth, the Egyptian sages' divination sets in motion the very event it seeks to forestall: the redemption of Israel. Pharaoh decrees newborn males must be murdered. One family manages to manipulate events so that their son survives, but only by being raised in the royal palace. In this way, he grows with an inner strength and independence of spirit difficult to nurture as a slave but likely prerequisite for leadership. His status enables him to escape Egypt, where he may learn to shepherd and come to hear the Divine call to lead Israel out of slavery. Such rich irony makes the narrative even more compelling. At the same time, the tale must justify itself exegetically, as the way in which Moses' speech became impeded, in order to persuade. The story breaches the canon by inventing this experience in his youth, but only by serving the canon's vision of Moses' destiny.

4. Moses and Zipporah

The narrative expands on several details from the biblical text, tying them together in a way that responds to unspoken questions: Why does Jethro have to instruct the young women to call for the visitor; did Moses not accompany them back to the family's tent? How can Moses let Jethro's daughters identify him as an Egyptian?[176]

Questions more suggestive of romance literature are also addressed, e.g.: Why Zipporah? Does she marry Moses simply because Jethro assigns her to him, or is there true merit and special attraction? Here the midrash both builds on her courage as portrayed in the biblical telling of the attack on Moses, and inserts a rabbinic value by assigning her the attribute of modesty. Moses' immediate attraction, Zipporah's divinely-inspired devotion to him, and her ingenuity and fearlessness in saving Moses' life transform a simple arranged marriage into more of a "first family" drama.

One laconic passage in the biblical text has long bothered exegetes: Why does God attempt to kill Moses en route to Egypt when he is going to fulfill the Divine charge? Why is circumcision the appropriate response and how could the great prophet Moses neglect such a central precept? The *Mekhilta Yitro 1* (HR 191:7ff) serves as witness to an earlier interpretive tradition that Moses agrees to an unseemly compromise in getting approval for the marriage, and it also provides a prooftext. Understanding ויואל as "he swore an oath" with the root א-ל-ה (Ex 2:21),[177] it claims that Jethro forces Moses to swear that the eldest child will become an idolator. Numerous texts (e.g., *Jubilees 48, b.Ned. 32a*) identify the attacker as a demon of some sort, not God, and others identify Dathan and Abiram as the two Hebrews who were struggling in Ex 2:13 (e.g., *Targ. Pseudo- Jonathan, Pirqe R. El. 48, Ex. Rab. 1:29*). Each of these interpretations addresses some difficulty in the text. *Midrash vaYosha* ingeniously adapts these exegeses to resolve an assortment of textual problems in a unified narrative:

a. Moses does not circumcise one of his sons because of the deal he is forced to make with Jethro.
b. Moses is not attacked en route to fulfill God's mission; it is a journey undertaken at his own initiative as a desperate response to the untenable agreement with his father-in-law.
c. The subsequent problem that is raised – what accounts for his return to Midian – is answered by bringing in the motif of Dathan and Abiram's opposition.
d. It is not God who attacks him, but Satan in the form of a snake.
e. Zipporah intuits that circumcision will resolve the issue, in part because that is why they flee Midian, and also because the snake cannot swallow Moses' circumcised member.
f. All of the uncertain pronominal identifications become clarified: It is the second son who is not circumcised, and the blood is cast on Moses' "leg."
g. Zipporah's strange exclamation, *A bridegroom of bloods to me on account of the circumcision* (Ex 4:26) is contextualized within the expanded narrative. "Bridegroom" is associated with the original condition Jethro makes in allowing Moses and Zipporah to marry. Crafting a tale which incorporates the circumcision of the two boys and vividly dramatizes Moses' circumcision as well, the plural of "blood" and the appearance of plural form for "circumcision" almost make sense.

While MV demonstrates less interest in linguistic prompts (like ויואל) to justify its exegesis, its focus on the contextual difficulties is impressive. An example of this distinction can be drawn from earlier in the lemma as well: The miracle of Moses' neck turning to marble appears as an imaginative, free-floating motif. As explicated in *Chronicles of Moses* (Eis 358) and *Ex. Rab. 1:31*, however, there is an exegetical stimulus in Ex 18:4: *And the other [son] was named Eliezer, meaning "The God of my father was my help, and He delivered me from the sword of Pharaoh."* Thus the method of Pharaoh's attempt to kill him is established. The intertextual exegesis is so obscured in MV that the reader might not recognize it unless s/he is familiar with the related traditions. It retains a contextual exegesis, however, explaining how it is that Moses could escape the powerful Pharaoh – and it applies that interpretation to reinforce the homiletical point of Divine salvation.

In this homily, sustained throughout the lemma, salvation is small and personal with lots of unrecognized angels doing God's work. It barely mentions the grand miracles of Moses' life leading up to the parting of the waters: the Divine charge at the burning bush, the ten plagues, etc. It is not historical in the way that *Chronicles of Moses* attempts to account for all the missing years in the hero's biography. Rather, with a clear message that we should acknowledge and be grateful for the constant care of the Most High – necessary for our very survival – this exegetical narrative is certainly didactic. Not surprisingly, its litany of praise accords with the stated reason for continuing exegetical expansion of the Torah reading for the seventh day of Passover: to "relate the wonders that God has done for us and for our ancestors."[178]

The fact that Moses can narrate the true nature of these events only in retrospect hints at a profoundly important aspect of medieval attitudes about causality. As Elaine Vitz explains, modern views are positivistic, asserting that we can understand why things happen. Medieval narrative reveals a different perspective, however, positing a world in which reasons are often mysterious to us and causality is Divine; everything is a story that only God knows. What unfolds to human beings as time and change is an eternal moment to God.[179] Trials and miracles alike become manifestations of God's will in human history. After the events have taken place, Moses can narrate the tale in which all these events, large and small, are attributable to the Most High.[180] Our hero relates his story in the first person so we discover these insights at his side. Synergetic in its divergent methods of persuasion, illuminating its purposes through "dialogue" between the biblical and midrashic tales, this passage is a compelling example of the genre of exegetical narrative.

II. The Staff of Moses

The idea that only the chosen one will be able to dislodge the powerful weapon is a relatively widespread folk motif. Catalogued among a group of "identity tests," the Stith Thompson index lists it as "Recognized by unique ability to dislodge sword from stone or tree" (H31.1), and it is found in Northern European cultures (English, Irish, Icelandic) as well as in India. The other striking theme, that the hero wins the maiden by prevailing over grave dangers, is known as a key element of romance tales from around the world.

Reflecting the rich exchange between Hebrew and Arabic legends,[181] the specific motif of Moses and the staff appears in the history of al-Tabari from tenth-century Persia, as well as *qişaş al-anbiya* (Tales of the Prophets) by al-Thalabi and al-Kisai in eleventh- to twelfth-century Iraq.[182] Jethro has possession of the staff, which comes to Moses' hand through semi-miraculous means and demonstrates that he is the intended owner. Al-Kisai relates the chain of ownership, while the others include a version of the "trial" by which Moses is the one who can raise it from the ground. Many of the themes of MV are found in Islamic tales of biblical figures, including some elements found only in Recension B (discussed in the introduction as part of the evidence that this more literary redaction of MV takes shape in the East, Sepharad or Italy, influenced by Muslim culture).

Nonetheless, Western readers might intuitively associate the theme of Moses' staff with the Excalibur legend of King Arthur, mixed with other European elements of the early medieval romance genre. Although the "dislodging a weapon" theme in Hebrew literature most likely derives from Arabic sources, comparison to the familiar Arthurian legend may be instructive in framing the specifically Jewish perspective on the tale. True to form for the adaptation of foreign motifs in rabbinic texts, there are characteristics that make the traditions more suitable for Jewish literature.

The initial act of setting the tale in an exegetical context and linking it to verses is a critical part of the Judaizing process.[183] In addition, the item is not enchanted; rather its power is Divinely inspired and it has existed since the dawn of time, carefully passed down to reach its intended owner. The words inscribed on its shaft are not promises of royal dominion, but tokens of God's power. Using imagery that is more stereotypically Jewish, a staff stands in place of the sword. To accentuate its very different sort of power and to place it more squarely in the realm of Jewish symbolism, it sprouts blossoms (and almonds in some manuscripts, establishing a more explicit link to Aaron's staff).

Other motifs also echo biblical narratives, e.g., clothing of many colors (Joseph-Moses as presented in court by Pharaoh's daughter), being thrown into a pit (Joseph-Moses), trickster subplots (Rebecca-Zipporah), and the seven-year cycle (Jacob for Rachel, Moses for Zipporah). These intertextual allusions – a more subtle but well-established rabbinic form of exegesis – yield unspoken meanings: the multi-colored cloak belongs to the chosen one; the descent into the pit presages a meteoric rise through God's providence; even when God's agents appear powerless, the Divine purpose will be achieved; seemingly insurmountable obstacles will be overcome in God's good time. They also serve to weave foreign traditions more tightly into a recognizable and evocative Jewish narrative fabric.

Exodus 15:3

יְהוָה אִישׁ מִלְחָמָה יְהוָה שְׁמוֹ׃

The Lord is a man of war, Lord is His name.

יי' איש מלחמה

אמרו רבותינו: בטכסיס מלך בשר ודם הביא עליהם את המכות. מלך בשר ודם כשהמדינה מורדת עליו מה עשה? משלח לגיונות עליה ומוסיפין [ומקיפין] עליה בתחילה היה סוכר המים שלה כדי שימותו. אם חזרו בהן הרי טוב ואם לאו מוליך עליהן קולנין. אם (fol. 237v) חזרו בהן הרי טוב ואם לאו הוא מורה בהם חצים. אם חזרו מוטב ואם לאו מוליך עליהן דרמסיאות, ואחר כך מגרה בהם לגיונות. ואחר כך אוסר אותם בבית האיסורין, ואחר כך הורג את הגדולים שבהם.

כך הב"ה בא על המצריים בטכסיסי מלכים: בתחלה סכר אמת המים שנאמר *ויהפוך [לדם] יאוריהם לדם*. לא עזבו את ישראל, הביא עליהן קולנים. אלו הצפרדעין שמקרקעין [שמקרקרין] במעיהן. לא עזבו את ישראל, הביא בהם חצים. אלו הכנים שהיו נכנסין בגופן של מצריים כחץ. לא עזבו את ישראל, הביא עליהן נבט. זה השחין. לא עזבו את ישראל הביא עליהן אבני בליסטרא. זה הברד. <לא עזבו את ישראל, נתן בהם בית האסורין. זה חשך.> לא עזבו את ישראל, הרג את הגדולים. [זה מכת בכורות.]

ולפי מה שעזבו [שחשבו] המצריים לעשות לישראל הביא הב"ה עליהם המכות. הם חשבו על ישראל שיהיו שואבין מימיהם, לפיכך יהפך מימיהם לדם. הם חשבו שהיו פרגמוטיהם, לפיכך שלח להם צפרדעים שיהיו מרקדין במעיהם. חשבו שיהיו [עובדים] אדמתם, לפיכך חזר עפרם לכנים. הם חשבו על ישראל שיהיו טוענין בניהם, לפיכך שלח בהם ערוב אריות וזאבים ונמרים ודובים. והיו למצרים עשרה בנים ונותנין ליהודי לטייל עמהם בשוק, ובא ארי וחטף אחד והדוב אחד, והנחש אחד, עד שיהיה לו חשבון מכלם. הם חשבו לעשות מישראל ~~משפטים במים לפיכ שקע~~ רועים למקניהם, לפיכך שלח בהם דבר. הם חשבו לעשות מישראל משפטים [במים], לפיכך שקע אותם במים, לפי שאין הב"ה דן את האדם אלא מדה כנגד מדה.

דעו כל המכות שהביא הב"ה על המצרים כן יביא על אדום כשיצאו ישראל מן הגלות בימות המשיח. במצרים הביא עליהם מכת דם תחלה, כמו כן יעשה לאדום, שנאמר *ונתתי מופתים בשמים ובארץ דם ואש ותמרות עשן, השמש יהפך*

The Lord is a man of war
(Exodus 15:3 – Recension B)

Our rabbis said: With the battle plan[184] of a human king, He brought the plagues against them. What does a human king do when the state rebels against him? He sends troops[185] to [surround] it,[186] first damming the water supply so that the [people] die. If they reconsider, good; but if not, he leads criers[187] against them. If they reconsider, good; but if not, he shoots arrows against them. If they reconsider, good; if not, he unleashes an epidemic[188] against them and then rouses troops against them. After that, he imprisons them in jail, and after that, kills their leaders.[189]

Similarly, the Blessed Holy One came against the Egyptians with the battle plans of kings. First, he closed off the flow of water, as it is said, *He turned their rivers into blood* (Ps 78:44).[190] They did not leave Israel alone, so He brought criers against them; these are the frogs who [croak] in their bellies.[191] They did not leave Israel alone, so He brought arrows against them; these are the lice who would enter the Egyptians' bodies like an arrow. They did not leave Israel alone, so he brought naphtha[192] against them; these are the boils.[193] They did not leave Israel alone, so He brought catapult stones[194] against them; this is the hail. <They did not leave Israel alone, so He gave them prison; this is darkness.>[195] They did not leave Israel alone, so He killed their leaders. [This is the plague of the first-born.][196]

Whatever the Egyptians [thought][197] to do to Israel, the Blessed Holy One brought a comparable plague against them. They thought to make Israel draw their water; therefore, He changed their water into blood. They thought they were their go-fers; therefore, He sent frogs against them who would dance around in their bellies.[198] They thought that they would [work][199] the earth; therefore He turned their dust into lice. They thought to make Israel carry their children; therefore, He sent a swarm of lions, wolves, leopards and bears.[200] Egyptians had ten children, and left it to the Jew to travel around with them in the market. A lion came and stole one away, and the bear took one, and the serpent took one – until all were accounted for. They thought to make some among Israel[201] shepherds for their herds; therefore, He sent cattle disease against them. They thought to execute judgments [in water]; therefore, He sunk them in water. Thus the Blessed Holy One judges a person only measure for measure.[202]

Know that all the plagues which the Blessed Holy One brought upon the Egyptians, He will also bring upon Edom when Israel goes forth from exile in the messianic age. In Egypt, He brought a plague of blood first. Similarly, He will do to Edom,[203] as it is said, *I will set portents in the sky and on earth: blood and fire and pillars of smoke. The sun shall turn into*

לחשך והירח לדם, שנאמר *לפני בוא יום יי' הגדול והנורא*.

למצרים הביא צפרדעים שהיה קולן (fol. 238r) גדול, כמו כן יעשה לאדום, שנאמר *קול שאון מעיר קול מהיכל קול יי' ישלם [משלם] גמול לאויביו*.

למצרים הביא עליהם כנים שהיו שורפין אותם, כמו כן יעשה לאדום, שנאמר *ונהפכו נחליה לזפת ועפרה לגפרית*.

למצרים הביא עליהם ערוב, אף באדום, כתיב *וירשוה קאת וקפוד ויגשוף ועורב ישכנו שם [בה]*.

במצרים הביא בהם דבר, אף באדום יעשה כן, *ונשפטתי אותם [אתו] בדבר ובדם*.

במצרים הביא שחין, אף באדום מכה אותן בשחין, שנאמר *וזאת [תהיה] המגפה אשר יגוף יי' את כל הגוים [העמים] אשר צבאו [על] בירושלם המק בשרו והוא עומד על רגליו ועיניו תמקנה בחוריהס[ן] ולשונו תמק בפיהם*.

במצרים הביא ברד, כמו כן יעשה באדום, שנאמר *ונשפטתי אותו [אתו] בדבר [...] ואבני אלגביש ואש וגפרית אמטיר עליו*.

במצרים הביא ארבה שהוא מן עופות, אף באדום כמו כן, שנאמר *בן אדם אמור לצפור כל כנף ולכל חית הארץ הקבצו ובאו*.

[במצרים הביא חשך, כמו כן יעשה באדום, שנאמר *ונטה עליה*] *קו תוהו ואבני בהו*.

במצרים נגף בכוריהם, אף באדום כתיב *שמה נסיכי צפון כלם*.

במצרים פרע ~~מאהליהם~~ {מאלהיהם}, אף באדום לאחר שפרע משר שלהם אחר כך הוא פורע מהם, שנאמר *והיה ביום ההוא יפקוד יי' על צבא המרום במרום ועל מלכי האדמה [על] בהאדמה*.

לכך כתיב *יי' איש מלחמה*.

darkness and the moon into blood – as it is said, *Before the great and terrible day of the Lord comes* (Joel 3:3–4).

Against Egypt He brought frogs, whose sound was tremendous. Similarly, He will do to Edom, as it is said, *Hark, tumult from the city, thunder from the Temple! It is the thunder of the Lord as He deals retribution to His foes* (Isa 66:6).

Against Egypt, He brought lice that burned them. Similarly He will do to Edom, as it is written, *Its streams shall be turned to pitch and its soil to sulphur* (Isa 34:9).[204]

Against Egypt, He brought a swarm of wild beasts. Regarding Edom, too, it is written, *Jackdaws and owls shall possess it; great owls and ravens*[205] *shall dwell there* (Isa 34:11).

Against Egypt, He brought cattle disease. He will do so against Edom as well: *I will punish [him] with pestilence and with bloodshed* (Ezek 38:22).

Against Egypt, He brought boils. Those in Edom, too, He strikes with boils, as it is said, *This is the plague with which the Lord will smite all the peoples that warred against Jerusalem: Their flesh shall rot away while they stand on their feet, their eyes shall rot in their sockets, and their tongues shall rot in their mouths* (Zech 14:12).

Against Egypt, He brought hail. Similarly, He will do to Edom, as it is said, *I will punish him with pestilence... hailstones and sulfurous fire I will rain down upon him* (Ezek 38:22).

Against Egypt, He brought locusts, which are among flying creatures. Similarly with Edom, as it is said, *You, O mortal, say to every winged bird and all the wild beasts: Assemble, come...* (Ezek 39:17).[206]

[Against Egypt, He brought darkness. Similarly, He will do to Edom, as it is said, *He shall measure it*] *with a line of chaos and weights of emptiness* (Isa 34:11).[207]

Against Egypt, He struck their first-born. So, too, with Edom it is written, *There are all the princes of the north [... and they lie uncircumcised with those who are slain by the sword]* (Ezek 32:30).[208]

Against Egypt, He punished their gods.[209] So, too, with Edom, after He punishes their [angelic] minister, He then punishes them, as it is said, *On that day, the Lord will punish the host of heaven in heaven, and the kings of the earth on earth* (Isa 24:21).

Thus it is written, *The Lord is a man of war* (Ex 15:3).[210]

יי' איש מלחמה יי' שמו

אמרו חכמים בטכסיסי בשר ודם בא הקב"ה על המצריים. מלך בשר ודם בשעת שצר על המדינה בתחילה מה הוא עושה? סוכר אמת המים שלהם שימותו בצמא, והקב"ה הפך מימיהם לדם.

{ואחר כך מתריע} ~~נגע - מרתיע~~ עליהם בקרנות ובבורקינוס, אף הקב"ה הביא עליהם צפרדעים שהיו קורסיין קשה מהם.

ואחר כך יורה להם (fol. 354r) חצים וצנים, אף הקב"ה נגפם במכות כנים שהיו בבשרם כחצים.

ואחר כך מגרה בהם אנשי מלחמה ומתערבין זה בזה, ואף הקב"ה הביא עליהם ערוב דובים ואריות שהיו מ<נ>לחמים בהם והורגים אותם.

ואחר כך משליך עליהם סם המות שמריחין אותם ומתים מריחה, ואף הקב"ה הביא עליהם את הדבר והיו מתים ומקניהם ובהמתם מריח עשבים שבשדה.

ואחר כך יורה בהם אש והוא שורף אותם, וכך השחין שורף כל גופם.

ואחר כך משליך עליהם אבנים, כך השליך עליהם הקב"ה אבני ברד.

ואחר כך נוקבים את החומות וכובשים אותם, כך הביא הקב"ה ארבה שהיה נכנס בחלונות.

ואחר כך נוטל אותם ואוסר אותם בשלשלאות של ברזל וחובשין אותם כדי שלא יברחו, כך הקב"ה מביא עליהם חושך וכולם נחבשין בחושך.

ולוקח הגבורים אנשי המלחמה והורג אותם והשאר מוליך בשבי, כך הקב"ה הורג כל בכוריהם והשאר הוליכם וטבעם בים.

לכך נאמר *יי' איש מלחמה יי' שמו.*

The Lord *is a man of war, Lord is His name* (Exodus 15:3 – Recension A)

The Sages said: The Blessed Holy One came against the Egyptians with human battle plans. What does a human king do first when he besieges a state? He closes off their flow of water so that they die of thirst. The Blessed Holy One transformed their water into blood.

[After that, he sounds alarm] against them with horns and trumpets.[211] So too, the Blessed Holy One brought frogs against them whose [clamor] was exceedingly difficult for them.[212]

After that, he shoots arrows and barbs[213] against them. So too, the Blessed Holy One afflicted them with a plague of lice which [dug] into their flesh like arrows.

After that, he rouses warriors against them, engaging them in battle.[214] So too, the Blessed Holy One brought a horde of bears and lions who would fight against them and kill them.

After that, he sends a deadly drug against them which they sniff and die from its smell. So too, the Blessed Holy One brought a pestilence against them; they died, along with their cattle and herds, from the scent of the grasses in the field.

After that, he shoots fire against them and burns them. Similarly, the boils burn their whole body.

After that, he hurls stones. Similarly, the Blessed Holy One hurled hailstones against them.

After that, they breach the walls and conquer them. Similarly, the Blessed Holy One brought locusts who entered through the windows.

After that, he takes them and imprisons them in iron chains, confining them so they will not escape. Similarly, the Blessed Holy One brings darkness upon them so they are all confined in the darkness.

And he takes the mighty ones, warriors, and kills them, leading the remainder into captivity. Similarly, the Blessed Holy One kills the first-born and leads the rest to drown them in the sea.

Thus it is said, *The Lord is a man of war, Lord is His name.*

Exodus 15:3 Commentary

I. God as a Human King Laying Siege

One might hope that the king's staged assault would indicate something about the time and place of MV's composition, especially since there are differences between recensions and manuscripts.[215] The battle strategies, however, are generally of ancient origin and most of the details are adopted from textual parallels. (Recension B especially reflects *Tanḥuma.*) Thus the details may simply derive from earlier texts, or be deliberately archaized to some extent in order to reflect medieval notions of earlier warfare. Nevertheless, it is interesting to explore historical bases for the strategies. As is frequently the case when Hebrew texts from Late Antiquity or the Middle Ages discuss military matters, there are a fair number of Greek/Latin loan-words and concepts.

1. Blood, Frogs, Lice

Denying a besieged city access to the water supply was common practice in ancient warfare, with numerous accounts in Greek and Roman histories. Philo of Byzantium, for example, states in a 3rd-century BCE manual for the Ptolemaic army that the enemy must be cut off from its source of water.[216]

The next pair of attacks in the sequence is supported by Josephus' report of the Roman siege against Yotvata in *The Jewish War 3:259–65*: He cautioned his troops to cover their ears against the common Roman strategy which sought to terrify the enemy with overwhelming noise, and he also instructed them to shield themselves against the subsequent volley of arrows. A medieval Catalan romance, *Tirant lo blanc,* depicts a pandemonium brought on by trumpets and battle cries during the long siege of Constantinople.[217]

Ceaseless noise may not only confuse or terrify the opposition; it was also employed to prevent the enemy from resting and to cover the sound of sappers working to undermine the city walls.[218] Rabbinic texts, however, tend to emphasize the fear factor of God's acoustic attack. R. Shimon b. Tzemaḥ Duran (1361–1444, "Rashbatz," Spain and N. Africa) includes a rendering of this interpretation in his *Haggadah* commentary on the ten plagues, and asserts that the purpose of the frogs was to terrify the Egyptians with their cries (similarly MS Mos 111). See also *m.Sotah 8:1* for a discussion of human warfare that mentions several times the intimidating power of loud noise.

2. Horde of beasts, Cattle disease

Because the list in MS Par 716 is incomplete, it is unclear whether it offers a parallel to the plague of wild beasts (ערוב) in this context. Recension A describes "men of war" who come to engage the rebellious province; the verb, מתערבין, literally means "mix it up" and operates as a word play on the name of the plague itself. *Pesiq. Rab. 17, Pesiq. Rab Kah. 7:11* and *Tanh. B. Bo 4* use the term לגיונית (troops, legions) as the "real-world" association for the horde of wild beasts God sends against Egypt; although the term is found twice in our manuscript, neither appears to fit the sequence. The term is used once at the onset of the siege as a general introduction, and then after the term דרמסיאות. If this latter term refers to spear carriers, as Wies-Campagner suggests, then it would be the association for the fourth plague (horde), and לגיונות – troops parallels the fifth (cattle disease). The sequence is plausible because Roman battle formations ordered troops relative to the strike distance of their weapon; it would not be uncommon to have archers (corresponding to lice, the third plague) followed by spear carriers, followed by regular infantry troops for the closest combat.

One challenge to this theory is that the close parallels in *Tanh. Bo 4* and MS Family B2 use a different term (ברברים – mercenaries) in relation to the horde of beasts, and connect דרמסיאות to the cattle plague. Also reflecting the realia of Roman practice, which frequently employed mercenaries and deployed them as a distinct regiment,[219] it suggests that Krauss' rendering of דרמסיאות is more apt. His *Lehnwörter* regards דורמסיאות as a derivative of אנדרולומוסיא (Greek: ανδροληµψια). The instances he cites discuss a mass death in which the innocent fall victim along with the guilty; the term would best be rendered, "epidemic." Such a definition fits nicely with the cattle plague, both because of the mass demise of the animals and because they did nothing wrong. They are merely "collateral damage," a term which aptly establishes the military context.[220]

According to Adrienne Mayor, biological warfare was definitely employed by the ancients. She notes that historians consider the catapulting of corpses in the siege of Kaffa in 1346 as the first documented case of deliberately spreading contagion to achieve military victory, but there are numerous mentions in earlier literature. Cuneiform Hittite tablets (1500–1200 BCE) record the citizens of Anatolia driving out infected animals and humans into enemy territory with the prayer, "The country that accepts them shall take this evil plague." The Latin expression *pestilentia manu facta* (hand-made pestilence) indicates that deliberately transmitted contagion was a weapon in the Roman period;

Livy (1st-century BCE) refers to such attacks without details, and the Roman historian Cassius Dio (2c. CE, writing in Greek) records two specific biological assaults against the Roman authority, each purposefully spreading a deadly disease.[221]

In Recension A, the cattle plague is associated with grass that has a toxic odor, and the human parallel is a poisonous drug that does the same. There is ancient record of battle strategies using poisonous smoke and compounds to kill livestock.[222] In addition, approximately one hundred fifty species of moths and butterflies have some degree of toxicity in their larval form (caterpillar). A species common in Southern Europe (currently moving throughout the continent due to climate change) could easily have given the impression that the odor of the grass it crawls in is toxic. The Oak Processionary Moth (*Thaumetopeoea processionea*), in its later stages of larval development, is armed with over sixty thousand poisonous defensive bristles that can detach in the wind and become airborne weapons. While some people simply break out in a rash, it is not uncommon to experience conjunctivitis, pharyngitis and respiratory distress (e.g., asthma, anaphylaxis).[223]

3. Boils

Most discussion of naphtha in the Talmud relates to it as a commodity, especially as a source of fire on Shabbat (e.g. *b.Shab. 24b, 26a, 46a; b.Yoma 38b–39a*), but the term is found in midrash as a weapon. This, too, is recorded in Roman annals of war. "Plutarch, Pliny, and Seneca, the historians who identified naphtha as Medea's secret weapon, based their speculation on firsthand accounts of liquid-fire weapons from Roman army veterans who had seen action in Asia in the first century BC[E]." Ammianus Marcellinus describes lakes of heavy liquid with "mortally noxious fumes" which, once burning, "human intelligence will find no other means of quenching it other than covering it with earth."[224] As with many weapons, naphtha remains in the military arsenal as its potency and delivery systems are developed; by the time of the Islamic conquest of the Middle East in the seventh century, for instance, naphtha projectiles were an indispensable siege weapon.

The textual parallel found in R. Shimon b. Tzemaḥ's *Haggadah* commentary elucidates the power of naphtha by describing a fierce battle between the Christians and the Muslims in which the Christian ship ran out of conventional weapons and resorted to throwing flammable liquid on the enemy, liquid that burned their flesh and caused the Muslim army to take flight. Recension A similarly emphasizes that this weapon is designed to burn the body.

4. Hail, Locusts

The catapult, its stones compared to the Divine hail against Egypt, is another weapon that was deployed over a long period with continuing technological advances. Its earliest design is generally credited to engineers working under Dionysius the Elder of Syracuse (399 BCE),[225] and it continued to serve as a critical siege weapon through the fourteenth century.

Locusts may have no parallel in MS Par 716, or they may be compared to the infantry troops who storm the city as its defenses are breached. In *Tanḥuma*, the association is to אוכלוסין הרבה (hordes), a Greek term that is not generally found as a stage of siegecraft but most likely represents the same idea. Samuel Krauss lists "soldiers" as a rare but acceptable translation.[226] Recension A has no special contingent mentioned; it simply states that the king breaches the walls and conquers the city, comparing this to the locusts who can invade even inside the homes by entering through the windows. It seems somewhat reminiscent of a motif found in Recension B at Ex 15:7, as part of the plague of wild beasts. There, the Egyptians lock themselves inside their homes in order to protect themselves from the rampaging animals, but God sends a mythical sea creature called the *siloni* (or *silonith*) to reach in through the windows and unlock the doors. See also *Sefer haYashar 80*, in which the *siloni* goes up on the roof, tears open the rafters and reaches in with its long arms.

In all of these articulations, the midrash reflects the historical reality that a conquering army must eventually conduct a house-to-house search for enemy troops, captives, booty, etc. Like locusts, they must sweep through every corner of the city.

5. Darkness, Death of the first-born

Imprisoning the enemy population and killing their leaders are relatively common tactics, with no loan-words required to express the concepts. They correspond neatly to the plagues of darkness and death of the first-born, completing the elaborate analogy of God's sequenced assault against Egypt to the battle plan of a human king.

II. Metaphor in Midrash vaYosha

One distinct metaphorical convention found within MV is the straightforward simile, e.g., Ishmael is kicked out like a divorced wife, the angel acts like a man in distress when he cries out twice to stop Abraham (14:30), Moses' neck is compared to a pillar of marble (15:2), lice pierce the body like arrows, locusts have mouths like leopards, teeth and fangs like lions (15:3,7). These images are simple but striking, able to convey emotion and drama. Their craft is perhaps best viewed in comparison to the similes in the Song itself; for all its poetic artistry, the explicit similes are routine: sinking like lead or a stone, waters heaped up like a mound, pursuers consumed like straw. Part of the difference is not the originality of the image in MV (in fact, most are found elsewhere), but the power of the narrative frame.

As mentioned in the introduction, Meir Sternberg offers a compelling analysis showing how the universal narrative dynamics of suspense, curiosity and surprise reshape non-narrative details around them. They "narrativize" other elements in the text so that static images become kinetic.[227] Extending this insight regarding biblical material to the broader canvas of *Midrash vaYosha*, the similes absorb and elaborate on their narrative contexts and cease to be merely descriptive. Ishmael is like a divorced wife because of the familiar albeit unstated biblical narrative in which he is sent away with his mother. That he now wants to come back and "inherit" the estate becomes pathetic, like a divorcée trying to reclaim her place in a man's bed. The angelic "man in distress" who tries to stay Abraham's hand becomes more than an image because we need to know if his tone of urgency will be sufficient to stop the sacrifice (suspense/prospection). We also need to understand how this turnabout unfolded (curiosity/retrospection), and what this test of Abraham's faith then means (surprise/recognition). It is bound up in a story in which all the characters are in distress: Abraham is weeping, the angels are distraught, and so the urgency of the man in distress is palpable – even audible (14:30). Moses' neck as "a pillar of marble" is not merely a picture of strength, but an evocation of miracle, a premonition of salvation (15:2). The description of the lice and locusts is not simply one of fierceness, but of weapons deployed in holy battle, enlivened on account of their exegetical association with the lengthy tale of the ten plagues (15:3,7).

Exodus 15:4

מַרְכְּבֹת פַּרְעֹה וְחֵילוֹ יָרָה בַיָּם
וּמִבְחַר שָׁלִשָׁיו טֻבְּעוּ בְיַם־סוּף׃

Pharaoh's chariots and his army He has cast into the sea;
And the pick of His officers are drowned in the Sea of Reeds.

מרכבות פרעה

אמרו חכמים: כשהיו ישראל במצרים היו המצרים משועבדים אותם בכל עבודה קשה שבעולם בחמר ובלבנים, ובכל יום היו אומרים לישראל לעשות כל אחד ואחד שש מאות לבנים. וכשהיה ישראל פוחת אחת היו משימין אותה בקיר כנגד מה שפיחת. לכך לקו המצרים ברדפם אחריהם בשש מאות רכב, שנאמר *ויקח שש מאות רכב בחור*.

וכשראו <ישראל> המצרים נוסעים אחריהם נבהלו וברחה נשמתם. אמרו מלאכי השרת לפני הב"ה: רבונו של עולם נרד ונעשה נקמה בלישראל במצרים ונשמור בניך.

וענה להם (fol. 238v) הקב"ה: אני בעצמי ארד ואשמור את בני, בשעה שעשה אברהם אביהם רצוני, שנאמר *וישכם אברהם בבקר*. וכשהגיע אותה שעה שעמד אברהם בתפלה לפניו, הסתכל *במחנה מצרים בעמוד אש וענן ויהם את מחנה מצרים*. לכך נאמר *מרכבות פרעה וחילו ירה בים ומבחר שלישיו טבעו בים סוף*.

Pharaoh's chariots
(Exodus 15:4 – Recension B)[228]

The Sages said: When the Israelites were in Egypt, the Egyptians enslaved them with every sort of of hard labor that exists, with mortar and with bricks. Every day they would tell Israel that each person had to make six hundred bricks. When an Israelite was one short, they put her in the wall in place of what was missing.[229] Thus the Egyptians were stricken when they chased after [Israel] with six hundred chariots, as it is said, *He took six hundred of his select chariots* (Ex 14:7).

When <Israel> saw the Egyptians traveling in pursuit, they were terrified and their soul fled.[230] The ministering angels said to the Blessed Holy One, "Master of the world, let us go down and exact vengeance for[231] Israel against Egypt, and let us protect Your children."

The Holy One answered them, "I Myself will go down, and I will protect My children [for] the time[232] when Abraham their father did My will, as it is said, *Abraham rose early in the morning..."* (Gen 22:3)" And when the moment arrived that Abraham stood in prayer before Him,[233] He looked upon *the Egyptian army from a pillar of fire and cloud, and threw the Egyptian army into panic* (Ex 14:24).[234] Thus it is said, *Pharaoh's chariots and his army He has cast into the sea; the pick of his officers are drowned in the Sea of Reeds* (Ex 15:4).[235]

***מרכבות** פרעה*

בשעה שטבעו המצריים בים אמרו ישראל למשה: משה שמא עלו מצריים מן הים כמו שעלינו.

באותה שעה אמר משה לפני הקב"ה: רבונו של עולם רבונו של עולם ישראל יש להם פחד, אינם מאמינים בשונאיהם שנטבעו. אלא אם יש רצונך הראה אותם להם.

באותה שעה אמר הקב"ה לים: הקיאם ליבשה.

אמר הים לפני הקב"ה: רבונו של עולם, יש אדון שנותן מתנה לעבדו ונוטלה?

אמר לה הקב"ה: אני אפרע לך אחד ומחצה שבהם.

אמרה לפניו: רבונו של עולם כלום יש עבד שתופש את רבו לדין בשביל חובו?

אמר לה הקב"ה: הרי נחל קישון הוא יהיה ערב לך והוא יפרעם לך.

מיד זרקם ליבשה וראום ישראל והאמינו שטבעו בים בים. ולכך פתחו שירה ואמרו *מרכבות פרעה וחילו*.

Pharaoh's ***chariots*** (Exodus 15:4 – Recension A)

When the Egyptians drowned in the sea, Israel said to Moses, "Moses, what if Egyptians rose up out of the water just as we rose up?"

Then Moses spoke before the Blessed Holy One, "Master of the world, Israel is afraid. They do not believe that their enemies are drowned. If it is Your will, show them to them."

Then the Blessed Holy One said to the sea, "Vomit them out onto dry land."

The sea spoke before the Blessed Holy One, "Master of the world, is there a master who presents his servant with a gift and takes it back?"

"I will compensate you one and one-half times their number."

"Master of the world, is there a servant who takes his master to court to collect his debt?"

The Blessed Holy One said, "Look, the Kishon River will be your surety, and it will compensate you."[236]

Then [the sea] threw them onto dry land. Israel saw them and believed that they drowned in the sea. Therefore they broke into song, "*Pharaoh's chariots and his army [He has cast into the sea]* (Ex 15:4).[237]

Exodus 15:4 Commentary

I. Midrash Migrations

Exegesis for this pericope is more varied among manuscript families than most passages in the midrash. While the broader issue of fluidity within the texts is addressed in the introduction's discussion of MV's literary-oral performance interface, the focus here is on how the traditions migrate from one lemma to another. Joseph Heinemann and James Kugel have highlighted traveling midrashic motifs in their extensive work on traditions history, commenting primarily on how they move over time between midrashim and adapt to their new contexts.[238] The extensive manuscript record of MV invites deeper reflection on how or why material moves *within* a midrash.

The striking quality of these wanderings is that they appear to find exegetical roots wherever they are set down, adding to the impression that exegetical prowess is demonstrated in part by being able to shuffle the deck and still play all the cards. Note how many moving pieces there are for the themes raised in this passage:

1. A potential contradiction between the Egyptian corpses displayed on the shore (Ex 14:30) or drowned in the sea (Ex 15:4) is resolved by imagining they are first hurled into the sea, but then vomited out. Recension A incorporates the tradition at 15:4; Recension B does so at 15:5, and then has God restore the dead to the "depths" after Israel is reassured.
2. Although both redactions personify the sea, the figure shifts place and purpose as well. The earlier recension may be concerned with the identity of figures who *remain* immersed in the depths, or the apparent "redundancy" of verses 4 and 5. (The song has already asserted that God drowned the Egyptians in the sea in v. 4, so v. 5 must convey the immersion of some other figure.) In exegesis of v. 5, Recension B seems more focused on establishing God's eternal authority over the sea and highlighting the love God demonstrates for Israel by accommodating their fears.
3. The mention of Pharaoh's chariots calls to mind Ex 14:7, which specifically mentions six hundred of them. Recension A associates it with nine hundred chariots of Sisera at 15:4. Recension B associates it with six hundred bricks as a daily quota here, and with the nine hundred chariots of Sisera at 15:5.
4. Pharaoh's chariots and soldiers are drowned, but the song does not specify that Pharaoh himself died in the sea. MS Family A2 imagines that Pharaoh repents and saves himself. Recension B incorporates this notion at 15:11, which is part of the reformed Pharaoh's testimony, *Who is like You among the gods, O Lord?*
5. The daily quota of bricks suggests Egyptian cruelty, leading Recension B to present the angels' desire to punish the Egyptians, but God insists on taking care of it personally. (Recension A at 15:1, Recension B at 15:4).
6. God is also motivated to save on account of Abraham's prayer. It is mentioned briefly in Recension A at 15:1 and more extensively in Recension B at 14:30. Family B2 roots the association exegetically in "morning watch" (Ex 14:24).

Other pericopes also demonstrate migrating patterns. The image of God destroying idols explicates how God *shatters the foe* (15:6) in Recension B, and how *You break Your opponents* (15:7) in Recension A. MS Family A2 *ad* 15:7 goes on to incorporate a tale of Egyptian magicians, Yoḥani and Mamre, also numbered among the opponents of the Most High who arrogate unto themselves semi-divine powers – although all other manuscript families set the magicians *ad* 15:10 where references to blowing and lead may have inspired magical associations. Recension B *ad* 15:7 repeats justification for the ten plagues (with different detail), which fits equally well there as a record of breaking Divine opponents, as *ad* 15:3 as a portrayal of God as a man of war.

The mare who lures Pharaoh's chariots into the seabed is anchored in MS Family A2 *ad* 15:1 by mention of a horse, and simply becomes part of Divine retribution against the enemy who hoped to overtake the Israelites in Recension B *ad* 15:9. Pharaoh's repentance, a radical innovation of the midrash, finds its way into various pericopes scattered among the manuscript families.

Within a single midrash, themes may shift for a number of reasons. The scribe or performer may not have received or may not understand the inherited exegesis, or may simply prefer a different one. Since story is generally most memorable, narratival elements may have been transmitted without a precise context. The choice may be a result of free association, or driven by didactic purposes. As noted in the introduction, most medieval collections of midrashic interpretations were considered "open books" for a long time.

The most intriguing possibility has to do with synagogue performance. It would require far too much time to explicate every verse of the song on a single occasion. If in fact parts of the midrash were originally performed, it is conceivable that motifs move in order to make it into the excerpted portion. The drama of Pharaoh's repentance, for instance, may be too inspiring to omit; over time, exegetes have found ways to work it into verses 4 (MS Family A2), 6 and 11. Even though I argue that Recension B is a literary rendering and does not directly reflect the performative stage of the midrash, it surely contains its traces.

Midrash vaYosha also demonstrates expectations regarding interpretive consistency. Once Recension A determines in this pericope that the Egyptians do *not* remain sunk at the bottom of the sea, then it must determine who *does* sink like a stone in its exegesis of the next verse; it is Rahab. This is another requisite skill for the midrashic "dealer."

Exodus 15:5

תְּהֹמֹת יְכַסְיֻמוּ
יָרְדוּ בִמְצוֹלֹת כְּמוֹ־אָבֶן׃

The deeps covered them;
They went down into the depths like a stone.

תהומות יכסיומו

אמרו חכמים: יתברך שמו של הב"ה שברא את עולמו בחכמה ובתבונה, ובנפלאותיו אין חקר ולתבונתו אין מספר, דכתיב *כונס כנד מי הים נותן באוצרות תהומות*. כשברא הב"ה את עולמו אמר לשר של ים: פתח פיך ובלע כל מימות שבעולם.

אמר לפניו: רבונו של עולם דיי שאעמוד בשלי, והתחיל לבכות. מיד הרגו הב"ה שנאמר *בכחו רגע הים ובתבונתו מחץ רהב*. מה עשה? כבשן וקבלן הים, שנאמר *ודורך על במתי ים*. ושם להם החול כמו בריח דלתים, שנאמר ***ויסם*** *[ויסך] בדלתים ים*.

אמר לו הים: רבונו של עולם אם כן יתערבו מימי המתוקים עם המלוחים.

אמר לו: כל אחד ואחד יהיה לו אוצר בפני עצמו, שנאמר *נותן באוצרות תהומות*.

בא וראה כמה חסדים עשה הב"ה עם ישראל יתברך שמו. כשהלכו ישראל במדבר היה *הולך לפניהם יומם בעמוד ענן לנחותם הדרך ולילה בעמוד אש להאיר להם ללכת יומם ולילה*.

ועוד שהיו שם נחשים ושרפים והב"ה מרוב אהבה שאהב את ישראל היה שולח לנחשים שהיו עושים עצמן כגשר, וישראל עוברין עליהם כאדם שעובר על הגשר. ועדיין מרוב אימה מן הנחשים שהיו במדבר ומפחד ואימה שהיה להם מן המצרים לאחר שטבעו בים, אמרו למשה: אתה אומר שטבעו המצרים בים, מתיראין אנו שלא יעלו מן הים כשם שעלינו אנחנו. אם רצונך הראה לנו מתים ונראה נקמה משונאינו.

מיד אמר משה להב"ה: רבונו של עולם מרוב אימה ופחד שהיה להם ממצרים אין מאמינים שטבעו בים. אם רצונך עשה (fol. 239r) להם נסים ונפלאות והראם להם ויראו נקמה מאויביהם.

מיד אמר הב"ה לשר של ים: השליכם ליבשה.

The deeps covered them
(Exodus 15:5 – Recension B)[239]

The Sages said: May the name of the Holy One be blessed, for He created His world with wisdom and understanding. There is no limit to His wonders and His understanding cannot be quantified, as it is written, *He heaps up the ocean waters like a mound, He stores the deeps in vaults* (Ps 33:7). When the Blessed Holy One created His world, He said to the prince of the sea, "Open your mouth and swallow all the waters in the world."

He replied, "Master of the world, it is sufficient for me that I hold (lit: stand in) my own," and he began to cry. Then the Blessed Holy One slew him, as it is said, *By His power He stilled the sea; by His skill He struck down Rahab* (Job 26:12). What did He do? He subdued and gathered the sea,[240] as it is said, *He trod on the back of the sea* (Job 9:8).[241] And he set sand as a bar (lit: door latch) for them, as it is said, *He [closed] the sea behind doors* (Job 38:8).[242]

The sea said to Him, "Master of the world, if you do that, the fresh (lit: sweet) waters will be mixed with the salty waters."

He replied, "Each will have its own storehouse," as it is said, *He stores the deeps in vaults* (Ps 33:7).

Come and see how many kindnesses the Blessed Holy One has done for Israel, may His name be praised. When Israel walked in the wilderness, *He went before them in a pillar of cloud by day, to guide them along the way, and in a pillar of fire by night, to give them light, that they might travel day and night* (Ex 13:21).

Further, there were snakes and fiery serpents there, but with abundant love for Israel the Blessed Holy One sent word to the snakes to make themselves like a bridge so Israel could cross; Israel crossed on them as a person crosses over on the bridge.[243] Still, out of overwhelming terror due to the snakes in the wilderness and from the fear and terror they had of the Egyptians even after they drowned in the sea, they said to Moses, "You say that the Egyptians drowned in the sea. We are afraid lest they rise up from the sea just as we did. If you please, show us the dead, and we will see that vengeance was exacted upon those who hate us."

Then Moses said to the Blessed Holy One, "Master of the world, due to overwhelming terror and fear that they had of Egypt, they do not believe that they are drowned in the sea. If You please, perform miracles and wonders for them, and show them to the [people] so they may see vengeance upon their enemies."

The Blessed Holy One told the prince of the sea, "Cast them out on dry land."[244]

אמר שר של ים לפני הב"ה: רבונו של עולם יש אדם שיתן מתנה לעבדו ויטלנה הימנה?

אמר הב"ה לשר של ים: אני אפרע לך אחד ומחצה כמותם.

אמר לפניו: רבונו של עולם יש עבד שתובע אדניו להן [לדין] בשביל חובו?

אמר לו: נחל קישון יהיה לך ערב.

מיד הוציאם לשפתיו וראו ישראל והכירו כל אחד שונאיו, ונטלו כל כספם וזהבם. ולאחר שראו נקמתם הצלילם הב"ה כאבן, לכך נאמר *תהומות יכסיומו ירדו במצולות כמו אבן*.

The prince of the sea responded to the Holy One, "Master of the world, is there a person who gives a gift to his servant and then takes it back from him?"

The Holy One said to the prince of the sea, "I will compensate you one and one-half times their like."[245]

"Master of the world, is there a servant who can sue[246] his master to collect his debt?"

"The Kishon River will be your surety."

Immediately, he brought them out onto his shores and Israel saw, each one recognizing his foes. They took all their silver and gold. After they saw their vengeance, the Blessed Holy One sunk them like a stone.[247] Thus it is said, *The deeps covered them, they went down into the depths like a stone* (Ex 15:5).

***תהומות** יכסיומו*

אמרו חכמים: הוא רהב שר של ים הוא וחילו שהכה הקב"ה אותם והרגם והשליכם במצולות ומהם הים מסריח, שנאמר *בכחו קרע [רגע] הים ובתבונתו מחץ רהב.*

ובשעה שביקש הקב"ה לקרוע ים לפני ישראל כדי שיטבע מצרים, פתח שר שלהם ואמר לפניו: רבונו של עולם מפני מה אתה רוצה להטביע המצריים? דיי להם לישראל שאתה מציל אותם מידם.

באותה שעה הרים הקב"ה ימינו והכה רהב שר של ים הכאה אחת הוא וכל חילו והרגו והשליכו במצולות ים. ומהם המים של ים מסריחין. וכשראו ישראל כך אמרו שירה: *תהומות יכסיומו ירדו במצולות כמו אבן.*

The deeps *covered them* (Exodus 15:5 – Recension A)[248]

The Sages said: It is Rahab, prince of the sea, and his army whom the Blessed Holy One struck, killed and cast into the depths, and on account of them the sea stinks – as it is said, *By His power He stilled*[249] *the sea; by His power He struck down Rahab* (Job 26:12).

When the Blessed Holy One sought to split the sea for Israel in order to drown Egypt, their prince[250] spoke up before Him, "Master of the world, why do You want to drown the Egyptians? Is it not enough for Israel that You save them from their hand?"

Then the Blessed Holy One raised His right hand and struck Rahab, prince of the sea, he and all his army with one blow, killing them and sending them down into the depths of the sea. On their account the sea stinks. When Israel saw this, they recited song, "*The deeps covered them. They went down into the depths like a stone*" (Ex 15:5).[251]

Exodus 15:5 Commentary

I. Rahab, Prince of the Sea – Mythology in Midrash

The Hebrew Bible strives valiantly to strip the creation narrative of explicit mythological influences, such as battles for control of the physical universe among competing divinities. Torah's final redaction posits a God with no peer, even if it occasionally intimates the existence of other gods (e.g. Ex 15:11). Rabbinic literature, firmly grounded in a monotheistic Judaism, does not feel similarly threatened by the lure of pagan imagery. Thus the traces of mythological figures such as Rahab that remain in the Bible are embraced as anchors for flights of midrashic fancy.[252]

Three biblical passages dramatically portray Rahab as the personification of the sea, each time controlled and contained by God's unequaled power:

Isaiah 51:9–10 Awake, awake, clothe yourself with splendor. O arm of the LORD! Awake as in days of old, as in former ages! It was You that hacked Rahab in pieces, that pierced the Dragon. [10] It was You that dried up the Sea, the waters of the great deep; that made the abysses of the Sea a road the redeemed might walk.

Psalm 89:9–11 O LORD, God of hosts, who is mighty like You, O LORD? Your faithfulness surrounds You; [10] You rule the swelling of the sea; when its waves surge, You still them. [11] You crushed Rahab; he was like a corpse; with Your powerful arm You scattered Your enemies.

Job 26:10–14 He drew a boundary on the surface of the waters, at the extreme where light and darkness meet. [11] The pillars of heaven tremble, astounded at His blast. [12] By His power He stilled the sea; By His skill He struck down Rahab. [13] By His wind the heavens were calmed; His hand pierced the Elusive Serpent. [14] These are but glimpses of His rule, The mere whisper that we perceive of Him; Who can absorb the thunder of His mighty deeds?

Rahab is not named in the Song at the Sea; still, its vivid descriptions of the waters invite association. It is unlikely that the rabbis understand the Hebrew term *Tehom* (deep) to be rooted in the Babylonian deity *Tiamat*, or that they recognize *Yam* (sea) as the name of the Canaanite sea-god, but they do intuit mythological traces in Exodus 15 and see affinities with the Rahab texts. The Isaiah passage actually invokes the parting of the Reed Sea, and Psalm 89 echoes the Song's language in several places. Job, awash in creation motifs, provides the imagery that the midrash seeks: waters that move as God instructs, a challenger silenced and struck down.

As the mythological universe gets reintroduced and expanded in midrash, the mythic battle becomes rabbinized, transformed into a logical argument. There does not appear to be any truly polytheistic threat of cosmic mutiny; the figures of the sea admit from the outset that God is Creator and Master of the universe. Such changes could strip the scene of its drama. As George Bernard Shaw points out, "...[E]very drama must present a conflict. The end may be reconciliation or destruction; or as in real life itself, there may be no end; but the conflict is indispensable: no conflict no drama."[253]

For rabbinic literature, however, dialectical reasoning *is* the stuff of drama. Recension B's extended arguments present real conflict; its collected Rahab traditions also deepen the drama of the text by heightening the conflict in different ways. One critical component is the transformation of the sea into a fully drawn character. Daniel Boyarin, presenting the *Mekhilta* passage in which the waters refuse to part for Israel, notes that Psalm 114 personifies the sea by imagining that it runs away in fear from the presence of the Lord, but "the midrash projects a world in which the Red Sea is not a personification, but a personality; not a metaphor, but a character."[254] In a later passage (*ad* 15:8), the sea ultimately recognizes the deep love God has for Israel and divides into twelve channels for the tribes to traverse, each with protective walls, windows and potable water.

Drama also develops through elaboration of the Israelites' fears, recognizing the abiding terror a nation of slaves would have of its captors. In addition to the pursuing Egyptians, the text incorporates a motif of fiery and fearsome serpents. A reader's growing empathy is but a shadow of God's infinite acts of grace; it is due to God's miraculous power and astounding love for Israel that the nation is able to move forward at all. Given the expository comments, "There is no limit to His wonders and His understanding cannot be quantified," and "Come and see how many kindnesses the Blessed Holy One has done for Israel," this drama seems to be the homiletical point.

1. Additional mythological figures in Midrash vaYosha

Although the transformation of the sea into a full-fledged character is one of the most salient examples, *Midrash vaYosha* contains other mythic figures, such as the frequent appearance of angels: Satan's agenda in trying to stop Abraham and Isaac, the seemingly autonomous actions of Uza (14:30), God subject to the court in heaven (14:15, 31). The earth, too, has its own ontological importance; not only is "she" integral to the salvation of the newborn Israelites in Egypt (15:1), she later worries about the curse laid upon her during the time of Cain, and what will happen if she allows the blood of the Egyptians to be upon her (15:12).

It is difficult to know if these motifs in MV are articulations of an actual belief in animate Nature and/or populated Heaven, or if they serve as literary tropes. Like dialogue and narrative, they enliven the text. As exegesis, they function to make sense of inconsistency in the biblical text and, as homily, they encourage faith in Divine sovereignty. Neutralization of mythic forces is but a foretaste of the ultimate triumph of God's purposes for creation. Literal or literary, they likely reflect a mystical intuition about the world, a stage of religious development Gershom Scholem describes as the world of mythology and that of revelation meeting in the soul of man.[255]

Exodus 15:6

יְמִינְךָ יְהוָה נֶאְדָּרִי בַּכֹּחַ
יְמִינְךָ יְהוָה תִּרְעַץ אוֹיֵב׃

Your right hand, O Lord, glorious in power;
Your right hand, O Lord, shatters the foe!

ימינך יי' נאדרי בכח

אמרו חכמים: בשעה שהביא הב"ה מכת בכורים על המצרים, קודם בא המכה על אלהיהם ועל כל צלמיהם, אותן שהיו מכסף וזהב ונחשת וברזל ובדיל ועופרת ניתכין ונמסין. וכל צלמים שהיו מעץ נרקבים ונשברים.

כשראה פרעה כן עמד בחצי הלילה וקרא למשה ולאהרן וצועק ובוכה בכל חוצות ישראל, ואומר: היכן משה ואהרן עומדים?

ונערים קטנים של ישראל משחקים ואומרים לו: ~~היאך~~ היכן אתה הולך ומי אתה מבקש?

ואמר להם: משה אוהבי אני מבקש.

והם אומרים לו: בכאן הוא דר, ואחד אומר לו: לא כי בכאן הוא דר, עד שמצא הבית.

ואומר לו: *קומו צאו מתוך עמי*!

אמר לו משה: וכי גנבים אנו שנצא בחצי הלילה? הב"ה אמר לנו, *ואתם לא תצאו איש מפתח ביתו עד בקר*.

אמר לו: בבקשה ממך קומו צאו.

מהו *ויהי בחצי הלילה*? זו שנאמרה ברוח הקדש על ידי דוד, שנאמר *חצות לילה אקום להודות לך על משפטי צדקך*. אמר רבי יוחנן: מלמד שאמר דוד לפני הב"ה: רבונו של עולם, מודה אני לפניך על אותה הלילה שנעשית לישראל במצרים.

ואמר: בוא וראה מה עשה הב"ה לישראל יתברך שמו ויתעלה זכרו, שלא גמר דינו במצרים עד שהודיע משפטיו למשה ולישראל. אמר לו הב"ה למשה: משה לך אמור להם, בני תהיו יודעים שאני יוצא בתוך (fol. 239v) מצרים, ואני בעצמי אפרע מהם ואשחט בכוריהם בשעה אחת, ואתם שחטו פסחיכם ותנו מדם הפסח על שתי מזוזות ועל גגות בתיכם ועל הכותלים. ויהיה זאת סימן לחיים.

משל למה הדבר דומה? למלך שהיה לו צאן והפריש מהם לחיים והפריש מהם למיתה. מה עשה? נטל את הסיקרא וסיקר אותם שהפריש לחיים, ושהפריש למיתה לא סיקר אותם. כך המלך זה הקב"ה, והצאן שרצה לשחוט אלו המצרים, והצאן שהפריש לחיים זה ישראל, ונתן עליהם סיקרא זה החיים

Your right hand, O Lord, is glorious in power
(Exodus 15:6 – Recension B)[256]

The Sages said: When the Blessed Holy One brought the plague of the first-born against the Egyptians, it struck first against their gods and all their images. Those made of silver, gold, copper, iron, tin and lead were melted and liquefied. All the images that were made of wood rotted and broke.[257]

When Pharaoh saw this, he got up *in the middle of the night* (Ex 12:29) and called to Moses and Aaron. He yelled, crying[258] throughout the Israelite neighborhood, "Where are Moses and Aaron staying?"

Young Israelite children were playing, and said to him, "Where are you going and whom do you seek?"[259]

"I am seeking my dear friend, Moses."

They told him, "He lives over here," but one said, "No, he lives over here," [and so it went] until he found the house.

He said, "*Up, depart from among my people*" (Ex 12:31).

Moses replied, "Are we thieves that we should leave in the middle of the night?[260] The Blessed Holy One told us, '*None of you shall go outside the door of his house until morning*'" (Ex 12:22).

"I beg of you, please get up and go."[261]

What is the significance of "*in the middle of the night*" *[the Lord struck down all the first-born]* (Ex 12:29)? It is as was spoken through the holy spirit by David, *I arise at midnight to thank You for Your righteous judgments* (Ps 119:62).[262] R. Yohanan said: It means that David spoke before the Blessed Holy One, "Ruler of the world, I am grateful to You for that night which was made[263] for Israel in Egypt."

And he said: Come and see what the Holy One did for Israel, may His name be blessed and His remembrance be exalted, that He did not complete His punishment of Egypt until He made known His judgments to Moses and Israel.[264] The Blessed Holy One said to Moses, "Moses, go say to them, 'My children, you should know that I am going out in the midst of Egypt, and I Myself will requite them, slaughtering their first-born in a single hour. And you – slaughter your paschal lambs and put some of their blood on the two doorposts and on the roofs of your homes, and on the walls. This will be a sign of life for you.'"

A parable: To what is this similar? To a king who had a flock of sheep. He set aside some for life and some for death. What did he do? He took red paint and marked those set aside for life, and did not mark the ones set aside for death. Analogously, the king is the Blessed Holy One, the sheep that He wanted to slaughter are the Egyptians, and the sheep that He designated for life are Israel, so He set the red mark of life on them,

זה הדם, שנאמר *ולקחו מן הדם ונתנו* עליהם סיקרא זה. החיים זה הדם, שנאמר *ולקחו מן הדם ונתנו על שתי המזוזות ועל המשקוף*.

וכן עשו ישראל: שחטו את פסחיהם ונתנו [מן הדם] על מזוזותיהם ועל כותל[י] בתיהם. אמר להם משה לישראל: כך אמר לי הב"ה, *זאת חקת הפסח כל בן נכר לא יאכל בו*. כששמעו ישראל דברו של הקב"ה עמדו על רגליהם בשמחה ובשירים. ומלו כל הערלים שהיו בישראל במהירות, והב"ה בא ורפאם.

כשהיה חצי הלילה עבר הב"ה בתוך מצרים וראה ישראל מלוכלכים בדם מילה ובתיהם מלוכלכים בדם פסח. ברך אותם ואמר להם: בני תהיו חיים לשנה הבאה, שנאמר *ואעבור עליך ואראך מתבוססת בדמיך ואומר לך בדמיך חיי ואומר לך בדמיך חיי*.

ואמר רבי יהושוע בן לוי: כשאמר משה לפרעה: דע שבכורי מצרים ימותו הלילה, התחיל להלעיג עליו ואמר: כמה יהיו בכורי מצרים – מאתים או שלש מאות? וטפש לא היה יודע שכלם בכורים, מפני שהיו שטופים בזמה, והיו כלם ממזרים. וכיון שמתו הבכורים וגדול הבית במקום הבכורים וראה פרעה שמתו רוב בניו ובניו עבדים ובני שפחות, אמר בלבו: מעולם לא אמר לי שקר. ואמר לעבדיו: כל זמן שהיה משה אצלי הייתי מפייס ממנו ומתפללין עלינו והיינו מתרפאין. עכשו כעסתי עליו ואמרתי, *אל תוסף ראות פני*. דין הוא שאני אלך בעצמי. מיד קם ממטתו בבכיה גדולה והלך עם שריו ועבדיו לפני פתחו של משה. צעק פרעה בקול (fol. 240r) גדול ובוכה במר נפש וקורא למשה: משה אוהבי, בבקשה ממך התפלל עלי לפני הב"ה.

ומשה ואהרן וכל ישראל אוכלים פסחיהם ושותין יין בהסבה ואומרים שירות ותושבחות להב"ה ויושבין בבתיהם. ואין אחד מהם יוצא בחוץ, אמר להם משה: *ואתם לא תצאו איש מפתח ביתו עד בקר*. וכשקרא פרעה לפתחו של משה אמר לו: מי אתה ומי שמך?

אמר לו: אני פרעה המושפל.

אמר לו משה: למה באת אלי אתה בעצמך? וכי דרכו של מלך לעמוד ולחזור על פתחי בני אדם?

אמר לו פרעה למשה: בבקשה ממך אדני בא והתפלל עלינו, עכשו לא ישאר אדם בכל ארץ מצרים.

namely the blood. As it is said, *They shall take some of the blood and put*[265] *it on the two doorposts and the lintel* (Ex 12:7).

That is what Israel did: They slaughtered their paschal lambs and put [some of the blood] on the doorposts and wall[s] of their homes. Moses said to Israel, "This is what the Blessed Holy One told me, *This is the law of the passover offering: No foreigner shall eat of it*" (Ex 12:43). When the Israelites heard the word of the Holy One, they rose to their feet with songs and rejoicing. They quickly circumcised all among Israel who were uncircumcised, and the Holy One came to heal them.[266]

When it was the middle of the night, the Blessed Holy One passed through Egypt and saw Israel stained with the blood of circumcision, and their homes stained with the blood of a passover offering. He blessed them, "My children, you will live to the next year," as it is said, *When I passed by you and saw you wallowing in your bloods, I said to you, "In your bloods, live!" I said to you, "In your bloods, live!"* (Ezek 16:6).[267]

Rabbi Joshua b. Levi said: When Moses said to Pharaoh, "Know that the first-born of Egypt will die tonight," he began to scoff at him. "How many first-born in Egypt are there – two hundred, three hundred?" The idiot did not know that they were all first-born because they were so steeped in licentiousness, and they were all bastards.[268] When the first-born died, and the eldest of the household in place of a first-born, and Pharaoh saw how most of his sons and the sons of the servants and maidservants died,[269] he said to himself, "He has never told me a lie." And he said to his servants, "All the while that Moses was staying with me, I would appease him and he would pray[270] for us and we would be healed. Now I lost my temper with him and said, '*You will not see my face again*' (Ex 10:28); it is right that I should go myself." He immediately arose from his bed, weeping profusely, and went with his ministers and servants to Moses' doorway. Pharaoh yelled loudly and wept bitterly, calling to Moses, "My dear Moses, I beg of you to pray for me to the Blessed Holy One."

Moses, Aaron and all Israel were eating their passover offerings and drinking wine, reclining and reciting songs and praises to the Holy One and sitting in their homes. Not one of them went outside, for Moses had told them, "*None of you shall go outside the door of his house until morning*" (Ex 12:22). So when Pharaoh called at Moses' doorway, he responded, "Who are you? What is your name?"[271]

"I am the humbled Pharaoh."

"Why did you come yourself to me? Is it customary for a king to go begging (lit: stand and return) at people's doorways?"

Pharaoh said to Moses, "I beseech you, my lord, come and pray for us, or there will not be a single man left in all the land of Egypt."

אמר לו: לא אוכל לצאת כי הב"ה צוה אותנו ואמר לנו: *ואתם לא תצאו איש מפתח ביתו עד בקר*.

ואמר פרעה למשה: בבקשה ממך צא אל <ה>חלון ודבר עמי, וכן עשה. ואמר לו: הלא אמרת לי אתמול, *ומת כל בכור בארץ מצרים*? ועכשו תשע ידות מתים.

אמר לו משה: אף על פי כן אם תרצה אלמוד לך דבר ותנצל אתה ולא תמות. הרם קולך ואמור, בני ישראל! הרי אתם ברשות עצמכם, קומו צאו מתוך עמי. עד עכשו הייתם עבדי פרעה, מכאן ואילך הרי אתם ברשות יי'. *עבדו את יי' אלהיכם*.

וכן עשה. אמר <לו> ~~ל~~משה: אמור כן פעם שנייה, וכן עשה. ואמר לו: אמור עוד פעם אחרת, וכן עשה. והב"ה השמיע קולו של פרעה בכל ארץ מצרים, שנאמר *ויקם פרעה לילה הוא ו<כל> עבדיו וכל מצרים ותהי צעקה גדולה במצרים כי אין בית אשר אין שם מת*.

ויאמר: *קומו צאו מתוך עמי*.

אמר לו משה לפרעה: למה אתה מטריח עצמך?

אמר לו: מתירא אני שלא אמות לפי שאני בכור.

אמר לו משה: אל תירא מדבר זה, לגדולה מזאת אתה מתוקן.

ולא תאמר פרעה לבדו היה דוחק אלא כל המצרים היו דוחקין, שנאמר *ותחזק מצרים על העם למהר לשלחם מן הארץ כי אמרו, כולנו מתים* – כאן אלא בים.

אמר רבי שמואל בר נחמני: בהערמה זאת באו ב מצריים על ישראל, אמרו: אם משועבדים אנו אותם נשבע שאינו יכול באש יכול אלהיהם להלחם בנו באש מלמעלה, כשם שהביא על סדום ועל עמורה. אלא נשבע (fol. 240v) שאינו יכול מביא מבול לעולם, בוא ונשעבדם במים.

ואמר להם הב"ה: שוטים! אני נשבעתי שלא יבא עוד מבול, חייכם אתם עצמכם תלכו אל המבול! לפיכך טבעם בים. לכך נאמר *ימינך יי' נאדרי בכח ימינך ה' תרעץ אויב*.

"I cannot go out, for the Blessed Holy One commanded us, saying, '*None of you shall go outside the door of his house until morning*'" (Ex 12:22).

Pharaoh said to Moses, "I beg you, come out to <the> window then and speak with me," and this he did.[272] [Pharaoh] said to him, "Didn't you tell me yesterday, '*Every first-born in the land of Egypt shall die*?' (Ex 11:5). Now nine tenths are dead!"

Moses said, "Nonetheless, if you wish, I will teach you something to save yourself so that you will not die. Lift up your voice and say, 'Children of Israel, behold you are free. Get up and go out from among my people. Until now you were slaves of Pharaoh; from now on you are in the keeping of the Lord. *Serve the Lord your God*'" (Ex 10:8).

So that is what he did. Moses told him,[273] "Say it a second time," and so he did. He told him, "Do it again," and so he did. The Blessed Holy One made Pharaoh's voice heard throughout the land of Egypt, as it is said, *Pharaoh arose in the night, with <all> his courtiers and all the Egyptians. There was a loud cry in Egypt, for there was no house where there was not someone dead* (Ex 12:30).[274]

He said, "*Up, depart from among my people*" (Ex 12:31).

Moses said to Pharaoh, "Why are you so agitated?"

"I am afraid lest I die because I am a first-born."

"Do not be afraid of this thing; you are being readied for something greater."

Do not presume that Pharaoh alone was pressing; rather, all the Egyptians were, as it is said, *The Egyptians urged the people on, eager to send them forth from the land, for they said, "We are all dying"* (Ex 12:33). Here, it means in the sea.[275]

R. Samuel b. Nahmani said: With this conceit, the[276] Egyptians came upon Israel, saying, "If we enslave them with fire,[277] their God could fight against us with fire from above just as He brought down upon Sodom and Gomorrah. But He swore never to bring a[nother] flood. Come let us [re]enslave them in water."

The Holy One said to them, "Idiots! I swore that another flood would not come. By your lives, you yourselves are going into the flood!" Thus He drowned them in the sea.[278] So it is said, *Your right hand, O Lord, is glorious*[279] *in power; Your right hand, O Lord, shatters the foe!* (Ex 15:6).

ימינך יי' נאדרי בכח

יתברך שמו של מלך מלכי המלכים הקב"ה בימינו קרע לנו את הים ושיקע צרינו בתוכו, דכתיב *ימינך יי' תרעץ אויב.* ובימינו נתן לנו את התורה, שנאמר *מימינו אש דת למו.*

אמרו חכמים: עליונים וכל מה שבהם נבראו בשמאלו בימינו, לפיכך הם חיים וקיימים לעולם. ותחתונים וכל מה שבהם נבראו בשמאלו, שנאמר *אף ידי יסדה ארץ וימיני טפחה שמים קורא אני אליהם ויעמדו יחדיו.* ועתיד הק' להחריבן, שנאמר *כי שמים כעשן נמ<ל>חו והארץ כבגד תבלה.*

וכן נשבע הק' לישראל שלא יהו מסורים ביד האומות, שנאמר *נשבע יי' בימינו ובזרוע עזו אם אתן את דגנך עוד מאכל לאויביך אם ישתו בני ניכר תירושך אשר יגעת בו כי מאספיו יאכלוהו והללו את יי' ומקבציו ישתוהו בחצרות קדשי.*

בשביל ירושלם שהייתה בנויה על ידי בשר ודם לכך נחרבה. ולעתיד לבא אני אבנה אותה בעצמי, שנאמר *בונה ירושלם יי' נדחי ישראל יכנס.*

וכיון שצפה משה ברוח הקודש נתנבא לישראל כל הניסים ונפלאות הללו מה שפירשנו למעלה. לכך פתחו ישראל בשירה שלהם ואמרו *ימינך יי' נאדרי בכח ימינך יי' תרעץ אויב.*

Your right hand, O Lord, is glorious in power
(Exodus 15:6 – Recension A)[280]

Blessed be the name of the king of kings – with His right hand, the Blessed Holy One rent the sea for us and sank our enemies in it, as it is written, *Your right hand, O Lord, shatters the foe* (Ex 15:6). With His right hand, He gave us the Torah, as it is said, *A fiery law for them from His right* (Deut 33:2).[281]

The Sages said: The celestial worlds and all that is in them were created with His right hand; therefore they exist eternally. The terrestrial worlds and all that is in them were created with His left hand, as it is said, *My other hand founded the earth, My right hand spread out the skies. I call unto them, let them stand together* (Isa 48:13).[282] In the future, the Holy One will destroy them, as it is said, *Though the heavens should melt away like smoke, and the earth wear out like a garment* (Isa 51:5).[283]

And so the Holy One swore to Israel that they would not be delivered into the hand of the nations, as it is said, *The Lord has sworn by His right hand, by His mighty arm: Nevermore will I give your new grain to your enemies for food, nor shall foreigners drink the new wine for which you have labored. But those who harvest it shall eat it and give praise to the Lord. And those who gather it shall drink it in My sacred courts* (Isa 62:8–9).

For the Jerusalem which was built by human beings is thus destroyed, but in the future I will build it Myself, as it is said, *The Lord rebuilds Jerusalem, He gathers in the exiles of Israel* (Ps 147:2).[284]

When Moses saw via the Holy Spirit, he prophesied unto Israel all these miracles and marvels which we explained above. Thus Israel let loose their song: *Your right hand, O Lord, is glorious in power; Your right hand, O Lord, shatters the foe* (Ex 15:6).[285]

Exodus 15:6 Commentary

I. Single Interpretive Thread

Although the multivalence of exegesis is frequently invoked as a defining characteristic of midrash, MV generally offers only a single interpretation of the verse (as is true of several other late midrashim with narrative tendencies like *Tanḥuma, Pirqe Rabbi Eliezer*, etc.). At times, it stitches together exegeses by creating a new narrative context, as in this pericope. Through the story of Pharaoh's actions beginning with the tenth plague, the passage contains the tradition about striking the idols of Egypt first, an interpretation of *in the middle of the night* (Ex 12:29), explanation of the blood on the doorposts, the Israelites' enthusiastic circumcision in order to participate in the Passover, the exegesis regarding "bloods" in Ezekiel 16, an indictment of Egyptian licentiousness, Pharaoh's decree of release as *the loud cry in Egypt* (Ex 12:30), an interpretation of *we are all dying* (Ex 12:33), and a story about the Egyptians' reasoning in attacking at the sea. This odd assortment of traditions reads like a single (though imperfect) recounting of the last night in Egypt to God's triumph at the sea. The rich multiplicity of midrash is sustained by utilizing several characters to represent different perspectives and possibilities of meaning.

Even in an instance where the text provides three separate sets of exegesis (15:3 – plagues as parallel to order of assault in war, each a punishment for a related Egyptian abuse, each to be seen again in the future against Edom), they appear narratively related rather than alternative or competing.[286]

II. Mashal – The Rabbinic Parable

The most classically framed mashal in MV is found here in 15:6: God instructs the Israelites to mark their homes with blood from the lamb, and the text compares the process to a king who marks with red paint those sheep among his flock that he plans to keep alive. The parable is presented as if it simply provides an explanation for how blood can be a sign of life. Yet David Stern has demonstrated that the form is designed to make the reader flesh out the interpretation, and to recognize that its few stock elements tell a deeper story; each character and action in the metaphor (משל – *mashal*) has a parabolic significance in the primary narrative (נמשל – *nimshal*), and even the gaps are full of meaning.[287]

Clearly the king is God and the sheep represent the Israelites in Egypt. The red paint brand is the paschal blood. The image of the flock, however, includes sheep [un]marked for death, i.e., the Egyptians, thus reinforcing God as the ruler of all peoples at the same time that the redemption of one nation unfolds. More pointedly, there is a gap in the comparison of the sheep to the people of Israel; in the mashal, the bodies themselves are marked (not the sheepfold) and in the nimshal it is their homes. Thus the true mark of redemption *is* a mark on the body, circumcision, and it is there that the larger narrative immediately turns. When the people hear the Divine instructions they rejoice and immediately circumcise all the men; thus when God passes by it is the pair of "bloods" (plural, as in the cited verse from Ezekiel 16) that preserve their lives.

Exodus 15:7

וּבְרֹב גְּאוֹנְךָ תַּהֲרֹס קָמֶיךָ
תְּשַׁלַּח חֲרֹנְךָ יֹאכְלֵמוֹ כַּקַּשׁ׃

In Your great triumph You break Your opponents;
You send forth Your fury and it consumes them like straw.

וברוב גאונך

אמרו חכמים: עשר מכות הביא הב"ה על המצרים במצרים. מכה ראשונה הביא עליהן [דם], ולמה הביא עליהם דם? מפני שהיו המצריים מונעים בנות ישראל לעשות טבילה, לכך הביא עליהם דם.

מכה שנייה הביא עליהם הב"ה צפרדעים שהיו נופלות בשארותם ובחדרי משכבם ומרקדין בפניהם, והיתה מכת צפרדעים קשה מכולם. ומפני מה הביא עליהם צפרדעים? לפי שהיו המצרים אומרים לישראל: לכו וצדו לנו דגים. לפיכך הביא עליהם צפרדעים.

מכה שלישית הביא עליהם כנים, והיו ברוב אמה על הארץ. וכשהיו המצרים לובשים בגדים נקיים מיד מתמלאים כנים. ומפני מה הביא עליהם כנים? לפי שהמצרים אמרו להם לישראל: לכו וטאטו בתנו חצרינו והשוקים, ולכך נהפך עפר מצרים לכנים.

מכה רביעית הביא עליהם ערוב אריות ודובים ונמרים, ונכנסין בבתיהם. והמצרים סוגרין דלתותיהם, והב"ה שלח להם חיה מן הים ושמה סילוני, והיתה נכנסת בחלונות ופותחות הדלתות והיו דובים ונמרים ואריות נכנסים ואוכלין המצרים. ומפני מה הביא ערוב? שהיו המצרים אומרים לישראל: לכו וצדו לנו חיות מן השדה, לפיכך הביא עליהם ~~ערוב~~ ערוב.

מכה חמישית הביא עליהם הב"ה דבר. ומפני מה הביא עליהם דבר? שהיו המצרים אומרים לישראל: לכו ורעו לנו את בהמתנו, ולכך הביא עליהם דבר שמתו כל בהמתם.

מכה ששית הביא עליהם הב"ה שחין באדם ובבהמה. ומפני מה הביא עליהם שחין? לפי שהיו המצרים אומרים לישראל: לכו תקנו אותנו מרחצאות לעדן עצמנו, ולפיכך הביא עליהם שחין שהיה מחמם את המזבח [בשרם].

(fol. 241r) מכה שביעית הביא עליהם הב"ה ברד על האדם ועל הבהמה. ומפני מה הביא עליהם ~~עליהם~~ ברד? לפי שהיו המצרים אומרים: לכו חרשו וזרעו את שדותינו, ולכך הביא הב"ה עליהם ברד ששיבר האלנות והזרעים.

ואמרו חכמים: בשעה שנשא משה את ידיו להקב"ה, עמד הברד בין השמים ובין הארץ, שנאמר *ויצא משה מעם פרעה את העיר ויפרוש כפיו אל יי'*

In Your great triumph
(Exodus 15:7 – Recension B)[288]

The Sages said: The Blessed Holy One brought ten plagues upon the Egyptians in Egypt. The first plague He brought upon them [was blood].[289] Why did He bring blood upon them? Because the Egyptians prevented the daughters of Israel from practicing ritual immersion, He brought blood against them.[290]

The second plague the Holy One brought against them was frogs, falling in their hair and their bedrooms, leaping all around them – so that frogs became the most difficult plague.[291] Why did He bring frogs upon them? Because the Egyptians would say to Israel, "Go catch fish for us," He brought frogs against them.

The third plague He brought against them was lice, which covered the land almost a cubit deep. When the Egyptians would put on clean clothes, they immediately would be filled with lice. Why did He bring lice upon them? Because the Egyptians would say to Israel, "Go and sweep our houses and our courtyards and the markets," the dust of Egypt was transformed into lice.

The fourth plague that He brought was a swarm of lions and bears and leopards that entered their homes. The Egyptians closed their doors, but the Blessed Holy One sent an animal from the sea called a *siloni*;[292] it entered through the windows and opened the doors so the bears and leopards and lions would come in and eat the Egyptians. Why did He bring such a swarm? Because the Egyptians said to Israel, "Go and hunt wild animals for us," He brought a swarm against them.

The fifth plague the Blessed Holy One brought against them was cattle disease. Why did He bring cattle disease against them? Because the Egyptians would say to Israel, "Go and herd our animals for us," He brought cattle disease against them in which all their animals died.

The sixth plague that the Blessed Holy One brought against them was boils [afflicting] man and beast. Why did He bring boils upon them? Because the Egyptians would say to Israel, "Go prepare baths for us in which to enjoy ourselves," He brought boils against them that would make their [flesh] hot.[293]

The seventh plague that the Blessed Holy One brought against them was hail upon man and beast. Why did He bring hail upon them?[294] Because the Egyptians would say, "Go plow and sow our fields," the Holy One brought hail against them that destroyed the trees and seeds.

The Sages said: When Moses lifted his hands to the Blessed Holy One, the hail stood between heaven and earth, as it is said, *Leaving Pharaoh, Moses went outside the city and spread out his hands to the Lord: the*

ויחדלו הקולות והברד ומטר לא נתך ארצה. אלא הוטל בין שמים וארץ, עד שבא יהושע ונלחם עם אותם מלכים שלשים ושתים והשליכה הב"ה עליהם, שנאמר *רבים אשר מתו ב[מ]אבני הברד מאשר מתו [הרגו בני ישראל] בחרב*. והנשאר ימטיר הב"ה על גוג ומגוג, שנאמר *ויצא ה' ונלחם בגוים ההם כיום הלחמו ביום קרב*.

מכה שמינית הביא עליהם הב"ה ארבה שהיה דומה פיו לנמר, ~~כב~~ שניו כשניו אריה, ומתלעותיו כמתלאות לביא. מפני מה הביא עליהם ארבה? מפני שהיו המצרים אומרים: לכו ונטעו לנו פירותיהן, לכך הביא עליהם ארבה, ואכל מה שנשאר מן הברד.

מכה <תשיעית> הביא הב"ה חשך של גהינם. מי שהיה יושב לא היה יכול לעמוד ומי שהיה עומד לא היה יכול לישב מפני כובד החשך. ומפני מה הביא עליהם חשך? מפני שהיו פושעים בישראל, ובקש הב"ה להמיתם בשלשת ימי האפילה וכדי שלא יראו המצרים במפלתם וישמחו בהם, לפיכך הביא עליהם הב"ה חשך.

מכה עשירית הביא עליהם מכת בכורים. וקודם שהביא עליהם המכה, הלך משה אצל בכורי מצרים ואמר להם: כה אמר יי', *כחצות הלילה אני יוצא בתוך מצרים ומת כל בכור בארץ מצרים*.

מיד הלכו בכורי מצרים אצל אבותיהם ואמרו להם: תדעו כי כל המכות שאמר משה כלם באו, ועכשו אמר, *ומת כל בכור בארץ מצרים*. ~~מיד הלכו בכורי מצרים~~

ענו להם אבותיהם: לכו אצל פרעה כי הוא בכור. וכן עשו, ואמרו לו: שלח את העם הזה. אם לא תשלחם ימות כל בכור בארץ מצרים.

אמר פרעה לעבדיו: הכום בכל מיני מרדות. אני אמרתי או נפשי תצא

(fol. 241v) או נפשותם של ישראל תצא, והם אומרים לי שאניחם. מיד הלכו בכורי מצרים ונטלו כל אחד ואחד חרבו והרגו אבותיהם, שנאמר *למכה מצרים בבכוריהם*. ועל כל זאת *בחצי הלילה ויי' הכה כל בכור בארץ מצרים*.

לכך נאמר *וברוב גאונך תהרוס קמיך תשלח חרונך יאכלמו כקש*.

thunder and the hail ceased, and no rain came pouring down upon the earth (Ex 9:33). Instead, it was held between heaven and earth – until Joshua came to fight with the thirty-two[295] kings, and the Blessed Holy One sent it against them, as it is said, *More perished from the hailstones than [the Israelites killed with a] sword* (Josh 10:11). And the remainder the Holy One will rain down upon Gog and Magog, as it is said, *Then the Lord will come forth and make war on those nations, as He is wont to fight on a day of battle* (Zech 14:3).[296]

The eighth plague that the Blessed Holy One brought against them was locusts; its mouth was like that of a leopard, its teeth like those of a lion, its fangs like those of a lion's whelp.[297] Why did He bring locusts upon them? Because the Egyptians would say, "Go and plant fruit trees (lit: their fruits) for us,"[298] He sent locusts against them which ate all that remained after the hail.

The <ninth> plague that the Blessed Holy One brought was the darkness of Gehenna. A person who was sitting could not stand and one who was standing could not sit due to the weight of the darkness. Why did He bring darkness upon them? Because there were sinners among Israel and the Blessed Holy One sought to kill them during the three days of deep darkness; so that the Egyptians would not see their fall and rejoice, the Holy One brought darkness against them.[299]

The tenth plague that He brought against them was the death of the first-born. Before He brought the plague upon them, Moses went to the first-born of Egypt and said to them, "Thus said the Lord, '*Toward midnight, I will go forth among the Egyptians, and every first-born in the land of Egypt shall die.*'" (Ex 11:4–5).

The first-born of Egypt immediately went to their fathers and said, "You know that all the plagues of which Moses spoke came to pass. Now he has said, '*Every first-born in the land of Egypt shall die.*'"[300]

Their fathers answered them, "Go to Pharaoh, because he is a first-born." So they did, saying to him, "Let this people go.[301] If you do not release them, every first-born in the land of Egypt will die."

Pharaoh said to his servants, "Strike them with all kinds of chastisement. I said they would leave over my dead body (lit: either my soul departs or the souls of Israel depart). And they are telling me to let them be!" The first-born of Egypt then went and each took his sword and they killed their fathers, as it is said, *Who struck Egypt through their first-born* (Ps 136:10).[302] For all this, *in the middle of the night, the Lord struck every first-born in the land of Egypt* (Ex 12:29).

Thus it is said, *In Your great triumph You break Your opponents; You send forth Your fury and it consumes them like straw* (Ex 15:7).[303]

***וברב** גאונך תהרוס קמיך*

בשעה שהביא (fol. 354v) הקב"ה על המצריים מכת בכורות בתחילה הביא על אלהיהם ואחר כך הביא עליהם, שנאמר *ובכל אלהי מצרים אעשה שפטים אני יי'*. ואיזו מכה הביא הקב"ה על אלהיהם? שכל צלם שהיה של אבן נשבר ונעשה כיתותין כיתותין. וזה שהיה מן כסף וזהב ונחשת ומן ברזל ועופרת ניתך ונעשה כטבלא על גבי קרקע.

וכשמתו המצריים בים ירדה אש על אלהיהם ושרפתם. לכך נאמר *וברוב גאונך תהרוס קמיך תשלח חרונך יאכלמו כקש*.

In Your great *triumph You break Your opponents* (Exodus 15:7 – Recension A)

When the Blessed Holy One brought the plague of the first-born against the Egyptians, He brought it first against their gods and, after that, against them. As it is said, *I will mete out punishments to all the gods of Egypt, I the Lord* (Ex 12:12). What sort of plague did the Holy One bring against their gods? Every image made of stone was broken, pulverized into tiny pieces. That which was made of silver, gold, or copper, from iron or lead, melted and became like a tablet on the ground.

And after the Egyptians died in the sea, fire came down upon their gods and burned them. Thus it is said, *In Your great triumph You break Your opponents; You send forth Your fury and it consumes them like straw* (Ex 15:7).[304]

Exodus 15:7 Commentary

I. Measure for Measure

Although Recension A's close reading of the text which imagines the idols of Egypt as "Your opponents" who are broken and burned is apt in terms of classic rabbinic exegesis, the later redaction offers an interpretation that hews more closely to the larger context. The Song at the Sea is a celebration of God's triumph over the *human* leadership of Egypt; Pharaoh's will is broken by the plagues and his troops are consumed in the sea. What the midrash adds is justification for such a debilitating series of blows. The justification, of course, takes the form of demonizing the Egyptians to some extent, inventing oppressive measures that correlate to each of the plagues – although the redactors appear more concerned with verbal or thematic similarity than moral parity.

In its first iteration of the motif in 15:3, the text employs the standard rabbinic term, מידה כנגד מידה, generally translated "measure for measure." Unfortunately, the English idiom is a bit misleading; it suggests a quantitative equivalence that explains God's actions. The rabbinic term, on the other hand, is designed to highlight a purposeful correspondence, not necessarily an equal balance. "With corresponding aspect" might be a better translation, were it not so inelegant; "poetic justice" captures a bit of what the rabbis had in mind. The Egyptians would not allow the Israelite women to ritually bathe themselves after their menses, so the waters become inundated with blood. They made Israel go hunt fresh game; now these dangerous animals invade Egyptian homes. Crops and fruit trees and animals, for which Israel was forced to do all the labor, are destroyed.

Yitzḥak Heinemann's important study of aggadic literature recognizes in rabbinic thought a similarity to myth: The object is not to explicate but to signify. Drawing out hidden connections between various elements in the world reveals order behind the seeming randomness of existence. For the rabbis, it unfolds the workings of Divine Providence in a world that would otherwise be bereft of meaning.[305] To this analysis of aggadic literature, Ishay Rosen-Zvi adds a vital clarification. The rabbis do not explore the world directly, but rather through investigation of biblical text – the blueprint for creation. Torah is that which reveals meaning within history.[306] Through exegesis, we come to "know" the additional labors and afflictions laid upon Israel, and thus the reasoning for the selection of these plagues among God's infinite arsenal.

Biblical precedent similarly highlights thematic or numerical correspondence rather than juridical equivalence. God's response to the scouts' discouraging report in Numbers 14, for instance, is to compel the Israelites to wander in the wilderness one year for each of the forty days the scouts investigated the land (v. 34). The people sought to return to Egypt or to die in the wilderness (vv. 2–3); they will get their wish, unfortunately. Scholars have identified the measure for measure theme within numerous biblical texts,[307] and early sources contain references to the exodus narrative that highlight this dynamic. The apocryphal text Wisdom of Solomon, for instance, identifies the plagues as a manifestation of God's poetic justice and emphasizes a pedagogical objective:

Wis 11:16: You sent upon them a multitude of irrational creatures for vengeance that they might learn, that by what things a man sins, by these he is punished.

Wis 18:4: For well did the Egyptians deserve the loss of light and imprisonment in darkness, they who had kept your sons imprisoned, through whom the incorruptible light of Torah was to be given to humanity.

Mekhilta Beshallaḥ 6 (HR 110) brings a series of prooftexts to reinforce thematic connection between sin and punishment,[308] leading up to Jethro's dramatic exclamation that he now fully recognizes the greatness of God on account of such exquisite correspondence. Egyptian troops are drowning, the precise scheme by which they intended to murder innocent Israelite infants.[309] The glory of Divine action here is distinct from halakhic requirements for direct, measured and equal justice; the aggadic principle illuminates how every moment intersects, every choice resounds with meaning, and all things can serve God's purpose.

II. Midrashic Motifs in Haggadot Illuminations

Art is also an interpretive medium, so "parallels" among textual illuminations are worthy of mention. A number of beautifully illuminated medieval haggadot incorporate midrashic motifs, including a few that correspond to MV's exegesis. Although many of the drawings depict scenes of the exodus (plagues, crossing the sea, etc.), they address a larger cycle of biblical narratives. One Golden Haggadah manuscript held in the British Library (Or. 2884) portrays Pharaoh's daughter presenting the young Moses to Pharaoh, and the caption makes reference to the magicians who warn that he will grow up to destroy Egypt (fol. 12r). Extant illuminations of the fourth plague elect the standard Jewish medieval interpretation of the plague as a horde of wild beasts (rather than a swarm of insects). Interestingly, the Sarajevo Haggadah includes an animal that resembles the description of the *siloni* (fol. 23v).

The early printed edition of the Venice Haggadah contains traditions scattered throughout MV. For example, artistic representation of the fifth plague includes broken idols (15:6). Another frame portrays husbands and wives abstaining from sexual intercourse in the wake of Pharaoh's decree (15:2).[310]

Given the multivocal nature of midrashic exegesis, some of the pictorial interpretations do not align with MV but rather find "echoes" in different texts. *Tanḥuma Bo 3*, for instance, offers an alternative explanation for the plague of darkness; it was designed so the Israelites could scout out the wealth in Egyptian homes and then identify the hiding places if the Egyptians pretended they had nothing to lend. In two frames, the Golden Haggadah illustrates Egyptians suffering the plague of darkness and the Israelites taking the hidden wealth of Egyptian homes (British Library Add. 27210 fol. 13r).[311]

Exodus 15:8

וּבְרוּחַ אַפֶּיךָ נֶעֶרְמוּ מַיִם
נִצְּבוּ כְמוֹ־נֵד נֹזְלִים
קָפְאוּ תְהֹמֹת בְּלֶב־יָם׃

At the blast of Your nostrils the waters piled up,
the floods stood straight like a wall,
the deeps congealed in the heart of the sea.

וברוח אפיך נערמו מים

כשראו מים של ים אהבה שאהב הב"ה את ישראל, השפילו המים עצמם בשביל כבוד ישראל. ואף הים השפיל את עצמו ועשה את עצמו לשנים עשר קרעים כנגד שנים עשר שבטי ישראל. והגביה את רגליו למעלה שש מאות מיל, והקפיא ע[צ]מו מלמטה. והמתיק את מימיו ונעשה להם כחומה, ונעשו בו חלונות שהיו ישראל רואין זה את זה. ומהללים להב"ה בשירות ותושבחות, ומהלכים בתוך הים כאדם שהיה מהלך בביתו, עד שיצאו ליבשה.

לכך נאמר *וברוח אפיך נערמו מים נצבו כמו נד נוזלים קפאו תהומות בלב ים.*

At the blast of Your nostrils the waters piled up
(Exodus 15:8 – Recension B)

When the waters of the sea saw how deeply the Blessed Holy One loved Israel, the waters humbled themselves for the honor of Israel. Even the sea humbled himself and divided into twelve sections, corresponding to the twelve tribes of Israel.[312] He raised his waves[313] six hundred mil upward and congealed himself[314] from below. He sweetened his waters[315] and made them like a wall, and there were windows in it so the Israelites could see one another. They praised the Blessed Holy One with songs and adorations as they went amidst the sea like a man walks in his own home, until they came out on dry land.

Thus it is said, *At the blast of Your nostrils the waters piled up, the floods stood straight like a wall, the deeps congealed in the heart of the sea* (Ex 15:8).[316]

***ובֿרוח** אפך נערמו מים*

בשעה שאמר הקב"ה למשה: נטה ידך על הים ובקעה, נטה משה ידו עליו ולא רצה הים לקרוע מפניו.

אמר משה לפני הקב"ה: רבונו של עולם אין הים רוצה להיבקע מפני בני ישראל. מיד נגלה הקב"ה על הים. וכיון שראה הים את הקב"ה מיד נבהל ונרתע ונזדעזע לחזר לאחוריו וברח, שנאמר *הים ראה וינוס הירדן תיסוב לאחור*. וכיון שנבקע הים נשמע קולו מסוף העולם ועד סופו וגבהו [המים] למעלה אלף ושש מאות מילין.

גער בו הקב"ה: מפני מה לא היתה נבקעת לפני בניי?

אמר לפניו: רבונו של עולם לא הייתי יודע שבאו בשליחותך, אלא מעכשו אני אעשה להם כל רצונך וכל רצונם. באותה שעה כפה הים את עצמו ונבקע לשנים עשר קרעים, ונעשה להם חומה מלמעלה. והמתיק להם מימיו, והצמיח להם כל אילני פירות וכל ריח טוב. והקפיא עצמו מלמטה ונעשה חומות להם מלמעלה. והיו ישראל מהלכין בתוכו כאדם שמהלך בביתו על גבי מצעות. וכל מה שהיה ישראל רוצים הוא היה עושה להם.

לכך נאמר *וברוח אפך נערמו מים נצבו כמו נד נוזלים קפאו תהומות בלב ים*.

At the blast *of Your nostrils the waters piled up* (Exodus 15:8 – Recension A)

When the Blessed Holy One said to Moses, "Extend your hand over the sea and split it,"[317] Moses extended his hand over it, but the sea did not want to divide before him.[318]

Moses said to the Blessed Holy One, "Master of the world, the sea does not want to be split before the children of Israel." Then the Blessed Holy One was revealed unto the sea; and when the sea saw the Holy One, he was immediately terrified, shaken and recoiling, fleeing to turn back upon himself – as it is said, *The sea saw and fled, the Jordan ran backward* (Ps 114:3). When the sea split, its sound was heard from one end of the world to the other, and [the waters] rose up sixteen hundred mil.[319]

The Blessed Holy One rebuked him, "Why would you not be split before My children?"

"Master of the world, I did not know that they came on Your mission. But now I will do Your will and theirs, whatever it be." Then the sea forced himself to split into twelve sections, building up walls for them. He sweetened the water for them and caused all kinds of fruit trees to sprout, with every lovely scent. He congealed himself below and was made into walls above so that Israel could walk through it the way a person walks in his house on carpet.[320] Anything the Israelites wanted, he would do for them.

Thus it is said, *At the blast of Your nostrils the waters piled up, the floods stood straight like a wall, the deeps congealed in the heart of the sea.* (Ex 15:8).

Exodus 15:8 Commentary

I. Twelve Channels at the Sea

Comparison with a partial parallel in *Ex. Rab. 21:6* raises the possibility of an exegetical foundation for the sea's twelve-lane highway. There, Ps 114 is invoked as a basis for the characterization of the sea. The motif of the channels may derive, as Daniel Boyarin implies, from a reading of חולי ארץ (v. 7): imagining it as the sea speaking to the earth to hollow (חלל) itself into channels.[321]

Given the prevalence of the twelve channels motif, it may not be surprising that the tradition is found among early Christian commentators as well. Origen supplies a more straightforward exegetical background:

> I have heard a tradition from the ancients that in that parting of the sea individual divisions of the waters were made for each individual tribe of the sons of Israel and a special way was opened in the sea for each tribe and I have proven it from that which is written in the Psalms: "*He who divided the Red Sea into divisions*" (Ps 136:13).[322]

Note that the verse continues, *His steadfast love is eternal*, suggesting a connection to God's deep affection for Israel as presented at the beginning of our lemma.

This motif is found traversing not only religious traditions, but also outside the boundaries of literature. The synagogue at Dura-Europus depicts the crossing of the Red Sea with twelve vertical lines delineating the path of the Israelites; at the top of each stands a small square that likely represents the windows suggested by the midrash. Constructed in the third-century, this synagogue fresco stands as a delightful witness to the multi-media nature of the midrashic imagination.[323]

Exodus 15:9

אָמַר אוֹיֵב אֶרְדֹּף אַשִּׂיג
אֲחַלֵּק שָׁלָל
תִּמְלָאֵמוֹ נַפְשִׁי
אָרִיק חַרְבִּי תּוֹרִישֵׁמוֹ יָדִי׃

The enemy said, "I will pursue, I will overtake,
I will divide the spoil.
My soul shall have its fill of them.
I will bare my sword – my hand shall subdue them."

אמר אויב

אמרו חכמים: בשעה שרדפו המצרים אחרי ישראל על הים נעשו שלש כתות. כת ראשונה אומרת: נטבע עצמנו בים. כת שניה אומרת: נשוב למצרים. כת שלישית אומרת: נערוך עמהם למלחמה.

כת שאומרת, נטבע בים אמר להם {משה}: *התיצבו וראו את ישועת יי'*. כת שאומרת, נחזור למצרים אמר להם משה: *לא תוסיפו לראותם עוד עד עולם*. כת שאומרת, נערוך עמהם למלחמה אמר להם משה: *יי' ילחם לכם ואתם תחרישון*.

וכיון שנבקע הים נשמע שמועתו מסוף העולם ועד סופו, וגבהו המים אלף ושש מאות מיל. ונבהל כל העולם ואחזום אימה ורעדה.

באותה שעה עמדו כל השבטין על שפת הים, זה אומר: מי ירד תחלה לים? וזה אומר: מי ירד תחלה? עד שקפץ שבט בנימין וירד תחלה ואחריו ירדו כל השבטים. לפיכך זכה בנימין שיצא ממנו מרדכי הצדיק שנפדו ישראל על ידו בין מות לחיים.

כיון שראו המצרים שנכנסו ישראל לים, אף (fol. 242r) הם נחלקו לשלש כתות. כת ראשונה אומרת: נחזירם למצרים. כת שנייה אומרת: נפשיטם ונעזבם ערומים. כת שלישית אומרת: נהרג אותם.

אותם שהיו אומרים נחזירם למצרים, נשף הב"ה ברוחו עליהם, שנאמר *נשפת ברוחך כסמו ים*. ואותם <שהיו> אומרים נפשיטם ונעזבם ערומים, נער הב"ה בים, שנאמר *וינער יי' את מצרים בתוך הים*. ואותם שהיו אומרים נהרגם, טבעם הב"ה בים, שנאמר *ומבחר שלישיו טבעו בים סוף*.

כיון שראו המצרים שהתחיל בהם פורענות אמרו: אלהיהם של ישראל גדול הוא מאד, נחזור ונברח במצרים. כיון שראה הב"ה כך, שיגר לפניהם מלאך בדמות סוס נקבה, ונכנסה לים ורצו כל הסוסים ונכנסו לים בעל כרחם. אמר הב"ה: *נטה ידך על הים וישובו המים על מצרים*.[...] *ויט משה את ידו על הים*. מיד בזזו ישראל ממונם של מצרים.

The enemy said
(Exodus 15:9 – Recension B)

The Sages said: When the Egyptians pursued Israel unto the sea, the [people] were of three camps. The first said, "Let us drown ourselves in the sea." The second group said, "Let us return to Egypt." The third group said, "Let us wage war against them."

To the group that said, "Let us drown ourselves in the sea," {Moses} said, "*Stand by and see the salvation of the Lord*" (Ex 14:13). To the group that said, "Let us return to Egypt," Moses said, "*You will never see them again*" (Ex 14:13). To the group that said, "Let us wage war against them," Moses said, "*The Lord will do battle for you; hold your peace*" (Ex 14:14).[324]

When the sea split, the sound was heard from one end of the earth to the other and the waters rose up sixteen hundred mil. All the world was terrified, seized with fear and trembling.

At that moment, all the tribes stood on the shore of the sea, with this one saying, "Who will go down first into the sea?" and that one saying, "Who will go down first?" – until the tribe of Benjamin jumped in first and all the tribes followed him down. Thus Benjamin merited that the righteous Mordechai would issue from its ranks, through whom Israel was rescued from death to life.[325]

When the Egyptians saw that Israel entered the sea, they too were divided into three camps. The first group said, "Let us return them to Egypt." The second group said, "Let us strip them and leave them naked." The third group said, "Let's kill them."

Those who said, "Let us return them to Egypt," the Holy One blew with His wind upon them,[326] as it is said, *You made Your wind blow, the sea covered them* (Ex 15:10). Those who said,[327] "Let us strip them and leave them naked," the Lord hurled into the sea, as it is said, *The Lord hurled*[328] *the Egyptians into the sea* (Ex 14:27). Those who said, "Let's kill them," the Holy One drowned in the sea, as it is said, *The pick of his officers are drowned in the Sea of Reeds* (Ex 15:4).[329]

When the Egyptians saw that retribution had begun against them, they said, "The God of Israel is very great. Let us turn back and escape into Egypt." When the Blessed Holy One saw this, He sent an angel before them with the appearance of a mare. She went into the sea and all the male horses ran in after her against their will.[330] The Holy One said, "*Hold out your arm over the sea, that the waters may come back upon the Egyptians....*" *Moses held out his arm over the sea* (Ex 14:26–27). Then the Israelites plundered the Egyptians' money.

לכך נאמר אמר אויב ארדוף אשיג אחלק שלל תמלאמו נפשי אריק חרבי תורישמו ידי.

Thus, it is said, *The enemy said, "I will pursue, I will overtake, I will divide the spoil. My soul shall have its fill of them. I will bare my sword – my hand shall subdue them*" (Ex 15:9).[331]

אמר *אויב ארדוף אשיג אחלק שלל*

בשעה שרדפו המצרים את ישראל נחלקו שלש כיתות. כת ראשונה אומרת: נשלול אותם ובניהם. כת שנייה: נחזירם אותם למצרים ונשעבד אותם בשעבוד קשה. כת שלישית אומרת: *אריק חרבי תורישמו ידי.*

אותם שהיו אומרים נשלול אותם, נשף הקב"ה עליהם ומתו, שנאמר *נשפת ברוחך כיסמו ים.* ואותם שהיו אומרים נחזירם למצרים ונשעבד בהם שעבוד קשה, ~~צלל~~ <צרר> הקב"ה נשמתם בים והיה הים משכשך אותם רוחן ומצערן. ואותם שהיו אומרים *אריק חרבי תורישמו ידי,* צללו הקב"ה בעימקי ים.

לכך נאמר *אמר אויב ארדוף אשיג אחלק שלל תמלאמו נפשי אריק חרבי תורישמו ידי.*

The enemy ***said****, "I will pursue, I will overtake, I will divide the spoil* (Exodus 15:9 – Recension A)

When the Egyptians pursued Israel, they were divided into three camps. The first group said, "Let us despoil them and their children." The second group said, "Let us return them to Egypt and subject them to difficult servitude." The third group said, "*I will bare my sword, my hand shall subdue them"* (Ex 15:9).

Those who said, "Let us despoil them," the Holy One blew upon them and they died, as it is said, *You made Your wind blow, the sea covered them* (Ex 15:10). Those who said, "Let us return them to Egypt and subject them to difficult servitude," the Holy One <bound> their souls in the sea and the sea suspended them [there] and afflicted their spirits. Those who said, "*I will bare my sword, my hand shall subdue them*," the Holy One sunk in the depths of the sea.

Thus it is said, *The enemy said, "I will pursue, I will overtake, I will divide the spoil. My soul shall have its fill of them. I will bare my sword – my hand shall subdue them"* (Ex 15:9).[332]

Exodus 15:9 Commentary

I. The Camps of the Egyptians and the Israelites

Recension B's camps among the Israelites present an elegant exegesis of Moses' exhortation, "*Have no fear! Stand by and see the salvation that the Lord will work for you today, for the Egyptians whom you see today, you will never see them again. The Lord will do battle for you; you hold your peace*" (Ex 14:13–4). Each of his directives thereby addresses a different concern and proposed strategy. In addition, it nicely complements the direct exegesis of the lemma from the Song in which three camps are identified among the Egyptian "enemy," each with a different idea for harming Israel – all of which are ultimately foiled by God.

Although the latter is likely the original exegesis of MV since it fits the lemmatic verse and is the only part found in Recension A, the camps of the Israelites quite possibly represent the older tradition. James Kugel suggests that its origin relates to Ps 106:7, which asserts that the Israelites rebelled at the Sea of Reeds.[333] According to Michael Klein, the interpretation belongs originally to Ex 14, and was moved to the Song as part of midrashic expansions on the Targum (*toseftot*) included for liturgical/homiletical purposes on seventh-day Passover.[334] In addition to the evidence he brings, it is interesting to note that both festival prayerbooks among the manuscripts (MSS Cam 667.1 and Prm 2736) contain an Aramaic version of the four camps in their targumic sections. Older parallels generally present four camps, a breakdown that fits Moses' speech most tidily. The reduction to three may be designed to parallel the three camps of the Egyptians in its new context. A tenth-century *piyyut* by Joseph Albardani in Baghdad which has the same three camps of Israelites as MV, however, suggests that the tradition may already be circulating in this alternative form.[335]

II. Irony in Midrash

As the mighty Egyptian army approaches a ragtag group of Israelites trapped at the sea, it is perfectly logical that the pursuers should presume to have their way. The contextual narrative in Exodus indicates they plan to return the people unto slavery; the verse in the Song uses language of a different sort of victory: to pursue, to overtake, to divide the spoil. Whatever the Egyptians' intentions, the Song at the Sea celebrates a stunning reversal: Those who anticipated triumph are instead utterly vanquished.

The situational irony evolves into a dramatic one as God's victory at the sea is rehearsed in midrash and liturgy. Surely Israelites who had just escaped slavery were as certain of their own defeat as Egyptians were of their victory, but a reader of MV knows that the best-laid plans of the Egyptians will come to naught in the face of Divine power. Our verse captures the troops in eternal ignorance – always before seeing the disaster that is to befall them – and so we know more than they do.

Similarly, Jethro's belated recognition of Moses as God's elect reverberates with dramatic irony (15:2). What the reader has known all along, Jethro should realize when Moses retrieves the staff; instead, he throws the man into a pit to die. The sea's misguided attempt to apply seniority to resist Moses (14:30), desperate Egyptian efforts to hunt down Israelite infants (15:1), Pharaoh's futile plan to screen out God's appointed redeemer (15:2) – all these reveal the value of dramatic irony in effective narrative.

There is also a rhetorical value, binding author and reader together in the pleasure of the puzzle:

> The very intricacy of our interpretive act builds for us, when we manage to do it right, a tight bond with the author; to understand him, we've had to assume that he is our kind of person, and that he knows that we will know that he knows that we will assume – etc. The result is that most literary effects that will allow for stable irony at all will be strengthened by it. Even though some readers or listeners may be left by the wayside, those who come along will be clamped inescapably into the author's patterns – they will in fact have the illusion of having built each point for themselves.[336]

As an essential tool in midrashic discourse, however, irony is doing much more. There is not only a dramatic quality but also a didactic purpose.[337] Recognizing the ambiguity of language and the multiplicity of meaning, rabbinic literature deploys a steady tension between the singular statement and its manifold possibilities of interpretation. One prominent purpose is to reveal

> the dissonance between the religion of the Rabbis and the Book from which it is supposed to be derived – and (at least a good part of the time) more precisely the dissonance between that book's supposedly unitary and harmonious message and its actually fragmentary and inconsistent components. Midrash, the perfect expression of rabbinic theology, is thus bound to be at the same time somewhat ironic and yet terribly in earnest.[338]

The challenges posed by Abraham and the angels exemplify this exegetical sort of purpose, revealing an irony in the Divine promise of the covenant. A straightforward understanding that Isaac will live to raise children is no longer tenable in the wake of the Divine command to offer him as a sacrifice on Mt. Moriah. The promise of reward for the righteous and the premise of a just God seem equally unfounded. Embracing contradiction with ironic (and earnest) tone and multiple voices, the midrash unfolds the Bible's messages in all their complexity (14:30).

Our current passage incorporates the other dimension described by Kugel. God's saving hand at the sea reflects a profound dissonance given the medieval Jewish community's experience. By the time of MV, the people have entered their second millenium of exile; their enemies have indeed bared their sword and subdued them, over and over again. Rabbinic use of irony, in the meeting of faith and experience, is also designed to strengthen faith in the underlying Reality that belies all appearances. God's will *is* unfolding in human history, the Jews will be restored, and redemption is again forthcoming.

Exodus 15:10

נָשַׁפְתָּ בְרוּחֲךָ כִּסָּמוֹ יָם
צָלֲלוּ כַּעוֹפֶרֶת בְּמַיִם אַדִּירִים׃

You made Your wind blow, the sea covered them.
They sank like lead in the majestic waters.

נשפת ברוחך

אמרו חכמים: בשעה שטבע המצריים בים, היו בהם שני מכשפים, ושמם יוחני וממרא. ואמרו לפרעה: אם ביד הב"ה יש נס זה אין אנו יכולין לו, אבל אם ביד מלאכים יש אנו יכולים לנערם. מיד עשו כשפיהם והורידו אותם אלהיהם.

אז אמרו המלאכים: הושיענו *אלהים כי באו מים עד נפש*, ואתה במאמרך טבעת אותם במים אדירים.

לכך נאמר *נשפת ברוחך כסמו ים צללו כעופרת במים אדירים.*

You made Your wind blow
(Exodus 15:10 – Recension B)

The Sages said: When He drowned the Egyptians in the sea, there were among them two magicians, named Yoḥani and Mamre.[339] They said to Pharaoh, "If this miracle is from the hand of the Blessed Holy One, we cannot prevail over Him, but if it is from the hand of angels, we can shake them."[340] So they cast their magic spells and their gods brought the [angels] down.[341]

The angels said, "Save us, *O God, for the water has become deadly* (Ps 69:2)[342] – and You with Your word drowned the [Egyptians] in the majestic waters."

Thus it is said, *You made Your wind blow, the sea covered them. They sank like lead in the majestic waters* (Ex 15:10).[343]

***נשפת** ברוחך כסמו ים*

בשעה שטבעו המצרים בים היה בהם בעלי כשפים, ועשו כשפים וברחו מן הים. אמר הים: פיקדון שפיקדני הקב"ה (fol. 355r) היאך אניח אותו? מיד שבו המים לפני כל אחד ואחד ועשו עצמן שבילין ומורידין המצריים לים, שנאמר *ומצרים נסים לקראתו* – לקראת כל מצרי ומצרי.

והיו בהם שני אנשים יוחנן וממרא, והרי שרי כשפים. מה עשו? עשו להם כשפים ועלו ברומו של עולם. והיו מיכאל וגבריאל רואין אותם, ואינם יכולין להם ואינם יודעים מה הם עושים. מיד צעקו לפני הקב"ה ואמרו לפניו: רבונו של עולם, הללו ששיעבדו בניך, עשה בהם דין.

מיד אמר לו הקב"ה למיכאל שר הגדול: לך והורידם והטביעם בים.

לכך נאמר *נשפת ברוחך כיסמו ים צללו כעופרת במים אדירים.*

You made *Your wind* ***blow****, the sea covered them*
(Exodus 15:10 – Recension A)

When the Egyptians drowned in the sea, there were magicians among them who performed tricks and escaped from the sea. The sea said, "How can I forsake the task with which the Blessed Holy One charged me?" The water immediately returned toward each one, making itself into pathways, and brought the Egyptians down to the sea. As it is said, *The Egyptians fled at its approach* (Ex 14:27) – it approached each Egyptian.[344]

There were among them two men, Yoḥani and Mamre, chiefs of the magicians. What did they do? They performed magic spells and rose to the heights. Michael and Gabriel saw them but could not prevail against them, and they did not know what they were doing. So they cried out before the Blessed Holy One, "Master of the world, execute judgment against these who subjugated Your children."

The Blessed Holy One answered Michael, the chief ministering angel, "Go – bring them down and drown them in the sea."[345]

Thus it is said, *You made Your wind blow, the sea covered them. They sank like lead in the majestic waters* (Ex 15:10).

Exodus 15:10 Commentary

I. Yoḥani and Mamre

These names were established as the chief magicians in Egypt before the composition of the Talmud. By the following shorthand reference found in *b. Men. 85a*, it is clear that they had already achieved proverbial status. Related to a discussion of the mishnaic requirement that agricultural offerings must come only from the choicest produce, the gemara continues:

אמרי ליה יוחנא וממרא למשה: תבן אתה מכניס לעפריים?
אמר להו: אמרי אינשי למתא ירקא ירקא שקול.

Yoḥani and Mamre said to Moses, "Would you bring straw to Afaraim?"
He said to them, "People say, 'Take vegetables to Veggietown.'"[346]

Yoḥani and Mamre are challenging Moses about the sense of bringing an item to a place where it is already plentiful, like "bringing coals to Newcastle" in the English idiom. It is understood to allude to Moses' efforts to impress Pharaoh with what are perceived as magic tricks, when Egypt is a bastion of magical practices. This presumption about Egypt can be found throughout rabbinic literature; see, for instance, *b. Kid. 49b, Avot d'Rabbi Natan A 28, Tanḥ. B. Vaera 12.* According to Rashi, Moses' reply means that it makes perfect sense to go to the leading market for a particular service or merchandise, because everyone who is interested in such things will be there.[347]

The notion that Egyptian magicians were none too impressed with God's first wonders as displayed by Moses is suggested already in Ex 7:11, where they match his feats with sorcery. There, however, they are not named. *Targum Pseudo-Jonathan* inserts the names Jannes and Jambres (יניס וימברים) in its translation of the verse, names believed to be interchangeable with the wily magicians of MV. Various forms of the names appear in ancient sources, along with various traditions ascribed to them. In the Damascus Document (7:19) published by Solomon Schechter, there is this brief mention: For in earlier times Moses and Aaron arose with the help of the Prince of Lights, while Belial raised up Yoḥanah and his brother in his cunning, when Israel was saved the first time.[348] A fragment of this tradition is also found in a scroll from Cave 6 at Qumran: DJD III 15,3-Plate 26.

According to Albert Pietersma, however, these references are to Israelite leaders gone astray, and he speculates about Second Temple figures and politics to clarify the intent of the passage. He goes on to list over forty traditions in assorted Greek, Christian and Jewish sources ranging from antiquity to the seventeenth century, including many that do identify the men as magicians in Pharaoh's court.[349] Generally, these texts portray the pair of magicians challenging Moses at the onset of the plagues, although the *Targum* states they predict the coming of a redeemer for Israel.

In other passages, they are described as the sons or assistants of Balaam, who is portrayed as an advisor to Pharaoh before being summoned by Balak to curse Israel as narrated in the Book of Numbers 22–24.[350] Some of these examples mention their magical skills as well. In fact, the Zohar has a motif very similar to MV, but it is located in its commentary on the defeat of Midian: Balaam and his sons fly into the air to escape, and it requires supernatural powers to capture them.[351]

Pietersma's primary interest, an ancient Greek source extant in three sets of fragments titled *The Apocryphon of Jannes and Jambres*, is among the texts that identify the pair as sons of Balaam and magicians at Pharaoh's court. While it includes an encounter with Moses, the imaginative narrative has numerous other plot elements, and the brothers die in Egypt, not at the sea.

An interesting strain of interpretation that conceivably weaves together Egyptian and Israelite identities describes the wizards as questionable proselytes who stir up the mixed multitude (ערב רב) in the incident of the golden calf.[352] *Tanḥuma Ki Tisa 19* includes an element of this tradition: Yoḥani and Mamre are among the multitude who demand a god to lead them, ultimately prompting the disaster.

In Pietersma's list, there are also a number of texts which reflect MV's notion that Yoḥani and Mamre remain in the service of Egypt and perish at the sea, e.g., *Yal. Shimoni 235, Yal. Reuveni 38a, Chronicles of Jeraḥmiel,* and King Alfred's version of Paulus Orosius' *History against the Pagans*.[353]

Although the men are described as brothers of Satan in *Questions of Bartholomew Lat. 2, IV:51*, none of the sources on Pietersma's list associate the "sons of Belial" found in the Damascus Document with the Egyptian magicians, a lacuna which leads him to question the connection presumed by modern scholarship. Thus it is of special interest that MS Mos 111, a fifteenth-century mixed recension of MV, presents the angels prosecuting these wicked wizards before God: "These are the men of Belial who have inflicted enormous servitude upon Your children; wreak vengeance upon them." This linkage suggests some continuation or rediscovery of the ancient motif from the Second Temple period.

Still, one wonders what inspires mention of wizards in the exegesis of this verse. It is possible that the phrase, "*They sank like lead in the majestic waters,"* conjures up images of sorcery because immersing metal objects into water was considered a magical act in the Middle Ages.[354] Lead became strongly associated with magic spells initially because lead tablets were easy to inscribe; later their heavy weight and dour coloring took on symbolic power as well.[355]

"You made Your wind blow" may be equally suggestive; the act of blowing on an object (a long-standing part of magical rites) may have no actual power, but the breath of God does.[356]

Exodus 15:11

מִי־כָמֹכָה בָּאֵלִם יְהֹוָה
מִי כָּמֹכָה נֶאְדָּר בַּקֹּדֶשׁ
נוֹרָא תְהִלֹּת עֹשֵׂה פֶלֶא׃

Who is like You among the gods, O Lord?
Who is like You, majestic in holiness,
awesome in splendor, doing wonders?

מי כמוך

אמרו חכמים ז"ל: בשעה שאמרו ישראל זאת השירה לפני הב"ה, שמע אותה פרעה שהיה מטורף בים. ונשא אצבעו לשמים ואמר: מאמין אני בך *שאתה הצדיק ואני ועמי הרשעים*, ולא יש אלוה בעולם אלא אתה.

באותה שעה ירד גבריאל והטיל על צוארו שלשלת של ברזל ואמר לו: רשע! אתמול אמרת, *מי יי' אשר אשמע בקולו*, ועתה אתה אמרת *יי' הצדיק*. מיד הורידו למצולות ים ועכבו שם חמשים יום, וציער אותו (fol. 242v) כדי שיכיר גבורותיו של הב"ה.

ולאחר כך המליכו *על נינוה העיר הגדולה*, וכשבא יונה לנינוה ואמר, *עוד ארבעים שנה [יום] ונינוה נהפכת*, מיד אחזו אימה ורעדה וקם מכסאו *ויכס שק וישב על האפר*. והוא בעצמו צועק ואמר: *האדם והבהמה הבקר והצאן, אל יטעמו מאומה ואל ירעו ומים אל ישתו*, כי יודע אני שאין אלוה אחר בכל העולם וכל דבריו אמת, וכל במשפט ובאמונה.

ועדין הוא פרעה חי ועומד על פתח גיהנם, וכשנכנסין מלכי אומות העולם, מיד הוא מודיע להם גבורותיו של הב"ה, ואמר להם: שוטים שבעולם! מפני מה לא למדתם ממני דעת, שהוא עני כפר [שהרי אני כפרתי] בהב"ה. לכן שלח בי עשר מכות, ואף טבעני בים ועכבני שם חמשים יום. ואחר כן העלני מן הים, ולבסוף האמנתי בו בעל כרחי.

ולפיכך שררו ישראל שירה זאת ואמרו כולם יחד: *מי כמוכה באלים יי' מי כמוכה נאדר בקודש נורא תהלות עושה פלא.*

Who is like You
(Exodus 15:11 – Recension B)

The Sages, may their memory be for a blessing, said: When Israel recited this song before the Blessed Holy One, Pharaoh heard it while he was foundering in the sea. He lifted up his finger toward the heavens and said, "I believe in You, that You are *the righteous one, while I and my people are the wicked ones* (Ex 9:27) – and there is no God in the world other than You."[357]

Just then, Gabriel descended and hung a chain of iron around his neck, saying, "Wicked one! Yesterday you said, '*Who is the Lord that I should listen to his voice*?' (Ex 5:2), and now you say, '*The Lord is the righteous one*!'" (Ex 9:27). Then he drew him down into the depths of the sea and detained him there for fifty days and afflicted him[358] so that he would recognize the great powers of the Blessed Holy One.

Afterwards, he appointed him king *over Nineveh, that great city* (Jonah 4:11)[359] and when Jonah came to say, "*Forty days more, and Nineveh shall be overthrown*" (Jonah 3:4),[360] fear and trembling immediately seized him. He rose from his throne, *covered himself in sackcloth and sat among the ashes* (Jonah 3:6). He himself cried out, "*Man and beast, cattle and flock: Don't taste a morsel, don't graze or drink water* (Jonah 3:7), because I know that there is no other God in all the world and all His words are true, with justice and faithfulness."

Even now, this Pharaoh lives at the entrance of Gehenna. As kings of the nations enter, he immediately makes known to them the great powers of the Holy One and says to them, "You are the biggest idiots in the world! Why did you not learn from me? See, [I] denied[361] the Blessed Holy One, so He sent ten plagues against me. Plus, He drowned me in the sea and detained me there for fifty days. Then He drew me up from the sea and in the end, I believed in Him against my will."

Thus, Israel sang this song and everyone recited together, *Who is like You among the gods, O Lord? Who is like You, majestic in holiness, awesome in splendor, doing wonders?* (Ex 15:11).[362]

מי כמוך באלים יי'

בשעה שאמרו ישראל שירה שמע פרעה קולם של ישראל כשהיה מטורף בים. נשא אצבעו לשמים ואמר: מאמין אני שכך הוא.

באותה שעה בא גבריאל ואמר לו: רשע! אמש היתה אומר *מי יי' אשר אשמע בקולו*, ועכשיו אתה אומר מאמין אני. הניח שלשלאות של ברזל על צוארו והורידו במצולות ים ועכבו שם חמשים יום בצער רוחו ונשמתו כדי שיכיר גבורותיו של הקב"ה.

ולאחר חמשים יום הוציאו מן הים והחזירו על כל אומה ולשון והיה מודיע להם גבורותיו של הקב"ה. ובסוף הכניסו בנינוה והמליכו עליו. וכשבא יונה הנביא וקרא, *עוד ארבעים יום ונינוה נהפכת*, באותה שעה נזדעזע פרעה ועמד מכסאו ואמר: יודע אני שאין אלוה בעולם אלא הקב"ה.

ופרעה עדיין הוא חי על שער גהינם. וכשמכניסין את הגוים ואת הממלכות לגהינם אומר להם: מפני מה לא למדתם ממני? שכפרתי בהקב"ה ולבסוף האמנתי אותו בעל כרחי. ומודיע להם גבורתו של הקב"ה.

לכך נאמר *מי כמוך באלים יי' מי כמוך נאדר בקדש נורא תהלות עושה פלא.*

***Who** is like You among the gods, O Lord?*
(Exodus 15:11 – Recension A)

When Israel recited song, Pharaoh heard their voice while he was foundering in the sea. He lifted up his finger toward the heavens and said, "I believe that it is so!"

Just then, Gabriel came and said to him, "Wicked one! Last night you were saying, '*Who is the Lord that I should listen to his voice*?' (Ex 5:2), and now you say, 'I believe!'" He laid iron chains around his neck and drew him down into the depths of the sea. He detained him there for fifty days with affliction of spirit and soul so that he would recognize the great powers of the Blessed Holy One.

After fifty days, he extracted him from the sea and sent him around to every people and language, and he made known to them the great powers of the Blessed Holy One.[363] In the end, he brought him to Nineveh and appointed him to rule over it. When Jonah the prophet came to proclaim, "*Forty days more, and Nineveh shall be overthrown*" (Jonah 3:4), Pharaoh was utterly shaken. He rose from his throne, saying, "I know there is no God in the world except the Blessed Holy One."

Even now, this Pharaoh lives at the entrance of Gehenna. As the nations and kingdoms are brought in, he says to them, "Why did you not learn from me? For I denied the Blessed Holy One, and in the end believed Him against my will." He makes known to them the great power of the Blessed Holy One.

Thus it is said, *Who is like You among the gods, O Lord? Who is like You, majestic in holiness, awesome in splendor, doing wonders?* (Ex 15:11).

Exodus 15:11 Commentary

I. Character Development – The Transformation of Pharaoh

Character development in midrash is rare. It is not uncommon for the reader of rabbinic exegesis to learn more about a character than is revealed in the Bible, but it is rather unusual for a character to learn more about him/herself during the course of the narrative. Within *Midrash vaYosha*'s Recension B, however, the literary qualities of the text evolve and consciousness of character allows for growth. Much of the character development is only implicit; the angels *should* come to understand the role of man in a different way since they move from questioning his creation to weeping about Abraham's trial. It could be argued that Abraham recognizes the nature of his relationship to God more fully through the course of the narrative – a reasonable expectation for enduring such a test of faith (14:30). More clearly expressed is the development of Jethro, who changes his mind about Moses, God and his own loyalty to Pharaoh (15:2). Perhaps, too, the nations of the world grow in spiritual understanding as they realize that their wickedness will exclude them from the world to come (15:14). Even the waters evolve, at first resisting God every step of the way and eventually coming to value the special relationship with Israel (15:5, 8).

The most radical and explicit transformation, however, is in the character of Pharaoh. In the Bible, the reader is reminded time and again that Pharaoh does not or cannot change. Recognizing that the whole point of the biblical narrative is to demonstrate the reality and power of God, however, the midrash begins with the premise that he cannot remain unmoved by the events. We see Pharaoh's defiance at the beginning in denying God and asserting his own divinity, as related by God at the heavenly tribunal (14:31). Pharaoh is cavalier when warned of the final plague, and cruel when his first-born subjects arrive to relay their concerns (15:6, 7). But we also follow him closely on the night that it strikes; in R. Joshua b. Levi's rendering, Pharaoh cries out in his search for Moses and Aaron once it is clear that Egypt is lost. Replacing the arrogant monarch of his earlier encounter, he presents himself as the "humbled Pharaoh," neatly indicating the tremendous shift that has taken place. Rather than sitting on his throne, he has had to leave the palace and stand awkwardly outside the window of a slave's home. Instead of asking his wise men to reproduce marvels to challenge the prophet's power and authority, he begs Moses to pray for Egypt. He negotiates for the welfare of his people (and his own life), and follows Moses' directions in announcing the release of the Israelites, even when Moses makes him do it again and again (15:6).

Finally, after Pharaoh founders in the sea, he admits God's righteousness and singularity. His newfound commitment is tested as Gabriel afflicts him in the watery depths for fifty days. Moving on to rule Nineveh, he demonstrates a wholly different response to the threat of Divine punishment, initiating a city-wide program of penitence. And ultimately, he serves as witness at the gate of Gehenna, clearly articulating the lesson he learned in coming to know God (15:11).

Again with a dramatic breach of the canon, the midrash creatively serves the purposes of the biblical agenda. It establishes the victory of God not merely through a display of awesome might, but through transformation of the most recalcitrant of human souls: Pharaoh.

1. Additional aspects of Pharaoh's portrait

Two variants add interesting dimensions to the narrative of Pharaoh's repentance. MS Parma 2736 speculates how Pharaoh got the job as king of Nineveh:

How did he come to rule there? He was wandering among the lands and telling about the mighty deeds of the Blessed Holy One. There was once a king of Nineveh without a son, and so they were divided among themselves, some saying this [one should rule] and some saying that [one]. They said, "Let us go outside the city and the first of everyone we meet will be king." They went out and found Pharaoh. They said, "It is fine for this one to be king, since he knows of the mighty deeds of the Blessed Holy One." Immediately, they made him king.

MS Family A2 sets the narrative as exegesis of Ex 15:4 (see note *ad loc.*) and elaborates in other ways:

Pharaoh who said, "*[My Nile is my own,] I made it for myself* (Ezek 29:3); *who is the Lord that I should listen to his voice?*" (Ex 5:2), the Holy One brought down into the depths and [then] he said, *"Who is like You among the gods, O Lord?"* (Ex 15:11). So He kept him there for fifty days, until he humbled himself, body and soul, in the heart of the sea. He did not die, but made repentance in the heart of the sea. He suspended his finger toward heaven and said: *Who is like You among the gods?*

The Blessed Holy One accepted him to make known that He does not regard stature or beauty, as it is written: *Man sees only what is visible, but the Lord sees into the heart* (I Sam 16:7). How many miracles did the Holy One do for the wicked Pharaoh, and he had neither stature nor beauty! As the Sages said: The Pharaoh who was in the days of Moses was a magus; he was a cubit tall and his beard was a cubit, his penis was a cubit plus a handsbreadth.[364]

When he returned in repentance, the Holy One did not regard his stature or body, but rather accepted him in repentance and brought him out to the dry land. He set him to rule over Nineveh for five hundred years, and he still exists – sitting and guarding the entrance of Gehenna. Some say that a hinge of the gate of Gehenna is set on his ear.[365]

Why does he still exist today? Because of the repentance he did in the heart of the sea. And the choice among his mighty men who did not repent drowned in the Sea of Reeds. Thus it is said: *Pharaoh's chariots and his army He has cast into the sea; and the pick of his officers are drowned in the Sea of Reeds* (Ex 15:4).

2. Exegetical foundations

There are exegetical anchors for pieces of this narrative, even though the midrash remains a radical revisioning of Pharaoh's character. First, it can be argued that Pharaoh survives the Sea of Reeds. A parallel in *Pirqe Rabbi Eliezer 43* offers Ex 9:15 (ואך אותך, understood as *[all] but you*) as a prooftext that Pharaoh does not drown; Jacob b. Asher's commentary brings Ex 14:28 instead, reading it as *no one remained among [the Egyptians] except one.* Alternatively, as intimated in MS Family A2's careful reading of Ex 15:4, the midrash may capitalize on the fact that it specifies Pharaoh's chariots and officers drowned, but does not mention the king himself.

It is more difficult to establish a prooftext for Pharaoh's repentance since it runs directly counter to the biblical exposition. Nonetheless, *Yalkut Shimoni 176* identifies parallel wordings by which Pharaoh recants, e.g. *Who is the Lord that I should heed Him* (Ex 5:2) and *Who is like You among the gods* (Ex 15:11).[366] It then interprets Ex 9:16 as God's explanation for allowing Pharaoh to live: *On account of this I have spared you.*[367]

Identifying a link to Jonah's Nineveh is also challenging. Jacob b. Asher notes the similar emphasis on faith in *they believed in the Lord and His servant Moses* (Ex 14:31) and *the people of Nineveh believed God* (Jonah 3:5). Alternatively, II Kings 23:29 mentions a later Pharaoh, king of Egypt who מלך-מצרים על-מלך אשור – translated in NJPS as *...king of Egypt marched against the king of Assyria.* Modern scholars, trying to determine the historical relationship between Egypt and Assyria at the time, have lifted up the potential ambiguity of the Hebrew. Could the rabbis have deliberately read with classic hyper-literality: *the king of Egypt is on the throne* (lit: king) *of Assyria?*[368]

Ultimately it is drama, not exegesis, that most effectively links the Egyptian sovereign to Nineveh, opening gateways to new meaning in both biblical texts. The Book of Jonah offers a perfect foil for Pharaoh; everyone believes and repents immediately, thereby avoiding retribution. Nineveh's instantaneous and complete return to God is without parallel in the Hebrew Bible, all the more remarkable for it being a pagan kingdom. If Nineveh's king is the Egyptian pharaoh who previously suffered grave consequences for resisting the Most High, his ready compliance has a compelling back story. Like Jonah himself, he comes to see the inevitability of Divine will while immersed in the depths of the sea. Pharaoh is given a chance to rule rightly and, although his "new" kingdom does go astray, the speech and actions of Nineveh's king after Jonah arrives convey that his transformative repentance is genuine.

Exodus 15:12

נָטִיתָ יְמִינְךָ תִּבְלָעֵמוֹ אָרֶץ׃

You put out Your right hand and the earth swallowed them.

נטית ימינך

אמרו חכמים: יכולים ללמוד מפסוק זה שלא רצה הים לקבלם, ולא רצה הארץ לבולעם. הים היה משליכם לארץ, והארץ משליכם לים. ולמה? שהיתה מתיראה הים מיום הדין, שלא יבקש אותם הב"ה ממנה. והארץ היתה מתיראה כמו כן מיום הדין, שלא יקלקלנה הב"ה כשם שקללה כשברא את עולמו. כשברא הב"ה היה רחב ושוה בכל ההרים, וכשעמד קין והרג הבל אחיו היה דמו תוסס בארץ וקללה הב"ה. מיד נעשו ההרים והגבעות, ובשביל כך לא רצתה לבלוע אותם הארץ. אז אמר הקב"ה: אל תראי. מיד פתחה האדמה את פיה ותבלע אותם.

לכך נאמר *נטית ימינך תבלעמו ארץ.*

You put out Your right hand
(Exodus 15:12 – Recension B)

The Sages said: We can learn from this verse that the sea did not want to receive the [Egyptians] and the land did not want to swallow them. The sea cast them out on the land and the land cast them back into the sea. Why? – Because the sea was afraid of Judgment Day, lest the Holy One hold it accountable (lit: lest the Holy One seek them from it).[369] And the land was similarly afraid of Judgment Day, that the Holy One not curse it the way He did when He created His world. When the Holy One created [it], it was broad and level in all the [now] mountainous regions. After Cain killed Abel his brother, his blood boiled up from the earth and the Holy One cursed [the land]. Then the mountains and valleys formed. This is why the land did not want to swallow them. So the Blessed Holy One said, "Do not be afraid." Immediately, the earth opened up its mouth and swallowed them.

Thus it is said, *You put out Your right hand and the earth swallowed them* (Ex 15:12).[370]

נטית *ימינך תבלעמו ארץ*

מלמד שהיה הים משליך אותם ליבשה, ואף היבשה לים. ולא הים רוצה לקבלם, ולא הארץ רוצה לבולעם שהיה מתייראת מיום הדין. באותה שעה נשבע הקב"ה שלא יתבעם ממנה ליום הדין. מיד פתחה הארץ פיה ובלעתהון.

לכך נאמר *נטית ימינך תבלעמו ארץ*.

You put out *Your right hand and the earth swallowed them* (Exodus 15:12 – Recension A)

It teaches that the sea cast them out onto the dry land, and the dry land into the sea. The sea did not want to receive them and the land did not want to swallow them, for it was afraid of Judgment Day. Then the Blessed Holy One swore that He would not demand them of it on Judgment Day.[371] Immediately, the earth opened its mouth and swallowed them.

Thus it is said, *You put out Your right hand and the earth swallowed them* (Ex 15:12).

Exodus 15:12 Commentary

I. God's Right Hand

The right hand has a number of associations in biblical and rabbinic literature, many of which express a presumed primacy.[372] Jacob's right hand in blessing his grandsons, for example, indicates the status of the first-born (Gen 48). With the right hand as a place of honor, God grasps one's right hand to signify election, or stands at one's right hand to assist in battle (e.g. Isa 45:1, Ps 110:5). Contextually, the Song at the Sea presents God's right hand as a symbol of strength in verses 6 and 12.[373]

Yet the midrash selects a different association, one that is highlighted in rabbinic literature. Recension A specifically asserts that God "swears" (נשבע), and several manuscripts are explicit: God swears with His right hand. Parallels in *Mek. Shir 9* (HR 145:5ff), *Pirqe R. El. 42, Midr. Ps.* (Buber) 22:17, *Lam. Rab. 1:3* explain: "The right hand signifies an oath, as it is said, *The Lord has sworn by His right hand* (Isa 62:8)."

Recension B drops mention of swearing; God simply says to the earth, "Do not be afraid." The text may still depend on the connection between God's right hand and a Divine promise, but it may also engage another common rabbinic association: the right hand represents the Attribute of Mercy. Many biblical mentions of God's right hand as an instrument of strength can be construed in this manner, e.g. Ps 17:7: *Show Your marvelous lovingkindnesses, You who deliver with Your right hand those who seek refuge from assailants.* Midrashic literature reinforces the interpretation[374] and MV Recension B could intend God's reassurance to convey Divine mercy. "Do not be afraid" is a promise to withhold judgment at the end of days, and not hold the earth accountable.

In either event, *Midrash vaYosha*'s brief discussion of Exodus 15:12 provides a simple illustration of the shifting emphasis from exegesis to narrative. The later texts recapture the drama evident in *Targum Pseudo-Jonathan*, not by restaging its direct argument between land and sea, but by elaborating on the reasons for their anxiety; interpretation of the verse takes a back seat.

Exodus 15:13

נָחִיתָ בְחַסְדְּךָ עַם־זוּ גָּאָלְתָּ
נֵהַלְתָּ בְעָזְּךָ אֶל־נְוֵה קָדְשֶׁךָ׃

In Your lovingkindness You lead the people You redeemed.
In Your strength, You guide them to Your holy abode.

נחית בחסדך

יתברך שמו של הב"ה שאין מדותיו של הב"ה כמדת בשר ודם. בשעה שיוצא בלילה, שריו ועבדיו מוליכין לפניו נרות ואבוקות כדי שלא ימצא צער בגופו. אבל הב"ה אינו כן, כי ברוב אהבה שאהב את ישראל הוא בעצמו הלך לפניהם. ואלמלא כתיב המקרא אי אפשר (fol. 243r) לאמרו, שכן כתיב *ויי' הולך לפניהם יומם בעמוד ענן [לנחותם הדרך] ולילה בעמוד אש [להאיר להם] ללכת יומם ולילה.*

ולכך נאמר *נחית בחסדך עם זו גאלת נהלת בעזך אל נוה קדשך.*

In Your lovingkindness You lead
(Exodus 15:13 – Recension B)

[375]May the name of the Holy One be blessed, for the traits of the Holy One are not like those of a human being. When [a king] goes out at night, his ministers and servants lead the way with candles and torches so he will not suffer physical injury. But the Blessed Holy One is not like that; due to the great love He had for Israel, He Himself went before them. If the verse were not written, it would be impossible to say this. But it is written, *The Lord went before them in a pillar of cloud during the day [to guide the way] and a pillar of fire at night [to give them light] that they might travel day and night* (Ex 13:21).[376]

Thus it is said, *In Your lovingkindness You lead the people You redeemed. In Your strength, You guide them to Your holy abode* (Ex 15:13).[377]

***נחית** בחסדך*

יתברך שמו של הקב"ה שאין מידותיו כמידת בשר ודם. מלך בשר ודם כשהוא הולך בדרך עבדיו מוליכין לפניו הנר בלילה ועושין לו צל ביום מפני החמה. אבל הקב"ה הוא בעצמו הלך לפני ישראל בעמוד ענן יומם ובעמוד אש לילה, שנאמר ויי' *הולך לפניהם יומם* וגו'.

לכך נאמר *נחית בחסדך עם זו גאלת נהלת בעוזך אל נוה קודשך*.

In Your lovingkindness ***You lead***
(Exodus 15:13 – Recension A)

May the name of the Blessed Holy One be blessed, for His traits are not like those of a human being. A human ruler, when he travels, has his servants lead the way with a candle at night and make shade during the day on account of the heat. But the Blessed Holy One went Himself before Israel, in a pillar of cloud by day and a pillar of fire at night. As it is said, *The Lord went before them in a pillar...* (Ex 13:21).

Thus it is said, *In Your lovingkindness You lead the people You redeemed. In Your strength, You guide them to Your holy abode* (Ex 15:13).

Exodus 15:13 Commentary

I. God is – and is Not – Like a King of Flesh and Blood

Although God is without compare, God is continually compared to a king of flesh and blood in rabbinic literature.[378] Within MV, the extended comparison of God to a human king laying siege to a city affirms that there *is* similarity (15:3). It works as exegesis for developing the concept of God as a *man of war*, but it also adds to the narrative and to the Divine portrait. As far as the story is concerned, it reinforces the notion that the intent of the plagues is not merely to free the Israelites, but to vanquish the enemy, to make Pharaoh subject to the Most High. It presents the figure of God operating strategically, penetrating the psychic fortress of Pharaoh; and in the refrains that repeatedly indicate all the opportunities for ending the assault, God's actions appear measured.

Perhaps more frequently, the comparison is presented in order to highlight a contrast – one that predictably shows God to be the greater sovereign. Human monarchs have limited power; God's power is infinite. Human monarchs are concerned primarily about their own interests; God cares about the well-being of the world and all who live in it. Or, as in this pericope: Human monarchs require their subjects to serve them, while God also serves the people. Providing light and shade for the Israelites is not a diminishment of Divine greatness, but an enhancement of it.[379] Divine חסד *is* strength: *In Your lovingkindness You lead the people You redeemed. In Your strength, You guide them to Your holy abode* (Ex 15:13).

With these distinctions, the metaphor emphasizes Divine grace; surely God could take advantage as human sovereigns are wont to do. Human experience of imperial power is harsh, but the rule of God is different. The marked critique of "flesh and blood" monarchy is also useful to contemporary readers who have little experience of or affection for royalty, and who frequently struggle with the image of God as king due to its gender implications and discredited form of governance. God is sovereign like no other.

1. If it were not written... it would be impossible to say

Rabbinic literature is also acutely aware of the dangers of anthropomorphizing God, making the Divine seem too human. Recension B explicitly engages the problem with a common textual caveat: *If it were not written... it would be impossible to say.* By directing our attention to the issue, the midrash guides us to process the information in a different way and to recognize that God's kindness does not render the Divine as a cosmic servant subject to our whim.

MS Family A2 also invokes this caveat; in an extended explication of our verse, it discusses how God repays kindness with kindness:

For all of the qualities that Joseph exhibited in dealing with his father, Jacob, at the time of his burial, the Holy One repaid him. When Israel went up from Egypt, Moses brought up the bones of Joseph with them. He was the most honored among his brothers and he kept the oath to his father; therefore Moses, who was the most prominent of prophets and father of sages, kept the oath to Joseph. He occupied himself with his father's burial, gathering all the elders of the land of Egypt, chariots and horsemen to honor his father. Thus it happened that Moses occupied himself with the coffin, and six hundred thousand Israelite footmen accompanied him. He brought his father up from Egypt to the land of Israel, so Moses and all Israel brought his bones up from Egypt to the land of Israel. As it is said: *Moses took the bones of Joseph with him* (Ex 13:19); and it is written: *Joseph's bones which the children of Israel brought up out of Egypt, they buried in Shechem* (Josh 24:32).

Why did all this happen? – To make known the power and might of the Holy One, for with what measure a man uses, so shall it be measured out to him.[380] The Holy One does not withhold the wage of any creature. Not only that, but the Holy One went Himself in Divine glory in front of Israel and in front of Joseph's coffin. If it were not written in the Bible, it would be impossible to say: *The Lord went before them in a pillar of cloud by day, to guide them along the way, and in a pillar of fire by night, to give them light, that they might travel day and night* (Ex 13:21).

Prompted to recognize the paradox, the reader understands that Divine kindness, even in this most humble form, does not compromise God's greatness. The exegesis concludes: Thus it says, *In Your love You lead the people You redeemed; in Your strength You guide them to Your holy abode* (Ex 15:13).

Exodus 15:14

שָׁמְעוּ עַמִּים יִרְגָּזוּן
חִיל אָחַז יֹשְׁבֵי פְּלָשֶׁת׃

The peoples hear, they tremble.
Agony grips the dwellers in Philistia.

שמעו עמים

אמר להם משה לישראל: ראיתם כל הניסים האלו שעשה לנו הב"ה בזמן הזה. כך עתיד לעשות על אדום בשעה שהוא גואל את ישראל. שכך אמרו חכמים: שלשה ימים קודם שיבא משיח יבא אליהו בתחלה, ויעמד על הרי ציון וצועק בקול מר ובוכה וסופד עליהם ואומר: עד מתי תהיו חרבים? וקול בכייתו נשמע מסוף העולם ועד סופו.

ואחר כך יבא ויאמר: בא שלום לעולם, שנאמר *הנה על ההרים רגלי מבשר משמיע שלום*. וכשישמעו הרשעים שבגהינם מיד יהיו שמחין ויאמרו: טובה באה לעולם. ביום השני יבא ויעמוד על הרי ישראל ויאמר: באה טובה לעולם, שנאמר *מבשר טוב*. ביום השלישי יבא ויאמר: ישועה באה לעולם, שנאמר *מבשר טוב [ו]משמיע ישועה*.

וכיון שרואין הרשעים שכך יאמר אליהו, *אומר לציון: מלך אלהיך*, ללמדך שכל [שעל] ציון ובניה יבא הישועה ולא לרשעים. באותה שעה יראה הב"ה מלכותו וכבודו לצדיקים ולכל אומה ולשון. מיד גואל את ישראל וירשו את הר ציון.

לכך *שמעו עמים ירגזון חיל אחז יושבי פלשת*.

The peoples hear
(Exodus 15:14 – Recension B)[381]

Moses said to Israel, "You have seen all these miracles that the Blessed Holy One has done for you in this era. In the future, He will do the same against Edom when He redeems Israel." For thus the Sages said: Three days before the Messiah comes, Elijah will come first and stand on the mountains of Zion and cry out in a bitter voice, weeping and eulogizing them, "How long will you be ravaged?" The sound of his cry will be heard from one end of the world to the other.

After that, he will come and announce, "Peace is coming to the world," as it is said, *Behold, on the hills, the footsteps of a herald announcing peace* (Nahum 2:1). When the wicked ones in Gehenna hear this, they will immediately become happy and say, "Goodness[382] is coming to the world." On the second day, he will come and stand on the mountains of Israel and say, "Goodness is coming to the world," as it is said, *heralding good fortune* (Isa 52:7). On the third day, he will come and say, "Salvation is coming to the world," as it is said, *heralding good fortune, announcing salvation* (Isa 52:7).

When the wicked see that Elijah is speaking in this way, *saying to Zion, "Your God is king!"* (Isa 52:7), they will understand (lit: to teach you) that salvation comes for Zion and her children but not for the wicked. At that moment, the Blessed Holy One will show His kingdom and honor to the righteous, and to every nation and language. He will immediately redeem Israel and they will inherit Mount Zion.

Thus, *The peoples hear, and they tremble. Agony grips the dwellers in Philistia* (Ex 15:14).[383]

***שמעו** עמים ירגזון*

כיון ששמעו כל מלכי אומות העולם יציאת מצרים וקריעת (fol. 355v) ים סוף רגזו וחלו וברחו ממקומם. אמר משה לפני הקב"ה: רבונו של עולם תן אימתך ופחדך שיהא לבם באימה עד יעברו ישראל את הים.

לכך נאמר *שמעו עמים ירגזין חיל אחז יושבי פלשת.*

The peoples ***hear****, and they tremble* (Exodus 15:14 – Recension A)[384]

When the kings of the nations of the world heard about the exodus from Egypt and the parting of the Sea of Reeds, they trembled and began to flee from their place. Moses said to the Blessed Holy One, "Master of the world, set Your dread and terror upon their hearts until Israel has crossed the sea."[385]

Thus it is said, *The peoples hear, they tremble. Agony grips the dwellers in Philistia* (Ex 15:14).[386]

Exodus 15:14 Commentary

I. Elijah as Harbinger of Redemption

Although the messianic promise comes into sustained focus beginning with exegesis of Ex 15:16, Recension B embellishes the earlier redaction by projecting the nations' fear into the future. After the wicked *hear* the message regarding the end of days, they *tremble* at their fate.

Casting Elijah as the harbinger of redemption can be traced back to the final verses in Malachi: *Lo, I will send the prophet Elijah to you before the coming of the awesome, fearful day of the Lord. He shall reconcile parents with children and children with their parents, so that, when I come, I do not strike the whole land with utter destruction* (Mal 3:23–4).

Maimonides associates this prophecy with the onset of the war of Gog and Magog, but acknowledges that some sages claim Elijah will appear to announce the coming of messiah beforehand. His response is to admit that we cannot know for certain until the events unfold; we have only exegetical clues that have led to a variety of opinions.[387] As with many apparently contradictory traditions, there have also been efforts to reconcile these two roles by sequencing them. Elijah can still be the messenger of Isaiah 52 to announce the coming of messiah, and then disappear until he returns to proclaim the *awesome, fearful day of the Lord.*[388]

Elijah's role as herald of the messiah seems to have been broadly recognized in antiquity. Ben Sira's paean to Elijah asserts that he is destined to calm the wrath of God, to turn hearts of parents to their children, and to restore the tribes of Jacob – all "at the appointed time" (Sir 48:10). Matthew and Mark both try to establish Jesus' claim as messiah by identifying John the Baptist with Elijah (Matt 11:10–14, 17:10–13; Mark 9:11–13).

Moses Auerbach speculates that it was against these apocalyptic and sectarian expectations that the Babylonian Talmud instead emphasizes Elijah's role in resolving halakhic disputes.[389] Yet he is also protector, advisor and peacemaker,[390] and his legacy grows as time moves on. A seat is set for him at every *brit milah* (covenantal circumcision) so that he may witness the ongoing flourishing of the covenant. In folklore, he comes in disguise to test and reward the righteous. In midrash and mysticism, he continues to convey messages from on high, including the good news that the time has come. It is the conviction that he will herald redemption which leads to his name being invoked in the grace after meals, the blessings after reading *haftarah*, and at the end of every Sabbath.[391]

He is best known by contemporary Jews as an invited guest at the Passover seder, an appearance that ultimately combines his role as halakhic arbiter and messianic harbinger. According to the Palestinian Talmud (*y.Pes. 10:1 (37c)*), the four cups of wine consumed at seder can be seen to correspond with four promises of redemption in Deut 6:6–7. Rabbinic literature records a dispute about whether to consume four cups or five, and this becomes linked to the exegetical symbolism as well; there is a fifth promise in verse 8 to bring Israel into the land which, because the exegetes are in exile at the time, takes on messianic significance. The cup is poured but not consumed and, around the seventeenth century, it becomes identified as Elijah's cup in Ashkenazi custom. Messianic hopes are high during Passover; human patterns of thinking echo the Talmudic assertion, "In Nisan, the people of Israel were redeemed, and in Nisan they will be redeemed in the time to come" (*b.Roš Haš. 11a*). The Vilna Gaon (1720–1797) explains that Elijah will resolve the halakhic question of the fifth cup, but Jews pouring the wine and opening the door for him are far more anxious to hear what else he might have to say.

Exodus 15:15

אָז נִבְהֲלוּ אַלּוּפֵי אֱדוֹם
אֵילֵי מוֹאָב יֹאחֲזֵמוֹ
רָעַד נָמֹגוּ כֹּל יֹשְׁבֵי כְנָעַן׃

Thus dismayed are the chiefs of Edom,
trembling grips the leaders of Moab;
and all the dwellers of Canaan are aghast.

אז נבהלו

אמרו חכמים: מפני מה נתיראו *יושבי פלשת*? מפני שהרגו בני אפרים מאתים אלף שמנו את הקץ ביציאת מצרים וטעו שלשים שנה. ויצאו בכח גבורתם וכעס עליהם הב"ה ומסרם ביד פלישתים. ועתה נתייראו ואמר: עתה יגלגלו עלינו ישראל, ויהרגו אותנו ויירשו את ארצנו.

ומפני מה נתייראו *אילי מואב*? יאמרו: עכשו יפקדו עלנו אותה מריבה שהיה בין רועי אברם לרועי לוט אבינו.

וכיון שראו מלכי כנען שכלם היו מתיראין, אמרו: ומה אלו שאינם רוצים [ישראל] לשוב לארצם יש להם אימה ופחד, אנו שארצנו נתנה הב"ה לאברהם אביהם, והם באים על אותה הבטחה, על אחת כמה וכמה.

לכך נאמר *[אז נבהלו] אלופי אדום אילי מואב יאחזמו רעד נמוגו כל יושבי כנען*.

Thus dismayed *[are the chiefs of Edom]* (Exodus 15:15 – Recension B)

The Sages said: Why were the *dwellers in Philistia* afraid (Ex 15:14)? Because they killed two hundred thousand[392] Ephraimites who calculated the end for the exodus from Egypt, and erred by thirty years.[393] They went out by their own power and the Blessed Holy One was angry with them, delivering them into the hand of the Philistines. Now the [latter] were afraid; they said, "Now Israel will get back at us; they will kill us and inherit our land."

Why were the *leaders of Moab* afraid (Ex 15:15)? They said, "Now they will avenge that dispute between the shepherds of Abram and those of Lot, our ancestor."[394]

When the kings of Canaan saw that everyone was afraid, they said, "If those whose land [Israel] does not wish to reclaim are distressed and afraid, how much the more so should we be [afraid], since the Holy One gave our land to Abraham, their ancestor, and they are coming based on that very promise."

So it is said, *[Thus dismayed are] the chiefs of Edom, trembling grips the leaders of Moab; and all the dwellers of Canaan are aghast* (Ex 15:15).[395]

***אז** נבהלו אלופי אדום*

מפני מה נתייראו *יושבי פלשת?* מפני שהרגו שבט אפרים מאתים אלף שמנו לקץ וטעו.

ו*אלופי אדום* כמו כן נתייראו. אמרו: עכשיו יפקדו עלינו שנאה שהיא בין עשו ובין יעקב.

ו*אילי מואב* כמו כן נתייראו. אמרו: יפקדו עלינו מריבה שהיה בין אברהם אביהם ובין רועי לוט אבינו.

כיון שראו *יושבי כנען* שהיו כולם מתייראין אמרו: מה אילו שאינם יושבים בארצם ואינם רוצים לבא עליהם מתייראין מהם, אנו שיושבים בארצם ורוצים לבא עלינו על אחת כמה וכמה.

לכך נאמר *אז נבהלו אלופי אדום אילי מואב יאחזימו רעד נמוגו כל יושבי כנען.*

***Thus** dismayed are the chiefs of Edom*
(Exodus 15:15 – Recension A)

Why were *the dwellers of Philistia* afraid? Because they killed two hundred thousand Ephraimites who calculated the end and erred.

And *the chiefs of Edom* similarly were afraid. They said, "Now [Israel] will avenge the hostility that was between Esau and Jacob."[396]

And *the leaders of Moab* similarly were afraid. They said, "[Israel] will avenge the dispute that was between the shepherds of Abram, their ancestor, and those of Lot, our ancestor."

When *the dwellers of Canaan* saw that everyone was afraid, they said, "If those who do not dwell in [Israel's] land, those against whom [Israel] does not wish to fight, are afraid of them, how much the more so should we be [afraid], since we dwell in their land and they want to fight against us."

Thus it is said, *Thus dismayed are the chiefs of Edom, trembling grips the leaders of Moab; and all the dwellers of Canaan are aghast* (Ex 15:15).

Exodus 15:15 Commentary

I. The Ephraimites Who Left Early

The tradition that a group of Ephraimites departed early is found within other midrashim; in *Mek. Beshallaḥ Petiḥta* (HR 76:16–77:1) and *Mek. R. Shimon b. Yoḥai 13:17*, for instance, God does not lead the Israelites the short way through the wilderness, lest they see the bones of the Ephraimites who died en route. They might get dissuaded from their path of liberation. Joseph Heinemann traces a traditions history and speculates the significance eventually becomes a cautionary tale about trying to hasten the end.[397]

In *b. Sanh. 92b*, we find a possible exegetical impetus for the Ephraimite tradition: 1 Chr 7:20–21 asserts that the people of Gath (=Philistines) killed Ephraim's descendants, although the biblical provocation is cattle rustling. Because the subsequent verse states they are mourned by "Ephraim their father," the Talmud presumes he is still alive and places the event during Egyptian bondage.

Related to this theme, MS Prm 2736 offers an example of expansive targumic tradition (*tosefta*) at Ex 13:17. The bones of the Ephraimites are those that Ezekiel raises, and they are also made to serve as chalices from which Nebuchadnezzar drinks. When the bones arise, they slap the king's face. Ezekiel asks why all the corpses rise except one, and he is told that the man charged interest. The passage concludes by explaining how the dry bones prophecy comes as a sign that the dead will be resurrected at the end of days and that, in the meantime, seeing the bones might make the fearful Israelites wish to return to Egypt.

II. Context in Midrash vaYosha

One of MV's creative strategies is to broaden the context without removing the verse from its narrative setting. It thereby draws intertextual connections and multiplies possibilities of meaning, but does not rely on the wholly atomistic reading of classical rabbinic literature. New interpretations are woven into the fabric of the story. The interpretation of the nations' fear in this verse, which could be read as a reasonable response to hearing about the fate of Egypt, becomes built instead on reviewing problems from the history of their relationship to Israel's forefathers. Similarly, the midrash replaces the straightforward contextual meaning of God's response, "*Why do You cry out to Me?*" in Ex 14:15 (in the first lemma) by taking into account the long history of covenant and salvation. The *loud cry in Egypt* (Ex 12:30, in exegesis of 15:6) becomes Pharaoh's rather than the Egyptians' because MV incorporates a long view of Pharaoh's character development. Such narrative consciousness is one of the key qualities of later darshanic stories. No longer built on a single verse and episode, they are more expansive and unified in their presentation.

As Ofra Meir points out, the story becomes a hermeneutic device, capable of imparting new meaning to a verse.[398] In this regard, contextual exegesis can be found through all the layers of rabbinic literature, but these new, extended narrative contexts operate a little differently than classical rabbinic midrash. At the same time, their exegesis remains more fanciful and far-reaching than the *peshat* of medieval commentary. Burt Visotzky succinctly articulates the shift from midrash to commentary:

> Whether explicit or implicit, the point of any commentary is the meaning of verse within its context. Even when quoting legendary comments that have little to do with the plain sense of the biblical text, the commentary tried to make some logical sense out of a verse within its context. That is emphatically not the case in the midrashic process, and this feature distinguishes the two types of literature from each other. Midrash atomizes scriptural verses and tears them out of context..... Not only verses but also individual words and even letters can be made the subject of midrashic exegesis, without regard for the context in which they appear in the Bible. Midrash places the scriptural text in a vacuum: commentary places it within a context.[399]

As a dynamic text that does not represent a single period style, *Midrash vaYosha* does both, in turn and in consort. Recension B's accentuated interest in narrative shifts the boundaries of what defines "contextual reading" and fashions essential poetics of the text.

Exodus 15:16

תִּפֹּל עֲלֵיהֶם אֵימָתָה וָפַחַד
בִּגְדֹל זְרוֹעֲךָ יִדְּמוּ כָּאָבֶן
עַד־יַעֲבֹר עַמְּךָ יְהוָה
עַד־יַעֲבֹר עַם־זוּ קָנִיתָ׃

Terror and dread will descend upon them;
through the might of Your arm, they are still as stone,
until Your people cross over, O Lord,
until this people whom You have ransomed cross over.

תפול עליהם (fol. 243v)

אמר משה לישראל: אחי ואחי! אתם יודעים שלא בחכמה ולא בתבונה ולא בכח ולא בעושר יכול אדם לכבוש אפילו עיר אחת, אלא בגבורותיו של הב"ה, שהרי כמה גבורים בחיילותיו של פרעה הרשע ולא הועיל להם גבורותיו לפני הב"ה. ועוד כמה גבורים עתידים להלחם עמכם ועתיד הב"ה לתת פחדכם ומוראכם [עליהם] ולא יתיצב איש לפניכם. ועתיד הב"ה לכתוב בתורתו, *אל יתהלל הגבור בגבורתו*. ואם אתם עושים רצונו של מקום הוא יושיעכם מיד אויביכם.

ואמר משה לפני הב"ה: רבונו של עולם, כשיבא עמלק להלחם עם ישראל *תפול עליהם אימתה ופחד*. וכשיבאו מלכי האמורי להטמין עצמן בנחלי ארנון *ידמו כאבן עד יעבור עמך* בנחלי ארנון *[...]עד יעבור עם זו קנית* עם יהושע את הירדן, ויבאו וירשו את ארצם. ושלם להם נדר שנדרת לאברהם אביהם.

ואף לימות המשיח עשה להם נסים ונפלאות, כמו שכתוב *כימי צאתך מ[ארץ] מצרים אראנו נפלאות*.

ולכך אמר משה: *תפול עליהם אימתה ופחד בגדול זרועך ידמו כאבן עד יעבור עמך יי' עד יעבור עם זו קנית*.

Will descend on them
(Exodus 15:16 – Recension B)

Moses said to Israel, "My brothers and sisters![400] You know that it is not through wisdom or understanding, not with strength or wealth that man is able to conquer even a single city – only through the great powers of the Holy One! Note how many mighty men there are among the wicked Pharaoh's soldiers, but [their] might was of no avail before the Blessed Holy One.[401] How many more mighty men will fight against you in the future, but the Holy One will set fear and terror of you [upon them][402] so that no one can stand before you. The Blessed Holy One is destined to write in His Torah, *Let not the strong man glory in his strength* (Jer 9:22). If you do the will of the Omnipresent, He will save you from the hand of your enemies."[403]

Moses said to the Holy One, "Master of the world, when Amalek comes to fight with Israel, let *fear and terror descend on them.* And when the Amorite kings come to hide themselves in the rivers of Arnon, let *them be like a stone until Your people cross over* the rivers of Arnon,[404] *until Your people, whom You have ransomed, cross over* (Ex 15:16) the Jordan with Joshua and come into their land to inherit it. Fulfill for them the vow You swore to Abraham their father.

"In the days of the Messiah, as well, do miracles and wonders for them, as it is written, *I will show him wondrous deeds as in the days when you went out of [the land of] Egypt*" (Micah 7:15).

Thus Moses said, *"Terror and dread will descend upon them; through the might of Your arm, they are still as stone, until Your people cross over, O Lord, until this people whom You have ransomed cross over*" (Ex 15:16).[405]

תפל *עליהם אימתה ופחד*
אמר משה לפני הקב"ה: רבונו של עולם, כשיבא עמלק להלחם עם ישראל תפל עליהם אימתה ופחד. וכשיבואו מלכי האמורי להכמין עצמן בנחל ארנן ידמו כאבן.

עד *יעבור עמך יי' עד יעבור עם זו קנית.* עד שיעברו שנות לימות המשיח, שנאמר *והחרים יי' את לשון ים מצרים והניף ידו על הנהר בעיים רוחו והכהו לשבעה נחלים והדריך בנעלים. והייתה מסלה לשאר עמו אשר ישאר מאשור* ממצרים *כאשר הייתה לישראל מ[ב]יום עלותו מ[ארץ] מצרים.*
לכך נאמר *עד יעבור עמך יי' עד יעבור עם זו קנית.*

Terror and dread **will descend** *on them* (Exodus 15:16 – Recension A)

Moses said to the Blessed Holy One, "Master of the world, when Amalek comes to fight against Israel, *let terror and dread descend on them* (Ex 15:16). And when the Amorite kings come to hide themselves in the Arnon River, *let them be like a stone.*

Until[406] *Your people cross over, O Lord, until this people whom You have ransomed cross over* (ibid.). – Until the time of the messiah comes to pass, as it is said, *The Lord will dry up the tongue of the Egyptian sea. With His spirit, He will raise His hand over the Euphrates and break it into seven wadis, so that it can be traveled dry-shod. Thus there shall be a highway for the remainder of His people out of Assyria*[407] *such as there was for Israel when it left the [land of] Egypt* (Isa 11:15–6)."[408]

Thus it is said, *Until Your people cross over, O Lord, until this people whom You have ransomed cross over* (Ex 15:16).

Exodus 15:16 Commentary

I. Variant Traditions about the Canaanites

MS Family A2 expands on the Canaanites' fear and connects it to larger themes, setting one passage *ad* Ex 15:14 and the other in this pericope. The first crafts a story in which their terror explains why the Israelites had to wander for a generation in the wilderness:

When the Canaanites heard news of Israel, they trembled and fell on their faces [in] agitation and turmoil. They bemoaned their fate, saying, "In vain we labored; others will come and enjoy all the crops we planted. Let's cut down all our trees and uproot all the crops we planted, and let's fell all our gardens and orchards, destroying our land." Then they cut and uprooted everything until there was not a shred or remnant left.

The Holy One said, "I promised my beloved Abraham to bring his descendants into an ample land full of all good things. But now they will find it ruined, and people will say, 'What of the promise He gave to Abraham?' Lo, I will encompass them in the wilderness for forty years so the Canaanites will stay; they will uproot the old trees from the days of Noah, and plant new trees, making the land as good as it was. My children will then come and find a good land, full of all good things, as it is said: *Houses full of all good things that you did not fill*" (Deut 7:11).

Therefore Israel was detained in the wilderness for forty years. The Canaanites gave up and (re-)built the land, so when Israel arrived they found the land as it should be. Thus it is said: *The people hear, they tremble; agony grips the dwellers in Philistia. [... All the dwellers in Canaan are aghast]* (Ex 15:14–15).[409]

The second passage presumes the facts of the first, and imagines the people of Israel actually crossing into the Promised Land. "Still as stone" describes the Canaanites' inability to reprise their destructive rampage because the Israelites come upon them too suddenly:

The Sages said: When the Canaanites heard that the Israelites were coming, they were like a stone. They wanted to uproot and cut down the trees like they did before, but they could not, because [the Israelites] came upon them suddenly like robbers. What did the Canaanites do? They took all the silver, gold, precious stones and jewels that they had and hid them in their homes, beneath the earth. At that time, the Israelites were hurting for money. The Holy One said, "My children, do not be troubled, I will bring plagues upon every house that has money buried inside. Through these plagues, you will recognize that there is money inside," as it is said: *When you enter the land...* (Lev 14:34).[410]

Thus when the Israelites entered the land of Canaan, leprosy broke out on all those houses inside which they had hidden money. When Israel saw the plague, they would recognize that there is money hidden inside and bring it out.

Both of these passages attempt to make vivid the exceptional situation of the Canaanites. While all the nations in the region may tremble, it is Canaan that the Israelites are coming to occupy. In narrating their dilemma, the text also manages to reinforce their unworthiness and God's faithfulness.

Exodus 15:17

תְּבִאֵמוֹ וְתִטָּעֵמוֹ בְּהַר נַחֲלָתְךָ
מָכוֹן לְשִׁבְתְּךָ פָּעַלְתָּ יְהוָה
מִקְּדָשׁ אֲדֹנָי כּוֹנְנוּ יָדֶיךָ׃

You will bring them and plant them in Your own mountain,
the place You made to dwell in O Lord,
the sanctuary, O Lord, which Your hands established.

תביאמו ותטעמו

ישתבח שמו של הב"ה שמרוב אהבה שאהב את ישראל קרא להם *בני בכורי*. בא וראה כמה חסדיו של הב"ה. עבד לובש את רבו אבל הב"ה לובש את ישראל, שנאמר *ואלבישך רקמה*. עבד רוחץ את אדניו אבל הב"ה רוחץ את ישראל, שנאמר *וארחצך במים*. עבד נעל את רבו והב"ה נעל את ישראל, שנאמר *ואנעלך תחש*.

ועל כל זאת הטובה בשגלו למצרים שכינה עמהם, שנאמר *אנכי ארד עמך מצרימ[ה]*. גלו לעילם שכינה עמהם, שנאמר ~~אנכי~~ *ושמתי כסאי בעילם*. גלו לבבל שכינה עמהם, שנאמר *למענכם שלחתי בבלה*.

ועתיד הב"ה להחזיר [את ישראל] להר קדשו, שנאמר *והביאותים אל הר קדשי*. וכתיב בתריה *ונטעתים אל [על] אדמתם*.

כיון שראה משה אהבתו של הב"ה, אמר לפניו: רבונו של עולם תביאם ותטעם שם, ותהיה אותה נטיעה שלא יהיה לך נתישה בעולם. (fol. 244r) ותוריד ירושלם מן השמים ולא תהרוס [אותה] לעולם, וכנס גליותיהם של ישראל לתוכה וישבו עליה לבטח.

לכך נאמר *תביאמו ותטעמו בהר נחלתך מכון לשבתך פעלת יי' מקדש יי' כוננו ידיך*.

You will bring them and plant them
(Exodus 15:17 – Recension B)

May the name of the Holy One be praised, for out of great love that He had for Israel, He called them, *My son, My first-born* (Ex 4:22). Come and see how numerous are the kindnesses of the Blessed Holy One. A servant dresses his master, but the Holy One dresses Israel, as it is said, *I clothed you in embroidered garments* (Ezek 16:10). A servant bathes his lord, but the Blessed Holy One bathes Israel, as it is said, *I bathed you in water* (Ezek 16:9). A servant puts on his master's shoes, but the Blessed Holy One provides shoes for Israel, as it is said, *I gave you sandals of dolphin-leather* (Ezek 16:10).[411]

On top of all this goodness, when they were exiled to Egypt, the Shekhinah went with them, as it is said, *I myself will go down with you to Egypt* (Gen 46:4). They were exiled to Elam and the Shekhinah went with them, as it is said, *I*[412] *will set My throne in Elam* (Jer 49:38).[413] They were exiled to Babylonia and the Shekhinah went with them, as it is said, *For your sakes, I am sent to Babylon* (Isa 43:14).[414]

In the future, the Blessed Holy One will return [Israel] to His holy mountain, as it is said, *I will bring them to My holy mountain* (Isa 56:7), and it is written afterwards, *I will plant them on their land* (Amos 9:15).

When Moses saw the great love of the Holy One, he said, "Master of the world, bring them and plant them there, and let it be a planting for which you will never have an uprooting.[415] Bring Jerusalem down from the heavens, and never destroy [it].[416] Gather together the exiles of Israel within it, so they may dwell there in security."

Thus it is said, *You will bring them and plant them in Your own mountain, the place You made to dwell in O Lord, the sanctuary, O Lord, which Your hands established* (Ex 15:17).[417]

תביאמו

אמר משה לפני הקב"ה: רבונו של עולם, כשם שעשית נס לעמך ישראל וגאלת אותם מבית עבדים, כך לעתיד לבא תפר<י>ש אותם מבין אומות העולם, ותבא אותם לבית מקדשך, ותיטע אותם נטיעה שאין לה עקירה לעולם. כשתוריד ירושלים שהיא בנויה בשמי מרום לא תנט<ת>ש ולא תהרס לעולם.

לכך נאמר *תביאמו ותטעמו בהר נחלתך מכון לשבתך פעלת יי' מקדש יי' כוננו ידיך.*

You will bring them
(Exodus 15:17 – Recension A)

Moses said to the Blessed Holy One, "Master of the world, just as You performed a miracle for Your people Israel and redeemed them from the house of bondage, so in the time to come may You separate them from among the nations of the world to bring them to Your sanctuary. Plant them in a planting that is never uprooted and, when You bring down the Jerusalem that was built in the heavenly spheres, let it never be removed or destroyed.

Thus it is said, *You will bring them and plant them in Your own mountain, the place You made to dwell in O Lord, the sanctuary, O Lord, which Your hands established* (Ex 15:17).

Exodus 15:17 Commentary

I. Heavenly Jerusalem

Tanakh occasionally alludes to the existence of a heavenly palace or sanctuary. In the psalmist's imagination, *The Lord is in His holy Temple; the Lord – His throne is in heaven* (Ps 11:4); and *Now I know that the Lord will give victory to His anointed, will answer him from His heavenly sanctuary* (Ps 20:7).[418] Later Second Temple literature expands upon these heavenly visions of the Divine Temple, with mystical ascents that reveal detailed interpretations of the Godhead.[419]

The relationship between celestial and terrestrial Temples is variously imagined. In biblical theology, the rituals of the earthly sanctuary connect heaven and earth, granting access to the Most High Sovereign. Through philosophical speculation, Philo determines that the "universal world is the highest and truest Temple of God," with heaven as its most sacred part and angels serving as God's priests. The earthly Temple is merely a shadow, a vehicle to facilitate human piety (*Special Laws I:12*). Although the image of the cosmos as a temple was common in the ancient Near East, Philo's preference for the heavenly abode may manifest the Platonic influence that pervaded Hellenistic Judaism and early Christianity – in this instance, the theory of forms.

Wisdom of Solomon, on the other hand, intimates a more integral relationship: *You gave a command to build a sanctuary in Your holy mountain, and an altar in the city of Your habitation, a copy of the holy tabernacle which You prepared beforehand from the beginning* (Wis 9:8). Rabbinic literature is not univocal, but tends to present a significant correspondence. With a wordplay on מכון (dwelling-place), *Mekhilta Beshallaḥ 10* (HR 149–50) establishes our verse in Exodus as one of the prooftexts that the earthly throne is a counterpart to a heavenly one. Reading with Rashi, who similarly understands the verse, one could translate: [The earthly Temple] *is designed to correspond [מכון] to what You made O Lord, the sanctuary, O Lord, which Your hands established* (Ex 15:17).

The most sustained biblical vision of an idealized Temple is found in Ezekiel 40–48. In overwhelming detail, he describes not a heavenly Temple, but a future one. Later eschatological projections frequently map this transformation onto the entire city of Jerusalem. The same apocalyptic texts that provide visions of God in the heavenly Temple also predict the eventual revelation of Zion, a city hidden until the end of days. Within rabbinic literature, there develops an abiding conception of ירושלם של מעלה (Heavenly Jerusalem) and ירושלם של מטה (Earthly Jerusalem).

> The upper, the celestial, Jerusalem is viewed in a radiant infinitely refined vision which bears only a remote resemblance to the terrestrial city. However, ...the idea of the celestial Jerusalem as it was conceived by Jewish thinkers, and even by mystic fancy, never lost its touch with down-to-earth reality. ...[N]ormative Judaism was less concerned with the meta-historical 'Heavenly Jerusalem' than with the latter-historical 'New Jerusalem' which a, in the main, restorative eschatology portrayed as an improved edition of its historic prototype.[420]

The relationship between the two realms in the interim remains significant. The Talmud (*b. Taanit 5a*) presents a pun on Ps 122:3, *Jerusalem built up, a city knit together (שֶׁחֻבְּרָה־לָּהּ יַחְדָּו)*, which again determines that the earthly city is a companion bound up (ח-ב-ר) with the heavenly one. Further, it is primary in significance. God will not enter celestial Jerusalem until God is re-enthroned in the terrestrial Jerusalem first. Similarly *Tanḥ. Pekudei 1* states that God built a heavenly Jerusalem on account of love for the earthly one, and sees no point in entering until the people are restored to their holy city.[421] Each articulation of the relationship, however, still points toward the eschaton.

In the end, there will only be one Jerusalem, the radiant eternal one. Some texts imagine the earthly Jerusalem will rise up toward the heavens as it becomes the city God destined it to be and spreads its influence through the world (e.g., *Pes. Rab 41, Song Rab. 7:5*). Others, like MV, call the heavenly city to descend into our midst – never to be removed or destroyed (e.g., *Midrash on the Ten Commandments*). The Temple built by God stands forever, and the nation too is planted in the land eternally.[422]

Exodus 15:18

יְהוָ֥ה ׀ יִמְלֹ֖ךְ לְעֹלָ֥ם וָעֶֽד׃

The Lord will reign forever and ever.

יי' ימלוך

אמר משה לישראל: ראיתם כל הנסים והגבורות והנפלאות שעשה לכם הב"ה. יותר ויותר הוא עתיד להם [לכם] לעשות לעתיד לבוא. ולא כעולם הזה העולם הבא: העולם הזה יש בו מלחמות וצרות ויצר הרע ושטן ומלאך המות ויש להם רשות לשלוט בעולם. אבל לעולם הבא אין בו לא צרות ולא שנאה ולא שטן ולא מלאך המות ולא אנחות ולא שעבוד ולא יצר הרע, שנאמר *הסיר [ומחה] יי' [אלהים] דמעה מעל כל פנים*, וכתיב *ואמר ביום ההוא הנה אל[ה]ינו זה קוינו לו ויושיענו*.

וכשיגיעו ימות המשיח יעלה גוג ומגוג על ארץ ישראל לפי שישמע שישראל בלא מלך ויושבים לבטח. מיד יקח עמו שבעים ואחד אומה ויעלה לירושלם. ואמר: פרעה היה שוטה שגזר להרוג הזכרים והניח הנקבות. בלק היה טפש {שרצה} לקללם והוא שלא היה יודע שאלהיהם היה מברכם. המן משוגע היה שרצה להרגם והוא לא היה יודע שאלהיהם היה יכול להצילם. אבל אני לא אעשה כן. אעלה אלחם עם אלהיהם תחלה, ואחר כך אהרוג אותם, שנאמר *יתיצבו מלכי ארץ ורוזנים נוסדו יחד על יי' ועל משיחו*.

ויאמר לו הב"ה: רשע! <עם> מי אתה מבקש לעשות מלחמה? בחייך אני אעשה עמך מלחמה. מיד יוריד עליו הב"ה אבני ברד שהן גנוזות ברקיע ויגוף אותם מגפה גדולה, שנאמר *וזאת תהיה המגפה אשר יגוף יי' את הגוים [כל העמים] אשר צבאו על ירושלם, המק בשרו והוא עומד על רגליו ועיניו תמקנה בחוריהן ולשונו תמק בפיהם*.

ואחריו יקום מלך אחד רשע ועז פנים ויעשה מלחמה עם ישראל שלשה חדשים. ושמו ארמילגוס, ואלו הן אותותיו: יהיה קרח, ועיניו אחת קטנה ואחת גדולה, וזרועו של ימין טפח ושל שמאל (fol. 244v) שתי אמות וחצי, ויהיה לו צרעת במצחו, ואזנו הימנית סתומה ואחרת פתוחה, וכשיבא אדם לדבר לו טובות מטה לו אזנו הפתוחה. ויעלה לירושלם ויהרג משיח בן יוסף, שנאמר *והביטו אליו את אשר דקרו וספדו עליו <כ>מספד על היחיד*.

The Lord will reign
(Exodus 15:18 – Recension B)

Moses said to Israel, "You have seen all the miracles, mighty acts and wonders that the Blessed Holy One has done for you. He will do even more for [you][423] in the time to come. The next world is not like this one: In this world, there are wars and sorrows. The evil inclination, Satan and the angel of death have authority to rule in the world. But in the next world, there are no sorrows, or hatred, or Satan, or angel of death, or laments, or subjugation, or evil inclination,[424] as it is said, *The Lord [God] will wipe*[425] *the tears from all faces* (Isa 25:8), and it is written, *In that day, they shall say, 'This is our God. We trusted in Him and He delivered us'* " (Isa 25:9).[426]

When the days of the Messiah arrive, Gog and Magog will rise against the land of Israel, for they will hear that Israel has no king and they dwell securely. He will take with him seventy-one nations and ascend to Jerusalem.[427] He will say, "Pharaoh was an idiot to decree killing the males but leaving the females alone. Balak was stupid {because he wanted}[428] to curse them, not knowing that their god would bless them. Haman was crazy because he wanted to kill them and didn't realize that their god could save them. But I will not do likewise. I will go up and fight with their god first, and then I will kill them." As it is said, *Kings of the earth take their stand and regents conspire together against the Lord and His anointed* (Ps 2:2).[429]

The Blessed Holy One will say to him, "O wicked one, {with}[430] whom are you seeking to wage war? By your life, I will wage war against you!" Then the Holy One will bring down on him hailstones hidden away in the firmament,[431] and He will strike them with a great plague, as it is written, *This will be the plague with which the Lord will strike [all the peoples]*[432] *that fought against Jerusalem: Their flesh shall rot away while they stand on their feet, and their eyes shall rot away in their sockets, and their tongues shall rot in their mouths* (Zech 14:12).

Afterwards, a wicked, insolent king will rise up and wage war against Israel for three months. His name is Armilgos,[433] and these are his features: He is bald, and he has one small eye and one large one. His right arm is a handbreath, and his left one is two and one half cubits. He has leprosy on his forehead. His right ear is stopped up, and the other one is open. When a person comes to say positive things to him, he extends the open ear.[434] He will ascend to Jerusalem and slay the Messiah, son of Joseph, as it is said, *They shall look to me regarding those who are slain, wailing over them as for a favorite son* (Zech 12:10).[435]

ואחר כך {יבא} משיח בן דוד בענן, שנאמר *וארו עם ענני שמיא כבר אינש*. וכתיב בתריה ולא *[ולה] יהיב שולטן ויקר ומלכו*. וימית ארמילגוס הרשע, שנאמר *וברוח שפתיו ימית רשע*.

ואחר כך יקבץ הב"ה ישראל הנפזרים לכאן ולכאן, שנאמר *אשרקה להם ואקבצם כי פדיתים ורבו כמו רבו*. ויהיו תלויים בירושלם שבעים ושתים מרגליות שהן מבהיקות מסוף העולם ועד סופו. ואומות העולם יהלכו לאותה אורה, כדכתיב *והלכו גוים לאורך ומלכים לנגה זרחך*. וההיכל יוריד הב"ה מן השמים כמו שהראהו הב"ה למשה, שנאמר *תביאמו ותטעמו בהר נחלתך וכו'*.

וישבו שם ישראל אלפים שנה ואוכלים את לויתן. ולקץ אלפים שנה ישב הב"ה על כסא לבנה ובושה החמה הדין בעמק יהושפט. מיד השמים והארץ חולפים וחמה ולבנה בושים שנאמר *וחפרה הלבנה ובושה החמה*. ומנין שביום השלישי יהיה הדין? שנאמר *יחיינו מיומים וביום השלישי יקימנו ונחיה לפניו*, זה דין.

והב"ה מביא כל אומה ולשון ואמר: למה עבדתם בעולם שהלך, ולמי השתחויתם?

והם אומרים: לאלילי כסף ולאלילי זהב.

ואומר להם הב"ה: עבדו אותם ואלהיכם אם יכולים להציל אתכם יצילו באש הזה. מיד הן עוברין ונשרפין שם, שנאמר *ישובו רשעים לשאולה כל גוים שכחי אלהים*.

ואחר כך ישראל באין ~~אמרי'~~ {ואומר} להם הב"ה: אתם למי עבדתם? מיד עונים: *כי אתה אבינו כי אברהם לא ידענו וישראל לא ה[נ]כירנו כי אתה ה' אבינו גואלינו מעולם שמך*. מיד הב"ה יצילם מדינה של גהינם ויושבין בגן עדן ומתעדנין בפירותיה, שנאמר *וענוים ירשו ארץ והתענגו* (fol. 245r) *על רוב שלום*.

ואחר כך מחדש להם הב"ה שמים וארץ, שנאמר *כי הנני בורא שמים חדשים והארץ החדשה*. והארץ שעתיד לחדש מוציא את האילנות וכל מיני מגדים, והכל חיים לעולם ולעולמי עולמים. מי

After that, the Messiah, son of David {will come} in a cloud,[436] as it is said, *One like a human being came with the clouds of heaven* (Dan 7:13). And it is written subsequently, *Dominion, glory and kingship were given to him* (Dan 7:14). He will kill the wicked Armilgos, as it is said, *He will slay the wicked with the breath of his lips* (Isa 11:4).[437]

Afterwards, the Holy One will gather Israel, scattered here and there, as it is said, *I will whistle to them and gather them, for I will redeem them; they will increase and continue increasing* (Zech 10:8). Hanging in Jerusalem, there will be seventy-two pearls which shine from one end of the earth to the other. The nations of the world will come to that very light, as it is written, *Nations shall walk by your light; kings, by your shining radiance* (Isa 60:3).[438] The Holy One will bring down the Temple from the heavens, as He showed it to Moses, for it is written, *You will bring them and plant them in Your own mountain, [the place You made to dwell in, O Lord, the sanctuary, Lord, which Your hands established]*[439] (Ex 15:17).

Israel shall dwell there for two thousand years,[440] eating Leviathan. After two thousand years, the Holy One will sit on the throne[441] of judgment in the Valley of Yehoshafat. The heavens and the earth will pass away, the sun and the moon will be ashamed, as it is said, *Then the moon shall be ashamed and the sun shall be abashed* (Isa 24:23).[442] How do we know that judgment will be on the third day?[443] For it is said, *In two days, He will make us whole; on the third day, He will raise us up and we shall live before Him* (Hosea 6:2) – this is judgment.

The Holy One brings every nation and language and says, "What did you serve in the world that is past, and to whom did you bow down?"

And they say, "To idols of silver and gold."

"Serve them and if your gods can save you, let them save you from this fire." So they pass through and are burned there, as it is said, *Let the wicked return to Sheol, all the nations who ignore God* (Ps 9:18).

Then Israel comes and the Holy One says[444] before them, "Whom did *you* serve?" They immediately answer, "*Surely You are our father – though Abraham regard us not and Israel not recognize us – You, O Lord, are our father. 'Our Redeemer' has always been Your name*" (Isa 63:16). Then the Blessed Holy One will save them from the sentence of Gehenna and they will dwell in the Garden of Eden, enjoying its fruits, as it is said, *The lowly shall inherit the land, and delight in abundant well-being* (Ps 37:11).[445]

Afterwards, the Holy One will renew heaven and earth for them, as it is said, *Behold, I am creating a new heaven and a new earth* (Isa 65:17). The earth that He will renew will bring forth the trees and all sorts of delicacies, and everything will live forever and ever. May the One who

שעשה נסים ונפלאות בימים האלה ובזמן הזה [ההם], הוא יעשה לנו נסים ונפלאות בימים האלה ובזמן הזה, ויקבוץ אותנו מארבע כנפות הארץ ויוליכנו לירושלם וישמחנו בה, ונאמר: אמ[ן], אמן. סלה.

performed miracles and wonders in days [past],[446] perform for us miracles and wonders in these days and this time [as well]. May He gather us from the four corners of the earth and lead us to Jerusalem so that we may rejoice in it.[447] Let us say: Amen, amen. Selah.[448]

יי' ימלוך

אמר משה לישראל: כל הגבורות וניסים ונפלאות הללו שעשה לכם הקב"ה, כנגדן הוא עתיד לעשות לכם לימות המשיח, ולא כעולם הזה. העולם הזה יש בו מלחמות וצרות ושעבוד מלכיות קשה וסטן ומלאך המות, יש להם רשות לשלוט בעולם הזה. אבל לעתיד לבא אין מלחמות ואין צרות ואין שעבוד ואין סטן ואין מלאך המות, שנאמר *ובלע המות לנצח ומחה יי' אלהים דמעה מעל כל פנים וחרפת עמו יסיר מעל כל* (fol. 356r) *הארץ כי יי' דבר*. ונאמר *והיה יי' למלך על כל הארץ ביום ההוא יהיה יי' אחד ושמו אחד*.

והקב"ה יסדר סידרן של צדיקים ושל חסידים ושל נביאים ושל חכמים ושל דור ודור ושל ברייא ובריא וכל נשמה ונשמה. ומעמיד כסאו לצד אחד ומוריד חנוך בן ירד ששמו מיטטרון, ומעלה עדת קרח מתהום רבה. ויסדר הקב"ה לעין כל ברייא ואומר להם: כלום ראיתם אלוה מבלעדי בשמים ממעל ועל הארץ מתחת, שנאמר *ואתם עדיי נאם יי' ואני אל*.

ומשיבין מיטטרון וחיות הקדש וקרח וכל עדתו ואמרו כולם בבת אחת ובקול אחת ובפה אחד לעיני כל: לא ראינו כמותך, ואין אלוה מבלעדיך *בשמים ממעל ועל הארץ מתחת אין עוד*. אתה ראשון ואתה אחרון ומבלעדיך אין אלהים.

מיד פתחו בשירה ואמרו: *יי' ימלוך לעולם ועד*.

נשלמו האגדות של ויושע

The Lord will reign (Exodus 15:18 – Recension A)

Moses said to Israel, "All these mighty acts, miracles and wonders that the Blessed Holy One has done for you – He will do their equivalent for you in the days of the Messiah, but not like this world. This world has wars, sorrows, and terrible subjugation to the kingdoms. Satan and the angel of death have authority to rule in this world. But in the time to come, there is no war or sorrow, no subjugation, Satan or angel of death. As it is said, *He will destroy death forever; the Lord God will remove tears from all faces. He will put an end to the reproach of His people over all the earth, for it is the Lord who has spoken* (Isa 25:8). And it is said, *The Lord shall be king over all the earth; in that day there shall be one Lord with one name* (Zech 14:9).

"The Blessed Holy One will arrange the disposition of the righteous, the pious, the prophets and the sages of every generation, making every creature and every soul stand before His throne. He will bring down Enoch son of Jared, whose name is Metatron, and raise up the congregation of Korah from the great depth. The Holy One will call to order, before the eyes of all, and say to them, 'Have you seen any God besides Me in the heavens above or on the earth below?'[449] As it is said, *And you are My witnesses, says the Lord, that I am God* (Isa 43:12).

"Metatron and the holy beings, Korah and all his congregation answer at once in a single voice before everyone, 'We have not seen anyone like You, and there is no God besides You *in the heavens above or on the earth below; there is no other* (Deut 4:32). You are first and last, and besides You there is no God.'"

Then they broke into song, "*The Lord will reign forever and ever*" (Ex 15:18).[450]

The aggadot of *Vayosha* are complete.

Exodus 15:18 Commentary

I. The Eschatological Vision

1. The end of days in Midrash vaYosha

Midrash vaYosha's vision of the end of days begins in 15:14, connecting the lemma with prophesies of Nahum (2:1) and Isaiah (52:7): *The peoples hear* – not about the dramatic rescue from Egypt, but about the coming redemption – and they are appalled because they will recognize too late the error of their ways. The idea that the broad canvas of redemption at the Sea should represent the precursor of a final redemption is demonstrated exegetically at the end of 15:16. There, the midrash cites Micah 7:15, *I will show him wondrous deeds as in the days when you went out of the land of Egypt.*[451]

When the Song at the Sea itself speaks of the future in its final verses, the midrashic eschatology begins in earnest. God's "bringing and planting" (Ex 15:17) the people of Israel in their land after the exodus is echoed by later prophets who use the same language to speak of a return (Isa 56:7, Amos 9:15). Each image in Moses' portrait of the time to come is imprinted with exegetical proof (15:18). The end of suffering, for instance, is supported by the verse, *God will remove tears from every face* (Isa 25:8); Gog and Magog's plot to attack God first and then the people is nicely paralleled by the verse, *Kings of the earth take their stand and regents conspire together against the Lord and His anointed* (Ps 2:2) – naming God first. And so it is for each stage of the apocalypse, rich with scriptural associations, except for the lemma itself. Oddly, Recension B never quite makes it back to the final verse of the Song to declare this vision as the enactment of God's eternal rule, *The Lord will reign forever and ever.*

Recension A, on the other hand, offers a precise exegesis of this verse in its relatively brief vision of the end of days: Korah and his band of followers will rise up from the earth, Metatron/Enoch will descend with his cohort and together they will attest to the singular, absolute and eternal dominion of God. Thus the song, *The Lord will reign forever and ever.*

The less developed eschatology again hints at the N. European origins of Recension A, where apocalyptic themes were not as pervasive. R. Moshe haDarshan in Provence (11c.) appears to have collected some elements from Pseudepigrapha, but Martha Himmelfarb makes a convincing argument that these are most likely mediated through Greek-speaking Jews of Byzantine Italy,[452] and Israel Ta-Shma points out that they were not quoted much by later European exegetes other than Rashi.[453]

2. Traces of traditions

Numerous aspects of *Midrash vaYosha*'s description of the end-time have ancient roots. The notions that Elijah will return as a herald (Malachi 3:23) and that Gog is the foreign ruler to be defeated at the end of days, for instance, can be traced back to the Hebrew Bible. Although rabbinic texts tend to treat Magog as a second king along with Gog rather than the place of his kingdom, they clearly build on Ezekiel's prophetic vision (38–39).[454]

Daniel 9:24–6 speaks of the death of a messiah. It is likely that this second-century BCE text intends merely an Israelite king who will preside over the return and rebuilding before his death.[455] The idea is found again, however, in 4 Ezra 7:27–30, a text that was written approximately two centuries later, after messianic speculation had further developed.[456]

There appears to be some delineation of stages within the eschatology; 2 Baruch 29–30, for instance, speaks of a messianic era in which those who are alive will feast on Leviathan, followed by resurrection. Within the Talmud, the concept of stages is further developed, although the varied terminology (ימות המשיח, עתיד לבוא, עולם הבא) is not consistently applied and there is disagreement about the details. Sequencing two messiahs so one appears after the other integrates otherwise conflicting traditions:[457] Messiah ben Yosef (occasionally referred to as Messiah ben Ephraim) will be killed, but he will be succeeded by Messiah ben David (*b. Suk. 52a*).[458] In describing public mourning for the former, the Talmudic text cites Zechariah 12 as does *Midrash vaYosha*.

Rabbinic texts and sages vary widely in imagining the differences between this world and the one to come. The Amora Samuel claims that the only change will be an end to Israel's subjugation under foreign rule; R. Yohanan, on the other hand, is cited as believing that all the prophesies about the end of days, presumably including supernatural elements, will come to pass in the days of the messiah – and that we can know nothing about the world to come after that (*b. Sanh. 99a, b. Pes. 68a*). In *b. Ber. 17a*, Rav describes the next world (עולם הבא) as a world transformed: no eating, drinking, propagation, business, jealousy, hatred or competition. Rather, the righteous sit with crowns on their heads and take sustenance from the radiance of the *Shekhinah*.[459] The Isa 25:8 prooftext cited in MV is also used in *Deut. Rab. 2:30* to demonstrate that God will rid the world of the evil inclination in the time to come (עתיד לבוא), which will in turn eliminate death. Debate about the nature of the world-to-come continues well into the Middle Ages, as philosophy compounds the unresolved questions.[460]

The concept of a heavenly Jerusalem is discussed in *b. Taanit 5a*, and a final judgment is mentioned in a number of the apocalyptic texts (e.g., 1 Enoch, 4 Ezra) from the Second Temple period. In *Lev. Rab. 27:11*, there is a nicely developed motif in which each enemy of Israel learns from the last what *not* to do, leading up to Gog and Magog who decide to attack the *patron* of Israel first. (MV uses the same prooftext.) It also includes God's threat to wage war, with very similar phrasing.

3. Sefer Zerubbabel[461] *and Near Eastern apocalypse*

Although many of MV's motifs can be found in Hebrew literature from Late Antiquity, it is *Sefer Zerubbabel*, a seventh-century apocalypse,[462] that is most often cited by scholars as the text that popularized the eschatological narrative found in many geonic and medieval Jewish texts. Joseph Dan calls this work, in which Metatron leads Zerubbabel through a tour of heaven and the world to come, "the seed around which messianic aggadah of the Middle Ages grew."[463] By the time of Saadiah Gaon (882–942), its major motifs have become authoritative. Seeing Armilos as the last powerful anti-Jewish king, Saadiah includes his victory over the descendant of Joseph and his subsequent defeat at the hand of the Messiah b. David. He calls this legend an "ancestral tradition," a term generally reserved for Talmudic teachings (*Beliefs and Opinions 8*). Hai Gaon (969–1038) also treats the Armilos tradition as definitive knowledge in his responsum detailing the sequence of events at the end of days, with many details that correspond to *Sefer Zerubbabel*.[464] Apocalyptic themes found in *Sefer Zerubbabel* appear in numerous medieval texts, including *Secrets of R. Shimon b. Yoḥai, Prayer of R. Shimon b. Yoḥai, Signs of the Messiah, Lekaḥ Tov* Num 24 and *Zohar 3:173b*, as well as MV.

Midrash vaYosha shares several elements of its eschatological narrative with details in *Sefer Zerubbabel*, including: a war against Gog and Magog, the death of the Messiah b. Yosef at the hands of Armilos, Messiah b. David's triumph over Armilos – slaying the enemy with his breath – and the descent of a Temple created in heaven.

Naturally, there are many aspects of *Sefer Zerubbabel* that are not incorporated into *Midrash vaYosha*, seeing that our text is not at its core an apocalyptic one. The whole story of Armilos' perverse origins, for instance, is not mentioned.[465] *Midrash vaYosha* similarly ignores the subplot of Hefzibah, the mother of the messiah; it does not mention a Persian king, nor does it speculate about the arrival date of the time to come.

Also useful for source analysis are those elements in *Midrash vaYosha* that are not found in *Sefer Zerubbabel*. Some of the motifs that have basis in earlier rabbinic literature, such as the suffering that will not exist in the world to come or the enemies' plotting based on past failures in attacking Israel, are not reflected in the *Sefer Zerubbabel* narrative. Elijah's role is not spelled out at all; he merely accompanies the messiah(s) at various points. The entire Elijah passage (*ad* 15:14), however, can be found in *Pesiqta Rabbati 35*. These substantial differences indicate that *Midrash vaYosha* did not simply adapt *Sefer Zerubbabel*; rather, it used a different source or itself continued the creative process of reassembling and revising a variety of Jewish (and non-Jewish) sources to create its own narrative of salvation.

Shared motifs frequently differ in detail, e.g. the physical description of Armilos. In *Midrash vaYosha*, he is more monstrous looking, bald and leprous, asymmetrical and misshapen in various body parts. The detail regarding his ears, using his stopped up one when anyone tries to say something good, adds a dimension to his character. In addition, it is interesting that this identical particular can be found in Arabic folklore describing the false messiah, *al-Dajjal*,[466] but not in the published editions of *Sefer Zerubbabel*. This description of Armilos is also found in *The Secrets of R. Shimon b. Yoḥai*, which makes thinly veiled references to the Arab conquest of the Land of Israel.[467]

These facts offer a modicum of additional support for the argument that Recension B was developed in the East under the aegis of Islam, and correlate with the overall development of eschatology in the Near East. John Reeves states:

> Near Eastern Jewish, Christian, and Muslim apocalypses of late antiquity and the early medieval era exhibit a series of remarkable structural correspondences that reach across the permeable boundaries of ethnic and religious affiliation. Despite the inevitable individual doctrinal variations, these apocalypses reveal a number of common motifs, dramatis personae, and discursive sequences.[468]

In Reeves' analysis, he identifies six main stages at the end of history found in Christian, Jewish and Muslim sources: 1) Deterioration of society and nature leading to war between the kingdoms and unprecedented pestilence, famine, earthquakes, etc.; 2) Advent of Gog and Magog (Yajûj wa-Majûj in Arabic); 3) Some change in the reigning power(s) necessary for the eschaton; 4) Advent of Antichrist/Armilos/Dajjal who is deformed or demonic; he marches on Jerusalem and deceives many people about his role; 5) Mission of a penultimate messianic figure who stands against the evil one; 6) Advent of the final messianic figure. Jewish and Christian sources have many more specific similarities at this last stage: The messiah is accompanied by angels, he restores the slain redemptive figure(s) who preceded him, there is a general resurrection of the faithful, the messiah slays the Antichrist/Armilos with his breath, there is reward and punishment. Examination of any single faith tradition reveals how Reeves' systemization oversimplifies a tremendously varied literature, but his insight regarding the commonalities is striking.[469]

An intriguing element of Reeves' thesis is that the rising dominance of written texts as a source of religious authority in Late Antiquity shaped this stage of apocalyptic imagination. In place of the self-authenticating revelations that were prevalent in the Hellenistic and Roman imperial periods, these apocalyptic eschatologies are grounded in exegesis, "awash with scriptural diction and citation."[470]

Each recension of MV presents a character whose portrayal invites a bit of investigation. Armilgos/Amrilos in Recension B, and Enoch/Metatron in Recension A both have key roles in the end of days.

4. Armilgos/Armilos

Aspects of the Armilos legend can be found on the cusp on Late Antiquity; *Targum Pseudo-Jonathan* on Deut 34:3 and *Targum Jonathan* to Isa 11:4 mention the name as a wicked man who will be punished.[471] They do not contain any detail, however, and some scholars speculate that the name may have been added later.[472] An anonymous *piyyut* is more evocative of the themes found in MV: "...and Harmalyos (הרמליוס) will come and stab the Messiah of God, the [other] Messiah will come and he will revive him by the word of God, and all Israel will have faith in him."[473] This liturgical poem is sometimes attributed to Qalir (6c.), but it appears to ground the coming apocalypse in the turbulent events of the early seventh century. As Wout Jac. van Beekum interprets the verse below, the *piyyut* alludes to decades of war in the Near East between Byzantium (the West/Edom) and the Sassanian empire (the East), followed by the dramatic invasion of Islam (Yoktan/Ishmael):

The king of the West and the king of the East,
they will crush each other;
and the king of the west will show strength in the country;
and from Yoktan a king will go forth:
his armies will be strengthened in the country[...]
Edomites and Ishmaelites will fight in the valley of Acre,
until their horses will sink in blood and panic.[474]

Sefer Zerubbabel is one of the earliest Hebrew texts in which the Armilos name and legend seem very similar to MV, even though his physical description is different.

There are numerous speculations about the origins of the name Armilos to identify the ultimate nemesis of Israel. Based on a history of destruction and oppression at the hands of the Roman empire and then its Christian successor, rabbinic texts frequently portray Rome/Edom as the long-standing enemy of the Jewish people. It is not surprising then, that many of the theories regarding the name of this monstrous king, who stands as the final obstacle to the kingdom of Heaven, revolve around Roman figures and Latin words. Most frequently mentioned is the clear homophonic similarity to Romulus, co-founder of Rome (and also the name of the last Roman Emperor 475–6 CE).[475] If the Armilos tradition is, in fact, rooted in events of the early seventh century, the figure could be a stand-in for the oppressive Byzantine emperor, Heraclius. He ruthlessly ruled over the Jews, including an edict mandating their conversion.[476] Raphael Patai also suggests the possibility that it draws from Suetonius' record of Caligula, who is described as tall and bald, with thin legs and a crooked eye: *armillatus in publicum processit* (processing in public wearing bracelets, Ch. 50, 52).[477]

David Berger completely rejects Patai's notion, however, as well as the theory proposed by some scholars that it relates to the Persian god of evil, Angra-Mainyu, which becomes 'Arimanoj or Ahriman in its Greek rendering.[478] Instead, he makes a compelling case supporting those who argue that the word is of Greek origin; thus this study opts for the spelling that best indicates its roots (Armilos, rather than the also prevalent Armilus).[479] A key manuscript of *Sefer Zerubbabel* (MS Oxford Heb. d.11) offers a gloss, although the text is corrupt in the critical section. According to Israel Lévi, the text intended the etymology, Erhmólaos, meaning, "destroyer of the people" (יחריב עם).[480] The actual name, Armilos, is found in Eusebius' *Chronicon I:47.7*, in which Armilos wars with Jupiter and is slain by a thunderbolt (early fourth-century Caesarea, writing in Greek). Another Greek record of the name is found in *Doctrina Jacobi nuper baptizati*, a Byzantine Christian text roughly contemporaneous with *Sefer Zerubbabel*.[481]

5. Metatron/Enoch

The portrait of Metatron/Enoch is strange; he is the heavenly representative that must descend and testify alongside Korah (each with his cohort) to the absolute uniqueness of God. Korah staged an infamous challenge to Divine authority (or so it was portrayed by Moses), but why would Metatron's testimony be of special importance? Medieval Jewish apocalyptic literature tends to portray Metatron as the revealer of secrets, a guide through heaven as in *3 Enoch, Sefer Zerubbabel, Midrash*

Katapuaḥ baAtzei haYa'ar, and the *Secrets of R. Shimon b. Yoḥai*, but that does not seem sufficient cast him as the celestial holdout.[482]

Yet there is another dimension of Metatron's portrait in apocalyptic and mystical literature that may make his role in MV more logical: *3 Enoch* (*synopse* 15, 73, 76), and later the *Zohar*, are among texts that refer to him as "the lesser YHWH."[483] In fact, this epithet could relate to the etymology of his name; Peter Schäfer reviews several possible derivations of Metatron and ultimately concludes that Saul Lieberman's thesis asserting Greek origins, μετα + θρονος is the most likely: a minor god whose *throne* is *beside* that of the great God.[484] Even though the portrait remains a positive one, it gives the angel something in common with Pharaoh: semi-divine status. If MV is familiar with this concept, it makes sense that each must at some point publicly attest to God's singularity.

A Talmudic narrative takes a dimmer view of Metatron's position and the possibility of seeing him as a deity (*b. Hag.15a*): As he sits in Heaven writing the merits of Israel, his activities cause Elisha b. Abuya to conclude that there are two powers in heaven and the angel receives lashes for not taking steps to avoid such a false impression. This tradition could highlight the value of Metatron's testimony at the end of days that there is only one God in heaven and on earth.

Enoch is similarly suspect in some of mainstream rabbinic literature: *Genesis Rabbah 25:1* suggests that Enoch was taken prematurely by God to prevent the evil dimension of his character from overwhelming his potential for good. Through this lens, framed more by classic rabbinic texts than by apocalyptic ones, the appearance of the angel alongside Korah seems logical.[485] It leads neatly to Recension A's brief but moving messianic peroration that concludes the midrash, all the while remaining focused on its exegetical point. At the end of days, God's sovereignty will be absolute.

The eschatological elements woven into the last several pericopes do not serve simply as a *simana d'neḥemta*, a token of consolation for the reader who is still mired in the muck of history and exile. Rather, they are integral components of the midrashic understanding of the Song, itself a celebration of God's activist role in redemption. Even after the midrash ceases to be linked to synagogue performance on the seventh day of Passover, its capacity to inspire the people with the miracles God has performed for them in the past, giving them hope for the future, continues. Divine faithfulness, kindness and unmatched power – reinforced at every turn in the elaborate expansion on the themes of Exodus – leads ineluctably to the messianic era. The vividness of its narration brings it close enough to touch.

Appendix: Manuscript Descriptions

The following descriptions rely heavily on information available at the Institute for Microfilmed Hebrew Manuscripts (IMHM) website, as well as the listed library catalog entries. IMHM lists 31 extant manuscripts of *Midrash vaYosha*, including several large fragments or substantial citations. In addition, there are two small genizah fragments that have been identified and two copies in the Jewish Theological Seminary collection that were not fully catalogued.[1]

I have reviewed the text of *Midrash vaYosha* within each manuscript and, in many cases, was able to review the microfilm of the entire manuscript to confirm and refine the information. JTS manuscripts were examined directly. A more extensive description and full listing of manuscript contents is available at http://jnul.huji.ac.il/imhm; much of the content detail is rendered in English in Mikva, "*Midrash vaYosha* and the Development of Narrative in Medieval Jewish Exegesis," Appendix B.

Manuscripts are listed within recensions, alphabetized according to the abbreviation used when it is specifically cited.

RECENSION A

(Cam 667.1) Cambridge University Library Add. 667.1, fol. 121r–124v
Copied 13–14th c. in N. France, in at least 2 Ashkenazi hands (new hand, fol. 193).
Vellum, 231 fols. 24 x 18 cm., generally 2 columns, 38 lines. Family A1

The manuscript is a prayerbook for the entire year according to the French rite (similar to *Mahzor Vitry*), although it it is missing fols. 1–5, 135–136, 192. *Midrash vaYosha* stands as commentary on the Torah reading for the 7th day of Passover; much earlier in the manuscript (fol 50v ff) there is a liturgy for the Passover seder and *Targum Pseudo-Jonathan* to Ex 14–15, with numerous midrashic expansions and piyyutim such as אזל משה. These passages contain two motifs similar to the text of Recension B: the sea refusing to obey Moses, and four camps of Israelites disagreeing on the best course of action. It includes a number of non-liturgical texts.

S.M. Schiller-Szinessy theorized that the compiler of the entire MS may have been Netanel b.Yosef of Chinon, although J. Laveen argued that only the calendrical lists can be proven to be his. Laveen identifies the prayerbook as deriving from the school of Rashi. There is an Italian censor mark on fol. 6r (suggesting that the 5 folios were already missing before the arrival of the MS in Italy: Fr[a] Vin[centiu]s de Mat[tellic]a dated 1597.

"Yaakov" is pointed out on numerous pages between fol. 124r and 182r. "Moshe" is pointed on fol. 5v, 105v; "David" is pointed out on fol. 69r. These may allude to the scribe and his family. On fol. 229v, there is a notation that "Joseph" owns the MS; at the end, it is claimed by Yehudah b. Yaakov Ḥaim Leon de Ancona (a city in Italy).

Except for the first lemma, it is not the verse citation at the beginning that is bold and enlarged, but rather the first words of the interpretation. The manuscript seems in good condition. The margins are even and the writing is steady with very few errors, although some letters are difficult to distinguish.

Related publications: 1) S.C.Reif, *Hebrew Manuscripts at Cambridge University Library* (Cambridge: 1997), 216–8. 2) J. Laveen, "A Maḥzor of the School of Rashi in the Cambridge University Library," in *REJ 125:2* (1966): 127–149. 3) S.M. Schiller-Szinessy, *Notices of Hebrew Manuscripts [in the University of Cambridge]*, 6 vol., Or. 1116–21, pp. 104–114.

(Cam 1505) Cambridge University Library Add. 1505, fols. 1r–9v
Copied in 17–18th c. in a Western (IMHM) or N. African (Reif) hand.
Paper, 11 fols. (fragment), 21 x 15 cm., 16–20 lines. Family A1

Containing MV and two collections related to Moses, this MS records a very different ending for *Midrash vaYosha* than other copies of Recension A. Although it does record the final lemma of MV, it does not mention Enoch or Korah as eschatological witnesses of God's eternal dominion, nor does it move toward the verse, יי' ימלוך לעולם ועד.

These folio pages at some point stood as part of a larger work; they are numbered in Hebrew 170–180. There is a frontispiece with some imperfect printing of animal forms and no calligraphy. Possibly owned by Eliakim Carmoly.

The beginning of the lemmas are bold and enlarged. The manuscript seems in relatively good condition, although folios are beginning to spot. The margins are approximate and the writing is clear but informal.

Related publication: S. C. Reif, *Hebrew Manuscripts at Cambridge University Library* (Cambridge: 1997), 152–3.

(Drm 25) Universitäts- und Landesbibliothek Darmstadt Cod. Or. 25, fol. 31v–34r
Copied in the late 14th c. in an Ashkenazi hand (fol. 83v notes the year 1383).
Parchment, bound with a leather back, 122 fols.
24 x 17 cm., 2 columns, 48–52 lines. Family A1
Scribe: Avraham haSofer (see fol. 92r).

An anthology of numerous brief midrashim and other religious writings. Among other types of texts, there are parts of Maimonides' *Mishneh Torah*, grammatical teachings by R. Eleazar of Worms, ethical treatises, calendars, a lexical work, riddles, mystical teachings, various *halakhot* – over 50 entries in all, few of them more than 5 folios.

The text of *Midrash vaYosha* does not include the lemma and crux of ויושע יי' at the beginning. The first word of the text is slightly enlarged; other divisions are marked by underlining the verse brought at the conclusion of a lemma. Some sections of MV seem abbreviated or lacking.

The MS also contains *Midrash on the Binding of Isaac*, similar to the narrative of the *Akeidah* found in MV Recension B, from Isaac's questioning his father to Abraham's plea that his obedience merit protection for their descendants in time of trouble. It appears to be the same text as found in MS War 258, which is more legible, and they both differ from MV in significant details and wording. There are notes of ownership on fol. 22r (in Frankfurt) and 180v. The manuscript has deteriorated somewhat, with a large degree of fading. The margins are approximate and the writing is clear but informal.

Related publication: 1) E. Roth, *Verzeichnis der Orientalischen Handschriften in Deutschland, Teil 2* (1965), 24–26.

(Esc G3) Real Biblioteca del Monasterio de El Escorial hebreo G-III-11, fol. 101r–114r
Copied in Portogruaro (Italy), 1501–1503,. in an Ashkenazi hand.
Paper, 21 x 10 cm., 199 fols., 19–21 lines. Family A2
Scribe: Kalonymus b. R. Azariel Yitzhak bar Kalonymus b. R. Gershom, (see colophons fols. 88v, 140r, 153r (150r, 163r in actual folios).

A miscellany of ethics, midrash, commentary, private accounts, kabbalah, philosophy and other writings.

Midrash vaYosha is followed by a note on synagogue recitation of Torah, "To the reader – The reading should continue up to רֹפאיך" [v. 26], which indicates the end of the scriptural reading for the 7th day of Passover.

Part of Family A2 (along with Ox 614 and Par 335), it contains a large amount of additional narrative material. MS Par 335 also features the same instruction to the reader, and shares several texts in common with this manuscript.

Generally in good condition, the manuscript has a few large spots. The lemmas are large and bold, frequently set apart like a title. There are occasional flourishes, such as the treatment of the first word and the infinity symbols over the word at the bottom that links to the next page. The left margin is uneven; the writing is clear.

The manuscript has an error in pagination; after fol. 102, it again paginates from fol. 93. Item #8 above is repeated on fols 131a–134b, with the signature of a different scribe: Moshe פרנקיטו b. Abraham Harari of Provence.

Related publications: 1) Nehemiah Allony and Ephraim Kupfer, *Reshimat tatzlumei kitvei-yad ha-ivri'im bamakhon, vol. 2* (Jerusalem: 1964), 94. 2) *Sepharad 3* (1943): 54–55.

(JTS 5000) New York – Jewish Theological Seminary 5000 (Rab. 1804), fol. 1b–3b
Copied in the 15th c. in an Ashkenazi hand
Paper, 23 fols. 19.5 x 13.3 cm., 23 lines. Family A1

In a collection of small midrashim, *Midrash vaYosha* (Family A1), has two lacunae: There is no mention of the heavenly tribunal in the case before God, and the interpretation is missing for Ex 15:17. It brings the lemma, but then transcribes the text found in 15:18 in other manuscripts.

Lemmas are slightly enlarged, with clear handwriting and even margins. The manuscript has a small amount of damage.

On fol. 1a, there are marks of ownership: "In this, too, God has been gracious to His servant Isaac the Kohen," followed by a statement from his sons similarly acknowledging the grace of God, as well as their esteemed father and teacher.

Related publication: Judah Brumer, *Rabbinics Manuscripts of the Jewish Theological Seminary of America* (NY: 1984–86), n. 1804.

(Mun 232) Munich – Bayerische Staatsbibliothek Cod. Heb. 232, fol. 47r–54v
Copied in the 14th c. in an Italian hand.
Paper and vellum, 142 fols. 19.6 x 13.8 cm., 21–23 lines. Family A1

A miscellany of teachings about prayer, ethics, midrash and halakha. *Midrash vaYosha* is introduced with a mythology of creation via Torah (as Divine names), similar to the one found at the beginning of MV in MS Vat 303 and at the end of MV in MS Prm 2269.

Like MS Ox 225, it uses the name Uziel to denote the Egyptian angel. On occasion, it abbreviates the exegesis, most noticeably in the lemma ה' איש מלחמה (v. 3).

Lemmas are slightly enlarged, and preceded by a small amount of blank space. The manuscript is in good condition. The left margin is uneven and the writing is clear but informal.

At the beginning of the MS, there is a mark of ownership: "When I divided books with my brother(s), [this was] in my portion: Shabbetai son of our honored teacher R. Moshe the Physician, may his memory be for a blessing." (Elsewhere: Shabb[etai] b. Yech[ial] b. Moses the Physician, 1383) A later owner: Joonis Alberti Widmestady (fol. 2r).

Related publication: M. Steinschneider, *Die hebraeishen Handschriften der K. Hof-und Staatsbibliothek in Muenchen* (Munich: 1895), 107–9.

(Ox 27) Oxford – Bodleian Library Or. 27 (Neubauer 268), fol. 230r–234v
Copied in the late 16th c., in two Ashkenazi cursive hands.
Paper, 347 fols. 30.5 x 21.5 cm., 35 lines. Family A1-ד

A collection of commentary and midrash. At first glance, the scribe appears to have had copies of both recensions. Although he copies Recension A, he occasionally adds a ד"א (alternative explication) that reflects Recension B. Upon close comparison, however, it is evident that the scribe is copying marginal notes from MS Wolf 36.25 or a related manuscript. (See discussion of manuscript families.)

There is a repeating (presumably printed) illuminated frontispiece inserted into the manuscript between texts, with space to write the title of the upcoming work(s). The scribe or collector titles *Midrash vaYosha* as: מדרש על שירת אז ישיר – *Midrash on the song az yashir* (Ex 15:1).

Lemmas are slightly enlarged and bold, until the final two pages. The penultimate page has four lemmas, with varying styles of more pronounced headings. The last page, which appears to be in a different hand, offers a stylized writing for the lemma. The manuscript is in good condition. The left margin is approximate, and the writing is clear.

Related publications: 1) A. Neubauer, *Catalogue of the Hebrew Manuscripts in the Bodleian Library* (Oxford: 1886), 52–3. 2) R. A. May, *Supplement of Addenda and Corrigenda to A. Neubauer's Catalogue* (Oxford: 1994), 39.

(Ox 135) Oxford – Bodleian Library Or. 135 (Neubauer 1466), fol. 352r–356r
Copied 13th c. (1215–1260) in Champagne region of N. France, in an Ashkenazi hand.
Vellum, 363 fols. 22 x 15 cm., 34 lines. Family A1
Scribe: (likely) Samuel, noticeably pointed on fol. 33r, 62v, 99v.

A miscellany of grammar, midrash and stories. The manuscript has received a fair amount of scholarly attention. Eli Yassif became interested because it contains early collections of stories. Although the manuscript also has lexical and grammatical works, it offers early textual evidence of an interest in narrative. A travelogue at the end of the manuscript with the date 1215 and other textual clues lead Yassif to conclude that the manuscript was written in the latter half of the thirteenth century.

Malachi Beit-Arie takes exception to Yassif's conclusion, primarily because it does not incorporate codicological information. A key piece of evidence is the preparation of the vellum, with a different texture on the hair side than the flesh side of the parchment, representing a technology that was superceded by the middle of the thirteenth century. Thus Beit-Arie is able to narrow the range between 1215 and 1260. Relying on the linguistic expertise of Menahem Banitt of Tel Aviv University, he is also able to narrow the geographical range; the dialect reflected in the lexical and grammatical texts is from the northern Champagne region of France.[2]

One interpretation is missing entirely (15:6); the scribe writes, "I did not find this explication." Others have minor lacunae and confusing elements. Although it is often alone in a minor variant, it still fits as an early representative of Family A1. A number of the biblical citations in MV have the Latin name and chapter number written in the interlinear space.

Lemmas are significantly enlarged and bold. The manuscript is in good condition; margins are even and the writing is clear.

Owners have made various notations at the beginning, indicating that the MS migrated from France to England: The signature of John Grandison, Bishop of Exeter (1328–69) is partly erased on fol. 1r and 363v. It was donated to a library by Sir Ro. Cotton Conningtonensis in 1603. Roman numeral pagination is evident at the top; according to this numbering MV is found on fol. 115r–119r.

Related publications: 1) A. Neubauer, *Catalogue of the Hebrew Manuscripts in the Bodleian Library* (Oxford: 1886), 519–21. 2) R. A. May, *Supplement of Addenda and Corrigenda to A. Neubauer's Catalogue* (Oxford: 1994), 244–5. 3) Y. Assif, "ספר המעשים:לאופיו, מקורותיו והשפעתו של קובץ סיפורים מזמנם של בעלי התוספות", *Tarbiz 53* (1983/4), pp. 409–29). 4) M. Beit-Arie, "כ"י אוכספורד 135 בשולי מאמרו של ע' יסיף," *Tarbitz 54* (1984/5): 631–5. 5) M. Beit-Arie, *The Only Dated Medieval Hebrew Manuscript Written in England (1189 CE) and the Problem of Pre-Expulsion Anglo-Hebrew Manuscripts* (London: 1985), 2–3, 16–17.

(Ox 225) Oxford – Bodleian Library Opp. 225 (Neubauer 970), fol. 135r–138v
Copied in the first half of the 16th c. in various Ashkenazi cursive hands.
Paper, 172 fols. 36–40 lines. Family A1-ק
Scribe: Ezriel b. Eliezer (1552) and others.

A miscellany of midrash, commentary and homiletical material, as well as dream interpretations, *takkanot*, and astrological teachings. This manuscript is the latest member of Family A1-ק, a group of three copies of MV that show the same minor variants.

No lemma citation is written at the beginning of each section, but the first two lines of exegesis are significantly indented, with the lemma verse at the end of the interpretation. The manuscript shows signs of deterioration, with fading and spotting. The left margin is approximate and the writing is clear, but informal.

Ezriel b. Eliezer copied several texts, completed in 1552. One text has watermarks similar to Briquet #3883 and 3884, dated 1473–1507.

Related publications: 1) A. Neubauer, *Catalogue of the Hebrew Manuscripts in the Bodleian Library* (Oxford: 1886), 208–9. 2) R. A. May, *Supplement of Addenda and Corrigenda to A. Neubauer's Catalogue* (Oxford: 1994), 152–3.

(Ox 614) Oxford – Bodleian Library Opp. 614 (Neubauer 2275), fol. 8r–15v
Copied in the late 13–early 14th c. in Germany, in several Ashkenazi hands.
Vellum, 65 fols., 20 lines. Family A2

A compilation of several different manuscripts containing midrash, halakah and biblical texts; *Midrash vaYosha* text may represent the oldest piece. This manuscript contains a fragment of the midrash, beginning in the middle of God's argument before the heavenly court regarding Pharaoh's sentence (וירא ישראל), and getting cut off just a few lines into the last lemma. Titled *Midrash VaYosha* (in script) at the top, it has numerous and sometimes lengthy additions to Recension A, although almost none reflect the direction of Recension B. It is the earliest representative of Family A2. Neubauer speculates that the manuscript may represent part of a prayerbook.

There are extended spaces between lemmas, but no change in the very precise paleography. The manuscript appears to be in good condition, with minor signs of aging on the edges. It left margin is approximate; the writing is very clear.

Related publications: 1) A. Neubauer, *Catalogue of the Hebrew Manuscripts in the Bodleian Library* (Oxford: 1886), 791. 2) R. A. May, *Supplement of Addenda and Corrigenda to A. Neubauer's Catalogue* (Oxford: 1994), 435.

(Par 335) Paris – Bibliothèque nationale de France 335, fol. 109r–115v
Mostly written in Venice in 1543 (see colophon, fol. 197v), in an Ashkenazi hand.
Paper, 300 fols. 34 x 25 cm., 30 lines. Family A2

A miscellany of Talmud and Bible commentary, midrash, medical science, homiletics, kabbalah. *Midrash vaYosha* is followed by a note on synagogue recitation of Torah, "To the reader: The reading should continue up to רֹפאיך" [v. 26], which indicates the end of the scriptural reading for the 7th day of Passover. Part of Family A2 (along with Ox 614 and Esc G3), it contains a large amount of additional narrative material. MS Esc G3 also features the same instruction to the reader, and shares several texts in common with this manuscript.

The text preceding MV is in a different hand, and is incomplete.

The lemmas are enlarged, bold and set apart, and the margins are even; this presentation creates a text with a very orderly feeling, even though the headings vary in style and there are occasional flourishes scattered through the manuscript. The paleography is consistent but it is occasionally difficult to distinguish the precise shape of the letters.

Related publication: *Catalogue des manuscrits hebreux et samaritains de la Bibliotheque imperiale* (Paris: 1866), 46–7.

(Prm 2269) Parma – Biblioteca Palatina 2269 (De Rossi 473), fol. 144r–149r
Copied in N. Italy in the mid-15th c., in an Ashkenazi semi-cursive script.
Paper, 163 fols. 21 x 15 cm., 24–27 lines. Family A1-ק
Scribe: Yoḥanan b. Yaakov Kohen (fols. 24r, 86v, 161r).

A miscellany of ethics, midrash, dream interpretation, halakha and other works. At the end of *Midrash vaYosha*, there is the same mythology of creation via Torah (as Divine names), found at the beginning of MSS Mun 232 and Vat 303. It is more similar to MS Vat 303.

Lemmas are enlarged, bold and set apart. Margins are even, with clear and consistent paleography. Unfortunately, the outer edge of the manuscript is damaged, with significant fading.

Notes of historical interest in the MS: An owner recorded family births 1520–22 at the beginning, and there is a censor mark by Domenico Irosolomit[an]o on fol. 161r. The manuscript is dark, damaged and somewhat difficult to read.

Related publications: 1) Benjamin Richler, *Hebrew Manuscripts in the Biblioteca Palatina in Parma* (Jerusalem: 2001), 146–8. 2) Giovanni Bernardo deRossi, *MSS codices hebraici Biblioth. I.B. deRossi* (Parma: 1803), 54–5.

(Vat 303) Vatican – Biblioteca Apostolica Ebr. 303, fol. 260r–262r
Most of the MS was copied in the late 14th c., in a Byzantine hand; MV and 3 additional midrashim were copied in the mid-13th c. in an Ashkenazi hand; attached at the end.
Paper and parchment, 265 fols. 28 x 20.9 (26.3 x 18) cm., 40 lines. Family A1

A miscellany of halakha, responsa, Talmudic commentary, midrash, philosophy and other writings. *Midrash vaYosha* begins with the same mythology of creation via Torah (as Divine names) as in Mun 232, although there are slight differences. It is almost identical to the passage found at the *end* of MV in Parma 2269.

Lemmas are not enlarged, but are set apart with space on each side, with a quotation mark on the end. Left margins are approximate, and the paleography is very clear and precise.

Related publications: 1) Nehemiah Allony and D. S. Löwinger, *Reshimat tatzlumei kitvei-yad ha-ivri'im bamakhon, vol. 3* (Jerusalem: 1968), 46–7. 2) Benjamin Richler, ed., *Hebrew Manuscripts in the Vatican Library* (Città del Vaticano: Biblioteca apostolica vaticana, 2008), 242–6.

(War 258) Warsaw – Uniwersytet Instytut Orientalistyczny 258, fol. 326r–327v
Copied in 1430 in an Ashkenazi hand, with some texts in different hands.
345 fols. 28.6 x 19.6 cm., 2 columns, 47–51 lines. Family A1-ק
Scribe: Shual b. R. Yisrael the Scribe (הלבלר).

A 15th-century collection of midrashim and stories, with many focused on the end of days, was appended to a 16th-century prayerbook. The incorporation of midrashic material into a prayerbook, along with the small midrash on the Binding of Isaac, are both worthy of note. Like MS Drm 25, it contains a condensed version of the opening narrative of Recension B, from Isaac questioning his father and figuring out the plan, to Abraham's plea that God remember his obedience when his descendents are in trouble. There are significant differences in the details and wording from MV.

Lemmas are occasionally unmarked, although the standard format is to set blank space before and after, with a quotation mark at the end. Frequently the only sign of a new text within the manuscript, the beginning has enlarged lettering. The left margin is approximate and the paleography is clear.

Signatures of the scribe can be found on fols. 331v (ספר המדות) and 338v (מסכת כלה). There are numerous ownership markings from men in Mainz, Glogow (Poland), Cologne, tracing its movement through the 17th c. (see fol. 1r).

(Wolf 36.25) Wolfenbüttel Cod. Guelf. 36. 25 Aug. 2^0, fol. 1v–4r
Copied in the 13–14th c., in an Ashkenazi hand.
Vellum, 12 fols. 31 x 23 cm., 2 columns, 41 lines. Family A1-ד
Scribe: The name "Yitzhak" is pointed on fol. 6r, potentially the scribe.

The manuscript is incomplete, containing only MV and *Midrash on the Ten Commandments*. There are several lengthy additions by a different hand in the margins, reflecting Recension B (as well as a few corrections). Marked as ד"א (דבר אחר)- "another interpretation," significant parts of these comments have faded to the point of illegibility. The remaining segments, however, are sufficient to identify the additions as the same texts inserted as ד"א into MS Oxford 27. Together, these two MSS comprise Family A1-ד.

Dr. Edna Engel at the Hebrew University was kind enough to review the dating.

Based on the pricking of the pages, the preparation of the vellum (with different textures for the skin and flesh sides), and the Middle Ashkenazi paleography, she assigns a 13–14c. range, with the most likely date toward the end of the 13th century.

Lemmas are bold, slightly enlarged, and almost always set at the beginning of a new paragraph. The margins are even, with clear and precise paleography.

There is a German dedication at the beginning by Geremias Jacob Jude in Halberstadt, presenting the "explication of Moses' song" to Augusten Herzogen Zu Braunschweig undt Lüneburg, a famous 17th-century book collector. In the dedication, he says the midrash was written and redacted by Rabbi Yehudah Gasith, a scholar who died 574 years previously. Although locating the origins of *Midrash vaYosha* in the appropriate time (11th century) and place (Askkenaz), no confirmation can be made of this authorship.[3]

Related publications: 1) Ernst Roth, *Hebraeische Handschriften*, in *Verzeichnis der orientalischen Handschriften in Deutschland VI:2* (Wiesbaden: 1965), 403–4. 2) Nehemiah Allony and Ephraim Kupfer, *Reshimat tatzlumei kitvei-yad ha-ivri'im bamakhon, vol. 1* (Jerusalem: 1957), 41. 3) Friedrich Adolph Ebert, *Catalogus codicum manuscriptorum orientalium Bibliothecae ducalis Guelferbytanae* in H. O. Fleischer, *Catalogus codicum manuscriptorum orientalium regiae Dresdensis* (Osnabrück: 1988), 77:7.

RECENSION B

(Bud A167) Budapest – Magyar tudomanyos akademia MS Kaufman A167, pp. 1–33

Copied in the 17th c., in Ashkenazi square (pp. 1–126) and cursive hands.
Paper, 146 pages. 19 lines. Family B2

A miscellany of midrash, kabbalah and philosophy. This manuscript is a member of family B2, the closer relative to the *editio princeps* of Recension B. In fact, it was copied after the work had already been printed.

Lemmas are bold and enlarged. The manuscript has even margins and a clear hand, but the microfilm is not of a high quality.

Related publication: M. Weisz, *Katalog der Hebraeischen Handschriften und Bucher in der Bibliothek des Prof. David Kaufman* (Frankfurt: 1906), 80.

(Cam 854) Cambridge University Library Add. 854, fol. 1r–21v

Copied in the 16–17th c., in an Eastern hand.
Paper, 25 fols. 16 x 11 cm., 18–21 lines. Family B2

This MS contains only two texts, MV and *King Solomon and the Ant*. The earliest extant manuscript of Family B2 that is complete, it is very similar to the *editio princeps* of Recension B. It is not clear whether it was copied before or after the printed edition was available.

Lemmas are enlarged and bold; the left margin is approximate and the paleography is very clear. The scribe left a large space between lines.

Related publication: S. C. Reif, *Hebrew Manuscripts at Cambridge University Library* (Cambridge: 1997), 154.

(Jer 3833) Jerusalem – The National Library of Israel MS Heb 3833*8, fol. 32r–39r
Copied in 1808 in Tunis and Tarabalus al-gharb in a Sephardic Tunisian hand.
Paper, 75 fols. 19 x 13 cm., 37–40 lines. Family B2
Scribe: Avraham HaTzair (the young one).

An anthology of midrash and kabbalah, it is a late member of Family B2 copied after the *editio princeps* of Recension B was already printed.

Lemmas are bold and enlarged; margins are approximate. The paleography is clear, but casual in its style.

On fol. 31v, the scribe writes: "So says the young Avraham b. Rafael.... When I was in Tunis in 5568 [1808 CE], God placed into my hand an old book... and within it... was *Midrash vaYosha* in an old printing which is not found, so I copied it. And after I copied... I said... I will collect some midrashim of the rabbis (z"l) about the exodus from Egypt and Moses our teacher, may he rest in peace. Since I saw differences among the midrashim, I decided [lit: said] to copy them all." A colophon on fol. 39v states: "Even though several familiar midrashim are copied from *Vayosha*, I went back and copied everything."

(Jer 6234) Jerusalem – The National Library of Israel 6234*28 (Sassoon 756), fol. 1r–14r
Copied in 1740, in a Persian cursive hand.
Paper, 214 fols. 16.5 x 11 cm., 22 lines. Family B2

A collection of familiar midrashim, with sage stories scattered among the texts. The MS also contains a few texts focusing on medicine, halakhah and ethics. A late member of Family B2, it was copied after the *editio princeps* of Recension B was already printed.

Lemmas are bold and slightly enlarged; the left margin are approximate. The paleography is clear and precise.

A colophon on fol. 203 gives the year. Several owners have left a record: Moshe b. Reuven haCohen in 1834; Yosef b. Gabirol; Ezra b. Yosef

Related publication: D.S. Sassoon, *Ohel David: A Descriptive Catalogue of the Hebrew and Samaritan Manuscripts in the Sassoon Collection* (Oxford: 1932), 470–72.

(Jer 7706) Jerusalem – The National Library of Israel Ms Heb 7706*38, fol. 1r–9r
Copied 1902 in Salmas (Iran), in a Persian hand.
Paper, 19 fols. 23 x 18 cm., 28–31 lines. 1–2 columns, 1 passage diag. Family B2
Scribe: Avraham b. R. Yitzhak (See colophons, fol. 10r, 19r).

The scribe describes the work as containing two precious pearls, MV and *Midrash Tadshe* accompanied by *The Story of the Ant by King Solomon.*

A late member of Family B2, the scribe apparently copied the text from the Warsaw printed edition (see "Printed Editions of Interest"). He ascribes *Midrash vaYosha* to the fourth-generation Tanna, R. Pinḥas b. Yair (son-in-law of R. Shimon b. Yoḥai). Frequently, the other work contained in this text (*Midrash Tadshe*) is identified with R. Pinḥas b. Yair, but I do not know of any other such attribution for *Midrash vaYosha*. It is most likely a misinterpretation of the title page of his source text.

Lemmas are bold and enlarged; the left margin is approximate. The paleography is clear, but casual in its style.

(JTS 4920) New York – Jewish Theological Seminary 4920 (Rab. 1730), fol. 1r–7v
Copied in the 15th c. in a Mizraḥi hand
Paper, 7 fols. 19.8 x 14.1 cm., 27 lines Family B2-ח

A fragment containing only *Midrash vaYosha* (not titled). It begins with אז ישיר משה (Ex 15:1) with decorations at the top of the page as if it was intended as a beginning, and is cut off after a few lines of אז נבהלו (Ex 15:15). It is the earliest member of Family B2.

Lemmas are enlarged and bold; one has outlines around the letters as if a later hand was "doodling." The left margin is approximate, with clear and precise paleography.

Related publication: Judah Brumer, *Rabbinics Manuscripts of the Jewish Theological Seminary of America* (NY: 1984–86), n. 1730.

(JTS 4966) New York – Jewish Theological Seminary 4966, fol. 109r–121r
Copied in 1819–20 in Salmas, Iran, in a Persian style script.
Paper, 122 leaves (6 in envelope). 17.2 x 11.8 cm., 19–29 lines. Family B2
Scribe: Gabirol b. Mordechai.

A miscellany of midrash, commentary and poetry. A late member of Family B2, the manuscript is similar to the *editio princeps* of Recension B.

There are numerous decorative elements in the manuscript: a geometric illuminated frame around a colophon, illustrations of animals and flora around another, and small boxes drawn around the key word at the bottom of the folio that indicates the next word (both *recto* and *verso*).

Lemmas are enlarged and bold; the margins are even, with clear paleography. Colophons may be found on fol. 77r, 99r and 121r, indicating the name and place of the scribe.

(JTS 4998) New York – Jewish Theological Seminary (Rab. 1771), fol. 68b–75a
Copied 1809–1816 in Tripoli, in a Western hand.
Paper, 112 fols. 22.8 x 17.0 cm., 31–42 lines. Family B2
Scribe: Avraham Khalfon.

Conceived as a collection of seven midrashic and mystical texts, titled by the scribe שבעה עינים – *Seven Eyes*, it has a good deal of other material as well. The end of the manuscript is missing, including a copy of *Midrash Temurah* identified as one of the seven texts.

A late member of Family B2, the scribe introduces the midrash by indicating he found it in an old printed book while in Tunisia. As material related to Moses and the Exodus, as well as messianic themes, it was of interest. The text has most of the variants identified for this group of manuscripts. In a few instances, it preserves the reading of Family B1, including: 1) When Abraham calls Satan a liar, it uses the term בדאי; 2) Jethro's deal is that half of Moses' children will be Egyptian (not Ishmaelite, as in the other B2 texts). Also, it is missing the detail about naphtha, so no comparison can be made there.

Related publication: Judah Brumer, *Rabbinics Manuscripts of the Jewish Theological Seminary of America* (NY: 1984–86), n. 1771.

(Lon 10851) London – British Library 10851 (Gaster 942), fol. 15r–21v
Copied in 1652, in a Babylonian or Greek hand.
98 fols. 34–40 lines. Family B2

A miscellany of midrash, kabbalah, liturgical and homiletical materials. The manuscript has sustained significant water damage and is difficult to read. It is also missing pages, including the end of MV. (It is truncated in the middle of explicating the verse that begins: תביאמו. The folio does indicate a continuation, however, which is simply not there.) Sections of the manuscript are from printed books: מעשיות שבתלמוד, סדר הלמוד – with some student writing in the blank areas.

Lemmas are slightly enlarged, bold and frequently set at the beginning of a new paragraph. The left margin is approximate and the paleography is not consistently clear.

Related publication: Neḥemiah Allony and D. S. Löwinger, *The Gaster Collection of Hebrew Manuscripts in the British Museum (Now British Library)*, Institute of Microfilmed Hebrew Manuscripts (Jerusalem: 1960), 89.

(Mon 279) London – Montefiore Library 279, fol. 62v–64r
Copied in the 16th c., in Italian (mostly) cursive characters.
71 fols. 24–27 lines. Family B-ע

A miscellany of commentary, ethics, halakha, kabbalah, lexical material and midrash. The sections from *Midrash vaYosha* appear to be copied from MS Vat 285 or similar manuscript that is not extant, as part of a larger text anthologizing aggadot from Talmud and midrash. These Family B-ע manuscripts share many texts in common, including an almost identical story collection with the same 3 sections of *Midrash vaYosha*, introduced in the same fashion.

The introductory language is bold and enlarged, but there are no "lemmas" per se. Margins are even and the paleography is clear, but the manuscript (or the microfilm) is damages, with severe fading on almost half the page.

At the beginning of the MS, there is a list of contents drawn up by Shlomo Chaim Zalman of Halberstadt. At the end of the MS, there is a note of ownership: אי"ש ג"ר אנכי בארץ. The acronym is the common signature of Abraham Joseph Solomon [b. Mordechai] Graziano (d. 1685), a well-known rabbinic authority in Modena. The end of the note indicates he may have been in Palestine when he acquired the manuscript.

Related publications: 1) H. Hirschfeld, *Descriptive Catalogue of the Hebrew Manuscripts of the Montefiore Library* (London: 1904), 89–90. 2) A. Berliner, *Magazin für die Wissenschaft des Judentum 9* (1882), 170.

(Ox 104) Oxford – Bodleian Library MS Selden Superius 104 (Neubauer 1267), fol. 139r–141r
Copied in the 15th c. in Byzantine semi-cursive hands.
Paper with a few vellum pages, 250 fols. 27 x 16.5 cm., 29–31 lines.Family B-ת

A miscellany of philosophy, ethics, midrash, kabbalah and other writings. MV is titled תשלום מדרש ויושע, the *Supplement of Midrash vaYosha*, and it contains Recension B from the beginning until the exegesis that stands as the start of Recension A. Thus it appears to be by a scribe familiar with Recension A who came across some form of Recension B. Either he did not recognize or care about differences further on in the MS, or they were not in evidence. The language of the supplement at times reflects Family

B1 and at other times Family B2. For purposes of this study, it is identified as Family B-ת (תשלום).

No letters are enlarged to separate the subsections. The left margin is approximate and the paleography is clear. However, the manuscript shows signs of damage, with leaching obliterating some words.

Several texts are explicitly dated (1436, 1441), and others are dated early- to mid-15th c. based on watermarks. Shabbetai Astruc owned the MS in 1549 (see fol. 216), and there are various extracts of שלשלת הקבלה in his handwriting. The name Yosef Algazi appears on fol. 72b.

Related publications: 1) A. Neubauer, *Catalogue of the Hebrew Manuscripts in the Bodleian Library* (Oxford: 1886), 445–7. 2) R. A. May, *Supplement of Addenda and Corrigenda to A. Neubauer's Catalogue* (Oxford: 1994), 207.

(Par 716) Paris – Bibliothèque nationale de France 716, fol. 231v–245r
Copied in the 14–15th c., in a Sephardic hand.
Vellum and paper, 299 fols., 25 lines. Family B1

A miscellany of midrash, grammar and halacha. Warsaw 374 is considered a copy of this manuscript; together, they comprise the base Family B1. There is a list of expenditures at the beginning, including book purchases and travel expenses (among them a trip to Perpignan, France).

There are a number of corrections written in the same hand with a segolate symbol for the place of insertion. Other errors are most likely marked by a later hand (primarily duplicate or erroneous words). There are a couple minor lacunae that actually interfere with the sense of the text, but it stands as the best choice for a base text because of its early date.

Lemmas are enlarged and slightly bolded; margins are even and the paleography is clear. There is a fair amount of space between the lines and most of the manuscript is in good condition, making the text relatively simple to read.

Related publication: 1) Zotenberg, *Catalogue des manuscrits hebreux et samaritains de la Bibliotheque imperiale* (Paris: 1866), 115–6.

(Vat 285) Vatican – Biblioteca Apostolica Ebr. 285, fol. 79v–81v
Copied in the 14–15th c. in a Byzantine hand.
Paper, 239 fols. 20.5 x 15 cm., 26 lines. Family B-ע

A miscellany of commentary, halacha, liturgy, midrash and other texts. The MS contains the same 3 sections of *Midrash vaYosha* as in MS Mon 279. The first is prefaced with the comment: "I also found written at the beginning of *Midrash vaYosha*" (fol. 79v), and it includes Satan's temptation of Abraham, Isaac and Sarah through the pointless argument between Ishmael and Eliezer (בעוד שהיו מהלכין בדרך.... ולא זה יירש). The next two segments are prefaced, "I also found written there...," and include elements of Recension B's messianic vision. They are essentially identical to Recension B on שמעו עמים and ה' ימלוך לעולם ועד. Like Family B1, the name of the enemy is Armilgos rather than Armilos.

The sections are separated by open space; two of them are decorated with a small pyramid of dots over the first word. Margins are even and the paleography is clear, with several marginal corrections that appear to be in the same hand.

Related publications: 1) Nehemiah Allony and D. S. Löwinger, *Reshimat tatzlumei kitvei-yad ha-ivri'im bamakhon, vol. 3* (Jerusalem, 1968), 42. 2) Benjamin Richler, ed.,

Hebrew Manuscripts in the Vatican Library (Città del Vaticano: Biblioteca apostolica vaticana, 2008), 211–215. 3) M. Hershler, *Genuzot* 2 (1985): 185–7.

(War 374) Warsaw – Zydowski Instytut Historyczny 374, fol. 205v–219r
Copied in the 14–15th c., in an Italian hand.
271 fols. 28.2 x 18.3 cm., 23 lines. Family B1

This MS is a copy of Par 716. In MV, all the marked errors and several unmarked ones have been corrected. In addition, there is a certain visual similarity to MS Par 716. Together, they comprise Family B1.

Lemmas are enlarged and bolded; margins are even and the paleography is clear and consistent. There is a fair amount of space between the lines and most of the manuscript is in good condition, making the text relatively simple to read.

Related publication: A.Z. Schwartz, *Die hebraeischen Handschriften in Oesterreich, no. 287.*

HYBRID RECENSIONS

(Mos 111) Moscow – Russian State Library, MS Guenzburg 111, fol. 137v–150r
Copied in 1462–68 in a Sephardic hand.
218 fols. 20 x 13 cm., 25 lines. Family AB2
Scribe: Chaim b. R. Mordechai b. Chaim Tzarfati (see colophons on fols. 97r, 179v).

A collection of midrash and ethics. MV is called דרש על ויושע; it mixes elements of Recension A and B (Family AB2), as well as a few flourishes not found in other MSS. It includes the long narrative about the Binding of Isaac, but does not conform to either recension at the end. Although it indicates a purposeful conclusion (תם ונשלם תהלה לאלהי עולם...), it does not complete the penultimate interpretation, nor does it include an explication for the final lemma. A later member of this family however, MS Zur 192, continues to the end, including parts of Recension A and material that is unique to this family.

(Prm 2736) Parma – Biblioteca Palatina 2736 (deRossi 804), fol. 85v–88r
Copied in Italy in the second half of the 14th c. in an Italian cursive script.
Parchment, 170 fols. 24 x 18 cm., 43–44 lines. Family AB1

The manuscript contains part of a *mahzor* according to the Roman rite, encompassing prayers for Sabbath, Rosh Hodesh, and festivals from Hanukkah to Shabbat Nahamu. Following the liturgy for Passover, there are midrashim on the beginning of Exodus (called מילי דפסח – *Milei d'Fesah*, fol. 82r) and then מילי דויושע – *Milei d'vaYosha*, fol. 83v, which begins with exegetical comments on *Parashat Beshallah* and segues (marked only by enlarged lemmas) to *Midrash vaYosha*. Following MV, there are other texts related to the holy day calendar: *Pirkei Avot* (traditionally read for the seven weeks between Passover and Shavuot), *Milei d'Shavuot*, (a variety of Shavuot material), and *Milei d'Tisha b'Av* (a shorter collection on the 9th of Av).

Although MV is most similar to Recension A, the preceding material contains numerous motifs and verbatim sections found in Recension B. In addition, there are elements of Recension B within MV itself.

DeRossi identified MS Parma 2737 as the complementary part of a single codex, but the two MSS are copied by different hands on differently numbered quires.

Lemmas are enlarged and bold, with a small amount of blank space surrounding them. The text is set with three lines that extend to the margins, alternating with three lines indented from both sides. The manuscript is in good condition, with even margins and precise (if blindingly small) paleography.

Related publications: 1) Benjamin Richler, *Hebrew Manuscripts in the Biblioteca Palatina in Parma* (Jerusalem: 2001), 214. 2) Giovanni Bernardo deRossi, *MSS codices hebraici Biblioth. I.B. deRossi* (Parma: 1803), 180.

(Zur 192) Zurich – Zentralbibliothek Zuerich, MS Heid. 192, fol. 81v–90r
Copied in 1682 in Bozzolo (N. Italy).
32 fols., 26–27 lines. Family AB2
Scribe: Yitzḥak Shalom Cohen of Bozzolo.

A miscellany of prayer customs, midrash, and other writings. This manuscript is a mixed recension, part of Family AB2 along with MS Moscow 111. MV contains the *Akeidah* narrative and most of the other "introductory" material found only in Recension B (but not the last paragraph of ועתה related to Uza). These sections combine aspects of Family B1 and Family B2. Most of the exegesis then follows Recension A, although there are several lemmas in which it incorporates material found in Recension B, and other instances in which it adds its own narrative expansion.

The explication for verses 9, 10 and 12 is missing in this manuscript. It continues to the end of the midrash, however (unlike MS Mos 111), containing some original material.

The lemmas are enlarged and bold, with approximate margins. The paleography is unusual and the manuscript is not in good condition, making the text difficult to read in many places.

Related publication: Nehemiah Allony and Ephraim Kupfer, *Reshimat tatzlumei kitvei-yad ha-ivri'im bamakhon, vol. 2* (Jerusalem: 1964), 122.

Geniza Fragments

(JTS ENA1) Jewish Theological Seminary ENA 2934.4–6
Paper, 3 fols. 17 x 13 cm., 18 lines.

This MS fragment contains Talmud commentary, *tafsir*, *Midrash vaYosha*, an Arabic treatise on the laws of witnesses, part of Maimonides' *Mishneh Torah*, a prayerbook, ספר השרשים, an Arabic poem and bible commentary.

Of *Midrash vaYosha*, there are fragments of Recension B on אז נבהלו, תפול עליהם, תבאמו ותטעמו and יי' ימלוך (Ex 15:15–18).

(JTS ENA2) Jewish Theological Seminary ENA 3142.1
Paper, 1 fol. 11 x 10 cm.

Midrash vaYosha is the only identified fragment of this MS; it contains a small piece of Recension B on the last verse of the midrash, יי' ימלוך.

Other Languages

Basel – Universitaetsbibliothek R II 3 (fragment)
Copied in the 17th c. in a Yiddish translation using rhymed prose.
Paper, 1 fol. 29 x 18 cm.

Related publication: Hans Niedermeier, "Der altjiddische Midrasch Wojoschah [The Old Yiddish Midrash Vayosha]," *Judaica* 21 (1965): 25–55.

Printed Editions of Interest

(Const 1519A) Constantinople 1519, Recension A, fol. 1r–4v
First printed edition.
4 fols., 18.5 x 14 cm., 32 lines.
No colophon information; related to MS Family A1.

Two copies are held at the Jewish Theological Seminary in New York (RB 5685, RB 5688).

Related publications: Moritz Steinschneider, *A Concise Catalogue of the Hebrew Printed Books of the Bodleian Library* (Oxford: Clarendon Press, 1929), #3736. Abraham Yaary, *Hebrew Printing at Constantinople: Its History and Bibliography* (Jerusalem: Magnes Press, 1967), #61.

(Const 1519B) Constantinople 1519, Recension B, pp. 84–103
First printed edition, in a collection titled לקוטים וחבורים.
119 pp., 17.5 x 13 cm., 32 lines.
Published by Astruc of Toulon; related to MS Family B2.

A copy is held at the Jewish Theological Seminary in New York (RB 117:20a). It is missing pp. 1–56, and begins in the middle of a collection of stories from the Talmud, מעשיות שבתלמוד, an alternative title for *A Beautiful Composition After Deliverance*, by R. Nissim b. Yaakov.

Related publications: Moritz Steinschneider, *A Concise Catalogue of the Hebrew Printed Books of the Bodleian Library* (Oxford: Clarendon Press, 1929), #3734. Abraham Yaary, *Hebrew Printing at Constantinople: Its History and Bibliography* (Jerusalem: Magnes Press, 1967), #60.

Eliezer Ashkenazi, דברי חכמים (Metz: J. Mayer Samuel, 1849), 2–16

88 pages plus fold-out calendar chart and French section at back by Josué Alorki. Introduction by Shlomo Munk. Related to Family B1. Described as "a collection of 11 old books... from expert scribes... most previously published, it includes: *Midrash vaYosha,* R. Joseph Karo's interpretation of Lamentations, Maimonides tract on pregnancy (*Ḥeshbon haIbbur*) and part of R. Avraham b. R. Ḥiyya's work on the same subject, an essay on free will by Moshe of Narbonne, correspondence, responsa and poetry.

Adolph Jellinek, בית המדרש (Jerusalem: Wahrmann Books, 1967), I:35–57.

Six sections of short midrashic texts, collected in two volumes. Originally published in 1853 in Leipzig, Jellinek consulted Eliezer Ashkenazi's דברי חכמים (1849), Constantinople (1519) and two manuscripts. He presents Recension B as the primary one (most often reflecting MS Family B1), but includes several segments of Recension A as well, identified as העתקה אחרת.

Chaim Kalter, שתי מרגוליות יקרות (Warsaw 1875), no pagination

The "two pearls" identified on the title page are *Midrash Tadshe* (attributed to Pinḥas b. Yair) and *Midrash vaYosha.* The miscellany also includes*, Ma'aseh haNemalah, Sefer Divrei Torah*, *Yad haḤazakah* (Part 2 of *Ma'asah Tzedakah*). It appears to be the edition used to copy MS Jer 7706.

Warsaw (Boymritter v'ḥatno Ganshar) 1886

Published with a commentary by Menaḥem Mendl Bliman called בית הגדול. *Midrash vaYosha* is bound with *The Story of the Ant by King Solomon*.

Vilna (Katzinelinboigen, 1893), pp. 1–34

Published with a commentary by R. Chaim Avraham Abba b. Shimon Goldblatt, called אשל חיים. He focuses on repairing errors that crept into the text, and providing parallels to be found in rabbinic literature. *Midrash vaYosha* is bound with R. Eliezer haGadol's *Orḥot Chaim* and *Midrash on the Ten Commandments.*

Yehudah David (J.D.) Eisenstein, ed., אוצר מדרשים (B'nei B'rak: Mishor, 1990), I:146–56.

Two volumes, organized alphabetically. Related to Family B2. These two volumes, originally published in 1915, gather short midrashim from various collections using manuscripts and available printed editions. Eisenstein's collection, in turn, was adopted in the Bar Ilan Responsa Project CD.

Endnotes

Chapter 1 – Introduction

1. Adolph Jellinek, ed., *בית המדרש [Bet ha-midrasch]* (Leipzig: 1853–57, Wien 1873–77; repr. Jerusalem: Wahrmann Books, 1967); Judah David Eisenstein, ed., *אוצר מדרשים [Otzar midrashim]* (NY: 1915; repr. Benei Berak: Sifrei Kodesh Mishor, 1990); Solomon Wertheimer and Abraham Wertheimer, eds., *במדרשי הגניזה - בתי מדרשות [Midrashim from the Genizah – Batei Midrashot]* (2nd ed.: Jerusalem: Ktav v'Sefer, 1968).
2. Each exegetical section is framed at the beginning by the verse from the source-text that prompts or anchors its interpretation, and frequently returns to the verse at the end of the section as well.
3. All of the manuscripts are described in the appendix. An additional text listed in the Institute for Microfilmed Hebrew Manuscripts (IMHM) catalog is rendered in Yiddish rhyme; it is not substantively addressed in this study, nor included in the stemmatic chart. See Hans Niedermeier, "Der altjiddische Midrasch Wojoschah [The Old Yiddish Midrash Vayosha]," *Judaica* 21 (1965): 25–55.
4. Daniel Boyarin, *Intertextuality and the Reading of Midrash* (Bloomington: Indiana University Press, 1990), 12.
5. Previous to this turn, MV has received only brief mention alongside other minor midrashim in comprehensive listings such as Leopold Zunz, *הדרשות בישראל [Derashot in Israel]* (trans. Chanoch Albeck; Jerusalem: Bialik Institute, 1946), 141–2, 429–30; Moshe Herr's article, "Midrashim, Smaller," *Encyclopaedia Judaica* (Jerusalem: Keter, 1972) 16:1515–18; H.L. Strack and Günter Stemberger, *Introduction to Talmud and Midrash* (Minneapolis: Fortress Press, 1992), 337.
6. Stemberger, "Midráš Wa-yoša'. Fuentes y tendencias de una narración medieval," *'Ilu: revista de ciencias de las religiones* 3 (2000): 11–27. He later published a slightly revised German translation of the article, "Midrasch Wa-yosha – Quellen und Tendenzen einer mittelalterlichen Erzählung," *Judaica Minora II* (Texts and Studies in Ancient Judaism, 138; Tübingen: Mohr Siebeck, 2010), 587–601. See also Zahara Pardes-Feinstein, "מדרש ויושע: מבוא, מהדורת טקסט ודיון [Midrash vaYosha: Introduction, Textual Edition and Discussion]" (Master's thesis, Hebrew University, 1993).
7. *Midrasch Wajoscha: Edition-Tradition-Interpretation* (Berlin: de Gruyter, 2009). See also my own dissertation, which frequently has more extensive footnotes and technical information than the present treatment, "*Midrash vaYosha* and the Development of Narrative in Medieval Jewish Exegesis" (Doctoral dissertation, Jewish Theological Seminary, 2008).

8. Kugel, *In Potiphar's House: The Interpretive Life of Biblical Texts* (San Francisco: Harper, 1990), 251.
9. Joshua Levinson, "Dialogical Reading in the Rabbinic Exegetical Narrative," *Poetics Today 3* (2004): 497.
10. E.g., Eisenstein, *Otzar midrashim* 1:146–56.
11. "Ashkenaz" is frequently used to represent the shared culture of Germany and Northern France. Israel Ta-Shma is among the scholars who argue that this perspective is most appropriate in consideration of medieval Jewish intellectual history. "Ashkenazi Jewry in the Eleventh Century," in *Creativity and Tradition* (Cambridge, Mass.: Harvard University Center for Jewish Studies, 2006), 1.
12. Stemberger, "Midráš Wa-yoša'," 23–4. [As is well-known, it deals with a motif that was of great importance after the First Crusade, reinforcing the religious meaning of recent history. Above all, it refers to the Jewish martyrs who, faced with the alternative of baptism or death, not only preferred suicide so as not to fall into the hands of the Christians, but even killed their own children, who many times freely consented to their parents' decision. (*Midrash VaYosha* and its parallels insist that Isaac obeyed not only God, but also his father.) I think that this historical context is precisely that of the first part of *Midrash vaYosha* and that, consequently, it cannot be previous to the twelfth century; its country of origin could be France or more probably Germany.]
13. He supports his hypothesis with a *piyyut* by R. Efraim b. Yaakov de Bonn (1132~1197), *I commemorate my ancestors* (את אבותי אני מזכיר), which alludes to Isaac's request that his ashes be brought to his mother after his death: "You shall gather my dust and it shall be brought unto the city, unto the tent of Sarah" (pp. 22–24). Regarding this motif (which is also found in MV) as somewhat scarce in rabbinic literature, Stemberger sees a regional, chronological and thematic confluence. Other parallel elements include: Satan approaches Abraham (most similar to *b.Sanh. 89b*), Isaac requests to be tightly bound so he does not invalidate the sacrifice, Abraham pins his son down with his knees.
14. Wies-Campagner, *Midrasch Wajoscha*, 366–99. For expansion on the themes of the *akeidah* in MV and piyyut, see also Rachel Mikva, "Weeping as Discourse Between Heaven and Earth: The Transformative Power of Tears in Medieval Jewish Literature," in *Crying in the Middle Ages: Tears of History* (ed. Elina Gertsman; Routledge: London, 2011), 156–72.
15. *Tanḥuma Vayera 22–23*. Other segments of MV reflect the European *Tanḥuma*, generally referred to as *Tanḥuma Buber*.
16. See, for example, James Kugel, "Nine Theses," *In Potiphar's House*, 255–59.
17. There is, however, a manuscript family (AB2) that includes the *akeidah* and omits several of the other expansions. It has numerous narrative elements not found in either major recension. See discussion in Section C.
18. Wies-Campagner tends to discount this evidence, arguing that only a small fragment of Ashkenazi manuscripts survive, and that Jews from N. Europe brought the tradition with them into the Muslim milieu as they fled persecution. This rationalization fails to account for two facts: Manuscripts of MV copied in an Ashkenazi hand continue to appear through the seventeenth century, but they belong to Recension A manuscript families. Ashkenazi scribes who relocated to the Mediterranean world would presumably still ply their trade and write in their original hand (*Midrasch Wajoscha*, 398). Both she and Stemberger continue to

advance the case made for redaction of Recension B in Ashkenaz, and their arguments in the cited works are worthy of consideration.

19. See Dan, *הסיפור העברי בימי הביניים [The Hebrew Story in the Middle Ages]* (Jerusalem: Keter, 1974), 60.
20. al-Tabari, *History of al-Tabari: The Children of Israel* (trans. William M. Brinner; Albany: State University of New York Press, 1991), 3:45; Ahmad al-Thalabi, *Lives of the Prophets* (trans. William M. Brinner; Leiden: Brill, 2002), 292–94; Muhammad al-Kisai, *Tales of the Prophets (Qiṣaṣ al-anbiya)*, (trans. Wheeler M. Thackston Jr.; Chicago: KAZI Publications, 1997), 222. The translator of al-Kisai speculates that the material served as a manual for preachers (p. xx). Cf. the thirteenth-century Syriac text by Solomon Bishop of Basra, *The Book of the Bee* (trans. Ernest A. Wallis Budge; Oxford: Clarendon Press, 1886), Chapter 30. For a more complete list of parallels, see Mikva, "*Midrash vaYosha*," 365.
21. Shinan, *תרגום ואגדה בו [The Embroidered Targum]* (Jerusalem: Magnes Press, 1992), 199. For a summary of research demonstrating awareness and influence of Islam in *Pirqe R. El.*, see Strack and Stemberger, *Introduction to the Talmud and Midrash*, 329. See also, Joseph Heinemann, *אגדות ותולדותיהן [Aggadah and its Development]* (Jerusalem: Keter, 1974), 181–99; Louis Ginzberg, *על הלכה ואגדה [On Law and Lore]* (Tel Aviv: 1960), 261.
22. They contain references to Islam and/or awareness of its traditions. See, e.g., Raymond Scheindlin, "Medieval Jewish Literature," in *From Mesopotamia to Modernity* (eds. Burton Visotzky and David Fishman; Boulder, CO: Westview Press, 1999), 133. These works did circulate in Ashkenaz by the time of Recension B's redaction, however, so the evidence must be weighed accordingly.

    It is also worth noting that Anat Shapira's analysis of *Midrash on the Ten Commandments* indicates its composition under the aegis of Islam. Potentially tracing a parallel synagogue-to-literature path, this text shares many qualities with MV. It is lemmatic with expanded narratives, it has links to festival observance, and it is found in shortened form with more focused exegesis in Ashkenazi *maḥzorim* manuscripts. It also happens to share a special interest in stories of Moses and Abraham. Shapira, *מדרש עשרת הדברות [Midrash on the Ten Commandments]* (Jerusalem: Bialik Institute, 2005), 185.
23. All the manuscripts of Recension B that include this word have the ב (*ad* 15:3); MS Family B2 compounds the Arabic-influenced variant with the ז at the end, and also changes the word בדאי (liar) to a synonym with an Arabic cognate (כוזב) *ad* 14:30. Family B2 manuscripts are generally late; the only one that certainly predates the printed text is a fragment that does not include exegesis of Ex 14:30 (JTS 4920).
24. Issachar Ben-Ami asserts that stories of magic and marvels are influenced by contact with Muslim culture, in Dan Ben-Amos, "Jewish Folktales: An Encyclopedia Survey," *Jewish Folklore and Ethnology Review* 14:1–2 (1992): 7. Several textual comparisons help to highlight the likelihood of this premise: *Tanhuma Buber Vaera*, reflecting a European recension, mentions Satan only once in the *akeidah* narrative (and altogether half as often as the other Tanḥuma). In the manuscript record of *Midrash on the Ten Commandments*, MS Par 716 – from the Sephardic world – has many more supernatural elements than its Polish counterpart (Shapira, *מדרש עשרת הדברות [Midrash on the Ten Commandments*, 148–53). Shinan establishes that *Targum Pseudo-Jonathan*, reflecting some Islamic influence, adds discussion of magic, angels and Satan; he also sees these elements as indicative of close connection to folk culture. Shinan, *תרגום ואגדה בו [The*

Embroidered Targum], 120–48; "האגדה בתרגומים הארמיים ה"ארץ-ישראליים" לתורה [The Form and Content of the Aggadah in the 'Palestinian' Targumim on the Pentateuch]" (Doctoral diss.; Hebrew University, 1977), 243–78.

25. John Reeves, *Trajectories in Near Eastern Apocalyptic* (Atlanta: SBL, 2005), 17.
26. See Commentary *ad* 15:18, "The Eschatological Vision," for more detail. This description of Armilos is also found in *The Secrets of R. Shimon b. Yoḥai*, which makes thinly veiled references to the Arab conquest of the Land of Israel.
27. Reeves, *Trajectories in Near Eastern Apocalyptic* , 19.
28. Himmelfarb, "Sefer Zerubbabel," in *Rabbinic Fantasies* (eds. David Stern and Mark Mirsky; Philadelphia: Jewish Publication Society, 1990), 67–8. *Otot haMashiaḥ* is the only midrash I know of that actually uses the term "antichrist," mentioning it as a term the gentiles use for Armilos.
29. See discussion in Even-Shemuel, *מדרשי גאולה [Midrashim on Redemption]* (Jerusalem: Bialik Institute, 1953), 162ff, 320.
30. For example, some manuscripts of *Mahzor Vitry* (11–12th c.) refer to *Sefer Zerubbabel* in a commentary on *Avot*. In *Sefer Rokeaḥ*, R. Eleazar b. Judah of Worms (*c.*1176–1238) discusses *Baraita d'Zerubbabel*. See Alexander Marx, "Studies in Gaonic History and Literature," *JQR 1* (1910–11): 76.
31. Steven Wasserstrom asserts that Jewish apocalyptic themes are well-represented within Muslim literature. ("Jewish Pseudepigrapha in Muslim Literature: A Bibliographical and Methodological Sketch," in *Tracing the Threads* (ed. John Reeves; Atlanta: Scholars Press, 1994), 87–88.) In addition, the somewhat more millennial character of Recension B is indicative of non-Ashkenazi attitudes. Stephen Sharot asserts that messianism among the Ashkenazim rarely carried with it transfigurative assumptions about the universe ("Jewish Millennial-Messianic Movements: A Comparison of Medieval Communities," in *Comparative Studies in Society and History* (ed. Todd Endelman; Ann Arbor: University of Michigan, 1997), 65–6).
32. "Kalila waDimna" borrows heavily from *Panchatantra*, an ancient Sanskrit collection of fables from India. It was first translated from Sanskrit to Pahlavi (Persia) in the sixth century, then to Syriac and Arabic in the eighth. Joseph Dan speaks of a similar pattern for *Parables of Sendebar* (*הסיפור העברי בימי הביניים [The Hebrew Story in the Middle Ages]*, 113–15).
33. See, e.g., Yassif, "הסיפורת העברית בארצות המזרח: התגבשותה בימי הביניים ומערבה לעת החדשה [Hebrew Narrative in the East: Its Crystallization in the Middle Ages and Its Western Movement Prior to the Modern Period]," *P'amim* (1986): 53–70. Jacob Elbaum also mentions Arabic influence in the shift of focus from exegesis to narrative. He cautions, however, that internal literary influences like the *piyyut* and esoteric literature, should not be overlooked. "המליצה, המוטיב והעניין [Style, Theme and Subject]," in *מחקרי ירושלים בפולקלור יהודי לכבוד דב נוי [Jerusalem Studies in Jewish Folklore in Honor of Dov Noy]* (eds. Tamar Alexander and Galit Hasan-Rokem; Jerusalem: Magnes Press, 1992), 99–126.
34. Dan, *הסיפור העברי בימי הביניים [The Hebrew Story in the Middle Ages]*, 23.
35. Strack and Stemberger, *Introduction to the Talmud and Midrash*, 337.
36. Stemberger, "Midrasch Wa-yosha," 601.
37. Wies-Campagner, *Midrasch Wajoscha,* 369–70.
38. Ta-Shma, *Creativity and Tradition*, 1, 4–5.
39. Stemberger, "Midrāš Wa-yoša‘," 24, 26.

40. *Akeidat Yitzhak* is found also in MS War 258. Both manuscripts differ from MV in significant details and wording, but the shared basis is unmistakable.
41. Building on a well-established rabbinic tradition that the Torah preceded creation and was used as a blueprint, it resembles *Midrash Konen* in regard to the notion that the names of God effect powers of creation. MS Prm 2269 has a similar text, set directly after MV.
42. Adolf Neubauer speculates that MS Ox 614 may be a fragment of a prayerbook manuscript: *Catalogue of the Hebrew Manuscripts in the Bodleian Library* (Oxford: 1886), 791.
43. Other manuscripts in MS Family B2 are: London – British Library 10851 (Lon 10851, 1562 Babylonian/Greek), Jerusalem – The National Library of Israel 6234*28 (Jer 6234, 1740 Persian), Jerusalem – The National Library of Israel 3833*8 (Jer 3833, 1808 Tunisian), Jewish Theological Seminary 4966 (JTS 4966, 1819 Persian), Jewish Theological Seminary 4998 (JTS 4988, 1809–16 Tripoli), Jerusalem – The National Library of Israel 7706*38* (Jer 7706, 1889–1902 Persian). MS JTS 4988 does *not* have the additional Arabic markers.
44. This section is adapted from Rachel S. Mikva, "Midrash in the Synagogue and the Attenuation of Targum," *Jewish Studies Quarterly* 18:4 (2011): 319-42. Additional discussion of *Midrash on the Ten Commandments* may be found there, along with more comprehensive notes.
45. In addition, certain versions of *Midrash Petirat Moshe* begin with the first verse of the Torah reading for Simhat Torah (Deut 33:1) and are assumed to have some relationship to the festival. See, e.g,, Jellinek, *בית המדרש [Bet ha-midrasch]*, 1.xxi, 115–29; Eisenstein, *אוצר מדרשים [Otzar midrashim]*, 2.361–68.
46. See Avigdor Shinan, "Live Translation: On the Nature of the Aramaic Targums to the Pentateuch," *Prooftexts* 3:1 (1983): 41–49.
47. Joseph Yahalom and Michael Sokoloff, *שירת בני מערבא [Jewish Palestinian Aramaic Poetry from Late Antiquity]* (Jerusalem: Israel Academy of Sciences and Humanities, 1999); Michael Sokoloff and Joseph Yahalom, "Aramaic Piyyutim from the Byzantine Period," *JQR* 85:3 (1985): 309–21; Menachem Schmelzer, "פירוש אלפביטין, פירוש על י"ג פיוטים ארמיים לר' בנימין בן אברהם מן הענוים *[Peirush Alfabeitin*: An Explication of Thirteen Aramaic Piyyutim by R. Benjamin Ben Abraham Min HaAnavim]," in *מחקרים ומקורות [Texts and Studies]* (ed. H. Z. Dimitrovsky; New York: Jewish Theological Seminary, 1977), 169. The most definitive evidence for the antiquity of the genre is a fourth- or fifth-century Egyptian papyrus with *Ezel Moshe*, a liturgical poem for the seventh day of Passover; see Yahalom, "אזל משה בפפירוס [*Ezel Moshe* According to a Papyrus]," *Tarbiz* 47 (1978): 173–82.
48. Expansive Aramaic exegesis exists for other holidays, however. For example: Rimon Kasher presents two Aramaic *piyyutim* in which Moses resists the decree that his death is nigh; although one of the manuscripts (MS Columbia X893 Z8V.1 n. 14) is an autonomous Targum text rather than a prayerbook, it specifies that the poem is a *tosefta* for the translation of Deut 34:1; see "שתי תוספתות תרגום על מות משה [Two Targumic Toseftot on the Death of Moses]," *Tarbiz* 54 (1985): 217–24. He speculates in n. 7 that it is possible the midrashim related to Moses' death played some role in the Torah reading as well, but he did not believe he had sufficient evidence to substantiate the theory.
49. Aryeh Goldschmidt, ed., *Mahzor Vitry* (Jerusalem: Otzar haPoskim, 2004), 2.474. Based on the Reggio manuscript (c. 1208), seventh-day Passover Targum is found

in 2:475–79; Shavuot Targum, 1:335–44, 2:487–570. Although the compiler, Simhah ben Samuel, died at the beginning of the twelfth century, the work continued to accumulate material.

Siddur Rashi similarly explains that a child translates every verse of the parasha in order to publicize the miracle of crossing the sea; see Salomon Buber and J. Freimann, eds., *Siddur Raschi* (Israel: 1980 repr.) #443, p. 225. Hizkuni (13c., France) mentions in his Torah commentary (*ad* Ex 20:13) that the Ten Commandments are translated into Aramaic during the Torah reading.

50. David Kimhi refers to *Targum shel tosefta* several times in his commentary; see Jud 11:1; 1 Sam 17:8; 1 Ki 22:20; and 2 Ki 4:1, 6 and 7, and 13:21. See also Shinan, "'Targumic Additions in Targum Pseudo-Jonathan," *Textus* 16 (1991): 139–55.
51. MSS Parma Palatina 3132 and 2887, respectively. Moses Ginsburger, "Aramäische Introductionen zum Thargumvortrag an Festtagen," *Zeitschrift der Deutschen Morgenländischen Gesellschaft* 54 (1900): 113–24, and Michael Klein, "The Targumic Tosefta to Exodus 15:2," *JJS* 26 (1975): 61–7. Italian prayerbooks record some of the most elaborate targumic traditions.
52. *Chag haShavuot*, section beginning *shacharit*. The name of this fourteenth- to fifteenth-century scholar reflects his location: Tyrnau, Slovakia. A German *posek*, Maharil (R. Yaakov Molin, d. 1427), cites his teacher R. Abraham Klausner of Vienna: On Shavuot the *Akdamut* is recited after the first verse of the Torah reading, there is more explication after Ex 20:1, and similar expansions on the second day of Shavuot as well. He mentions some variety in regional custom (*Sefer Maharil, Hilkhot Shavuot 4*).
53. This discussion does not deal with the unique customs of the Yemenite Jewish community, where targumic tradition has been preserved to this day.
54. E.g., Judah ibn Kuraish (c. 900), Hai Gaon (d. 1038), Shmuel haNagid (d. 1056). See Wilhelm Bacher, "Targum," www.JewishEncyclopedia.com; Benjamin Lewin, *אוצר הגאונים: תשובות גאוני בבל ופירושיהם, ברכות [Otzar HaGeonim: Responsa of the Babylonian Geonim and Their Explication, Tractate Berakhot]* (Haifa: 1928), 18–19 (#33); Joel Müller, *מפתח לתשובות הגאונים [Index of Geonic Responsa]* (New York: Menorah, 1956), 106, 211.

    As the Gaon Sar Shalom (c. 850) indicated in a responsum, the Targum the Babylonian sages intended is *Targum Onkelos*, although Hai Gaon specifically authorized Palestinian versions as well, based on ancient tradition; see Abraham Berliner, *Targum Onkelos* (Berlin: 1884), 172–75.
55. Ta-Shma, *Creativity and Tradition*, 1, 4–5, 23, 75–6. Cf. Talya Fishman, *Becoming the People of the Talmud* (Philadelphia: University of Pennsylvania Press, 2011), 91–120, 176–81, 222–4.
56. See, e.g., *y. Meg. 4:1 (74d)*.
57. *M. Meg. 4:6* states that children *may* read from the Torah scroll or translate the text, but the medieval prayerbooks present it as customary for a minor (*katan*) to recite the Aramaic Targum.
58. See, for instance, *peirush* on Shavuot exegesis in Goldschmidt, *Mahzor Vitry* 1:319–34; MSS Cambridge 667.1, JTS 4460.
59. Avigdor Shinan, *מקרא אחד ותרגומים הרבה [Biblical Story as Reflected in its Aramaic Translations]* (Tel Aviv: Hakibbutz Hameuchad, 1993), 25. Joseph Heinemann makes a similar claim in "שרידים מיצירתם הפיוטית של המתורגמנים הקדומים [Fragments of Poetic Composition of the Early Meturgemans]," *HaSifrut* 4 (1973): 369.

60. There is evidence that various communities supplemented or replaced Aramaic with vernacular explication (aside from the Arabic trend already mentioned). Persian Jews in Bokhara, for instance, read the Targum and a Farsi paraphrase of the haftarah for eighth-day Passover. See Rachamim b. Chakham Eliyahu, *הפטרה ליום שמיני של פסח עם התפסיר בלשון פרסי כפי מה שנהגו בני עמי יושבי בוכאר"א ואגפיה [Haftarah for Eighth-Day Passover with a Farsi Translation According to the Custom of the Residents of Bukhara and its Environs]* (Jerusalem: A.M. Lunts, 1898).

    There is a Sicilian-Jewish translation of the expanded Targum for Shavuot, with extant manuscripts from the fourteenth and fifteenth centuries. See Yahalom, "The Aramaic *Alfabetin*: From Eretz-Israel to Italy," *Materia Giudaica* 3 (1997): 56–60, and Giuseppe Sermoneta, *Alfabetin. Traduzione giudeo-siciliana in caratteri ebraici del servizio della Pentecoste*, *Collezione di testi siciliani dei secoli XIV e XV* (Palermo: Centro di Studi Filologici e Linguistici, 1994).
61. See Shinan's discussion of parallels between midrashic literature and *Targum Pseudo-Jonathan*: *תרגום ואגדה בו [The Embroidered Targum]*.

    A large number of parallel motifs can also be found in *Pirqe Rabbi Eliezer*, including a few that have more precise parallel details. Scholars have suggested that this midrash, too, has some relationship to Targum, perhaps an attempt to set into Hebrew a fluent narrative incorporating many of the earlier synagogue targumic traditions (as well as written rabbinic exegesis). See Gerald Friedlander, ed., *Pirke de Rabbi Eliezer* (London, 1916; repr. New York: Hermon, 1965), and Miguel Pérez Fernández, *Los capítulos de Rabbí Eliezer* (Biblioteca Midrásica 1; Valencia: Institución S. Jerónimo para la Investigación Bíblica, 1984).
62. For instance, Pharaoh's expanded rejection of God's demand, found in two manuscript families of MV (A2, AB2), is recorded in the targumic explication of MS Parma 2736: How many troops and chariots does God have? How many countries has He conquered, etc.? *Mahzor Vitry* and *Targum Pseudo-Jonathan Ex 15:12* briefly mention Abel's blood crying out from the ground as a reason for the land's hesitation to absorb the Egyptian corpses, a theme expanded in several manuscripts of MV (Family A2, MS Oxford 225).
63. They also contain the *Midrash on the Ten Commandments* and expansive Targum for the seventh day of Passover and Shavuot. Two additional manuscripts could be counted in this category. MS War 258, a collection of midrashic material including *Midrash vaYosha* (dated 1430), is appended to an Ashkenazi prayerbook from the sixteenth century. MS Oxford 614 is a thirteenth- or fourteenth-century Ashkenazi fragment which Adolf Neubauer speculates may have been part of a prayerbook.
64. Interestingly, the Targum includes a number of passages titled *Alfabeitin*, even though they are neither acrostic nor poetic.
65. A number of the early manuscripts title the works "*Aggadot shel...*" or "*Haggadah shel...*," again potentially suggesting interpretive traditions offered in public on the festival days. Various *piyyutim* and other liturgical passages are called "____ *d'vaYosha*," identifying the holy day by the key introductory passage to the Song at the Sea (Ex 14:30). *Milei d'Fesah* collects material primarily from *Mekhilta d'Rabbi Ishmael* related to the Exodus and to the Torah reading for the first day of Passover.
66. The fact that these sixteenth-century Ashkenazi MSS are relatively late and are not *mahzorim* suggests they may be descendants of a copy used in the synagogue. The early manuscript of this family, MS Ox 614 (13–14c. Ashkenazi), might well

conclude with this notation since it may be a *mahzor*, but is cut off before the end. *Midrash on the Ten Commandments* also contains instances in which Targum is interwoven with the midrash and instructions for recitation.

67. Shinan, *מקרא אחד [Biblical Story]*, 152.
68. Prayerbooks: MS Cambridge 667.1 (Family A1: 13–14c. Ashkenazi); MS Prm 2736 (Family AB1: 14c. Italian). The two texts containing the note to the Torah reader are from MS Family A2, adding substantial narrative homilies about songs of praise, Pharaoh's repentance, raising the lowly and humbling the proud, and God siding with the pursued against the pursuer. Motifs move and scores of details change. Copies of *Midrash on the Ten Commandments* located in prayerbook manuscripts display even more variety (as does the midrash in general).
69. Alexander, "Jewish Aramaic Translations of Hebrew Scriptures," in *Mikra: Text, Translation, Reading and Interpretation of the Hebrew Bible in Ancient Judaism and Early Christianity* (ed. Martin Jan Mulder; Peabody, Mass.: Hendrickson, 2004), 217–53.
70. See Israel Ta-Shma, "The 'Open Book' in Medieval Hebrew Literature," *Bulletin of the John Rylands University Library* 75:3 (1993): 7–24; Lewis Barth, "Is Every Hebrew Manuscript a New Composition?" in *Agendas for the Study of Midrash in the Twenty-first Century* (ed. Marc Lee Raphael; Williamsburg: College of William and Mary, 1999), 43–62; and Malachi Beit-Arié, "Publication and Reproduction of Literary Texts in Medieval Jewish Civilization: Jewish Scribality and its Impact on the Texts Transmitted," in *Transmitting Jewish Traditions* (eds. Yaakov Elman and Israel Gershoni; New Haven: Yale University Press, 2000), 225–47.
71. See, e.g., discussion in the Tur and subsequent halakhic literature/commentary reflecting Sephardi practice. *Orah Hayyim 145–6* describes Targum as an outdated rabbinic practice and prohibits speaking during the Torah reading.
72. The themes of MV do not leave the synagogue just because the text does; they remain material for sermonizing in Jewish communities under Islamic rule. Numerous motifs of MV (including Moses' staff and others found only in Recension B) are included in the homilies of ibn Shueib in Spain (14c.) and the *peirush* on the haggadah by Maimonides' grandson, David haNagid, in Egypt (13c.). See *דרשות ר"י אבן שועיב* [*Sermons of R. Joshua ibn Shueib*], (ed. R. Zeev Metzger; Jerusalem: Wagshel, 1992), 1:108, 128–30, 226–7; *מדרש רבי דוד הנגיד הגדה של פסח* [*Midrash of Rabbi David haNagid on the Haggadah of Passover*] (Jerusalem: Wagshel, 1981), 80–95.

    In general, Jewish preachers within Sephardi tradition exhibit a greater interest in narrative within their sermons, perhaps influenced to some extent by the Islamic *qaṣaṣ*, a storyteller who frequently fulfilled worship and preaching duties as well. See Ignaz Goldziher, *Muslim Studies* (trans. C.R. Barber and S.M. Stern; London: Allen and Unwin, 1971), 152–3. The synagogue was a locus for storytelling in various areas within the reach of Islam: professional storytellers in North Africa practiced their craft while waiting for synagogue to begin or between scheduled prayers; the story of Hannah and her seven sons was narrated for simple folk and women in the Iraqi synagogue on Tisha b'Av; tales related to the Torah reading of the week were read aloud for illiterate men and women in Kurdistan. See Ben-Amos, "Jewish Folktales," 3–25.
73. Emden, *סדור בית יעקב מעמדין [Siddur Beit Yaakov of Emden]* (1904; repr. Lemburg: David Balaban, 2003), 306a–b. Earlier, R. David b. Shmuel haLevi (d. 1667) complained about the practice of *Akdamut* in his *Turei Zahav*; R. Aryeh

Gunzberg (d. 1785) tried to change the custom after he became Chief Rabbi of Metz, but the community refused. See Gunzberg, *שאגת אריה [Sha'agat Aryeh: Questions and Responsa]* (Vilna, 1874; repr. Jerusalem: Hatam Sofer Institute, 1974), 98. Other *posekim* of the eighteenth century ruled against the practice as well; see *Shevut Yaakov* (Jacob b. Joseph Reischer, d. 1733) 1:12 and *Panim Meirot* (Meir b. Isaac Eisenstaat, d. 1744) 3:31.

74. Elizabeth Shanks Alexander, "The Orality of Rabbinic Writing," in *The Cambridge Companion to the Talmud and Rabbinic Literature* (eds. Charlotte Fonrobert and Martin S. Jaffee; Cambridge: Cambridge University Press, 2007), 38–57; Yaakov Elman and Israel Gershoni, eds., *Transmitting Jewish Traditions*; Steven Fraade, "Literary Composition and Oral Performance in Early Midrashim," *Oral Tradition* 14 (1999): 33–51; Martin Jaffee, "Oral Tradition and Rabbinic Studies," *Oral Tradition* 18 (2003): 37–39; Talya Fishman, *Becoming the People of the Talmud, passim*. See also the article by Werner Kelber ("Orality and Biblical Studies: A Review Essay," *Review of Biblical Literature* [cited 3 December 2007]. Online: www.bookreviews.org/pdf/2107_6748.pdf), which discusses the trend among scholars now to negate the "great divide" theories between oral and written literatures.
75. For a discussion of this process in non-Jewish literature, see Bruce Rosenberg, *Folklore and Literature: Rival Siblings* (Knoxville: University of Tennessee Press, 1991), 144, and Francesca Sautman et al., eds., *Telling Tales: Medieval Narratives and the Folk Tradition* (New York: St. Martin's, 1998), 3–4.
76. Marc Saperstein discusses the language of medieval preaching and its literature in *Jewish Preaching 1200–1800: An Anthology* (New Haven: Yale University Press, 1989), 39–44.
77. See the introduction to Eli Yassif, *The Hebrew Folktale* (trans. Jacqueline Teitelbaum; Bloomington: Indiana University Press, 1999), xii–xiii.
78. *Die gottesdienstlichen Vorträge der Juden historisch entwickelt* (Berlin:1832). Zunz clearly had an agenda in trying to establish the antiquity and continuity of synagogue preaching as justification for its place in the progressive synagogues of his day. He folded his argument into a study of midrashic texts, claiming that they record the historical development of synagogue homily. Other scholars advanced the thesis with analyses of midrash as the "stuff" of sermons, especially focusing on the *petiḥta* or proem form. See, for example, Julius Theodor, "Zur Composition der agadischen Homilien," *MGWJ* 28–30 (1879–1881); Phillipp Bloch, "Studien zur Agadah," *MGWJ* 34 (1885): 165–187; and Wilhelm Bacher, *Die Proömien der alten jüdischen Homilie* (Leipzig: Hinrich, 1913).
79. See questions raised by Joseph Heinemann, "The Proem in the Aggadic Midrashim," *Scripta Hierosolymitana* 22 (1971): 100–22; Richard Sarason, "The Petiḥot in Leviticus Rabba: 'Oral Homilies' or Redactional Constructions?" *JJS* 33 (1982): 557–65; Yonah Fraenkel, *דרכי האגדה והמדרש [Methods of Aggadah and Midrash]* (Givatayim: Masada, 1991); David Stern, *Parables in Midrash* (Cambridge, Mass.: Harvard University Press, 1991); Jacob Neusner, *Introduction to Rabbinic Literature* (New York: Doubleday, 1994); Steven Fraade, "Sifre Deuteronomy 26 (*ad* Deut 3:23): How Conscious the Composition?" *HUCA* 54 (1983): 245–301; Burton Visotzky, *Golden Bells and Pomegranates* (Tübingen: Mohr Siebeck, 2003) and "The Misnomers *'Petihah'* and 'Homiletic Midrash' as Descriptions for Leviticus Rabbah and Pesikta De-Rav Kahana," *JSQ* 18 (2011): 19–31.

80. Adrian Tudor, "Preaching, Storytelling, and the Performance of Short Pious Narratives," in *Performing Medieval Narrative* (eds. Evelyn Vitz, Nancy Regalado and Marilyn Lawrence; Cambridge: D.S. Brewer, 2005), 153.
81. Jellinek, *בית המדרש [Bet ha-midrasch]*; Eisenstein, אוצר מדרשים *[Otzar midrashim]*; Wertheimer, *במדרשי הגניזה [Midrashim from the Genizah]*.
82. See Joseph Dan, "Fiction, Hebrew," in *EJ* 6:1261–71; Moshe Herr, "Midrashim, Smaller," 16:1515–18; Moses Gaster, *Studies and Texts in Folklore, Magic, Mediaeval Romance, Hebrew Apocrypha, and Samaritan Archaeology*, Vol. 3 (New York: Ktav, 1971).
83. Joseph Dan, *הסיפור העברי בימי הביניים [The Hebrew Story in the Middle Ages]*, 21–2, 134–36. He also asserts that the return of apocryphal and pseudepigraphic works to Hebrew literature helped to open the door to narrative, especially retold Bible.
84. *Ibid.*, 15–22. He discusses the development of expanded biblical narrative in Chapter 15, specifying three primary differences from earlier midrash: 1) primacy of narrative elements over ethical or exegetical ones, 2) return of apocalyptic literature, 3) greater reliance on external sources: Quran, Hadith, apocrypha, etc.
85. Rosen and Yassif, "Hebrew Literature in the Middle Ages," in *The Oxford Handbook of Jewish Studies* (ed. Martin Goodman; Oxford: Oxford University Press, 2002), 277.
86. Yassif, "הסיפורת העברית בארצות המזרח [Hebrew Narrative in the East]," 56–60.
87. C.S. Lewis, *The Discarded Image* (Cambridge: Cambridge University Press, 1964), 211; as cited in Rosenberg, *Folklore and Literature*, 148–9.
88. Indeed, scholars examining the rise of *peshat* exegesis mention increased interest in Scriptural study and rationalism in Islam as well as the impact of grammatical studies. Karaite exegesis may also have exerted some influence. Those focusing on northern Europe add other factors, e.g., polemical and cooperative responses to Christian biblical interpretation; experience with Talmudic exposition; the twelfth-century Renaissance with its dialectic of faith and rationalism, scriptural authority and interpretation, historical consciousness and curricular expansion. See Eleazar Touitou, *הפשטות המתחדשים בכל יום [Exegesis in Perpetual Motion]* (Ramat Gan: University of Bar Ilan, 2003), 11–47; Avraham Grossman, "The School of Literal Jewish Exegesis in Northern France," in *Hebrew Bible/Old Testament* (ed. Magne Sæbo; Göttingen: Vandenhoeck and Ruprecht, 1996), 2:323–31; Nahum Sarna, "Hebrew and Bible Studies in Medieval Spain," in *The Sephardi Heritage* (ed. Richard David Barnett; London: Valentine, Mitchell, 1971), 323–66.
89. Beryl Smalley, *The Study of the Bible in the Middle Ages* (Oxford: Basil Blackwell and Mott, 1940; reprint Notre Dame, Ind., 1964), 370–72.
90. Sternberg, "How Narrativity Makes a Difference," *Narrative* 9 (2001): 117.
91. Like most aspects of MV's poetics, this quality is not unique to our midrash. See, for example, the medieval text *Midrash on Proverbs*, which also presents expanded narratives within an otherwise straightforward exegetical frame (e.g., the story told about the Queen of Sheba in Chapter 1).
92. Meir, "הסיפור 'הדרשני' במדרש קדום ומאוחר [The Darshanic Story in Early and Late Midrash]," *Sinai* 86 (1980): 247. See also her book, *הסיפור הדרשני בבראשית רבה [The Darshanic Story in Bereshit Rabbah]* (Tel Aviv: HaKibbutz HaMeuchad, 1987), which expands upon this concept, 63–70. The term *darshani* is generally left

untranslated in mention of her book title because it communicates aspects of exegesis as well as homiletics, and no English term quite matches it.

93. Levinson, "Dialogical Reading," 497–506. See also his book, *הסיפור שלא סופר: אמנות הסיפור המקראי המורחב במדרשי חז"ל [The Twice Told Tale: A Poetics of the Exegetical Narrative in Rabbinic Midrash]* (Jerusalem: Magnes Press, 2005), 29–101, 192–238.
94. Levinson, "Dialogical Reading," 524.
95. See, for example, Elman and Gershoni, *Transmitting Jewish Traditions*, 5.
96. Steven Fraade, "Literary Composition and Oral Performance, 45.
97. See Meir Sternberg, *Expositional Modes and Temporal Ordering in Fiction* (Bloomington: Indiana University Press, 1993), 90–158.
98. This motif may be borrowed from *Pirqe R. El. 31*, which deliberately set about creating narrative backgrounds for each of the prayers in this rubric of the service. The structure in *Pirqe Rabbi Eliezer* is incomplete. Less specific, but still utilizing established prayer language, are 1) the blessings offered by the mothers when they awake after giving birth (15:1), and 2) Jethro's embrace of Moses and his God after he survives the ordeal in the pit (15:2).

Chapter 2 – *Midrash vaYosha* with Translation and Commentary

1. Israel is frequently identified as the dove of Song 2:14: *O my dove, in the cranny of the rocks*, leading to numerous midrashic analogies. A more fully drawn comparison between Israel at the sea and the trapped dove can be found in *Song Rab. 2:14:2*. Since it cannot take cover in the nest because of the serpent, nor can it fly away on account of the hawk, the dove begins to cry and beat its wings so the owner of the cote will come to its rescue. Cf. *Mek. R. Shimon b. Yoḥai 14:13*, *Mek. Beshallaḥ 2* (HR 94:8–12), *Tanh. Shofetim 13.*
2. Left untranslated is the common term מיד (lit: immediately). Like באותה שעה (lit: at the same time), it is in medieval literature most often a generic literary conjunction without clear indication of time relationships.
3. Literally: He accepted in love. א-ה-ב (love) connotes willing agreement or obeisance. See Yochanan Muffs, *Love and Joy* (New York: Jewish Theological Seminary, 1992), 122–32, 186–7.
4. The rabbinic tradition regarding the identity of the young men is well-established. See, for instance, *Lev. Rab. 26:7, 20:2; Eccl. Rab. 9:6; Pirqe R. El. 31, Targ. Pseudo-Jonathan Gen 22:3.*
5. There may be some allusion to another midrashic tradition. The fleeting quotation from Genesis 22:5 within Abraham's response (*עד כה*, ad koh – *up to there*) is associated with the verse: *Look toward heaven and count the stars, if you are able to count them.... So* (*כה*, koh) *shall your offspring be* (Gen 15:5). Several midrashim (e.g. *Gen. Rab. 56:2, Pesiq. Rab. 40*) connect the two instances of the word, highlighting the irony that God's own promise seems destined to be undone by the command to sacrifice Isaac.

   There are marks above רחוק (far) in the MS, used to indicate words that may not belong, and it is not found in the other MSS; consequently, it is not reflected in the translation.

6. Presumably the same question as before, although Abraham offers a purpose rather than a place in response.
7. *Gen. Rab. 55:7, Pesiq. Rab. 40, Yal. Shimoni 96* put the challenge regarding priestly officiation in Abraham's mouth, to which God responds that he is authorized to perform the ritual. Here, it is possible that the author has Abraham name Shem to hint that God (haShem) is ultimately responsible for the offering, but Shem is frequently the paradigmatic early priest in midrash. See, for example, *Gen. Rab. 30:6, Lev. Rab. 25:6.*
8. The midrash changes the tone of Isaac's biblical question, making it an urgent query. In MS Family AB2, Isaac first becomes afraid after his father offers the elusive biblical response to Isaac's question about the burnt offering: *God will see to the sheep for the burnt offering, my son* (Gen 22:8).
9. Rabbinic literature tends to presume Isaac was a willing participant, a pervasive notion since the Second Temple period. See, e.g., 4 Macc 13:12, Pseudo-Philo's *Biblical Antiquities 32:2–3,* Josephus' *Jewish Antiquities 1:232.* Early Christian exegetes see the Binding of Isaac as an allegory for the crucifixion, so Isaac's embrace of the Divine command is also critical for them. In the Quran as well (Sura 37), Abraham's son is a willing participant in the sacrifice.
10. Isaac's statement calls to mind one that is attributed to Rabban Gamaliel in *m. Avot 2:4*: Do God's will like your own, so that He may do your will like His. Here, Isaac's urging will seem prescient, because Abraham does have an important request of God at the end of the pericope. References to God as owner can be found in the liturgy. See also Isa 1:3 in which the prophet chastises the people for not recognizing God; even the ox knows its owner.
11. The word "Deceiver" is not in our MS, leaving the biblical verse as God's command. Except for our MS and its copy (MS War 374), all the other MSS and printed editions have either המשטין (the Deceiver) or שטן (Satan), thus depicting the true Deceiver cleverly undermining the Divine charge. Based on such evidence and the fact that Abraham's response makes more sense in this context, the text has been emended.
12. The verse is interrupted by an additional word, ברכתי (My blessing), marked as incorrect with a double slash above the word in the MS. It is not found in other MSS.
13. Interestingly, Abraham paraphrases the end of the verse, "and make a burnt offering before Me," an ambiguous statement that fits the eventual ending; it does not specify that the sacrifice will be Isaac.
14. Alternatively, one might play with the ambiguity of the words to suggest: *Is not your piety your folly, your hope the path of naiveté?* This part of the dialogue is an abbreviated rendering of *b.Sanh. 89b.* Based on Rashi's comments there, the translation renders Satan's challenge as one that draws into question Divine justice, seeing as Abraham's piety offers no surety, only sorrow.

    The talmudic passage exegetically links the *akeidah* (Gen 22:1, *After these things, God tested Abraham.*) with Job 4:2: *הנסה דבר אליך תלאה,* which Rashi understands as, *What if He should test you in a matter that overwhelms you?* (In the biblical context, this question which Eliphaz asks Job is best translated, *"If one ventures a word with you, will it be too much?"* and the remainder of the verses affirm God's justice rather than challenge it.) MV reworks the tradition, removing it from the Talmudic frame in which Satan is also the catalyst for Abraham's trial.

The adaptation lends greater legitimacy to Satan's complaint since he did not provoke God to take this action.

15. All the other manuscripts use the actual verse from Job 4:7: *מי הוא נקי אבד ואיפה ישרים נכחדו* – *What innocent man ever perished, where have the upright been destroyed?* Although it appears most likely that the scribe made an error, it is interesting to contemplate the possibilities of meaning for the text as a deliberate word play: Abraham refutes Satan's challenge of Divine justice by emphasizing that it is Satan who causes the righteous to suffer and who seduces the wicked to succumb.
16. The word קבל (accept) is in the margin of our MS, and found in almost all other MSS and printed editions of Recension B.
17. MS Family B2 (except JTS 4998) and Const 1519B use the synonym כוזב. Although the term is found in the Hebrew Bible, the word choice in these primarily Sephardi and Eastern transcriptions may be related to the Arabic cognate, *kadab*. The proverb is also found in *Avot d'Rabbi Natan (A) 30*.
18. The expression in general means to vex; ק-ה-ה (to blunt) suggests the image of grinding one's teeth. In Ezek 18:2 and Jer 31:29, it is cited proverbially: Parents have eaten sour grapes and children's teeth are set on edge (although the prophets challenge this notion of vicarious justice). Satan exclaims thus to Isaac and to Sarah, both of whom vicariously suffer the fierce devotion of Abraham to his God.

    MS Family B2 and Const 1519B have: היכן שני ילדותך (Wherefore the years of your youth?). Examining the manuscript record, it appears likely that the change was effected through a series of scribal errors. היאך יקהו שניך (How they set your teeth on edge) may have first been altered to היאך יקחו שניך (How they take your years away), with only one misread letter, and then other variations followed.
19. The *Gen. Rab. 56:4* parallel does not present Isaac as already knowing his fate. It imagines that Isaac still rebuffs Samael, but the temptation succeeds in part; he speaks to his father in such as way as to elicit sympathy, perhaps to dissuade him from the deed. Samael also plays on the tension between Sarah, Ishmael and Isaac, warning that all the tunics Sarah made for Isaac will pass to Ishmael. *Tanḥ. Vayera 22* and *Pesiq. Rab. 40* present Satan tempting Isaac by inviting him to consider his mother who fasted and prayed for his birth – about to be undone by this old man. Isaac asks his father if he heard this, and Abraham advises him that the interloper has come merely to cause trouble.
20. *Sefer haYashar 23* records a conversation in which Abraham actually tells Sarah that is where they are going; the chapter shares many motifs with MV.
21. The juxtaposition of the *akeidah* and Sarah's death in Genesis prompts rabbinic midrash to see a causative link. *Pirqe R. El. 32* states that Samael visits Sarah after the trial has ended but before Abraham's return; he tells her that Isaac was, in fact, sacrificed and she dies in response to the terrible news. *Tanḥ. Vayera 23* imagines that Satan takes on the appearance of Isaac and describes the ordeal in such detail that Sarah dies before the tale comes to a close. Cf. *Lev. Rab. 20:2, Yal. Shimoni 102.*

    Muslim tradition also records Satan *(al-Shaytan)* trying to deter Abraham and Isaac/Ishmael, and going to Sarah to report the sacrifice. See Reuven Firestone, *Journeys in Holy Lands: The Evolution of the Abraham-Ishmael Legends in Islamic Exegesis* (Albany: State University of New York Press, 1990), 110–15.
22. MS has לקבל (to receive), but the word found in all other Recension B families and Const 1519B, לבטל (to prevent), seems correct. Parallel texts also read לבטל.

23. The midrash here cleverly finds a way for Abraham to articulate the conflict without questioning God's command. Similarly, *Gen. Rab. 56:10, y.Taanit 2:4 (65d), Lev. Rab. 29:9, Pesiq. Rab. 40.* In *Gen. Rab. 56:8*, Abraham juxtaposes the seemingly contradictory Divine statements and God reconciles them.

    MS Family B2 and Const 1519B are different: ואני מהרתי לומר ישמעאל כי על יצחק אמרת לי *כי ביצחק יקרא לך זרע* – I quickly spoke up, "(You mean) Ishmael, because regarding Isaac You told me, '*It is through Isaac that offspring shall be continued for you.*'" This tradition may have emerged because of the Arabic milieu, articulating the competition between Judaism and Islam for the legacy of the Abrahamic covenant.
24. The Hebrew words for "unique" and "unify" share the same root, shaping the logic of Abraham's challenge.
25. Similarity to the waters of the sea drying up in Ex 14:22, 15:19 is surely deliberate.

    Satan plays the critical role of articulating all the doubts in the reader's mind about leading Isaac to sacrifice. Until the trickery at the river, he is unusually straightforward and constructive in his arguments. The closest parallel for the temptations of Satan is *Tanḥ. Vayera 22*. Other partial parallels include *Yal. Shimoni 96, b. Sanḥ. 89b, Gen. Rab. 56:4,* In the *Gen. Rab.* passage, Samael (Satan) also attempts to deter Abraham by suggesting God will accuse him of murder after the deed is done (similarly *Tanḥuma*).
26. The earlier identification of these two young men now takes on substance. Joseph Heinemann, *אגדות ותולדותיהן [Aggadah and its Development]*, 186–9, hypothesizes a typological significance to the argument as found in *Pirqe R. El. 31*: Ishmael represents Islam (a well-established typology) and Eliezer represents Christianity. (The latter identification is more speculative, but Christian lore builds on the midrashic connection of Eliezer with the gematria value of his name (318, found in *Gen. Rab. 43:2*) and assigns religious significance, e.g. asserting that there were 318 bishops at the Council of Nicaea. Cf. *Epistle of Barnabus 9*.) They each claim the spiritual inheritance of Judaism, but the midrash denies both their claims: Judaism (Isaac, the covenantal seed of Abraham) is not about to die. In the context of MV, the narrative works with or without the typology. Serving as foils for Abraham and Isaac who are committed to fulfilling God's severe command, Ishmael and Eliezer haggle about "stuff."
27. *Tanh. Vayera 23* and *Yal. Shimoni 101* describe the two of them working together on the altar, although the former lacks any detail or comparison to preparations for a wedding. Other midrashim express concern that Isaac might injure himself while building and thereby render himself unfit for sacrifice (e.g., *Gen. Rab. 56:5, Pesiq. Rab. 40*). The latter group may be playing off the fact that the verse mentions only Abraham building; MV seems more interested in demonstrating Isaac's complete cooperation.
28. In a *seliḥah* (penitential prayer) on the Binding of Isaac entitled "אמונים בני מאמינים [Faithful Ones, Children of the Faithful]," Benjamin b. Zeraḥ (11c.) uses the image of Isaac exulting as if under a bridal canopy. See Commentary for additional examples and discussion.
29. MS Family AB2 portrays Isaac as a young boy, not yet educated regarding the commandments.
30. Once it is established that Isaac is just as committed to the sacrifice as his father, the question may arise why he needs to be bound at all. This dialogue offers an answer. Cf. *Pesiq. Rab. 40, Tanḥ. Vayera 23, Gen. Rab. 56:8, Targum*

Pseudo-Jonathan, Fragment-Targums Gen 22:9–10, Pirqe R. El. 31. Also worth comparison is a fifth- to sixth-century Syriac verse homily that similarly develops the narrative through dialogue, including: "Draw me near, father, and bind me, tie tightly for me my bonds, lest my limbs should shake, and there be a blemish in your sacrifice." See Sebastian Brock, "Two Syriac Verse Homilies on the Binding of Isaac," *Le Muséon* 99:1–2 (1986): 124.

31. Notice that Abraham does not answer his son's first question. The dialogue suggests a certain consciousness of narrative flow, anticipating long-term effects of an event not addressed in the biblical text.

    Yal. Shimoni 101 parallels several elements of the dialogue: Isaac tells his father to hasten to do the will of his Creator and to send the ashes to Sarah; he also asks what Abraham and Sarah will do in their dotage without him. *Tanḥ. Vayera 23* presents a related concern for how the event is communicated to Sarah. Many of the themes are also found in an early Aramaic *piyyut*, "Isaac Said to His Father Abraham." See Joseph Yahalom and Michael Sokoloff, *שירת בני מערבא [Jewish Palestinian Aramaic Poetry]*, 124–31.

32. It appears a word is missing. The MS uses a f.s. verb (נטבלת), but a plural noun (עצים). MS Family B2 and Const 1519B have the *knife* immersed in tears, a f.s. noun that agrees with the passive verb. MS Ox 104 utilizes a plural verb, agreeing with the plural noun, wood. Family AB2 has the altar filled with tears.

33. There is a midrashic tradition connecting the psalm with Abraham because Ps 8:5 speaks of God being mindful (ז-כ-ר) and Gen 19:29 states, *ויזכר אלהים את אברהם*, *God was mindful of Abraham*. The next part of the Psalm verse speaks of פ-ק-ד, taking note, and God takes note of Sarah in Gen 21:1. See *Tanḥ. Vayera 18, Midr. Ps. 8:7*.

34. The preceding verse makes it an especially apt quote: *Hark, the Arielites cry aloud; the angels of peace cry bitterly* (Isa 33:7). *Pirqe R. El. 31* cites v. 7 and then imagines the angels arguing that Isaac is bound like an animal, and God is known to save animals.

35. Abraham's reputation for hospitality becomes a frequent refrain in rabbinic literature. See, e.g., *Avot d'Rabbi Natan (B) 14*, *t. Sotah 4*.

36. Similarly, *Pesiq. Rab. 40, Gen. Rab. 56:5*. The angels' argument is not that Abraham has successfully passed the test, so it is time to stop; rather, God's command is unjust and inconsistent.

37. *Gen. Rab. 56:7* records that the angels' tears dissolved the knife, explaining why Abraham is instructed not to extend his *hand* against the boy. *Gen. Rab. 65:10* relates how the angels' tears dropped into Isaac's eyes and dimmed his vision, the condition described when he mistakes Jacob for Esau (Gen 27:1).

38. The MS is missing the bracketed words, presumably in error. The paragraph is filled in from MS Families B2, B-ת, AB2 and Const 1519B. Cf. *Pesiq. Rab. 40, Tanḥ. Vayera 23, Ex. Rab. 2:6*.

39. MS Families B2, B-ת, AB2 and Const 1519B have a more extended conversation between Abraham and the angel: אמר לו אברהם למלאך: לא אשחטהו אלא אחנקהו? אמר לו: *ואל תעש לו מאומה*. – Abraham said to the angel, "I am not to butcher him; should I strangle him?" He said, "*Don't do anything to him*."

    It suggests exegetical nuance for the apparent redundancy of the angel's command: 1) do not raise your hand, and 2) do not do anything to him. *Gen. Rab. 56:7, Pesiq. Rab. 40* also contain this extension of the conversation. The notion that

Abraham could find it difficult to abandon the mission, to walk away from the precipice, is both compelling and disturbing.

40. This expression is found in a variety of contexts in the Babylonian Talmud: *Qidd. 42b, B. Qam. 56a, Sanh. 29a, Tem. 25a. Tanḥ. Vayera 23* contains a somewhat different exchange in which Abraham simply states that, since it was God's command in the first place, let the Holy One come to cancel the decree.
41. The crux is the fact that the angel speaks twice, and the midrash picks up on the detail that the second time he specifically invokes God.
42. *Pirqe R. El. 31* also describes Isaac dying on the altar, coming back to life, and reciting the blessing. There, it is part of a large but incomplete construct to develop narrative origins for the חתימות (closing sentences) of the blessings in the *Amidah.*
43. Grammatically, Isaac is the last referent and could be the speaker. There is certainly precedent in rabbinic literature for Isaac to invoke his own sacrifice in pleading before God (e.g. *b. Shab. 89b*). However, MS Family B2 and Const 1519B specify Abraham here, and the frame for the story recounts how God calls to mind Abraham's prayer.
44. "And now" self-consciously marks the return of the midrash to the conversation between God and Moses (Ex 14:15) that was interrupted by the long excursus about Abraham. It is written in large letters, but should not be considered a separate pericope. See Commentary, "The Seam."
45. Moses' question accentuates the somewhat perplexing first response of God to the Israelites' dire predicament. "Why do you cry out to Me?" clearly implies that Moses should do something himself, but he cannot possibly know what it is. The midrash also addresses the purpose of the staff, which is not specified in the biblical narrative. Perhaps evoking the 'speak' versus 'strike' tension of producing water in the subsequent biblical narrative, it conjures a conversation with the sea that involves both actions. Cf. *b. Sotah 37a*.
46. Our MS repeats לא נבראתי (I was not created) but MS Family B2 and Const 1519B have the correct form (נבראת). The motif of the sea's initial refusal is found in Recension A at Ex 15:8.

    אזל משה ("Moses went") is an Aramaic acrostic *piyyut* that speaks of the sea's refusal on these two grounds: You are born of woman, and I am older than you. Similar motifs are found in *Yal. Shimoni 234, Midr. Hallel, Ex. Rab. 21:6.* Cf. *Midr. Ps. 114:9, Tibat Marqe 2:12* (a Samaritan midrashic composition that includes many ancient traditions, with parts that were redacted perhaps as late as the ninth century).
47. The scribe or a later reader recognized the dittography; "Moses" is repeated, but the first one appears to be crossed out.
48. *Mek. Beshallaḥ 4* (HR 102:13), *Pirqe R. El. 42* have a different rendering of the sea's refusal to obey Moses, in which it does not move until God's own presence is manifest.
49. The tradition of Naḥshon being the first to brave the sea is recorded also in *Mek. Beshallaḥ 5* (HR 105:17), following a contrasting midrash that relates how the tribes were all competing to be first. Various forms of the tale can be found in *Mek. R. Shimon b. Yoḥai 14:22, b. Sotah 37a, Pirqe R. El. 42, Yal. Shimoni 234* and other midrashim. In comments on Ex 15:9, MV credits the tribe of Benjamin.
50. There appears to be a visible seam left from the earlier version of the midrash, repeating the lemmatic verse and "the Sages" formulaic opening. The most

compelling evidence is that Recension A *begins* only at this point (see Commentary).

51. Some MSS read: *from* the hand of Egypt, as in the verse. If our MS is not in error, then the crux would seem to be: Was not Israel already extracted from Egyptian bondage? Were they delivered *into* the hands of the Egyptians to need rescuing again? *Yal. Shimoni 241*, a close parallel to this passage with Uza's suit, explicitly asks whether Israel was then *in* the hands of the Egyptians.

    Emphasizing ביום ההוא (on that day), MS Prm 2736 remarks that there were a number of days on which God saved the people. Thus the crux becomes a question of whether or not the seventh day after leaving Egypt can properly be considered the day on which God delivered the people.

52. The commentary of Bahya b. Asher (d. 1340) explicitly cites MV as a source for this name (*ad* Ex 14:10): "So I saw in *Midrash vaYosha*: Uza is the guardian angel of Egypt." MSS Mun 232, War 258 and Ox 225 call him Uziel.

    It is likely that the singular verbs attached to Egypt encourage exegetical license to posit a single figure who represents the nation; see, for example *Ex. Rab. 21:5, 22:2.*

53. MS Family AB1 brings Dan 12:1 as evidence that Michael stands for Israel in time of distress: *At that time, the great prince, Michael, who stands [beside the sons of your people, will appear. It will be a time of trouble...].* Then it employs Job 32:16 as a prooftext to demonstrate how we know he was silent: *For they stood and answered no more.*

54. The image of a court of judgment in heaven with angels present is already suggested in the Hebrew Bible, e.g. Ps 82:1 and the beginning chapter of Job. The latter is key in supporting the rabbinic notion of *beit din shel maalah*, where suits even against God could be brought. Numerous texts incorporate the motif; see Yisroel Klapholtz, *Tales of the Heavenly Court* (trans. Sheindel Weinbach; Bene Brak: Peer haSefer, 1982).

55. Many manuscripts (A and B) use the rabbinic term, פ-ת-ח, opened, to indicate the beginning of an address.

56. Recension A adds the prooftext from Gen 15:13, *[Know well that your offspring shall be strangers in a land not theirs;] and they shall be enslaved and oppressed for four hundred years*. In this and other minor details, *Yal. Shimoni 241* is similar to Recension A (especially A1-ק).

57. Calculating that Moses was eighty years old upon his return to Egypt, Miriam was 5 years older, and the plagues took a year. MSS Ox 135, Cam 667.1, JTS 4966 and JTS 5000 state eighty years, probably a scribal error.

58. Uza associates the first two letters in Miriam's name, מ-ר, with the root מ-ר-ר, to embitter. In Ex 1:14, it states *וימררו את חייהם בעבדה קשה, they embittered their lives with hard labor*. This pun is found in *Pesiq. Rab Kah. 5:9, Pesiq. Rab. 15, Song Rab. 2:11, Tanḥ. Bo 7:7, S. 'Olam Rab. 3, Lekaḥ Tov Ex 15:20.* The implication is that the period of four hundred years begins with the birth of Miriam because it was then that the status of the Israelites changed from guests to slaves, and her family chose the name to reflect the recent change in status.

    There is also a strong thematic association between קיים (exist, endure) and גזירה (decree), each with covenantal overtones.

59. MS Mos 111 and Recension A use the term "oath" in place of "decree." In these MSS and MS Prm 2736, Uza explicitly asks permission to return them to Egypt for an additional three hundred fourteen years.

60. Michael's silence gives fresh significance to the obvious: It is *God* who delivers the people.
61. It is possible that our family of manuscripts reads להחזירן (to return them) as do most other MSS, but the transcription here better fits the preposition, "in."
62. The notion that slavery in Egypt came to pass as a result of Abraham's question is also found in *b. Ned. 32a, S. Eli. Rab. 14.*
63. Many midrashim address the apparent inconsistency between the four-hundred-year sentence decreed to Abraham in Gen 15:13, and the four hundred thirty years mentioned in Ex 12:40 (or the two hundred ten years that rabbinic tradition calculates as the actual time in Egypt). The idea that one begins counting four hundred years with the birth of Isaac is found in numerous texts, e.g., *Mek. Bo 14* (HR 50:4ff), *Mek. R. Shimon b. Yohai 12:40, S. 'Olam Rab. 3, Pirqe R. El. 48, Targum Pseudo-Jonathan Ex 12:40.* They do not include, however, the clever distinction clarifying that God's decree to Abraham does not specify Egypt.
64. Recension A begins here, with what now stands as the middle of the Recension B. This chapter continues to alternate the redactions to facilitate comparison.

    Vayosha was frequently used to indicate the seventh day of Passover and various liturgical elements of the day absorb the word into their title.
65. This line makes God's frustration with Michael's silence more palpable, representing one of the few instances in which Recension A seems to offer a slightly more developed dramatic sensibility.
66. Like Recension B manuscripts, MS Family A1-ק does not include a derogatory reference to Cush, but Family A2 elaborates slightly on the motif.
67. See, e.g. *Gen. Rab. 56:10, Lev. Rab. 29:9, Pesiq. Rab Kah. 154a–b, y.Taanit 2:4 (65d), Pesiq. Rab. 40, Tanḥ. Vayera 23, Fragment-Targums Gen 22:14*, which presume that Abraham offers a prayer at Mt. Moriah. Other texts do not mention Abraham's supplication, but simply argue that the *akeidah* perpetually merits forgiveness: *Lev. Rab. 29:3, b.Roš Haš. 16a, Pesiq. Rab Kah. 151b.*
68. *Mek. R. Shimon b. Yoḥai 14:21, Gen. Rab. 55:8, Ex. Rab. 21:8, Midr. haGadol Ex 14:15. Mek. Beshallaḥ 3* (HR 98:2) also presents the exegetical link, mentioning Abraham's merit along with several other possible factors in moving God to divide the sea. Further on (HR 100:2), it states that once Israel walked into the sea, Mt. Moriah uproots from its place with the scene of Isaac's binding displayed on its crest, and God then urges Moses to act.
69. For a full discussion of the motif of tears in this pericope, see Rachel Mikva, "Weeping as Discourse Between Heaven and Earth: The Transformative Power of Tears in a Medieval Jewish Exegesis," in *Crying in the Middle Ages* (ed. Elina Gertsman; Routledge: London, 2011), 156–72. Some discussion of the bridal canopy metaphor may also be found there.
70. Shalom Spiegel, *The Last Trial* (trans. Judah Goldin; New York: Behrman House, 1979), 135–7. "It is for us to praise" is the beginning of a standard liturgical doxology originally recited during Rosh haShanah musaf and, at least since the twelfth century, at the close of daily worship (first during the morning service, and later at every communal worship service).
71. "O God, do not silence the shedding of my blood," in Heinrich Brody, *מבחר השירה העברית [Selection of Hebrew Poetry]* (Leipzig: Insel-Verlag, 1922), 221. An English translation of significant portions of the *piyyut* is available in Alan Mintz, *Hurban: Responses to Catastrophe in Jewish Literature* (Syracuse: Syracuse University Press, 1996), 94–5.

72. "I shall speak in the grief of my spirit," as cited in Spiegel, *The Last Trial*, 20.
73. The usual exegetical foundation is Isa 33:7: *Hark! The Arielites cry aloud; Shalom's messengers cry bitterly*.
74. It begins with Isaac's questions before reconciling with the sacrifice; then Satan accosts Abraham en route to Mt. Moriah, with the same guise and similar dialogue. Next, Satan goes to Isaac but the young man resists him. Instead, he asks his father to bind him tightly lest he kick and make the sacrifice unfit. After all, he is young and Abraham is old. Satan tempts Sarah and transforms into a river; Isaac requests his ashes be delivered to Sarah and asks what will happen after he is gone; God observes the hearts of binder and bound are equal; everyone weeps and angels' tears dull the knife; Isaac dies and is resurrected. Other details are there as well – including Abraham's request that his faithfulness serve to protect Israel in time of trouble. However, Satan goes to Sarah after Isaac has died and before he comes back to life; thus news of his death kills her. *Akeidat Yitzhak* also goes on to discuss the ram substitute in detail. Once incorporated into MV, the denouement involving the ram disappears; since the midrash is prelude to salvation at the sea, the resolution of the drama now lies squarely in Abraham receiving (and invoking) the Divine promise of blessing for his descendants.
75. Stemberger and Wies-Campagner argue for a historical catalyst; see Introduction.
76. Since Abraham extends the citation to include Isaac's name, his verse can also be understood as a belated answer to Isaac's question in A4. Cf. *Gen. Rab. 56:4, Pirqe R. El. 30, Yal. Shimoni 101, 714* which read Gen 22:8, *God will see to the burnt offering, my son*, as a way of hinting that "my son" is the burnt offering.
77. See Rachel Mikva, "Talking Back to God: An Examination of *Hutzpa K'lapei Shamaya* in the Babylonian Talmud" (Rabbinic Thesis, Hebrew Union College, 1990), 19–24, 149–55.
78. MS Family AB2 enlarges *ויושע יי'* (*The Lord delivered*) as if it were a new pericope.
79. Bahya b. Asher notes the singular form of נסע (journey) in his commentary on Ex 14:10, and specifically cites *Midrash vaYosha* as his source for identifying the Egyptian angel by name; Jacob b. Asher (*circa* 1303, Spain) specifies the name as well, adding a word play on the name Uza (עוזא) and the epithet in Ex 15:2: עזי (*Ba'al haTurim* Ex 14:10). Rashi *ad loc.* offers the explanation that it might be Egypt's patron angel, but brings no name. *Ex. Rab. 21:5* has the most extensive and explicit discussion of this crux, noting the singular form of נסע (journey) in Ex 14:10 and סוס ורכבו (horse and its rider) in Ex 15:4, 21; it maintains that these indicate God's punishment of Egypt's guardian angel before the Egyptians themselves. Cf. *Mek. Shir 2* (HR 124:20ff), *Mek. R. Shimon b. Yoḥai 15:1*. Eleazar of Worms (Rokeah) includes the tradition of Uza's suit in his thirteenth-century siddur commentary, *פרושי סדור התפילה לרוקח [Rokeah's Explications of the Prayerbook]* (ed. Moshe and Yehudah Alter Hershler; Jerusalem: Wagshal, 1992), 212.
80. In some of these traditions, the name is Aza. See, e.g., *b. Yoma 67b, 3 Enoch 5, Aggadat Bereshit (Buber, 39), Pesiq. Rab. 34:2, S. Eli. Zuta 25, 49, Zohar 1: 9b, 19b, 23a, 126a.* For a convenient collection of many such texts, see Reuben Margulies, *מלאכי עליון [Heavenly Angels]* (Jerusalem: Mosad haRav Kook, 1945), 274–80. See also, Bernard Bamberger, *Fallen Angels* (Philadelphia: Jewish Publication Society of America, 1952); Leo Jung, *Fallen Angels in Jewish, Christian, and Mohammedan Literature* (New York: Ktav, 1974); Annette Reed,

Fallen Angels and the History of Judaism and Christianity: The Reception of Enochic Literature (Cambridge: Cambridge University Press, 2005).

81. Wies-Campagner, *Midrasch Wajoscha*, 349–53.
82. Stemberger, "Samael und Uzza: zur Rolle der Dämonen im späten Midrasch," in *Die Dämonen: die Dämonologie der israelitisch-jüdischen und frühchristlichen Literatur im Kontext ihrer Umwelt* (ed. Armin Lange; Tübingen: Mohr Siebeck, 2003), 636–61.
83. For a full discussion of the historical implications of racializing the lineage of Ham, see Stephen R. Haynes, *Noah's Curse* (Oxford: Oxford University Press, 2002).
84. This section appears to be accidentally omitted from the manuscript; it is found in Family B2. The homeoteleuton (due to the reiteration of the word להטביע) is partially restored in MS War 374, a copy of our MS; it then leaves space for what the scribe correctly considered to be additional missing text. Recension A contains the omitted words and also a rhetorical strategy by Uza, who declares that God is called righteous and upright, never demonstrating injustice or favoritism – thus hoping to prevent Israel from advantage in this case.

    Having unsuccessfully argued for continued Israelite enslavement in the previous pericope, Uza brings a second dispute, hoping to forestall judgment against the Egyptians.
85. Given that MS War 374, Family B2 and Recension A all have נטלו (took) in place of בטלו (nullified), and that our scribe uses נטלו at the end of the sentence, the appearance of בטלו here is deemed an error.
86. Two letters are transposed: פלמיא instead of the correct פמליא.
87. Many manuscripts of Recension A have דיינין in place of שפטו, but they both mean "judge." MSS Wolf 36.25, Vat 303 and Prm 2736 (as well as Const 1519A) say, "Then I will judge," relegating the heavenly retinue to a role as proctor rather than arbiter.
88. In Recension A, באמת is clearly attached to the previous thought: Judge Me honestly (even though I am God). Although it is the preferred rendering, the additional space before the word, which the scribe for MS Paris 716 often uses to indicate the end of a "sentence," suggests the translation given for this text.

    The prefixed *bet* is crossed out and a small *mem* (possibly in a different hand) is written above.
89. Many manuscripts of Recension A continue, "thundering against My name." *Tanḥ. Vaera 5:5, Ex. Rab. 5:14* imagine that Moses and Aaron have arrived on the day during which Pharaoh receives ambassadors (using the Greek term *prozbotai*), with all of the expected ceremony. A number of other midrashim also relate aspects of this appearance by Moses and Aaron before Pharaoh: *Chronicles of Moses* (Eis 360), *Alpha-beta d'Rabbi Akiva: Koof* (Eis 422), and *Sefer haYashar 79*.
90. The minor emendation is based on MSS War 374 and MS Family B2. Recension A has: לא ידעתי אותו, I don't know him.

    In *Quran 28:38–40*, Pharaoh claims to know no god for the Israelites other than himself. For this arrogance, the text explains, he is cast into the sea.
91. It appears to be בנקביו (in his orifices) in the MS. It should read בפנקסיו, from the Greek word *pinaks,* tablet, as do all the other manuscript families of Recension B. It is probable that the Greek term was not familiar to the scribe; it seems unlikely (although fun to imagine) that this copy of the midrash deliberately portrays Pharaoh in a perverse way that could crudely but appropriately be rendered, "He looked up his ass for the records but didn't find anything." The scribe of MS War

374 felt the text was not correct and left a blank space. *Yal. Shimoni 181* has an episode in which Pharaoh needs to move his bowels (הוצרך פרעה לנקביו) just before he challenges Moses and Aaron regarding this god who has not sent any tribute; perhaps the confusion is somehow related to this passage. Rabbinic literature imagines that Pharaoh pretended, as a "god," never to need to relieve himself; see, e.g. *Tanh. Vaera 14, Ex. Rab. 9:8.*

92. It would make better sense if it said he found no record of God's name or sending a gift, as does Recension A.
93. The dialogue does not make sense without the addition, which is found in MS Family B2 and Const 1519B.
94. Cf. Isa 19:11 which derides the idiocy of Pharaoh's advisors with these words. צדק (righteous) is not in the other manuscripts, and has slashes above it in MS Par 716.
95. See Ezek 29:3, cited explicitly in Recension A. The condemnation of Pharaoh for believing himself to be a god is a recurring midrashic motif. See, e.g., *Mek. Shir 8* (HR 142:16ff.).
96. Our MS presents a word that looks like Him (בו) rather than Me (בי), but the preferred reading is supported by the other MSS.
97. The midrash may presume a connection because Pharaoh denied God as Creator, who fashioned the world with ten utterances as in *m. Avot 5:1*; Pharaoh's sin is requited with ten plagues, measure for measure. The idea that God will drown the supposed creator of the Nile in a body of water also has a certain poetic justice.
98. Conceivably, the royal we, even though arguing before the heavenly court, which normally comprises the plural. Possibly God and Michael, or the Hebrews.
99. The word is misspelled again, although differently than its first appearance; given that this is the second Greek term confused by the scribe, it is likely he did not know Greek – not even the limited vocabulary found in rabbinic texts.
100. Rabbinic tradition frequently invokes the dialectical aspects of Divine mercy and justice/judgment, identifying both as essential qualities of the Most High. The passage focuses on an affirmation of Divine judgment against the Egyptians (and their advocate). The Israelites' faith in God and in Moses stands in sharp contrast to Pharaoh's challenge.
101. Uza's rhetorical strategy, announcing from the outset God's reputation for integrity, seems effective. Here, God specifically charges the angels to judge Him honestly – presumably guarding against the tendency to take God's side automatically.
102. A reference to the indenture of Egyptians as they sold their property in exchange for the stored food. This fine point is neglected in Recension B.
103. MS Families A2 and AB2 add a more extensive challenge by Pharaoh for God to declare his royal merits (how many countries does he rule, how many wars has he fought and won, etc.), and a longer list of attributes by Moses and Aaron. MS Parma 2736 has a similar expansion in its Targum for the Torah reading.

    In MS Family AB2, God offers a parable portraying the nations as a foolish servant who goes to find his priestly master in a cemetery, teaching that a living God (the Kohen) would not be found among these lifeless idols (the dead bodies). It also offers the challenge for God to declare his royal merits and expands on Pharaoh's assertion of self-reliance. The MS family is similar to parallels in *Tanh. Vaera 5:5, Ex. Rab. 5:14.*
104. The Ezekiel verse could also be understood to say, *I made myself*. The Isaiah verse which provides the foundation for the advisors' response is more fully cited in MS Families A1-ק and A2. The latter texts continue with a dramatic refutation by God:

"Surely the princes of Zoan are fools, the counsel of the wise counsellors of Pharaoh have become stupid. How can you say to Pharaoh [that] I am the son of sages, the scion of Kedemite kings (Isa 19:11)? I answered from the heights of heaven, 'What idiots there are in the world! You call yourselves sages and call Me the son of sages?! By your lives, I will destroy your wisdom,' as it is said: *The Lord has mixed within her a spirit of distortion [which shall lead Egypt astray in all her undertakings, as a drunken man staggers in his vomit]; Egypt has been led astray by the chiefs of her tribes* (Isa 19:14, 13)."

105. There is a very close parallel in *Yal. Shimoni 241*, following Recension A almost verbatim; Isaac Shiloni indicates in his notes on *Yalkut Shimoni* (II: 301) that the source is MV, even though the manuscript evidence is not specific and later printings name *Midrash Avkir* as the source. It contains the narrative of Pharaoh's court as part of God's testimony against Uza before the heavenly tribunal.
106. Ofra Meir offers a useful discussion of "The Story as a Hermeneutic Device," *AJS Review 7* (1982): 231–62.
107. Hasan-Rokem, *Tales of the Neighborhood: Jewish Narrative Dialogues in Late Antiquity* (Berkeley: University of California Press, 2003), 2.
108. Emphasis on his intransigence here highlights the dramatic power of his eventual repentance; see exegesis on Ex 15:6, 11.
109. Naomi Schor, *Reading in Detail* (NY: Methuen, 1987), 122. Many scholars of narrative theory have sketched some version of this literary element, e.g. Wolfgang Iser's implied reader, Gerald Prince's narratee, etc. The closest parallel is perhaps David Stern's analysis of the rabbinic parable (mashal), in which he discusses the implied interpreter. See Stern, *Parables in Midrash*, 87.
110. MS Family A1 begins by emphasizing God's personal involvement, although it eventually arrives at very similar exegesis. Other manuscript families convey a very different exegesis; see Commentary.
111. Because Moses and Israel are described as singing but the actual song begins in the first-person singular form, the midrash may be responding to this crux by presenting a debate about who will sing first. There are discussions in rabbinic literature of how the song was recited, e.g., *b. Sotah 30b*, but I did not find a direct parallel. The mutual deference shown by Moses and Israel in leading the song stands in a slightly expanded form at the beginning Recension A 15:2, which specifies that Israel and Moses ultimately sing together. Cf. *Mek. Shir 1* (HR 116).

    MV also demonstrates its larger contextual consciousness here, recognizing the recurrent use of water and birth imagery of Exodus 1–15, and linking it to a tale of miraculous Israelite births.
112. MS War 374 has על in place of עד, an appropriate correction.
113. Other MSS: בידינו, in our hands.
114. Recension A uses the synonymous phrase: מתאספים עדרים ונכנסנו, gather in large groups and we entered.... The change in Recension B is most likely the result of having lost its exegetical origins. Avigdor Shinan, "מדרשת הפסוק אל האגדה החופשית: פרק בתולדות הסיפור המקראי המורחב [From Exegesis of a Verse to Free-standing Aggadah: A Chapter in the History of the Expanded Biblical Narrative]," *Mech'k'rei Yerushalayim b'sifrut ivrit* 5 (1984): 208–10, theorizes that many of the motifs within the narrative trace back to the extended metaphor in Ezekiel 16, with the midrashist actualizing each element in a narrative-historical context. See Commentary.

115. Cf. *Targ. Pseudo-Jonathan Ex 15:1–2, Fragment-Targ. op. cit., b. Sotah 11b, Pirqe R. El. 42, Ex. Rab. 1:12, 23:8, Deut. Rab. Lieberman 14–15, Pesiq. Rab. 47, Tibat Marqe 4:73.*
116. Cf. Recension B at 15:4.
117. The brief invocation of Abraham's merit is suggestive of the later expanded narrative in Recension B *ad* 14:30. Here, it stands at what appears as a subtle seam, with an entirely different train of thought that follows – namely the exegesis found for this verse in Recension B.
118. This motif is found at least as early as the *Mek. Shir 1* (HR 120:16ff), which also goes on to specify the reasons for which Israel is moved to glorify God. In MS Prm 2736, the fetuses use a standard blessing formula. See Gwynn Kessler, *Conceiving Israel: The Fetus in Rabbinic Narratives* (Philadelphia: University of Pennsylvania Press, 2009), for additional discussion of the fetuses singing God's praise.
119. The text has an indecipherable word; the substitute is based on other MSS.
120. This recension is closer to the *b. Sotah 11b* parallel than the later redaction of MV, including the notion that the Egyptians plough the birthing ground in search of the newborns (similarly, *Chronicles of Moses* (Eis 356)). Parallels in *Lekaḥ Tov Ex. 1:14, Yal. Shimoni 164, Yal. Shimoni Ezek 354, Sekhel Tov Ex 2* lead up to Ex 15:2, *This is my God and I will enshrine Him, <u>the God of my father</u>, and I will exalt Him.* Perhaps prompted by the parallel structure, they understand the second part of the verse to be spoken in the voice of the newborn. The parallel in *Deut. Rab.* (Lieberman 14–15) indicates exegetical grounding in the word זה (this), pointing as they indicate: *This is my God.*
121. As explicated in the *b.Sotah* parallel, the return of the groups (עדרים) is "proven" by Ezekiel 16:7: "*You continued to grow up until you came into womanhood* (בעדי עדים, an unusual Hebrew phrase). Don't read בעדי עדים, but rather בעדרי עדרים." See Commentary.
122. Recension A utilizes the second part of the verse as the conclusion of the lemma; its emphatic doubling of the verb ג-א-ה (triumph, be exalted) reflects the wondrous aspects of God's salvific power in Egypt and at the sea. Rashbam explicates: He has triumphed over the *proud* – utilizing another meaning of the root which also fits this narrative of God subverting Egyptian efforts to murder Israelite newborns, and saving the people from being forcibly returned to Egyptian servitude. Robert Alter, *The Five Books of Moses* (New York: W.W. Norton, 2004), 397, illuminates a different pun; ג-א-ה refers also to the rising tide of the sea, making it especially apt as the action by which God vanquishes the Egyptians with surging waters.
123. Recension A relates that Pharaoh's daughter later puts a golden *chain* (רביד) *around his neck* (v. 11). Cf. Gen 41:42, in which a golden chain marks Joseph's appointment as vizier.
124. The images of God clothing, bathing and providing shoes are repeated, with prooftexts from Ezekiel, in the interpretation of Ex 15:17. There, Moses contrasts God with a human king, for the latter would expect his servants to provide for him.
125. Shinan, "מדרשת הפסוק אל האגדה החופשית [From Exegesis of a Verse to Free-standing Aggadah,]" 203–220. On the other hand, Ofra Meir asserts that the purpose of extending darshanic stories in later rabbinic literature is not for a literary aesthetic, but in order to unify the disparate elements of tradition, ""הסיפור ה"דרשני במדרש קדום ומאוחר [The Darshanic Story in Early and Late Midrash]," *Sinai* 86 (1980): 266. For a thorough treatment of Ezekiel 16 in rabbinic literature, see

Gerhard Bodendorfer, *Das Drama des Bundes: Ezechiel 16 in rabbinischer Perspektive* (Freiberg im Breisgau: Herder, 1997).

126. *Ex. Rab.* explicitly cites Song 5:10, and *Deut. Rab.* simply describes a young man with beautiful curls, as pictured in Song 5:11.
127. "This" is often understood in rabbinic thought to accompany a gesture, and other texts imagine Israelites pointing to God at this juncture in the Song at the Sea. See, e.g., *Mek. Shir 3* (HR 126–7).
128. The pericope begins as does MS Family A1, celebrating the fact that God attends personally to the people's salvation at the sea.
129. Cf. *Mek. Shir 1* (HR 116).
130. The common midrashic reading of the verse renders literally the unusual אשדת into two words, making one noun the modifier of the other: *fiery law*.
131. The midrash conflates Ex 13:16 and Deut 6:8 (unless the redactor's text was different than the masoretic text). Still, the familiar rabbinic methodology of *notarikon* is clear; the unusual spelling of ידכה is divided into two words (and expanded).
132. The relationship to "front" is self-evident. Cf. *Mek. Beshallaḥ 6* (HR 112), *Ex. Rab. 4:3, Song Rab. 1:4, Yal. Shimoni 238.*
133. The mare motif appears in Recension B in 15:9 and is discussed there.
134. NJPS: "my strength and my might."
135. See Commentary for a discussion of Miriam's prophecy.
136. The MS paraphrases Ex 2:3–4, preserving the first person voice of the narrative.
137. *B. Sotah 12b* offers a different motivation for Pharaoh's daughter to go to the river: to cleanse herself of her father's idols, i.e. to convert (similarly, *Ex. Rab. 1:23*). *Pirqe R. El. 48* suggests she was afflicted with skin ailments and needed the cool water of the river; when she reached out to touch Moses, she was healed. *Tanḥ. Shemot 7, Yal. Shimoni 166* offer both of these alternative interpretations.

    While MV emphasizes God's saving power in motivating Pharaoh's daughter to be at the right place at the right time, the Talmud suggests the young woman's righteousness, and *Pirqe R. El.* focuses on Moses' miraculous gifts.
138. *B. Sotah 12b* elaborates: The handmaidens urged her to kill the infant, arguing that at least the members of Pharaoh's household should observe the decree. (See also *Ex. Rab. 1:23.*)
139. *B. Sotah 12b* explains that Moses is unwilling to suckle from an Egyptian woman because he is destined to speak with God. For similar reasons, *Tanḥ. Shemot 7* and *Ex. Rab. 1:25* note Moses does not suckle even though it is halakhically permissible (*b.ʿAbod. Zar. 26a*). *Chronicles of Moses* (Eis 358) imagines a series of Egyptian nurses attempting to suckle Moses; similarly *Quran 28:12*.
140. There is a longstanding tradition that the Egyptians had predicted a savior would be born for Israel, in some cases divined by the magicians and in others learned from one of Pharaoh's dreams. Early versions do not include a subsequent test; instead they appear to explain why Pharaoh commands the drowning of male Israelite infants at birth (e.g., Josephus *Antiquities II:205–7, Targ. Pseudo-Jonathan Ex 1:15*, the poem אזדעזע עלמה in *Fragment Targums ad* Ex 12:1). It might seem counterintuitive to order such a radical diminishment of Egypt's slave labor force. *B. Sotah 11a* notes that Ex 1:10 speaks of a single entity, *Let us deal shrewdly with him/it*, which opens the door to imagining an individual figure. Cf. *Pirqe R. El. 48, Chronicles of Moses, Ex. Rab. 1:18.*

141. *B. Sotah 11a* mentions Jethro as an advisor to Pharaoh, along with Balaam and Job. Balaam is slain for agreeing with Pharaoh's plan to kill all the infant sons, and Job is afflicted with suffering for silently acquiescing. Jethro, however, is rewarded for fleeing and refusing to be part of the plan; his descendants sit at the Chamber of Hewn Stone. (A similar passage can be found in *b. Sanh. 106a, Ex. Rab. 1:9.*) Josephus asserts that Pharaoh's daughter saves Moses without such a test, and MS Family AB2 appears to meld the traditions so that Jethro uses her love as part of his argument in persuading Pharaoh to administer the test (thus avoiding summary judgment). See also Judith Baskin, *Pharaoh's Counselors: Job, Jethro and Balaam in Rabbinic and Patristic Tradition* (Brown Judaic Studies 47; Chico, Calif.: Scholars Press, 1983).
142. A ת is missing in the MS, but the emendation is supported by other MSS.
143. Reference to Ex 6:12, 30 – generally understood as a speech impediment. *Ex. Rab. 1:26* presents a very similar narrative and exegesis. *Chronicles of Moses* is slightly different: When Moses takes the crown, Balaam reminds Pharaoh of the dream he had regarding Israel's redeemer and advises Pharaoh to cut off Moses' head. Gabriel is sent by God in the guise of an Egyptian advisor, suggesting a test similar to Jethro's but with a precious stone in place of the gold coin.
144. MS has נשאתי, presumed to be a scribal error. Theoretically, it could be intended as נשאתי את עיני (I lifted up my eyes) or a misspelling of נסעתי (I journeyed), but the preferred reading is יצאתי (I went out), as found in other MSS.
145. Ex 2:11, except for preserving the first person voice of the midrash.
146. Similarly, *Chronicles of Moses* (Eis 358), *Ex. Rab. 1:31.* The former presents the catalyst for this narrative motif, Ex 18:4: *And the other [son] was named Eliezer, meaning, "The God of my father was my help, and He delivered me from the sword of Pharaoh."* The latter presents an explicit crux: How did Moses escape from Pharaoh? Cf. *y.Ber. 9:1 (13a), Tanḥ. Shemot 10, Mek. Yitro 1* (HR 192:8ff), *Mek. R. Shimon b. Yohai 18:2.* Stith Thompson's *Motif Index of Folk Literature* (D2072.1, D2086.1) has similar motifs, with the sword dulled or otherwise rendered useless against the hero.
147. Jethro does not throw Moses in jail until the drama unfolds. Although the statement may serve as foreshadowing to build suspense, it may also reveal a literary seam in the evolution of the text. Recension A, which lacks the test of retrieving the staff, has Moses imprisoned upon meeting Jethro – presumably for slaying the taskmaster (similarly *Chronicles of Moses* (Eis 359).
148. Our MS has אביו (his father), which is clearly incorrect. The emendation is based on other MSS of Recension B and Const 1519B.
149. Each Hebrew letter of the acronym represents the first letter of one of the plagues, organized in the order of their narration in Exodus. (Ps 88 relates the plagues in a different sequence.) Cf. *Sif. Deut. 301, Haggadah shel Pesah, Ex. Rab. 8:3.* Other sources mention the Explicit Name of God engraved on the staff; see, e.g. *Pesiq. R. Kah. 19, Deut. Rab. 3:8.*
150. MS Family B2 and Const 1519B add: "ויגמול שקדים והניחו שם, and brought forth almonds. So he left it there." Note the biblical allusion to Num 17, in which Aaron's staff blossoms overnight when challenged to prove he is chosen for priestly leadership.
151. The midrash uses a first-person rendering of Ex 2:19, including the biblical doubling with an infinitive absolute.

152. *Ex. Rab. 1:32* similarly notes that Moses is described as an Egyptian by Jethro's daughters, but explains how they made the error rather than discussing the repercussions for Moses. Cf. *Deut. Rab. 2:8*, which contrasts Moses with Joseph; the latter *does* claim his ancestry and therefore merits burial in the Land of Israel.
153. The closest parallel (and possible source) is *Pirqe R. El. 40*. Cf. *S. Eli. Rab. 2, Targum Pseudo-Jonathan Ex 2:21, 4:20, Chronicles of Moses* (Eis 359–60). Although Western readers likely hear echoes of the King Arthur romance with his claiming of Excalibur, passages actually dealing with Moses and the staff can be found in the *qiṣaṣ al-anbiya* (Lives of the Prophets) literature of Islam; a related tradition can also be found in the thirteenth-century Syriac work by Solomon Bishop of Basra, *The Book of the Bee*, Chapter 30. See Commentary.
154. Other MSS, including War 374, have "sages of Egypt." There are traditions of Israelite expectations of the redeemer; Josephus *Antiquities II:215–17*, for example, recounts a vision given to Amram.
155. *Sefer haYashar 76–77* recounts a similar tale of imprisonment during which he is sustained by Zipporah. After his release, he finds a sapphire staff in the garden of Jethro; it has the name of God engraved on it and was passed down a similar chain from Adam to Joseph. Although other men have tried to dislodge it in order to win Zipporah's hand, Moses is the only one who can do it. Thus it becomes evidence of his merit rather than his dangerous power.
156. MS Family B2: בכל יום ויום, Every single day – probably a better reading.
157. The rabbinic trope of kissing a person on the head is a common shorthand for indicating approval, frequently with a measure of delighted surprise. See, e.g. *m. Roš Haš. 2:9, t. Ḥag. 2:1.*
158. MS Family B2 (except JTS 4998) and Const 1519B: ישמאלים, Ishmaelite. In the Bible, Jethro is identified as Midianite and in the midrash he is an advisor in the Egyptian court. Midianite and Ishmaelite identities are conflated in Gen 37:28, slightly confusing who rescues Joseph from the pit. The midrashic mention of Ishmael is possibly influenced by the presence of Islam, perhaps a covert polemic: Although Muslims do circumcise their sons, some Islamic traditions dictate the procedure be done at age 13, so the infant would not yet have been circumcised – and God clearly does not approve.
159. Troubled by the idea that someone as great as Moses failed to circumcise his son, the midrash offers an ingenious explanation: The temporary lapse was due to an unavoidable deal with Jethro, and Moses' own horror at the prospect led him to take drastic action. See Commentary for the exegetical background of this tradition.

    Among the Church Fathers, there is a tendency to blame Zipporah for preventing the circumcision; see *Ephraem I:200, Aphraat 110*; her valorization in MV is more appealing, but the Christian exegesis adds an interesting tone to Zipporah's exclamation about Moses being a bridegroom of blood.
160. Although the biblical context suggests that it is God who assaults Moses (Ex 4:24), the attacker is identified merely as "he," thus enabling the many interpretations (including the Septuagint translation) which describe an angel or demon of some sort.
161. "Leg" is likely a euphemism for his sexual organ.
162. See Commentary for discussion of Zipporah's unusual exclamation. See also, Geza Vermès, *Scripture and Tradition in Judaism* (Leiden: E.J. Brill, 1961), 178–92, with numerous translations and interpretations from antiquity.

    The more fully developed portrayal of Zipporah and other women prompted

Stemberger to speculate that women may have been in the audience at times when MV was presented ("Midráš Wa-yoša'," 18). Alternatively, Charlotte Fonrobert highlights the conservative function of aggadic midrash. For all the possibilities of "filling in the missing voices of women in biblical literature," it would be a mistake to overlook the fact that the androcentric universe which produced these texts generally directs expanded portraits toward traditional supportive roles ("The Handmaid, the Trickster, and the Birth of the Messiah," in *Current Trends in the Study of Midrash* (ed. Carol Bakhos; Leiden: Brill, 2006), 245–75). Even Zipporah's decisive actions serve such a function: to protect this man Moses who is special for reasons personal and Divine.

163. Several texts identify Dathan and Abiram as the two Hebrews who were struggling in Ex 2:13. See, e.g., *Targ. Pseudo-Jonathan 2:13–14, Pirqe R. El. 48, Ex. Rab. 1:29.*
164. The first-person singular nature of this verse in the Song provides a natural catalyst for recounting God's saving power in Moses' life. Recension A records a *very* abbreviated form of the stories about Moses' life before his mission.
165. The motif of mutual deference is found in Recension B *ad* Ex 15:1. As presented here, it still serves as exegesis of that verse, even though it is located in the subsequent pericope. It explains how "Moses and Israel" sang with a singular verb; they sang together as one.
166. Cf. Joseph's appointment as vizier, when he receives from Pharaoh fine clothes and a golden chain on his neck, Gen 41:42.
167. A parallel in *Chronicles of Moses* and *Sefer haYashar 70* adds a speech by Balaam that claims the child surely knew what he was doing because he is a Hebrew, citing patriarchal biographies to support his point. Cf. *Lekah Tov Ex 4:10*, *Yal. Shimoni 166.*
168. "Reader" stands for the recipient of the material, although it may well have frequently been in oral form.
169. See also the illumination in the Venice Haggadah (1609) of husband and wife in separate beds, abstaining from sexual relations (Online: http://www.library.yale .edu /judaica/site/exhibits/venicehaggadah/images/HVenice8.jpg).
170. *Ex. Rab. 1:12, Yal. Shimoni 165* are similar, although the argument about two worlds is replaced with one which posits that Amram's decree is more likely to be fulfilled because he is righteous. Miriam's advice is referenced again in *Ex. Rab. 1:19*. Further on in *b. Sotah (12b–13a)*, it does mention Miriam's prophecy that her mother will bear a son who is to become the savior of Israel. See also: *Chronicles of Moses,* which contains a strong parallel to many aspects of this lemma, and *y. Sotah 1:9 (17b), Mek. Shir 10* (HR 151), *Mid. Prov 14, Ex. Rab. 1:22.*
171. Joshua Levinson, "Dialogical Reading in the Rabbinic Exegetical Narrative," 508.
172. Some rabbinic texts, such as *Tanh Shemot 8*, incorporate only the symbolism of taking Pharaoh's crown as an allusion to his eventual downfall; Moses does not set the crown on his own head (which might be interpreted as seeking to rule in his stead). In Josephus, Moses stomps on the crown after Pharaoh places it on his head, but the Egyptians decide not to kill Moses because they presume he might be intended to inherit the throne (*Antiquities 2:232–37*).

    It is interesting that the extended legend is not found in rabbinic sources until a rather late period. In medieval Jewish texts, however, the motif is quite popular, e.g. *Ex. Rab. 1:26, Chronicle of Moses, Yal. Shimoni 166, Sefer haYashar 70, Lekah Tov Ex 4:10*. David Flusser, "*Palaea Historica:* An Unknown Source of Biblical

Legends," *Scripta Hierosolymitana* 22 (1977): 67, speculates about its likely origins in Jewish Hellenistic literature. *Palaea Historica*, a Byzantine Christian work, resembles Josephus at the beginning but includes the test (without the culminating exegesis). The theme is also found in the Armenian Apocrypha, *History of Moses* as cited in James Kugel, *The Bible as it Was* (Cambridge, Mass.: Belknap Press, 1997), 298.

173. This detail is not in Recension A, or in the textual witnesses from Late Antiquity. It is found in most of the medieval parallels, suggestive of the broader embrace of supernatural elements; its incorporation here, however, becomes part of the homiletical persuasion.
174. Jeffrey Rubenstein makes a similar point about Talmudic stories: *Talmudic Stories: Narrative Art, Composition, and Culture* (Baltimore: Johns Hopkins University Press, 1999), 2.
175. Zornberg, *The Particulars of Rapture: Reflections on Exodus* (New York: Doubleday, 2001), 90. She cites Robert Paul, *Moses and Civilization* (New Haven: Yale University Press, 1996), 79.
176. The latter problem is attested in *Deut. Rab. 2:8* as well, which contrasts Moses with Joseph. Because Joseph *does* claim his Hebrew ancestry, he merits burial in the Land of Israel.
177. Similarly, *Yal. Shimoni 169*. The *Mekhilta* compares the appearance of the word here to I Sam 14:24, where it is generally understood as an oath. Rashi cites a related tradition in which Jethro forces Moses to swear that he will not take his family and leave Midian without his father-in-law's permission. This fits the context of the verse better, yielding the translation: *And Moses swore to dwell with the man, so he gave his daughter Zipporah to Moses* (Ex 2:21). Cf. *Targ. Pseudo-Jonathan Ex 4:24, Fragment-Targums (P) Ex 4:25, Sefer haYashar 79.*
178. *Sefer Kolbo 52* (see Introduction).
179. This principle is most clearly conveyed in MV by the somewhat confusing juxtaposition of Abraham's prayer and the cloud that protects Israel from the Egyptians in the exegesis of Ex 15:4.
180. Vitz, *Medieval Narrative and Modern Narratology,* (New York: NYU Press, 1989), 112–19, 176–212.
181. See Joseph Dan, *הסיפור העברי בימי הביניים [The Hebrew Story in the Middle Ages]*, 60.
182. al-Tabari, *History of al-Tabari: The Children of Israel,* 3:45; al-Thalabi, *Lives of the Prophets*, 292–94; al-Kisai, *Tales of the Prophets*, 222. See also Brannon Wheeler's discussion of the rod motif in al-Zamakhshari (1074–1143) and other Islamic exegetes (*Moses in the Quran and Islamic Exegesis* (London: Routledge Curzon, 2002), 59–63).

    Roderick Beaton, in his study of the medieval romance genre in Greece, *The Medieval Greek Romance* (London: Routledge, 1996), 20, 32–4, identifies tales of romance and adventure in the Eastern Mediterranean with story themes from Arabic and Persian literature dating from the eighth–twelfth centuries. One motif that he mentions (from *Digenes, Akrites*, c. 1100) is that of a girl who warns that her father threatens suitors with death.
183. Eli Yassif, *The Hebrew Folktale*, 79.
184. טכסיס, from the Greek: ταξις (lit: order). See Commentary for discussion of these battle plans. Note also the exegesis begins by invoking the rabbis rather the sages; it is the only instance.

There are strong parallels in *Tanḥ. Bo 4, Tanḥ. B. Bo 4–6* and *Yal. Shimoni 182*: comparisons to a king at war, matching Egyptian afflictions measure for measure, and prophecies against Edom. (The *Yalkut*, however, identifies a vague future enemy rather than Edom, and it does not include the final statement about striking the gods/idols first.) *Pesiq. Rab Kah. 7:11, Pesiq. Rab. 17* are more approximate to the MV text, and contain only the first and third of these sets. Cf. *Pesiq. Rab. Supplement 1:2, Lekaḥ Tov Ex 11:9, Song Rab. 1:49, Ex. Rab. 15:27,* Torah commentary of R. Baḥya b. Asher.

185. לגיונות (legion), from the Greek/Latin: λεγεων = *legio*. This term is used both to describe the most common contingent of foot soldiers, and as a general term for troops of all sorts (Samuel Krauss, *פרס ורומי בתלמוד ובמדרשים [Persia and Rome in Talmud and Midrash]* (Jerusalem: Mosad haRav Kook, 1948), 174).
186. MS Family B2 and Const 1519B have the preferred reading, "surround," while our MS has מוסיפין (add).
187. The nineteenth-century Prussian commentator on *Tanḥuma*, R. Chanoch Zundel b'Rav Yosef (Etz Yosef) states that these קלאנים are בעלי קול, masters of voice, presumably interpreted as people whose job it is to make noise (criers). Cf. *Sefer Arukh haShalem* ק-ל-ן and קילוני. From Joshua's trumpets at Jericho to modern stun grenades, the potential power of noise as a weapon is well documented.
188. Krauss, *Griechische und lateinische Lehnwörter im Talmud, Midrasch und Targum [Greek and Latin Loanwords in Talmud, Midrash and Targum]* (Berlin: S. Calvary, 1898), refers the listing דורמסיאות to אנדרולומוסיא (Greek: ανδρολημψια), defined as "epidemic," a mass death of innocent and guilty alike. Similarly, *Sefer Arukh haShalem*, listed under דרלמוס.

    Wies-Campagner, *Midrasch Wajoscha*, 272, proposes a different definition, "spear carrier," presumably a Hebrew derivative of the Greek δοριμηστω (lit: master of the spear). Roman and medieval warfare strategy included ranks of soldiers in a strategic formation, with spear carriers in the middle.
189. Recension A aligns the human and divine assaults so God's actions immediately follow the human example, and its list is complete. It does not continue with the other two lists (parallel Egyptian cruelties, or comparable plagues that will strike Edom).
190. In MS Prm 2736, the narrator marvels that the same vessel of liquid provided water to an Israelite, but turned to blood for an Egyptian who tried to drink from it. A similar comment is found in MS Family AB2 at Ex 15:7. Cf. *Ex. Rab. 9:10.*
191. Recension A adds that the frogs' croaking was especially difficult for them, a detail found in Recension B at Ex 15:7. The *Tanḥuma* parallel states that the croaking of the frogs was worse than the destruction they wrought, and R. Shimon b. Tzemaḥ comments that the emphasis on the *sound* of the frogs suggests word play between דבר (plague) and דבור (utterance). A unique detail is found in MS Prm 2736: When a person would speak to his fellow, a frog would answer from within the fellow's gut.
192. MS Family AB2 substitutes the biblical phrase, *fire and brimstone*, for the Greek loan-word. Naphtha has been a tool of siege-craft since the Assyrian empire; the parallel with boils is apt, because they also burn and water provides no relief.

    Recension A transcribes the word as נפט, and Recension B substitutes a ב for the פ; since there is no voiceless bilabial stop ("p" sound) in Arabic, this substitution is a common Arabism (even though there is an "f" phoneme and the actual Arabic cognate is *neft*). In several manuscripts, the ט at the end is replaced with a ז, a shift also found occasionally in Arabic-influenced Hebrew.

193. MS Prm 2736 expands on the miraculous notion that Moses can throw a handful of dust into the air and it can result in boils spread for hundreds of miles; MS Family AB2 does the same at Ex 15:7.
194. בליסטרא (*ballistra*) probably refers to the Roman-style ballista, a catapult for firing stones or arrows commonly used in siege tactics. MSS Vat 303 and Drm 25 substitute אבני ליטריות (litra-weight stones), perhaps not recognizing the military loan-word.
195. The marginal insertion is underscored by ל"א (לשנא אחרינא\לשון אחר, alternative wording) suggesting the editor-scribe had an additional manuscript.
196. The emendation is based on MS War 374, which added the obvious completion of the parallels to the gapped text.
197. The emendation is based on MS Family B2 and Const 1519B. Although our MS has עזבו (they abandoned) here, it uses חשבו (they thought) in the rest of the section.
198. פרגמטיהם might more conventionally be translated "merchandise," related to the Greek term, πραγματεια (trade, trade goods); see, for instance, *b. Shab. 127b*. Later manuscripts of MV add the verb "carry," so that the common denotation makes sense. The midrash may imagine Israelites conducting market business, as servants in the Middle Ages often were. "Go-fer" suggests the running to and fro required, whether selling or toting the goods, to parallel the frogs dancing about.
199. As in MS Family B2, Const 1519B.
200. Frequently, the swarm (ערוב) is imagined as one of flies or other insects (e.g. Septuagint, Vulgate, Philo, and many modern commentaries). There is a tannaitic dispute recorded in *Ex. Rab. 11:4*, in which R. Nehemiah claims the plague consisted of flies, and R. Yehudah insists the swarm was one of wild beasts; most Jewish medieval writings reflect the latter opinion. Rashi, Rashbam, ibn Ezra, Radak, and the targums describe various collections of wild beasts.
201. Four words, משפטים במים לפיכ' שקע – judgments in water, so He sunk...., are marked as an error. The dittography is most likely due to the reappearance of the word מישראל in the next line where the words belong.
202. *S. Eli. Rab. 8* has an extended discussion of the Egyptian cruelties that made them liable for each of the plagues. Other texts mention the concept of certain plagues being "measure for measure," but do not recite the list. *Pirqe R. El. 48*, for instance, equates the death of the first-born with the midrashic notion that the Egyptians burned the Israelite first-born children alive (with Deut 4:20 as prooftext). See Commentary *ad* 15:7 on the concept of measure for measure.

    Using the close parallels in *Tanḥ. Bo 4, Tanḥ. B. Bo 5, Yal. Shimoni 182*, it is possible to surmise associations missing here in MV: 1) Boils – the Egyptians made Israel heat their water/be their bath attendants, 2) Hail – they stoned the Israelites, 3) Locusts – they made Israel be their vinedressers, 4) Darkness – they imprisoned the Israelites, 5) First-born – they killed the Israelites. Cf. MV at 15:7.
203. MS Family B2 and Const 1519B frequently insert "the wicked" as a modifier for Edom; here, they also add: כשנעקר, when it will be uprooted. Wies-Campagner notes the typological significance of Edom as archetype for Christianity, *Midrasch Wajoscha*, 321.
204. Isa 34:7 identifies "a great slaughter against Edom." The chapter is cited three times in this chain of parallels; other prophecies used as prooftexts are directed to

Gog, to Egypt or to a general audience, but they invoke the messianic tones of "on that day," etc.

205. In addition to the parallel overtaking of the land by animals, note the similar root: עָרוֹב (swarm) and עֹרֵב (raven).

206. The midrash groups locusts with other winged creatures. In the biblical verse, the animals are invited to dine on the flesh and blood of warriors whom God will defeat in the future.

207. The emendation is based on MS Family B2; the Isaiah verse fragment does not make sense without the addition.

תהו ובהו – chaos and emptiness describes the darkness and nothingness that pervaded the world before creation.

208. The previous verse, Ezek 32:29, similarly clarifies the parallel to the death of the first-born (here "chieftains"): *Edom is there, her kings and all her chieftains who, for all their might, are laid among those who are slain by the sword.*

209. Two letters are transposed so that it actually reads "tents," but the word is crossed out and "gods" is written in the margin in what appears to be a different hand.

210. The "battles" God wages against Egypt and Edom (Parts I and III) make apt analogies to a man of war, enhanced by the association between specific battle technologies and the ten plagues. The justification of the plagues (Part II) in this lemma makes less exegetical sense here; it is repeated in expanded form at Ex 15:7.

This three-part association of plagues with Divine actions, not found in Recension A, is most likely influenced by the identical sequence in the *Tanḥuma.* Wies-Campagner, *Midrasch Wajoscha*, 397, suggests reading Edom as part of an anti-Christian polemic. Present in both *Tanḥuma* texts and built on biblical imagery in Isaiah, however, the messianic anticipation of vindication against imperial forces need not be that specific.

211. בורקינוס is a Greek loan word, βυκινος (Lat: *buccina*) for trumpet.

212. קורסיין (here and in MS Cam 667.1) most likely should be קרקרין or קרקורן as in other MSS. Using the biblical root (v. Isa 46:2), it could conceivably be rendered "who made them cower [in fear] of them."

Recension B 15:7 similarly states that the frogs constitute an especially difficult plague; one possible exegetical catalyst for this relative judgment is that Moses "cries out" (צ-ע-ק) to God for relief from the frogs, and this term is not used for other plagues (see Etz Yosef on *Tanh. Bo 4*). MS Family A2 states: Hearing the frogs was more difficult than hearing human criers and horns.

213. According to the Brown-Driver-Briggs lexicon (צֵן), A.A. Bevan proposes "barbed spears" as the meaning in another context.

214. The verb מתערבין literally means "mix it up" and operates as a word play on the name of the plague itself ערוב (swarm or horde).

215. Joseph Dan, *הסיפור העברי בימי הביניים [The Hebrew Story in the Middle Ages]*, 21, notes that it is very common in Hebrew narrative of the Middle Ages to idealize the biblical period in rabbinic and medieval concepts; one specific category he identifies is the insertion of medieval aspects of weapons and warfare.

216. *Poliorketika*, as cited in Gwyn Davies, *Roman Siege Works* (Stroud, Gloucestershire: Tempus, 2006), 16–7.

217. Michael Harney, "Siege Warfare in Medieval Hispanic Epic and Romance," in *The Medieval City Under Siege* (eds. Ivy Corfis and Michael Wolfe; Woodbridge, Suffolk: Boydell Press, 1995) 183.

218. Roman Vinokur, "Acoustic Noise as a Non-lethal Weapon," *Sound and Vibration* (2004): 20, suggests the latter could have been the actual purpose of Joshua's trumpets at Jericho.
219. Samuel Krauss, *פרס ורומי בתלמוד ובמדרשים*, 174–5. Cf. Daniel Sperber's discussion, *Magic and Folklore in Rabbinic Literature* (Ramat-Gan: Bar-Ilan University Press, 1994), 139–40, of ברברים in a different context: "It surely refers to the Berbers...wild Saharan tribesmen, who on a number of occasions in Roman and Byzantine history overran areas of North Africa, wreaking havoc and slaughter wherever they went." Footnote 1003 in the Yitzhaki edition of R. Shimon b. Tzemaḥ's Haggadah commentary cites *Torat Chaim* with an early Tosafist gloss on ברברים: a people who strike aggressively (suggesting some of the modern connotation of "barbarian"). Images of marauding soldiers were likely all too familiar to a medieval Jewish community.
220. Some rabbinic texts include discussion of bestiality as part of the licentiousness that leads to cross-species plague (e.g. *Gen. Rab. 26:5*). Baḥya b. Asher glosses the term דורמסאות as horsemen who charge around the area deliberately killing all the cattle (*ad* Ex 12:29).
221. Adrienne Mayor, *Greek Fire, Poison Arrows, and Scorpion Bombs: Biological and Chemical Warfare in the Ancient World* (Woodstock: Overlook, 2003), 119–126. "Epidemic" is definitely a better rendering for the *Tanḥuma* and MS Family B2 texts, but our manuscript is less clear. Aside from the more ambiguous sequence in the latter passage, the accompanying verb does not fit the deliberate spreading of a plague. While the king "brings" the דורמוסיות in *Tanḥuma*, which might mean to bring on an epidemic, he "leads" דרמסיאות in MV; this phrasing better fits the image of leading spear carriers or rampaging horsemen. Given the weight of textual evidence, however, the translation utilizes Krauss' definition, theorizing that the scribe might not have understood the term.
222. E.g., Kautilya's *Arthashastra* (4c. BCE), as cited in Mayor, *Greek Fire,* 111.
223. H. Maier, et al. "The Oak Processionary Caterpillar as the Cause of an Epidemic Airborne Disease: Survey and Analysis," *British Journal of Dermatology* 149:5 (2003): 990–7; Charles Clover, "Moth that Can Kill Humans is Found Breeding in Britain." *Daily Telegraph* (October 14, 2007).
224. Mayor, *Greek Fire*, 234–5.
225. Paul E. Chevedden, "Artillery in Late Antiquity" in Corfis and Wolfe, *The Medieval City Under Siege*, 134–64.
226. Krauss, *Lehnwörter*, 18.
227. Sternberg, "How Narrativity Makes a Difference," 117.
228. Recension A has an entirely different midrash here, found at the end of the next lemma in Recension B. The exegesis found in MS Par 716 focuses on justifying the drowning of Pharaoh's chariots and army, and emphasizing that God took care of it "personally," in keeping with the masculine singular verb, ירה – He cast. MS Prm 2736 combines elements of both recensions, crafting a tidy narrative.
229. Other MSS do not use the feminine pronoun. *Sefer haYashar 77* has a similar motif. MS JTS 4998 specifies that an infant would be put into the wall. *Mek. R. Shimon b. Yoḥai 3:1* and *Pirqe R. El.* 48 mention Israelites placed into the walls, but not as punishment for failing to meet the quota of bricks. It was merely a sign of tremendous cruelty on the part of the Egyptians, explaining the doubling of the verb ראה ראיתי – *I have marked well [the plight of My people]* (Ex 3:7), or the cause for the people's cry to reach God after enduring generations of slavery (Ex 2:24).

Gerald Friedlander, in his annotation to *Pirqe R. El.*, suggests that the root ל-ח-צ (oppress) could be the exegetical link for the interpretation: Balaam's donkey presses (תלחץ) his foot into the wall. In this view, the verb alludes to plastering Israelites into the wall.

230. MS Family B2 and Const 1519B: פרחה נשמתם, their soul hovered/flew – the more common idiomatic expression. Translating as "took flight" captures aspects of each. The replacement of the phoneme "p/f" with "b/v" may be an indication of the linguistic influence of Arabic, or simply a scribal shift.
231. The prefix מ (from) is crossed out and replaced with a ל (for, to) above.
232. MS Family B2 (not including B2-ח) and Const 1519B specify that it is a reward (שכר in place of שעה). It appears to be the preferred reading.
233. Note the similarities to motifs in Recension A *ad* Ex 15:1.
234. MS Family B2 (except JTS 4998) and Const 1519B add the essential part of the prooftext: As it is said, *At the morning watch, the Lord looked down upon the Egyptian army [from a pillar of fire and cloud, and threw them into a panic]* (Ex 14:24). The midrash connects it with the "morning" of Abraham's trial. *Mek. R. Shimon b. Yoḥai 14:24* claims that God brought the cloud based on the merit of Abraham who rose early in the morning, and five other biblical figures who tried to fulfill God's wishes in the morning.

    In the first lemma, Abraham expressly invokes protection for his descendants immediately after the *akeidah*; here the text seems to present Abraham offering a prayer in response to the Israelites' specific dilemma at the sea. Alternatively, the apparent simultaneity of Abraham's prayer and God's redemption of Israel may depend on Divine perception of time and change in the medieval imagination. Elaine Vitz discusses its impact on medieval notions of narrativity, *Medieval Narrative and Modern Narratology*, 119.
235. MS Family A2 describes Pharaoh's repentance and God's forgiveness, based neither on stature nor beauty, but on the heart. MS Ox 614 actually has a graphic description of Pharaoh's ugliness, but it seems to be censored in the other two MSS of the family. Then all three MSS in the family continue with Pharaoh's assignment to rule Nineveh for five hundred years and later to sit at the gate of Gehenna. These last elements bear some resemblance to the motifs found in Recension B *ad* Ex 15:11, which at first seems to be a more apt setting for Pharaoh's acceptance of God: *Who is like You among the gods?* On close reading of Ex 15:4, however, one notices that the verse says that Pharaoh was cast into the sea, but it does not say that Pharaoh drowned with his men. Such an omission opens up the exegetical possibility of Pharaoh's repentance here. For further discussion of Pharaoh's repentance, see Commentary on Exodus 15:11.
236. This is a reference to the nine hundred iron chariots of Sisera, one and one-half times Pharaoh's six hundred chariots (Judg 4:3, 13). Although the prose narrative of the battle does not mention them being sunk in the sea, Deborah's song says that the Kishon River swept the Canaanite kings away (Judg 5:21). Thus the Kishon is the surety for God's promise. MS Families A2 and AB2 spell out the connection to Sisera. The motif is incorporated into Recension B in the following pericope.
237. The exegesis appears to reconcile the contradiction of Ex 14:30, which states the Israelites saw the Egyptians dead on the shore, versus the exultation in the song that describes them drowned in the sea (Ex 15:4). They *did* drown, and then are cast up on the shore to verify their deaths.

238. See, for example, Joseph Heinemann, *אגדות ותולדותיהן* and James Kugel, *In Potiphar's House*.

239. The exegetical prompt may be *tehomot* (deeps), which are the clear subject and actor of the first strophe: *the deeps covered them*. Lingering mythological connotations for *Tehom* as a personification of the sea, derived from the Babylonian Tiamat, could contribute to the portrayal of Rahab and his army vanquished in the watery depths. See Commentary.

This section has close parallels in *Tanh.* and *Tanh. B. Hukkat 1* and *Num. Rab. 18:22*. A fraction of this tradition, with the slaying of Rahab for resisting the Divine command to swallow the waters and his burial in the sea, can be found in *Yal. Shimoni Isa 510* and *Job 913*. All of these texts also connect the smell of the sea to the presence of the slain Rahab, as does Recension A.

The critical issue for Recension B is demonstration of Divine power over terrestrial creatures and God's boundless love for Israel – thus setting the stage for the miraculous post-mortem display of the Egyptians out of the depths (presented in Recension A in the previous pericope).

240. Arguably, the text should read בים in place of הים, rendering the Hebrew more precisely, "He conquered and gathered them [the waters] in the sea." In a different hand, there is marginal note with the word תהומות, but it is not completely legible (folio 238v).

241. Older translations read *waves of the sea*. The image is one in which God compresses the sea by "walking" on the waters to press all the air out of them; in this way they can be confined in more limited space. See *Gen. Rab. 5:2*.

242. The MS has וישם (placed) in place of ויסך (covered). There are a number of traditions about separating and storing the waters in *Gen. Rab. 5*.

243. *Ex. Rab. 24:4* offers a related motif, in which the dangerous animals of the wilderness crouch before Israel as they pass, so they will not be afraid. Stith Thompson's *Motif Index of Folk-Literature* (B555) identifies the theme of animals forming a bridge over water within Persian, Iranian and Jewish lore.

244. Presumably a new prince stands in place of the one destroyed during creation. Parallels in *b. Pes. 118b* and *b. Arak. 15a* treat Israel's fear as an act of rebellion. Cf. Wis 10:18–20, Rashi *ad* Ex 14:30.

245. This is a reference to the nine hundred iron chariots of Sisera, one and one-half times Pharaoh's six hundred chariots (Judg 4:3, 13). Cf. Recension A 15:4.

246. The manuscript appears to have copied the word לדין incorrectly.

247. The midrash crafts the multiple reasons for temporarily drawing the Egyptians out of the sea found in *Mek. Beshallah 6* (HR 113:10–16) into a sequential narrative.

248. The other manuscripts in MS Family A1 and Const 1519A ask explicitly: Did the Egyptians descend to the bottom of the sea? Didn't the text already say Israel saw them dead on the shore (Ex 14:30)? Also, this exegesis follows immediately upon the portrayal of the Egyptians vomited out on the shore in the previous lemma. *Someone*, however, appears to have sunk to the depths and remained. Unlike Recension B which clearly states that God ultimately returns the Egyptians to the sea and sinks them like a stone, this version resolves the crux by positing that it is Rahab and his army who are buried in the sea.

249. The manuscript has קרע (tore) rather than the masoretic text's רגע (stilled).

250. שר can mean minister, prince, angel. In 14:31, שר שלהם was translated "their guardian angel." Given the lack of clear referent, it could again refer to Egypt's guardian angel; the argument is quite similar to the one Uza poses in the earlier

lemma. Almost certainly, however, this instance refers to the celestial guardian of the sea, which is generally rendered in mythological terms as a prince rather than an angel.

251. After the closing lemma, MS Family A2 continues with a tangent about God raising and lowering people; it leads back to sinking Pharaoh and his people in the depths, repeating the verse at the end of the pericope.
252. See discussion by Shalom Spiegel in his introduction to *Legends of the Jews* by Louis Ginzberg (Philadelphia: Jewish Publication Society, 1909; repr. 2003), xxxi–xxxix. Jeffrey Rubenstein asserts that medieval texts articulate the mythic perspective more fully and creatively than classical rabbinic literature, and kabbalistic texts take it further still ("From Mythic Motifs to Sustained Myth: The Revision of Rabbinic Traditions in Medieval Midrashim," *Harvard Theological Review* 89 (1996): 131–59). Rabbinic midrash is not the only medium for integrating mythic motifs with biblical narratives, of course; they become artistic conventions as in Ravenna's Arian Baptistery's mosaic (10c.), which presents Jesus' baptism with the Jordan River portrayed as an old man. Cf. the Nile River as an old man in Beit Shean's "House of Leontis."
253. Shaw, 1898 Preface to *Plays Pleasant* (London: Penguin Classics, 2003), 8.
254. Boyarin, *Intertextuality and the Reading of Midrash*, 96.
255. Scholem, *Major Trends in Jewish Mysticism* (New York: Schocken Books, 1961), 8.
256. The first paragraph of this interpretation is similar to Recension A in the next lemma. In this pericope, the early redaction focuses on traditions associated with God's right hand, while this one crafts a meandering narrative about the last plague and Egyptian deaths at the sea, perhaps catalyzed by the end of the verse which describes how God *shatters the foe*.
257. Punishment or destruction of idols according to their various construction materials is found in other texts, e.g. *Mek. Bo 7* (HR 24:3–8), *Mek. R. Shimon b. Yoḥai 12:12, Yal. Shimoni 199, Ex. Rab. 15:15.*
258. *Mek. Bo 13* (HR 44:15–16) ponders the verb in Ex 12:31, *ויקרא ל-* – *he called for*, and presents Pharaoh as wandering around Egypt asking where Moses and Aaron dwell.
259. What are the children doing outside playing in the middle of the night? Certainly they would not be out on the night of the plague of the first-born! *Yal. Shimoni 208* uses "playing" with the clear connotation that they were making sport of Pharaoh, but it does not resolve the underlying problem with the interpretation.

    "How" is the first word of their response, but it has slash marks above it to indicate that the word does not belong; it is followed by "where."
260. Similarly, *Tanḥ. Bo 7, Midr. Ps. 113:2, Sefer haYashar 80.*
261. From the search for Moses to this point, MV has close parallels in *Tanḥ. B. Bo 19, Yal. Shimoni 208*. They pick up again when Moses asks Pharaoh why he is so agitated, and continue through the Egyptian scheme of battling in water.
262. *"In the middle of the night"* could be read as seemingly extraneous information; thus midrash uncovers its cryptic significance through association with another passage that identifies the same time frame (albeit generations apart). *Pesiq. Rab Kah. 7:4* understands משפטי צדקך (frequently translated as "righteous judgments") as two distinct acts: judgment (משפט) against Egypt and justification (granting merit, even if not deserved – one possible understanding of צדק) for Israel. Cf. *Ex. Rab. 18:2, Yal. Shimoni 186.*

For a discussion of midrashim with the formula, “It is as was spoken through the holy spirit by David,” see Jacob Mann, *The Bible as Read and Preached in the Old Synagogue* (Cincinnati: Hebrew Union College, 1940), 44–68; Albeck’s note in Zunz, *הדרשות בישראל [Derashot in Israel]*, 400 n. 84; Marc Bregman, "פתיחתאות מעגליות ופתיחתאות 'זו שנאמרה ברוח הקודש' [Circular Proems and 'This is what was spoken through the Holy Spirit' Proems]," in *מחקרים באגדה, תרגומים ותפילות ישראל לזכר יוסף היינמן [Studies in the Aggadah, Targum and Liturgy of Israel, in memory of Joseph Heinemann]* (ed. Ezra Fleischer and Jakob Petuchowski; Jerusalem: Hebrew Union College Press, 1971), 40–51. The mention of David also calls to mind the haftarah reading for the seventh day of Passover, 2 Sam 22, which presents David’s song of deliverance.

263. A slightly better reading is found in MS Family B2 and Const 1519B: שעשית נס, on which You made a miracle. They then specifically attribute the next sentence to David; it is crafted, however, more like a direct rabbinic statement. In our MS, “And he said” could refer to David or to R. Yoḥanan.

264. The midrash is playing with the multiple meanings of משפט. While the term can mean the execution of justice (e.g. Lev 24:22), it also refers to the special rules God commands Israel to perform as part of the covenant (e.g. Deut. 8:11). Its dual significance may be considered parallel to the two appearances of “right hand” in the verse of the Song; *Ex. Rab. 22:2* explicitly relates the doubling to the Divine hand which both saves Israel and requites the Egyptians.

Mek. Shir 5 (HR 134) uses *notarikon* to interpret the term נאדרי בכח (glorious in power), describing God as pleasant (נאה) in exhibiting Divine might (אדיר). It notes that God does not completely destroy evildoers until they have committed their full measure of wickedness, e.g. the gradual punishment of the ten plagues. MV does not offer the play on words, but similarly portrays God administering punishment with a measure of consideration (this time for Israel’s sake).

265. It seems incongruous that the Israelites are “marked for life” by smearing blood on their homes; the parable offers a context in which the “brand” is indeed set on those the rancher intends to keep. *Ex. Rab. 18:7* also compares the marking of Israelite houses to the marking of livestock before slaughter. The MS has dittography of 11 words, likely prompted by the repeated appearance of ונתנו.

266. “Foreigner” is interpreted here as one who is uncircumcised, as clarified in Ex 12:44–48.

267. Note that the midrash returns to the “middle of the night” language, most likely to help the disparate traditions hang together. There are numerous partial parallels explicating the plural of bloods in Ezekiel as the blood of circumcision and the blood of the passover offering, assigning these two *mitzvot* as the acts that merited redemption. See, e.g., *Pesiq. R. Kah. 7:4*, *Ex. Rab. 17:3* and *19:5, Song Rab. 5:2, Ruth Rab. 6:1, Tanh. Vayera 4, Pirqe R. El. 29, Pesiq. Rab. 17.*

268. Every union yielded only one child before the partners mated with someone else. The crux appears to be Ex 12:33, in which the Egyptians lament, *"כלנו מתים – We shall all be dead."* MS Family AB2 and *Tanhuma B. Bo 19* specify that each man had five wives and each woman had five husbands, with every union producing a first-born. MS Family AB2 and *Yal. Shimoni 208* state that, if the first-born died previously, he was temporarily raised up from the dead so that the loss would be felt acutely on that fateful night. Cf. *Mek. Bo 13* (HR 45:18ff), *Mek. R. Shimon b. Yoḥai 12:33*, *Pesiq. Rab Kah. 7:6, Yal. Shimoni 186.*

Note this lemma is the only one that designates rabbinic tradents: R. Joshua b. Levi here and R. Samuel b. Nahmani below.

269. Family B2 offers the preferred reading, as edited. MS War 374 tries to repair its flawed model, with little success.
270. MS has a m.pl. participle; it could be referring to Moses and Aaron. Family B2 has the m.s. perfect verb, which better fits the context.
271. There is a certain echoing effect, perhaps deliberate: 1) Pharaoh decides he should go himself, as God does in previous pericopes; 2) Moses asks Pharaoh, "Who are you," somewhat resonant of Pharaoh's question when they first met, *Who is the Lord that I should listen to His voice?*
272. Other midrashim also note that Pharaoh summons Moses and Aaron during the night on which no Israelite is allowed outside (Ex 12:31), and they imagine a conversation through a window or peeking out from a balcony. See, for example, *Mek. R. Shimon b. Yohai 12:31.*
273. The prefix -ל is crossed out, and לו (to him) is added in the margin. With the corrections, it denotes the accurate direction of the dialogue.
274. The "loud cry" becomes Pharaoh's voice rather than the outcry resulting from mass grief. Cf. *Targ. Pseudo-Jonathan Ex 12:31, y.Pes. 5:4 (32b–c), Midr. Ps. 103:2.*
275. This problematic sentence fragment is not found elsewhere, and the translation takes liberties to give it the sense of the more complete expression, found only in MS JTS 4920: ובת קול יוצאת ואומרת אין אתם מתים כאן אלא בים, "A heavenly voice issued forth, saying, 'You are not dying here, but rather in the sea'" (similarly, *Tanh. B. Bo 19*). Even with the gap, one can sense the crux that some Egyptians clearly survive the tenth plague; their plaint that they are *all* dying will be fulfilled at the sea.
276. There is a loose ב in the MS, marked as an error.
277. Presumably using fire in the process of recapturing them. The MS seems to have extraneous words likely copied from the next line: נשבע שאינו יכול. The error is found only in this MS and its copy, MS War 374.
278. *B. Sotah 11a* similarly makes the distinction between God *bringing* a flood versus the Egyptians rushing headlong into one. The passage also justifies the punishment as fitting recompense for Pharaoh's decree to drown the male infants in the river. Cf. *Ex. Rab. 1:9.*
279. There may be a pun, playing with the similarity of God's oath (נדר) not to bring a flood, and God's gloriousness (נאדרי) in power. God's right hand is also also associated with taking an oath; see Isa 62:8 and Commentary on Ex 15:12.
280. Here, MS Ox 135 presents the lemma with the comment: הדרשה לא מצאתי, "I did not find the interpretation [of this section]," but other MSS of Recension A and Const 1519A contain the missing material. This text relies on MS Wolf 36.25.

    For a discussion of God's "right hand," see Commentary *ad* 15:12.
281. The common midrashic reading of the verse renders literally the unusual אשדת into two words, making one noun the modifier of the other: *fiery law* (NJPS: lightning flashing). The Septuagint has αγγελοι (angels).
282. The odd phrasing אף ידי could literally be translated "also my hand" (NJPS: My own hand); the midrash understands it to be the "other" (i.e. left) hand.
283. MS Family A2 adds brief exegetical traditions explaining that mortality among earthly creatures is evidenced by the fact that acts of terrestrial creation use only a partial name of God, while celestial ones use the full name.

284. MS Family A2 again expands slightly: The eternality of a rebuilt Jerusalem is evidenced by a verbal association with God's heavenly throne. Each is described as enduring through the ages (Lam 5:19, Joel 4:20).
285. Moses prophesying to Israel about future events (not included in MS Family A2) explains how the nation could be celebrating them at the sea.
286. MS Family A1-ד does specifically mention alternative explanations (דבר אחר), but they are incorporated from different manuscript traditions of MV.
287. Stern, *Parables in Midrash*, 1–9, 16–19, 71–82.
288. Recension A presents a brief discussion of God destroying the idols of Egypt before the tenth plague, similar to the beginning of Recension B 15:6. The interpretation fits nicely as exegesis of the verse, with God breaking *His* opponents, consuming them like straw. MS Family A2 goes on to discuss Yoḥani and Mamre (found in other manuscripts *ad* 15:10), along with traditions about ten measures of various qualities (magic, licentiousness, beauty) distributed unevenly in the world.

    Recension B's correlation of plagues with Egyptian actions is also found in the lemma יי' איש מלחמה, *The Lord is a man of war* (Ex 15:3), albeit with different detail. Although the repetition makes one of the iterations appear superfluous, the plagues are also appropriate here as symbols of God's triumph over His foes.
289. As in MS Family B2 and Const 1519B. The syntax is clearer, and corresponds to the remainder of the passage.
290. See discussion of "measure for measure" in Commentary. One miraculous aspect of the blood plague, according to MS Family AB2, is that the same vessel provided water for an Israelite but turned to blood if an Egyptian tried to drink. *Ex. Rab. 9:10* offers the same reasoning for the blood plague and includes this detail. See also MS Prm 2736 *ad* Ex 15:3.
291. It is also possible to understand that the frogs leapt *inside* them. In this case, it would be akin to MS Prm 2736 *ad* Ex 15:3, which imagines that frogs spoke from within the guts of the Egyptians.
292. According to Aryeh Kaplan in his translation of the eighteenth-century work begun by Jacob Culi, *Me'am Lo'ez: The Torah Anthology* (New York: Moznaim, 1977), 4:208, 254 n. 18, the creature is an octopus or giant squid, i.e., an animal with tentacles that could do the slithery reaching described in the midrash. In a footnote, Kaplan mentions the likely root of the word, סילון (pipe), descriptive of its many cylindrical body parts. He admits that a number of authorities, however, identify the term as a mermaid or siren; the *Arukh* and Raavad actually read *sironith*, clearly derived from the Greek σειρην (siren). See also *Sefer haYashar 80*, in which the *siloni* goes up on the roof, tears open the rafters and reaches in with its long arms.
293. The emendation is based on MS Family B2 and Const 1519B; our MS has "the altar" (המזבח). MS Family AB2 calls it a great miracle that a man throws fistfuls of soot into the air and it results in boils spread for hundreds of miles; MS Prm 2736 does the same at Ex 15:3. The term for boils, שחין, is related to one word for hot: שחון.
294. "Upon them" is accidentally repeated, but crossed out in the MS. MS Family AB2 offers a parable explaining the fiery ice, comparing it to two warring legions brought together to fight on behalf of the king.
295. All the other manuscripts of Recension B mention thirty-one kings, the number listed in Joshua 12:7–24.

296. *Ex. Rab. 12:7* also discusses hail suspended between heaven and earth. The deployment of the stones in the time of Joshua and at the end of days is found in *Tanh. Vaera 16.*
297. The phrase resembles Joel 1:6. There are two letters in the MS (כב), possibly marked with a slash as extraneous.
   MS Family AB2 claims that the Egyptians ate the locusts, enjoying the plague, so God drove the insects away.
298. MS Family B2 is clearer: By adding אילנות ושמרו, it reads: plant *trees* for us *and guard* their fruits.
299. *Targ. Pseudo-Jonathan Ex 10:23* mentions light within the homes of Israel so they could bury the wicked among the community who had died.
300. The words מיד הלכו בכורי מצרים are marked as an error; they are repeated from the line above, prompted by the presence of מצרים before both instances.
301. Paraphrase of a repeated refrain in the biblical narrative.
302. Reading the verse to mean that the first-born were the instrument of attack (-ב as "with"). See *Tanh. B. Bo 18, Pesiq. Rab. 17, Midr. Ps. 136:6, Yal. Shimoni 186, Midr. Aggadah Ex 11:5.*
303. A close parallel of the whole sequence is found in *Chronicles of Moses* (Eis 360–1). It narrates the attack by the first-born more clearly: Pharaoh commands them to kill their fathers once he learns who sent them to plead for Israel's release. Thus the measure for measure quality of the punishment is evident; as they murdered their fathers, so too will they be killed. MS Family AB2 is similar. Cf. *Yal. Shimoni 182, S. Eli. Rab. 8.*
304. Similar to the beginning of Recension B Ex 15:6, it fits better here with precise articulations of how God breaks and burns the gods of Egypt – those who rise against the Most High. (This distinguishes their fate from that of the Egyptians, whose primary crime is the oppression of Israel, and whose deaths are by plague and by drowning.)
305. Heinemann, *דרכי האגדה [The Methods of Aggadah]* (Jerusalem: Magnes Press, 1954), 64–8. His discussion of myth relies on Ernst Cassirer, *The Philosophy of Symbolic Forms, Volume 2: Mythical Thought.*
306. Rosen-Zvi, "Measure for Measure as a Hermeneutical Tool in Early Rabbinic Literature," *Journal of Jewish Studies* 57:2 (2006): 280.
307. See, e.g. Sarah ben-Reuven, "מידה כנגד מידה בסיפור יוסף [Measure for Measure in the Story of Joseph]," *Beit Miqra* 49:4 (2004): 185–90; Yael Shemesh, "Measure for Measure in the David Stories," *Scandinavian Journal of the Old Testament* 17:1 (2003): 89–109.
308. Ps 7:16–17, Prov 26:27, Eccl 10:8–9, Prov 18:20, Isa 59:18, 65:7, Jer 32:19, 50:29. Some fit the profile better than others.
309. The midrash is thus interpreting a syntactically challenging verse: in Jethro's speech: *Now I know that the Lord is greater than all gods, yes, by the result of their very schemes against [the people]* (Ex 18:11).
310. The Golden Haggadah and Sarajevo Haggadah manuscripts both trace back to the mid-fourteenth century. The Venice Haggadah is an early printed work with illuminations (Venice: Giovanni da Gara, 1609); select pages are available online: http://www.library.yale.edu/judaica/site/exhibits/venicehaggadah/VeniceHaggadah html.
311. The rabbinic penchant for close reading must note that God's instruction to "borrow" the wealth of the Egyptians is given after the plague of darkness has

fallen and before it is lifted. Since the illumination clearly portrays the Israelites *taking* the objects, it must either represent a slightly different tradition, or relate events after the Egyptians agree to give them their wealth. *Ex. Rab. 14:3* offers an honorable conclusion in which the Egyptians realize the Israelites could simply have taken it all during the darkness but did not, and so they become favorably disposed to provide their riches.

312. Splitting of the sea into twelve channels is a prevalent motif. See, e.g., *Pirqe R. El. 42, ARN A 33, Tanh. Beshallah 10, Targ. Pseudo-Jonathan Ex 14:21*, *Ex. Rab. 24:1, Deut. Rab. 11:10, Sefer haYashar 81.*

313. The text could be translated without emendation as "his legs," but the clearer reading as rendered is found in MS Family B2.

314. MS reads עמו instead of עצמו, but it seems to be simply a scribal error. One "mil" measures approximately one kilometer.

315. *Mek. Shir* (HR 138:1–4) presents prooftexts for נוזלים indicating sweet waters (=fresh water vs. salt water): Ps 78:16, Song 4:15, Prov 5:15. A different prooftext can be found in Jacob b. Asher's commentary on Ex 15:2, linking the verse to its echo in Isa 12:2, which then goes on to speak of drawing water in great celebration.

316. Congealing the waters and sweetening them are among the ten miracles which tradition reports took place at the Sea of Reeds. See, e.g., *Mek. Beshallah 4* (HR 100:11ff), *Midr. Ps. 114:7*. For an amalgamation of related traditions and sources, see Louis Ginzberg, *Legends of the Jews*, I:555–8.

The pericope serves as rather direct exegesis; it concretizes the images presented in the verse – God "blasting" the sea, waters standing like walls, deeps congealing – and crafts them into a narrative.

317. A paraphrase of Ex 14:16.

318. Recension A's portrayal of the sea's initial unwillingness to cooperate is found in Recension B *ad* Ex 14:30. MS Family A2 does not portray the sea refusing to split. Instead, when the waters form walls between the tribes, the people subsequently fear for their fellows whom they cannot see. God prompts the sea to fashion windows, and the sea also prepares all sorts of delicacies that the people share.

319. "The waters" is found in most other manuscripts. If the word order of the numbers was shifted, it could suggest six hundred thousand mil, one per each adult male.

320. The term generally refers to beds of straw, leaves, etc., that are spread out.

321. Boyarin, *Intertextuality*, 100, 153 n. 25.

322. *Homilies on Genesis and Exodus* (FC 71; Washington, D.C.: Catholic University, 1982), 282–3. Cf. Eusebius *ad* Psalm 77:13.

323. See Carl Kraeling, *The Excavations at Dura-Europos: The Synagogue* (New Haven: Yale University Press, 1956), 84–5. At the same site, there is a fresco of Miriam's well which also has twelve channels of waters coming from it, one for each tribe.

324. *Mek. Beshallah 2* (HR 96:1–6), *Mek. R. Shimon b. Yohai 14:13*, *y. Taanit 65d, Targum Pseudo-Jonathan Ex 14:13–14, Targum Neofiti Ex 14:13–14* and the *Fragment-Targums* (Ex 14:13–14, and at the Song) present an additional group that advocates shouting at the Egyptians to confound them. Moses' response to that camp is to keep silent, and sing praise to God. Some parallels mix up the elements. A similar exegesis (with three groups) is found in *Tibat Marqe 4:63*, but the Israelites advocate submitting, fleeing (rather than drowning themselves in the sea) and waging war. Pseudo-Philo's *Biblical Antiquities 10* also contains a trace of this motif which explains the reasoning of each group.

325. The midrash weaves together different exegeses with a narrative thread: The Israelites had three different ideas about how to react before the sea split – all wrong – and still most of the people are too fearful to embrace God's path until the tribe of Benjamin takes the lead. The image of the waters risen sixteen hundred mil into the air is set here, adding vivid justification for their dread.

The tradition that Nahshon jumped in first is recorded above, *ad* Ex 14:30; other texts recall the tribe of Benjamin leading the way. Cf. *b. Sotah 37a, Midr. Ps. 68:14, Yal. Shimoni 234, Lekaḥ Tov Ex 14:22.* MS Prm 2736 spells out the exegesis in its מילי דויושע section: Playing on the description of Benjamin in Ps 68:28, *There is little Benjamin who rules them* (רדם), it reads instead that "he went down into the sea" (רד ים). Joseph Heinemann offers a traditions history of the motif in *אגדות ותולדותיהן [Aggadah and its Development]*, 78–84.

326. רוח has multiple meanings, all of which speak to this instance: wind, breath, spirit.

327. Added in the margin of the manuscript in the same hand: שהיו.

328. וינער is a perfect pun; it means to hurl or shake, but can also have the connotation "to strip bare" (e.g., *נעור ורק – shaken out and stripped* (of property), Neh 5:13). What they threaten to do to the Israelites, God does to them.

329. The motif of the three Egyptian camps, not as common as the Israelite camps, is also found in *Mek. Beshallaḥ 7* (HR 140:11–15), *Mek. R. Shimon b. Yoḥai 15:9.*

330. Probably meaning against the riders' will. Some midrashic traditions note the phrasing of Ex 15:19, *For the horse(s) of Pharaoh went, with its chariot and horsemen, into the sea*, and interpret that the horses moved against their riders' will (e.g., *Mek. Shir 2* (HR 125:7–8), *Mek. R. Shimon b. Yoḥai 15:1*). Mares are not generally used in chariotry; the uncanny image of a mare among Pharaoh's chariots likely derives from Song 1:9. Cf. *Pirqe R. El. 42.*

As a military stratagem, sending in a mare to distract the male horses in battle is documented in a fifteenth-century BCE Egyptian inscription. See James Pritchard, *ANET*, I:241 (lines 27–29 and note 37).

331. Recension A does not discuss the three camps among Israelites, nor the attempted escape of the Egyptians foiled by a mare who lures them into the sea. It includes only the exegesis most relevant to this lemma: a parsing of the enemies' threats and what becomes of them. MS Family A2 gives different responses to the three Egyptian camps, and then presents a motif about the pursued; the patriarchs and the people of Israel are frequently pursued by enemies, and God will always take the side of the pursued.

332. Although the phrases of Ex 15:9 are not directly assigned to the different camps, it seems that the claim "*I will pursue, I will overtake*" could represent those who want to drag the Israelites back into slavery; "*I will divide the spoil*" parallels the group who wants to strip the Israelites and leave them bare; and the rest of the verse speaks of dealing death as urged by the last group.

333. Kugel, *The Bible as it Was*, 339.

334. Klein, *The Fragment-Targums of the Pentateuch*, I:19–21.

335. Albardani's "אמנם שלוש כתות" is available in English translation as "The Three Factions" in T. Carmi, ed., *The Penguin Book of Hebrew Verse* (London: Penguin, 1981): 259–60.

336. Wayne Booth, "The Pleasures and Pitfalls of Irony: Or Why Don't You Say What You Mean?" in *Rhetoric, Philosophy and Literature: An Exploration* (ed. Don M. Burks; West Lafayette, Ind.: Purdue University Press, 1978), 11–12.

337. See Rubenstein, *Talmudic Stories*, 247–8; Yonah Fraenkel, *דרכי האגדה והמדרש* *[Methods of Aggadah and Midrash]* (Givatayim: Masada, 1991), 266–71.
338. James Kugel, "Two Introductions to Midrash," *Prooftexts* 3:2 (1983): 134–5. He states that there is "something a bit joking about midrash," but always with a point. As Jakob Jonsson points out in *Humor and Irony in the New Testament* (Reykjavík: Bókaútgáfa Menningarsjóôs, 1965; repr. Leiden: Brill, 1985), 86–7, the role of humor is not to ridicule the holy, but to deploy the comical with a sacred cause.
339. See Commentary for discussion of Yoḥani and Mamre. MS Family A2 discusses the magicians at Ex 15:7. Here, it offers a midrash on all those called "mighty" (similar to *Mek. Shir 7* (HR 141)).
340. Note that it is the same verb used when God hurls the Egyptians into the sea who want to strip Israel and leave them naked (נ-ע-ר).
341. The MS has אלהיהם, which yields two difficult readings. Grammatically, it is best rendered: "So they did their magic and their gods brought them down," but it seems strange that idols would be accorded "divine" status. Allowing for one understanding of the word *elohim*, it could be translated: "So they did their magic and brought down their angels." Neither of these seems as apt as the alternative transcription found in MS Family B2 and Const 1519B: אל הים, yielding, "So they did their magic and brought them (the angels) down to the sea."
342. Ps 69:2, but preserving the plural rather than singular first-person voice, "save *us*." Eisenstein claims that part of the narrative is missing: the Holy One comes to the aid of the angels, drowning Yoḥani and Mamre in their stead and prompting the angels to praise Him. It would make sense of the latter section of direct address since, in the current articulation, the second half of the sentence does not fit perfectly either as a part of the angelic plea for help, or alongside the third person narration of God's saving arm. Recension A does have a more elaborate tale, but it does not coincide with his hypothesis.
343. Origen links this verse to Zechariah 5, in which leaden weight is associated with wickedness (*Homilies on Genesis and Exodus*, 289).

    Yal. Shimoni 235 states that Yoḥani and Mamre made branches with their magic and flew in the air (broomsticks!). Gabriel states, *In Your great triumph You break Your opponents* (Ex 15:7), and the Holy One immediately tells Michael to go deal with them. Michael grabs them by their hair and destroys them in the water, bringing the verse, *It was You who drove back the sea with Your might, who smashed the heads of the monsters in the water* (Ps 74:13). Cf. Stith Thompson's *Motif Index of Folk Literature* (D2165.1) for traditions of escape by flying in the air.
344. *Mek. Beshallaḥ 6* (HR 111:2–3), *Yal. Shimoni 237, Ex. Rab. 15:15* similarly portray the sea pursuing the fleeing Egyptians. The last of these parallels identifies a crux: The language of the verse suggests that the Egyptians fled *toward* the water rather than away from it.
345. In MS Mos 111, God instructs the prince of the sea to do it. Also, the angels call Yoḥani and Mamre "the children of Belial," a demon.
346. Similarly, *Ex. Rab. 9:7, Yal. Shimoni 182*. In the Talmud, the story is brought as a comment on the Mishnah because it may seem to make little sense to bring even the choicest fruits to God, who is the owner of all and lacks for nothing.
347. Thus one can fetch a good price for the vegetables.
348. Schechter, "Fragments of a Zadokite Work," *Documents of Jewish Sectaries edited from Hebrew MSS. in the Cairo Genizah Collection, vol. I* (Cambridge: Cambridge

University Press, 1910; reprint New York: Ktav, 1970). Modern editions locate the text at 5:18. Cf. Robert H. Charles, ed., *The Apocrypha and Pseudepigrapha of the Old Testament in English* (Oxford: Clarendon Press, 1913), II:785–834; he rejects Schechter's emendation and translates the end, "when the former rescued Israel" (810).

349. E.g., Numenius Book 3, Ambrosiaster on 2 Tim 3:8, John Malalas *Chron. 30*, John of Nikiu *Chron. 30*, *Targum Pseudo-Jonathan Ex 1:15, Palaea historica 231–34, Zohar Ki Tisa 2:191a.*
350. E.g., *Targum Pseudo-Jonathan Num 22:22, Chronicles of Moses, Yal. Shimoni 168, 176, Sefer haYashar 79, Zohar Balak 3:194a.*
351. Pinchas sends a soldier to fly after them. With spells of his own, Pinchas is able to foil their escape and has the evil magicians killed. The *Zohar* recognizes there is a conflicting tradition that they die after the golden calf, and it tries to reconcile the texts.
352. See *Yal. Reuveni 19a, 80a, 81a, 85a; Zohar Ki Tisa 191a, Tiqqune haZohar 142a.*
353. Pietersma, ed., *The Apocryphon of Jannes and Jambres the Magicians* (Leiden: E.J. Brill, 1994), 12–33. Other scholars have investigated the diverse sources for Jannes and Jambres traditions. See, for instance, H. L. Strack and P. Billerbeck, *Kommentar zum neuen Testament aus Talmud und Midrasch* (Munich: Beck, 1965), 660–64; Martin McNamara, "The New Testament and the Palestinian Targum to the Pentateuch" (Thesis, Pontifical Biblical Institute, 1966), 82–96; John G. Gager, *Moses in Greco-Roman Paganism* (Nashville: Abingdon Press, 1972), 137–40 with primarily pagan sources; Albert-Marie Denis, *Introduction aux pseudépigraphes grecs d'ancien testament* (Leiden: Brill, 1970), 146–49 with primarily Christian sources.
354. Michael Garcia, "Medieval Medicine, Magic and Water," *Peregrinations* 1:3 [cited 13 November 2007]. Online: http://peregrinations.kenyon.edu/vol1-3.pdf.
355. Fritz Graf, "How to Cope with a Difficult Life: A View of Ancient Magic," in *Envisioning Magic* (ed. Peter Schäfer and Hans Kippenberg; Leiden: Brill, 1997), 100.
356. See Reginald Thompson, *Semitic Magic: Its Origins and Development* (NY: Ktav, 1971), 73, 162, 168. Idries Shah, *Oriental Magic* (London: Octagon Press, 1968), 156, describes a pre-Islamic Arab death spell involving vigorous blowing on a string of knots.
357. The midrash turns Israel's rhetorical question into a moment of transformation for Pharaoh, someone who actually *did* believe in other gods.
358. In *Mek. Beshallaḥ Petiḥta* (HR 75:7–9) and *Mek. R. Shimon b. Yohai 12:32*, Pharaoh's dramatic change of heart is noted, but he is rewarded for seeing the light rather than punished for insincerity or opportunism.
359. *Chronicles of Moses* (Eis 361), *Pirqe R. El. 43* and *Yal. Shimoni 176* mention Pharaoh coming to believe in God and becoming king of Nineveh. MS Prm 2736 and Family A2 provide interesting variants; see Commentary.
360. MS reads "years," but it is an error. It is otherwise a quote of Jonah 3:4. Other MSS (including War 374) and Recension A are correct.
361. It could be rendered as is: This unfortunate one denied..., but the emendation is based on the sense of Rec. A, MS Family B2 and Const 1519B.
362. MS Family A2 goes on to offer two additional exegeses of the verse, one related to Mi-chael (lit: who is like God), and the other celebrating the uniqueness of God and Israel.

363. Establishing Pharaoh as an evangelical believer spreading the faith.
364. פרמשתק is a Persian loan word for penis. See *b.MK 18a*, which may be the source of this tradition, a parody of Zoroastrian men and customs. Cf. *Targ. Pseudo-Jonathan Ex 7:15, 8:16*. MSS Par 335 and Esc G3 are missing the entire physical description, but there is blank space there suggesting it was censored (or self-censored). A Christian censor may have determined that insulting a magus (Zoroastrian priest) was akin to insulting the magi who ostensibly visited the infant Jesus, or the passage may simply have been deemed vulgar.
365. See *y.Hag. 2:2 (77d)*. A woman under discussion in the *sugya* suffers this fate. MS Ox 614 has an extra word the other two do not, but it is partially obliterated.
366. In the biblical context, Pharaoh is not among those who sing about God's incomparability.
367. In the biblical context, this statement is indeed directed at Pharaoh to make known God's greatness, but it precedes the plague of hail.
368. There are other biblical connections between Egypt and Assyria which themselves may have invited midrashic imagination. Ezek 31, for example, describes to Pharaoh the fall of Nineveh's king.
369. The land is clearly afraid of being held accountable, but the sea's fear may be more literal: It does not want to be expected to produce the bodies at the end of days. Jewish sources express a great deal of anxiety about the disposition of bodies and souls that are not properly buried; it is this concern, perhaps, being set in the mouth of the sea. See Saul Lieberman, *Texts and Studies* (New York: Ktav, 1974), 527–30.
370. MS Family A1-ק and Cam 667.1 specify that God swears with His right hand. Recension A clearly relies on this association to connect stretching out God's hand and the earth swallowing the Egyptians. Recension B may depend on this as well, or on the rabbinic portrayal of God's right hand as an instrument of mercy. See Commentary.

    Targum parallels *(Neofiti, Pseudo-Jonathan, Fragment Ex 15:12)* present the sea and land in direct argument, as does MS Family A2. The latter then offers a new element (also MS Ox 225): Since the earth was cursed on account of the blood of a single man (Abel), it assumes that the large number of Egyptian corpses would have a more severe impact. MS Prm 2736, which is more similar to Recension B here, adds a motif about the earth being cursed in the days of Noah.
371. Although the biblical text uses God's right hand as a symbol of strength, the midrash associates it with taking an oath, specifically stating that God "swears" the earth will not be held accountable on Judgment Day. A number of rabbinic texts highlight this connotation, citing Isa 62:8: *The Lord has sworn by His right hand*. See Commentary.
372. See Louis Rabinowitz and Stephen Wald, "Right and Left," in *EJ* 17:302–3 (2d ed.). They identify four biblical usages (right as opposed to left, directions, strength, merism) and briefly discuss rabbinic development of the concepts.
373. See also Isa 62:8, Ps 20:7, 98:1, 110:5, etc.
374. E.g., *Mek. Shir 5* (HR 134) enumerates Divine graces that ensue when Israel obeys God's will, as they "make the left hand right." In *Song Rab. 1:9:1*, the midrash interprets that the right hand leans toward acquittal and the left hand toward condemnation. Given the well-established tradition of the right hand as primary, the exegesis reflects rabbinic prioritization of Divine mercy over Divine justice.

375. Note: There is no "The Sages said..." introduction. Many of the lemmas that follow also lack the phrase, although it had been a relatively consistent feature until this point. The manuscripts vary in terms of the frequency of the introductory formula.
376. Cf. *Tanḥ. B. Beshallaḥ 10, Mek R. Shimon b. Yoḥai 13:21, Pesiq. Rab Kah. 11, Ex. Rab. 25:6, Midr. Aggadah Ex 13:17.*
377. God's constant presence leading Israel through the wilderness is considered a premier act of חסד (*ḥesed*), lovingkindness. The comparison to a human king who is always protected on a journey rather than protector, creates a dramatic foil. The unspoken difference lies in the destination; God's holy abode is not simply a royal residence for the king, but a spiritual home for the people as well.

    MS Family A2 then segues into repayment for *ḥesed*, recycling an ancient motif lauding Joseph for attending to his father's burial; Moses consequently attends to the promise to bring his bones out of Egypt. See Commentary.
378. See the collection of such texts by Ignaz Ziegler, *Die Königsgleichnisse des Midrasch* (Breslau: S. Schottlaender, 1903). Many utilize the mashal form, which David Stern identifies as the greatest effort in all of rabbinic literature to imagine God (*Parables in Midrash*, 93).
379. Similarly, *ad* 15:17 God clothes, bathes and provides shoes for the people the way a servant does for his master.
380. Parallels can be found in *m. Sotah 1:9, t. Sotah 4*. The measure for measure nature of God's justice is a well-established rabbinic principle; see Commentary on Ex 15:7.
381. *Pesiq. Rab. 35* contains this midrash of Elijah's pronouncements, connecting it to Zech 2:14–15: *Shout for joy, fair Zion!... In that day, many nations will attach themselves to the Lord and become His people.* Since it seems likely that MV is based on this earlier tradition, the exegesis of the verse takes on a dramatic twist: The wicked among the nations hear news that at first makes them rejoice, thinking that they will benefit in the coming redemption; once they understand the whole picture, however, they begin to tremble.
382. In MS Family B2 and Const 1519B, the language and sequence of Elijah's pronouncements are clearer: On the first day, he announces that peace is coming, and no reaction is recorded. On the second day, he announces that goodness is coming and even the wicked rejoice. On the third day, he proclaims that deliverance is coming. When the wicked *in Gehenna* see that it applies only to Israel and to the righteous, they are seized with fear and trembling.
383. This passage addresses the first part of the verse, with nations trembling upon learning they may not be redeemed. It appears that salvation is available to the righteous of every language and nation but, as detailed in the next lemma, the surrounding peoples all have cause to suspect the worst when judgment comes. The Philistines' specific fear is addressed in exegesis of Ex 15:15.
384. *Pirqe R. El. 42* is similar. Cf. *Mek. Shir 9* (HR 148), *Targ. Pseudo-Jonathan Ex 15:15–16.*
385. Some MSS present Moses' request that the terror last until Israel crosses the Jordan – 40 years later! MS Family A2 explicates the reasons why the Israelites could not go directly to the Promised Land; see Commentary on Ex 15:16.
386. The midrash attempts to concretize the image of being gripped, immobilized by fear.
387. *Mishneh Torah Hilkhot Melakhim 12:2.*
388. E.g., *Yal. Shimoni Melakhim 207, S. 'Olam Rab. 17.*

389. E.g., *b. Ber. 35b, Men. 45a*. See Auerbach, "Elijah," *EJ* 6:333 (2d ed.).
390. E.g., *b. Sanh. 63b, b. B. Metsia 59b, 85b, m. 'Ed. 8:7*.
391. See also Kristen Lindbeck, *Elijah and the Rabbis: Story and Theology* (Columbia University Press, 2010).
392. There is some dispute about the meaning of אלף; commonly translated "one thousand" (thus 200 x 1,000) in modern Hebrew, some biblical scholars argue that it is a designation for a much smaller but defined troop or group.
393. Similarly, *Sefer haYashar 75*. The standard calculation for four hundred years is from the birth of Isaac; instead, the Ephraimites calculated from the day the prophecy was received at the covenant of the pieces, thirty years before. See Commentary.
394. *Viz.* Gen 13:7.
395. Giving biblical background for each nation's fear and presenting them as foils for the Canaanites is an elegant exegesis of the stylistic redundancy of the Song. It also suggests a more intense connotation for the dread expressed by the Canaanites in the verse. Other midrashim capture part of the drama; *Mek. Shir 9* (HR 147:11ff), *Mek. R. Shimon b. Yoḥai 15:15*, *Yal. Shimoni 251* and *Lekaḥ Tov Ex 15:15*, for instance, put the fear of dredging up old rivalries into the mouths of the nations to give shape to the Canaanites' terror.
396. MS Family B2 also has this additional example (*viz.* Gen 25–27). It fits the shape of the verse more precisely.
397. Heinemann, *אגדות ותולדותיהן*, 137–41. Cf. *Mek. R. Shimon b. Yoḥai 13:17, Pirqe R. El. 48, Ex. Rab. 20:11*, Baḥya b. Asher *ad* Ex 15:14.
398. "The Story as a Hermeneutic Device," 231. Chapter 3 of her book, *סוגיות בפואטיקה של סיפורי חז"ל [The Poetics of Rabbinic Stories]* (Tel Aviv: Sifriat haPoalim, 1993) develops a similar argument.
399. Visotzky, *The Midrash on Proverbs* (New Haven: Yale University Press 1992), 2.
400. Literally, "my brother and my brothers." The translation is an updated, inclusive rendering of its emphatic tone.
401. The MS actually reads "*his* might." MS Family B2 and Const 1519B do not have the sentence about Pharaoh's warriors.
402. עליהם (upon them) is implied in the MS, and explicit in MS Family B2 and Const 1519B.
403. "Omnipresent" is a translation of מקום, literally "place," one of the traditional rabbinic names for God. It is invoked in only one other instance in MV (*ad* Ex 15:1). Another unusual quality of this address is that Moses imagines God communicating through future writing of Torah – namely the prophecy to Jeremiah which, in Moses' time, was still many centuries away. For the reader who sits many centuries *after* the people fail to listen to Jeremiah and are thrust into exile, the text potentially reawakens consciousness that the choice to observe God's will or not is made anew in every moment.
404. Numbers 21 details battle with the Amorites, whose border with Moab was the Arnon. Specifically invoking the fear and dread set to fall upon all the nations, Moses recounts victory over the Amorites and anticipates the battles yet to come (Deut 2); many *midrashim* develop the parallel wish that future enemies be paralyzed, e.g. *Mek. Beshallaḥ 9* (HR 148). *B. Ber. 54a–b* portrays the battle with the Amorites hiding in mountain caves to ambush the Israelites as they cross the river, and God crushes them by moving the mountains together. Cf. *Mek. R. Shimon b. Yoḥai 15:16*, *Fragment-Targums Ex 15:16*, *Tanḥ. Ḥukkat 20*, *Num. Rab. 19:25*).

Rashi *ad* Ex 15:16 grounds the historical allusions to the repetition of עד יעבור, *until [Your people] pass over.*

405. Apparently emphasizing the imperfect form of תפול (it will fall) and יעבור (will cross over) as well as the repetition of the latter phrase, the midrash applies God's protection to a future time as well. Although the imperfect is used sporadically in the Song, this verse uses it repeatedly to describe an action that has already taken place in the biblical narrative, offering an ideal springboard to incorporate future redemptions. In Ex 15:1, the word ישיר (will sing) also inspires messianic musings in midrash (e.g. *Mek. Shir 1* (HR 116 ff)).

    MS Family AB2 presents a more graphic set of protections for the Israelites in their journeys. In MS Family A2, an expansion on the terror of the Canaanites comes first; see Commentary.
406. The word עד (until) is enlarged, but it is not the beginning of a new pericope.
407. The word ממצרים (out of Egypt) erroneously appears here as well.
408. The midrash lifts up the association already articulated by Isaiah. Relying on the imagery of the exodus from Egypt, he prophesies waters that dry up so the people may pass out of exile, and he proclaims a future redemption as glorious as the first.
409. Similarly, *Mek. Beshallah 1* (HR 76), *Tanh. Beshallah 1, Eccl. Rab. 3:2.*
410. The midrash understands "when you enter the land" as the actual moment of entry, not simply a status that abides once they arrive. MS Ox 614 indicates a different biblical verse (Num 15:2). It is more likely, however, that the Leviticus passage is intended, since it deals with leprosy of houses.
411. A similar motif is found in *Pesiq. Rab Kah. 11:8, Tanh. B. Beshallah 10, Ex. Rab. 25:6, Midr. Aggadah Ex 13:7, Yal. Shimoni 226.*
412. There is a scribal error, adding אנכי (doubling the "I") at beginning of verse.
413. Elam=Persia (see Isa 21:2).
414. Reading the verb in a passive form. *Mek. Bo 14* (HR 52), *Sif. Num. 84, 161, y.Taanit 1:1 (64a), b. Meg. 29a, Lam. Rab. 1:54, Num. Rab. 7:10, Yal. Shimoni 210, 731,* similarly explain God's descent into exiles with Israel.

    MS Zur 192 has a long tangent with the motif that God advances the healing before inflicting the wound. The examples given are Nebuchadnezzar's forced idolatry, met by the faith of Daniel and his fellows; and Ahasuerus' (Haman's) plan to eliminate the Jews that was foiled by Mordechai and Esther.
415. Evokes the image of Amos 9:16, Jer 24:6.
416. Heavenly Jerusalem, a concept quite prevalent within rabbinic literature, fits well here. Its sanctuary is not the one that Israel builds after the exodus, but the one God builds: *the sanctuary, O Lord, which Your hands established.* Recension A *ad* 15:6 similarly suggests that the future Jerusalem, established by God, will be eternal. See Commentary.
417. Recension B expands on the theme of God's kindnesses as precedent, as if to make the prospect of the impending redemption more convincing. MS Family A2 elaborates on the relationship between the earthly and heavenly Temples; it also posits that Moses excluded himself from entry by saying, *bring <u>them</u> and plant <u>them</u>.* Cf. *Mek. Shir 10* (HR 149), *Mek. R. Shimon b. Yohai 15:17, Pirqe R. El. 42, b. Taanit 5a.* See also Even-Shemuel, *מדרשי גאולה [Midrashim on Redemption]*, 11–22.
418. The first utilizes the Hebrew term היכל, the second שמי קדשו. Another candidate is Isaiah's visionary call amidst the seraphim, which begins: *In the year that King Uzziah died, I beheld my Lord seated on a high and lofty throne; and the skirts of*

His robe filled the Temple (Isa 6:1). More likely, however, Isaiah perceives the connection between heaven and earth enabled by the Temple in Jerusalem, and it is the terrestrial space flooded with God's skirts, which drape extravagantly from the heavenly throne.

419. See, for instance, 1 Enoch, 2 Baruch, 4 Ezra.
420. Shemaryahu Talmon, "Biblical Concept of Jerusalem," *The Journal of Ecumenical Studies* 8 (1971): 309. For a collection of exegetical traditions related to Heavenly Temple/Jerusalem, see also, Victor Aptowitzer, "The Celestial Temple as Viewed in the Aggadah," in *Binah Vol. 2* (ed. Joseph Dan; New York: Praeger, 1989; orig. published in Hebrew, 1931), 1–29.
421. Both relate the exegesis to Hosea 11:9, which speaks of God not entering the city.
422. Ps 78:69 invokes the biblical aspiration that the Temple is modeled on heaven and earth, established by God forever.
423. MS has להם, for them – but it appears to be an error.
424. The list varies somewhat in the manuscripts, but they share the basic premise. See Commentary for discussion of rabbinic eschatology.
425. MS has והסיר; the masoretic text (MT) and most other MSS read ומחה. Recension A includes the first part of the verse (as in MT), which seems key to the dramatic and specific change mentioned in the midrash: בלע המות לנצח, *He will destroy death forever.* A note in NJPS, however, suggests the biblical context is speaking only of putting an end to mass killings, like those committed by the Assyrians.
426. The most significant element that this verse adds to the previous one is ביום ההוא (on that day), making Isaiah's predictions a description of the time to come.

    The New Testament contains similar imagery for the future redemption. Revelation 21:1–4, for instance, speaks of a heavenly Jerusalem descending to earth (see previous lemma) and a world without death, mourning or sadness. Cf. *Alphabet of R. Akiba 12.*

    Recension A delivers the entire description of the time to come in Moses' voice. It is possible to read much of this redaction in the same way, but there is a reference to Moses in the third person. Thus the translation ends Moses' direct speech here, and the concluding messianic peroration is best imagined as a narrator inviting readers to comprise the first-person plural address along with the community of Israel.
427. Gog and Magog are common figures in Jewish imaginings of the apocalypse. The basic framework for this part of the narrative can be found in Ezek 38 and 39, although there Magog is a place. (In Gen 10:2, it is the name of a person, a descendant of Japhet.) Gog is most likely part of ancient Babylonian-Assyrian creation myths which find their way into Jewish (and Christian) eschatology.

    Seventy is generally the symbolic universal number of nations in rabbinic literature.
428. It appears that שרצה (because he wanted) is written in the interlinear space; it is not in MS War 374. Without the insertion, it would read: Balak was stupid to curse them....
429. *Esther Rab. 7:23* contains a parallel, with Haman as the ultimate adversary. *Lev. Rab. 27:11, Midr. Ps. 2:4* and *Tanḥ. Emor 13* contain a similar motif, with each enemy of Israel trying to learn from or outdo the last. Gog and Magog decide to attack their *patron* first, using the same prooftext that mentions God (and *then* His anointed) as the designated target.
430. עם (with) is written interlinearly; it is integrated within MS War 374.

431. See exegesis at Ex 15:7 for a fuller discussion of the hail that was stored away. Some manuscripts use a different term for hailstones (also meteors), אבני אלגביש, as in Ezek 38:22.
432. MS has הגוים (the nations) in place of MT's כל העמים (all the peoples).
433. MS Family B1 and Vat 285 consistently have the name as Armilgos, but the others use the now standard Armilos. See Commentary for discussion of this figure.
434. Most Recension B manuscripts reverse the image and offer its complement: וכשיבא האדם לדבר אליו טובות מטה לו אזנו הסתומה ואם ירצה אדם לדבר אליו רעה יטה לו אזנו הפתוחה., When a person comes to say positive things, he extends the stopped up ear, but when a person wishes to tell him bad things, he extends the open ear to him. Although MS Par 716 seems to have a faulty reading, both versions portray a perverse king: either one who deliberately seeks out negative things (possibly in order to fuel his anger and justify his cruelty), or one who listens only to good news and sycophants, so he hears what he wants to hear.
435. Using the same biblical verse, *b. Suk 52a* discusses the death of Messiah b. Yosef, killed in a war between the nations prior to the final redemption led by Messiah b. David. Identifying this monstrous enemy as Armilos can be traced back to *Sefer Zerubbabel* (7c.), which had a great impact on the messianic speculation of the gaonic and medieval periods. See Commentary.
436. This image and its accompanying prooftext is mentioned in a discussion regarding messiah in *b. Sanh. 98a*, where it is contrasted with the notion that he will enter in a lowlier fashion, riding on an ass.
437. This verse is part of the haftarah reading for the eighth day of Passover. The theme of the prophetic reading for the seventh day is David's celebration of being rescued from enemies; the theme for the eighth-day reading is messianic.

    Jesus is reputed to destroy the Antichrist with the "breath of his lips" in 2 Thessalonians 2:8.
438. A tradition that God will set gems in the gates of Jerusalem in the time to come can be found in *b. BB 75a, b. Sanh. 100a.* The theme of the city descending adorned with precious stones can be found in apocalyptic literature such as *Sefer Eliahu, Secrets of R. Shimon b. Yohai*. See Even-Shemuel, *מדרשי גאולה [Midrashim on Redemption]*, 48, 196–7. Cf. Isa 54:11–12, Rev 21:21.
439. The verse is frequently brought as evidence that the third Temple will be built by God and thus stand forever; see, e.g. *Tanh. Noah 13, Pesiq. Rab. 29.*
440. *B. Sanh. 97a* and *b. AZ 9a* mention a messianic era that lasts two thousand years.
441. Several words in the MS appear out of place, similar to a phrase on the next line; the dittography is not found in other manuscripts, except MS War 374.
442. *S. Eli. Zuta 20* clarifies the idea that the sun and moon, created by the Holy One, are ashamed for all the injustice they "oversaw" during their existence. Then God makes a new heaven and earth for the world to come, as MV indicates below. Rashi, discussing *b. Sanh. 91b*, claims that their shame simply means that they will fade in comparison to the light that will emanate from the righteous. (The Talmud has a similar passage in *b. Pes. 68a.*) Isa 60:20 describes sun and moon both shining, an image illuminated in the Venice Haggadah (Online: www.library.yale.edu/judaice/site/exhibits/venicehaggadah/ images/HVenice21.jpg.
443. Rabbinic midrash frequently interprets a day as one thousand years based on Ps 90:4: *For in Your sight a thousand years are like yesterday that has passed.*
444. An abbreviated plural verb form is written, crossed out and replaced with the singular.

445. *Secrets of Rabbi Shimon b. Yoḥai* contains many of the motifs of MV's eschatological vision. *S. Eli. Rab. 5* emphasizes the comforts and joy the righteous will enjoy in the world to come, but it has very different language and context.
446. There appears to be dittography, referring to present/future time twice and not to the past. MS Family B2 and Const 1519B present a more cogent phrasing on which the minor revision is based.
447. Ingathering of the exiles from the "four corners of the earth" is invoked in daily liturgy, most notably in the *Ahavah Rabbah* prayer and the *Amidah*. In place of the phrase about rejoicing, MS Family B2 and Const 1519B read: תבנה ותכונן במהרה בימינו, may it be built and established speedily, in our days.
448. Rather than a concluding citation of the lemma verse, *The Lord will reign forever*, the midrash offers a classic messianic peroration. Recension A does repeat the verse at the end, although several MSS then add a brief peroration. The exegesis is a vision of how it comes to pass that God's reign is established on earth: through the defeat of Israel's enemies, evidence and universal testimony of God's singular power, and the abiding establishment of Israel in Jerusalem.
449. It is presumably by design that God has one witness from each place.
450. Due to the fact that the text does not refer to Israel in the third person until the end, the translation is punctuated to present the whole speech as Moses prophesying to the people about the time to come. Thus inspired, they sing the climactic culmination of the midrash, *The Lord will reign forever and ever.* Alternatively, however, the omniscient narrator could absorb the role after the first paragraph, and the final line would be in the voice of those assembled before God's throne.

    MS Family A2 expands on praise for God and the messianic peroration.
451. Cf. Deutero-Isaiah (e.g., Ch. 43), who also makes use of Exodus imagery to describe the future redemption.
452. *Bereshit Rabbati*, one text attributed to this school, discusses apocalyptic traditions related to the advent of Elijah, the *Testaments of the Twelve Patriarchs*, and the *Assumption of Moses*. Himmelfarb, "Rabbi Moses the Preacher and the Testaments of the Twelve Patriarchs," *AJS Review 9:1* (1984): 73–4; "Some Echoes of *Jubilees* in Medieval Hebrew Literature," in *Tracing the Threads: Studies in the Vitality of Jewish Pseudepigrapha* (ed. John Reeves; Atlanta: Scholars Press, 1994), 115–6.
453. Ta-Shma, "רבי משה הדרשן והספרות החיצונית [Rabbi Moshe haDarshan and the Pseudepigrapha]," in *כנסת מחקרים [A Collection of Studies]* (Jerusalem: Bialik Institute, 2001), 3:188–201.
454. See, for example, *Lev. Rab. 9:6, b. Sanh. 94a, b. 'Abod. Zar. 3b*. Ezek 37–40 also frames the broad sequence of events: a messianic kingdom, Gog from Magog and his destruction, a new Jerusalem. Cf. Rev 20:4–21:1.
455. Set in sixth-century BCE Babylonia, the Book of Daniel is generally considered to have been composed of various second- to third-century BCE apocalyptic sources. Chapter 9 indicates a date shortly after the outbreak of the Maccabean revolt. See Harold Ginsberg, "Daniel, Book of," in *EJ* 5:1277–1286.
456. Cf. James Charlesworth, ed., *The Messiah: Developments in Earliest Judaism and Christianity* (Minneapolis: Fortress Press, 1992).
457. See also the discussion of stages in Chaim Milikowsky's work on *Seder Olam*, including his essay, "Trajectories of Return, Restoration and Redemption in Rabbinic Judaism: Elijah, the Messiah, the War of Gog and the World to Come," in *Restoration: Old Testament, Jewish, and Christian Perspectives* (ed. James M. Scott; Leiden: Brill, 2001), 265–80.

458. Some of the Second Temple literature, such as the *Testament of the Twelve Patriarchs* and certain Dead Sea Scrolls, also mention two messianic figures, but they are a king from Judah and a priest from Levi.
459. Apocalyptic works such as 2 Baruch (Chapters 73–4) elaborate greatly on the transformation of the natural world.
460. See, e.g., Maimonides, *Helek-Sanhedrin Ch. 10* and *Essay on Resurrection.*
461. For an excellent discussion of *Sefer Zerubbabel* (along with an English translation) and related Jewish apocalyptic texts, see John Reeves, *Trajectories in Near Eastern Apocalyptic*. Eli Yassif has published a transcription of a fourteenth-century Ashkenazi manuscript, MS Oxford Bodleian Library Heb. d.11 (Neubauer 2797) in *ספר הזכרונות הוא דברי הימים לירחמיאל [Book of Remembrances: Chronicles of Yerahmiel]* (Ramat Aviv: Tel Aviv University, 2001), 427–35. According to the Institute of Microfilmed Hebrew Manuscripts, however, the oldest extant manuscript (10–11c.) is from the East: MS Cambridge Add. 3353. It remains unpublished to the best of my knowledge.
462. Graetz and some of his contemporaries identify *Sefer Zerubbabel* as an eleventh-century text, and Joseph Dan believes it may date between the third and sixth centuries ("Armilus: The Jewish Antichrist," in *Toward the Millenium* (ed. Peter Schäfer and Mark R. Cohen; Leiden: Brill, 1998) 80, 98–100. This thesis supplants his earlier acceptance of the seventh-century dating, as found in *הסיפור העברי בימי-הביניים [Hebrew Story in the Middle Ages]*, 43.)

    Most modern scholars, however, still affirm its redaction in Palestine in the first half of the seventh century. See, e.g., Martha Himmelfarb, "Sefer Zerubbabel," 67–90; Israel Lévi, "L'apocalypse de Zorobabel et le roi de Perse Siroès," *Revue des études juives* 69 (1919):108–15; Walter E. Kaegi, *Byzantium and the Early Islamic Conquests* (Cambridge: Cambridge University Press, 1992), 207; David Biale, "Counter-History and Jewish Polemics Against Christianity: The *Sefer Toldot Yeshu* and the *Sefer Zerubavel*," *Jewish Social Studies 6:1* (1999): 137.
463. Dan, *הסיפור העברי בימי-הבימיים [Hebrew Story in the Middle Ages]*, 35. Its widespread appeal, he asserts, is based on its literary power and its avoidance of a specific ideology. By not partaking of one of the three great medieval Jewish movements (philosophy, ḥasidei Ashkenaz, mysticism), the apocalyptic vision raised little dissension (pp. 44–6). Dan also points out that, in the broader history of Jewish messianic themes, the elements of *Sefer Zerubbabel* that have been most influential are those which elaborated and systematized earlier traditions ("Armilus: The Jewish Antichrist," 103).
464. Patai, ed., *The Messiah Texts*, 168–9. A transcription can be found in Even-Shemuel's *מדרשי גאולה [Midrashim on Redemption]*, 135–41, translated by Reeves in *Trajectories in Near Eastern Apocalyptic*, 134–43.
465. According to *Sefer Zerubbabel*, Armilos is the offspring of Satan and a marble statue in the shape of a virgin with whom he had sexual relations. In medieval folklore, there was a legendary "marble virgin" in Rome, somehow associated with Virgil, and Romans were rumored to engage in immoral sexual acts with it. Some scholars have suggested that, as fodder for the Jewish imagination, the tale has the added power of satirizing Christian worship of the Virgin Mary. See, e.g., Israel Lévi, "L'apocalypse de Zorobabel," 71:58–61; Jacob Klatzkin, "Armilus," in *EJ* 3:476–7; Martha Himmelfarb, "Sefer Zerubbabel," 67–90; Joseph Dan, "Armilus: The Jewish Antichrist," 81–2; David Biale, "Counter-History and Jewish Polemics Against Christianity," 130–45; Peter Schäfer, *Mirror of His Beauty: Feminine*

Images of God from the Bible to the Early Kabbalah (Princeton: Princeton University Press, 2002), 212–16. Although MV's omission of this significant theme could then be seen as a hint of Christian censorship or as a minor indication of redaction in a non-Christian environment since the satire would have little significance, Reeves argues that there is little to substantiate the connection to Christian iconography, *Trajectories in Near Eastern Apocalyptic*, 21.

466. Even-Shemuel, *מדרשי גאולה [Midrashim on Redemption]*, 177, 195. David Cook, *Studies in Muslim Apocalyptic* (Princeton, N.J.: Darwin Press, 2002), 96–7, mentions one tradent who describes *al-Dajjal* with his ears cut off.
467. See Reeves, *Trajectories in Near Eastern Apocalyptic*, 77, 80–85.
468. *ibid.*, 17. It is important to note, however, that many Hebrew texts composed within the aegis of Islam had travelled to Western Europe by the time of Recension B's redaction.
469. See, for instance, Cook, *Studies in Muslim Apocalyptic*, to understand the broad differences in detail, sequence and even primary figures of the eschaton.
470. Reeves, *Trajectories in Near Eastern Apocalyptic*, 6.
471. *Targ. Pseudo-Jonathan* Deut 34:3 expands on the biblical narrative, with God showing Moses various events of the future including "the punishment of the wicked Armilgos and the battle orders of Gog." (Note the text's insertion of a "g," as in MS Family B1 and Vat 285.) In the targum of Isa 11:4, one finds "*shall slay the wicked,*" becomes "*shall slay the wicked* Armilos." It may be worth noting that Isa 11:4 is part of the haftarah reading for the eighth day of Passover.
472. See, for example, Zunz, *הדרשות בישראל [Derashot in Israel]*, 35, and Albeck's notes, 252 n. 9, 429–30 n. 31; Even-Shemuel, *מדרשי גאולה [Midrashim on Redemption]*, 90ff.
473. Wout Jac. van Bekkum, "Jewish Messianic Expectations in the Age of Heraclius," in *The Reign of Heraclius (610–641): Crisis and Confrontation* (ed. G. J. Reinink and Bernard Stolte; Leuven, Belgium: Peeters, 2002), 108. Joseph Yahalom published the *piyyut* in "על תוקפן של יצירות ספרות כמקור לבירור שאלות היסטוריות [On the Strength of Literary Works as a Source for Clarification of Historical Questions]," *Cathedra* 11 (1979): 130–33. Also see his chapter, "The Temple and the City in Liturgical Hebrew Poetry," in *The History of Jerusalem* (ed. Joshua Prawer and Haggai ben-Shammai; Jerusalem: Yad Izhak ben-Zvi, 1996), 278–80. Cf. *Targ. Tos.* Zech. 12:10, which attributes the murder to Gog: "Afterwards the Messiah b. Ephraim will emerge and fight a battle with Gog, but Gog will slay him before the gate in Jerusalem. Then...they will mourn for him as a father and mother mourn for an only child."
474. van Bekkum, "Jewish Messianic Expectations," 108.
475. Joseph Dan is among those scholars who incline toward this historical reference, consistent with his earlier dating: "Armilus: The Jewish Antichrist," 80, 98–100.
476. John Meyendorff, *Imperial Unity and Christian Divisions: The Church 450–680* (Crestwood, N.Y.: St. Vladimir's Seminary Press, 1989), 341–2.

    Sefer Eliahu (most likely also a seventh-century text) mentions a variety of names, including Harmalet and Tarmila, which sound a bit like Armilos, although it ultimately favors Hakashra.
477. Raphael Patai, *The Messiah Texts* (Detroit: Wayne State University Press, 1979), 157, 195. This notion is first found in Ferdinand Hitzig, *Das Buch Daniel* (Leipzig: Weidmann, 1850), 125, but has been generally ignored by the scholarly community.

478. Kaufmann Kohler is among those promoting the association with the Persian deity ("Armilus," *Jewish Encyclopedia, I:296–7*), emphasizing the "g" sound found in some renderings of Armilos (Armilgos).
479. Berger, "Three Typological Themes in Early Jewish Messianism: Messiah son of Joseph, Rabbinic Calculations, and the Figure of Armilus," *AJS Review 10:2* (1985): 155–62. He provides a tidy analysis of the various arguments, as does Joseph Dan, *הסיפור העברי בימי-הביניים [Hebrew Story in the Middle Ages]*, 41–3. Berger does not discount the Romulus theories, preferring to see an amalgamation of associations that compound the evocative power of the name.
480. Israel Lévi, "L'apocalypse de Zorobabel," 71: 57–65. According to Reeves, *Trajectories in Near Eastern Apocalyptic*, 20, Graetz was the first modern scholar to propose this derivation.
481. Reeves, *Trajectories in Near Eastern Apocalyptic*, 18–19.
482. See Reeves, "Metatron as Apocalyptic Persona," in *Trajectories in Near Eastern Apocalyptic*, 179–86. Some Elijah tales share motifs with Metatron, e.g., revealer of secrets (*b. B. Metsia 85b*), recorder of merits (*Lev. Rab. 34:8*).
483. For discussion of Metatron as the lesser YHWH, see Andrei Orlov, *The Enoch-Metatron Tradition* (Tübingen: Mohr Siebeck, 2005), 136–43. See also: Gershom Scholem, *Jewish Gnosticism, Merkabah Mysticism and Talmudic Tradition* (New York: Jewish Theological Seminary, 1960), 41–2; Alan Segal, *Two Powers in Heaven: Early Rabbinic Reports About Christianity and Gnosticism* (Boston: Brill, 2002), 63. Moshe Idel presents the Enoch-Metatron transformation in the larger context of mystical and mainstream rabbinic literature: "Enoch is Metatron," *Immanuel 24/25* (1990): 220–40.
484. Schäfer, *The Hidden and Manifest God: Some Major Themes in Early Jewish Mysticism* (Albany: SUNY Press, 1992), 29 n. 70.
485. Gershom Scholem, in his study of Jewish gnosticism, asserts that the Talmud and major midrashim do not conceive of Metatron as a human being (Enoch) transfigured into an angel; although this lore can be traced as a distinct stream in Targum and other aggadic texts, elsewhere Scholem ascribes the absence "to a reluctance of the talmudists to regard Enoch in a favorable light." Apocalyptic texts integrate the disparate traditions. See *Jewish Gnosticism*, 41–51, and his article on "Metatron" in *EJ 11:1445*.

Appendix: Manuscript Descriptions

1. The two manuscripts not identified by IMHM as containing MV are JTS 4998 and JTS 5000. A search of the database for *Midrash vaYosha* also yields a manuscript that collects interpretations related to the ten plagues (MS London 10416). This 18–19th-century text, copied in an Eastern hand, includes material from MV's treatment of the plagues, but it is not included in this study.
2. In Yassif's later work, *The Hebrew Folktale*, xii, he integrates Beit-Arie's refinements regarding the origin of the manuscript.
3. Wies-Campagner provides a transcription of the dedication, *Midrasch Wajoscha,* 8–9.

Bibliography

Alexander, Elizabeth Shanks. "The Orality of Rabbinic Writing." Pages 38–57 in *The Cambridge Companion to the Talmud and Rabbinic Literature*. Edited by Charlotte Fonrobert and Martin S. Jaffee. Cambridge: Cambridge University Press, 2007.

Alexander, Philip. "Jewish Aramaic Translations of Hebrew Scriptures." Pages 217–53 in *Mikra: Text, Translation, Reading and Interpretation of the Hebrew Bible in Ancient Judaism and Early Christianity*. Edited by Martin Jan Mulder. Peabody, Mass.: Hendrickson, 2004.

al-Kisai, Muhammad ibn Abd Allah. *Tales of the Prophets (Qiṣaṣ al-anbiya)*. Translated by Wheeler M. Thackston Jr. Chicago: KAZI Publications, 1997.

Allen, Roger. *An Introduction to Arabic Literature*. Cambridge: Cambridge University Press, 2000.

al-Tabari, Abu Jafar Muhammad. *History of al-Tabari: Prophets and Patriarchs*. Translated by William M. Brinner. Albany: State University of New York Press, 1987.

–. *History of al-Tabari: The Children of Israel*. Translated by William M. Brinner. Albany: State University of New York Press, 1991.

Alter, Robert. *The Art of Biblical Narrative*. New York: Basic Books, 1981.

–. *The Five Books of Moses*. New York: W.W. Norton, 2004.

al-Thalabi, Ahmad ibn Muhammad ibn. *Lives of the Prophets*. Translated by William M. Brinner. Leiden: Brill, 2002.

Anderson, Gary A. "Law and Lawgiving." Pages 475–77 in *Encyclopedia of the Dead Sea Scrolls*. Oxford: Oxford University Press, 2000.

Anderson, Robert T., and Terry Giles. *Tradition Kept: The Literature of the Samaritans*. Peabody, Mass.: Hendrickson Publishers, 2005.

Aptowitzer, Victor. "The Celestial Temple as Viewed in the Aggadah." Pages 1–29 in *Binah Vol. 2*. Edited by Joseph Dan. New York: Praeger, 1989. Originally published in Hebrew, *Tarbiz* 2 (1931).

Ashkenazi, Eliezer, ed. *דברי חכמים [Divre hakhamim]*. Metz, 1849.

Astren, Fred. "The Dead Sea Scrolls and Medieval Jewish Studies: Methods and Problems." *Dead Sea Discoveries* 8:2 (2001): 106–23.

Auerbach, Moses. "Elijah – In the *Aggadah*." Pages 6:333–4 in *Encyclopaedia Judaica*. 2d ed. Macmillan Reference USA, 2006.

Bacher, Wilhelm. *Die Proömien der alten jüdischen Homilie*. Leipzig: Hinrich, 1913.

–. "Targum," in *Jewish Encyclopedia*. New York: Funk and Wagnalls, 1906. Online: www.jewishencyclopedia.com.

–. "Zum Schrifttum und Ritus der persischen Juden von Buchara." *Zeitschrift fur Hebraeische Bibliographie* 4 (1900): 180–85.

Bak, János M., Heinz Quirin, and Paul M. Hollingsworth, eds. *Medieval Narrative Sources : A Chronological Guide*. New York: Garland, 1987.

Bal, Mieke. *Narratology : Introduction to the Theory of Narrative*. Toronto: University of Toronto Press, 1985.

Bal, Mieke, and David Jobling. *On Story-telling: Essays in Narratology*. Sonoma, Calif.: Polebridge Press, 1991.

Bamberger, Bernard Jacob. *Fallen Angels*. Philadelphia: Jewish Publication Society of America, 1952.

Bar Ilan Responsa Project, Version 17. Ramat Gan: Bar Ilan University,1972–2009.

Barth, Lewis. "Is Every Medieval Hebrew Manuscript a New Composition?" Pages 43–62 in *Agendas for the Study of Midrash in the Twenty-first Century*. Edited by Marc Lee Raphael. Williamsburg: College of William and Mary, 1999.

Baskin, Judith. *Pharaoh's Counselors: Job, Jethro and Balaam in Rabbinic and Patristic Tradition*. Brown Judaic Studies 47. Chico, Calif.: Scholars Press, 1983.

Beaton, Roderick. *The Medieval Greek Romance*. London: Routledge, 1996.

Beit-Arie, Malachi. *Hebrew Manuscripts of East and West: Towards a Comparative Codicology*. London: British Library, 1993.

–. "Publication and Reproduction of Literary Texts in Medieval Jewish Civilization: Jewish Scribality and its Impact on the Texts Transmitted." Pages 225–47 in *Transmitting Jewish Traditions: Orality, Textuality, and Cultural Diffusion*. Edited by Yaakov Elman and Israel Gershoni. New Haven: Yale University Press, 2000.

–. "Transmission of Texts by Scribes and Copyists: Unconscious and Critical Interferences." *Bulletin of the John Rylands University Library* 75:3 (1993): 32–51.

–. "כ"י אוכספורד 135: בשולי מאמרו של ע' יסיף, תרביץ נג (תשמ"ד), עמ' 409 ואילך [MS Oxford-Bodleian Or. 135: Regarding E. Yassif's Article in Tarbiz 53]." *Tarbiz* 54 (1985): 631–34.

Bekker-Nielsen, Hans, ed. *Medieval Narrative: A Symposium*. Odense: Odense University Press, 1979.

Bekker-Nielsen, Hans, Marianne Børch, and Bengt Algot Sørensen, eds. *From Script to Book : A Symposium*. Odense: Odense University Press, 1986.

Ben-Amos, Dan. *Folktales of the Jews*. Philadelphia: Jewish Publication Society, 2006.

Ben-Amos, Dan, ed. "Jewish Folktales: An Encyclopedic Survey." *Jewish Folklore and Ethnology Review* 14:1-2 (1992): 3–25.

ben Asher, Bahya. ביאור על התורה *[Torah Commentary]*. Jerusalem: Mosad haRav Kook, 1967.

–. כד הקמח *[Kad haKemah]*. Jerusalem: Mosad haRav Kook, 1991.

Ben-Chaim, Zev, ed. *תיבת מרקה [Tibat Marqe]*. Jerusalem: Israel Academy of Sciences and Humanities, 1988.

ben Chakham Eliyahu, Rachamim. *הפטרה ליום שמיני של פסח עם התפסיר בלשון פרסי כפי מה שנהגו בני עמי יושבי בוכאר"א ואגפיה [Haftarah for Eighth-Day Passover with a Farsi Translation According to the Custom of the Residents of Bukhara and its Environs]*. Jerusalem: A.M. Lunts, 1898.

ben Eliezer, Tobiah. *מדרש לקח טוב [Midrash lekah tov]*. Jerusalem, 1959.

"ben Hyrcanus, Rabbi Eliezer". *פרקי דרבי אליעזר [Pirkei d'Rabbi Eliezer]*. Jerusalem: Eshkol.

ben-Reuven, Sarah. "מידה כנגד מידה בסיפור יוסף [Measure for Measure in the Story of Joseph]." *Beit Miqra* 49:4 (2004): 185–90.

Berger, David. "Three Typological Themes in Early Jewish Messianism: Messiah son of Joseph, Rabbinic Calculations, and the Figure of Armilus." *Association for Jewish Studies Review* 10:2 (1985): 141–64.

Berliner, Abraham. *Targum Onkelos*. Berlin: 1884.

Bettan, Israel. *Studies in Jewish Preaching*. Cincinnati: Hebrew Union College Press, 1939.

Bezold, Carl. *Die Schatzhöhle*. Leipzig: J.C. Hinrichs, 1883.

Biale, David. "Counter-history and Jewish Polemics Against Christianity: The *Sefer Toldot Yeshu* and the *Sefer Zerubavel*." *Jewish Social Studies* 6:1 (1999): 130–45.

–, ed. *Cultures of the Jews : A New History*. New York: Schocken Books, 2002.

Bible Works, Version 6.0. Norfolk, VA: Bible Works LLC, 2003.

Bloch, Phillipp. "Studien zur Agadah." *MGJW* 34 (1885): 165–87.

Bodendorfer (=Langer), Gerhard. *Das Drama des Bundes: Ezechiel 16 in rabbinischer Perspektive*. Freiberg im Breisgau: Herder, 1997.

Booth, Wayne. "The Pleasures and Pitfalls of Irony: Or Why Don't You Say What You Mean?" Pages 1–13 in *Rhetoric, Philosophy and Literature: An Exploration*. Edited by Don M. Burks. West Lafayette, Ind.: Purdue University Press, 1978.

Borges, Jorge Luis. *Seven Nights*. Translated by Eliot Weinberger. New York: New Directions, 1984.

Bowman, Steven B. *The Jews of Byzantium (1204–1453)*. University, Ala.: University of Alabama Press, 1985.

Boyarin, Daniel. *Intertextuality and the Reading of Midrash*. Bloomington: Indiana University Press, 1990.

Braude, William G., and Israel J. Kapstein, eds. *Tanna debe Eliyyahu*. Philadelphia: Jewish Publication Society of America, 1981.

Bregman, Marc. "Midrash Rabbah and the Medieval Collector Mentality." *Prooftexts* 17:1 (1997): 63–76.

–. "Pseudepigraphy in Rabbinic Literature." Pages 27–41 in *Pseudepigraphic Perspectives: The Apocrypha and Pseudepigrapha in Light of the Dead Sea Scrolls*. Edited by Esther G. Chazon and Michael E. Stone. Leiden: Brill, 1999.

–. *ספרות תנחומא-ילמדנו: תיאור נוסחיה ועיונים בדרכי התהוותם [The Tanhuma-Yelamdenu Literature: Studies in the Evolutions of the Versions]*. Piscataway, NJ: Gorgias Press, 2003.

–. "פתיחתאות מעגליות ופתיחתאות 'זו שנאמרה ברוח הקודש' [Circular Proems and 'This is what was spoken through the Holy Spirit' Proems]." Pages 34–51 in *מחקרים באגדה, תרגומים ותפילות ישראל לזכר יוסף היינמן [Studies in the Aggadah, Targum and Liturgy of Israel, in memory of Joseph Heinemann]*. Edited by Ezra Fleischer and Jakob Petuchowski. Jerusalem: Hebrew Union College Press, 1971.

Briggs, Charles F. "Literacy, Reading and Writing in the Medieval West." *Journal of Medieval History* 26:4 (December 2000): 397–420.

Brock, Sebastian. "Sarah and the Aqedah." *Le Muséon* 87:1-2 (1974): 67–77.

–. "Syriac Dialogue Poems: Marginalia to a Recent Edition." *Le Muséon* 97 (1984): 29–58.

–. "Syriac Dispute Poems: The Various Types." Pages 109–19 in *Dispute Poems and Dialogues*. Edited by G. J. Reinink and H. L. J. Vanstiphout. Leuven: Department of Oriëntalstiek, 1991.

–. "Two Syriac Verse Homilies on the Binding of Isaac." *Le Muséon* 99:1–2 (1986): 61–129.

Brody, Heinrich. *מבחר השירה העברית [Selection of Hebrew Poetry]*. Leipzig: Insel-Verlag, 1922.

Brooke, George J. "Rewritten Bible." Pages 777–81 in *Encyclopedia of the Dead Sea Scrolls*. Edited by Lawrence H. Schiffman and James C. VanderKam. New York: Oxford University Press, 2000.

Brown, Francis, Samuel Driver and Charles Briggs, *A Hebrew and English Lexicon of the Old Testament*. Oxford: Clarendon Press, 1936.

Brown, Raymond Edward. *The Birth of the Messiah: A Commentary on the Infancy Narratives in Matthew and Luke*. Garden City, N.Y.: Doubleday, 1977.

Buber, Solomon. *מדרש תנחומא, הקדום והישן [The Earlier Midrash Tanhuma]*. New York, 1885. Repr., 1945.

Buber, Solomon, and J. Freimann, eds. *Siddur Raschi*. Berlin, 1911. Repr., Israel: 1980.

Campbell, Duncan B. *Besieged: Siege Warfare in the Ancient World*. Oxford: Osprey, 2006.

Cargill, Oscar. *Drama and Liturgy*. New York: Columbia University Press, 1930.

Carmi, T., ed. *The Penguin Book of Hebrew Verse*. London: Penguin Books, 1981.

Charles, Robert Henry, ed. *The Apocrypha and Pseudepigrapha of the Old Testament in English*. Oxford: Clarendon Press, 1913.

Charlesworth, James H. "The Pseudepigrapha as Biblical Exegesis." Pages 139–52 in *Early Jewish and Christian Exegesis: Studies in Memory of William Hugh Brownlee*. Edited by William Hugh Brownlee, Craig A. Evans and William F. Stinespring. Atlanta: Scholars Press, 1987.

–, ed. *The Messiah: Developments in Earliest Judaism and Christianity*. Minneapolis: Fortress Press, 1992.

Chernick, Michael. "Marie de France in the Synagogue." *Exemplaria* 19:1 (2006): 183–205.

Chiat, Marilyn Joyce Segal, and Kathryn Reyerson, eds. *The Medieval Mediterranean: Cross-cultural Contacts*. St. Cloud, Minn.: North Star Press, 1988.

Clover, Charles. "Moth that Can Kill Humans is Found Breeding in Britain." *Daily Telegraph* October 14, 2006. Cited 25 September 2007. Online: http://www.telegraph.co.uk/news/main.jhtml?xml=/news/2006/10/14/noak14.xml.

Cohen, Gerson D. *Studies in the Variety of Rabbinic Cultures*. Philadelphia: Jewish Publication Society, 1991.

Cohen, Mark R. "Medieval Jewry in the World of Islam." Pages 193–218 in *The Oxford Handbook of Jewish Studies*. Edited by Martin Goodman. Oxford: Oxford University Press, 2002.

Cook, David. *Studies in Muslim Apocalyptic*. Princeton, N.J.: Darwin Press, 2002.

Copeland, Rita. *Rhetoric, Hermeneutics, and Translation in the Middle Ages: Academic Traditions and Vernacular Texts*. Cambridge: Cambridge University Press, 1991.

Corfis, Ivy A., and Michael Wolfe, eds. *The Medieval City Under Siege*. Woodbridge, Suffolk: Boydell Press, 1995.

Culi, Jacob. *Me'am Lo'ez: The Torah Anthology*. Translated by Aryeh Kaplan. New York: Moznaim, 1977 (orig. 18th c.).

Dan, Joseph. "Armilus: The Jewish Antichrist and the Origins and Dating of *Sefer Zerubbavel*." Pages 73–104 in *Toward the Millenium*. Edited by Peter Schäfer and Mark R. Cohen. Leiden: Brill, 1998.

–. "Fiction, Hebrew." Pages 6:1261–71 in *Encyclopaedia Judaica*. Jerusalem: Keter, 1972.

–. "The Narratives of Medieval Jewish History." Pages 141–52 in *The Oxford Handbook of Jewish Studies*. Edited by Martin Goodman. Oxford: Oxford University Press, 2002.

–. *הסיפור העברי בימי הביניים [The Hebrew Story in the Middle Ages]*. Jerusalem: Keter, 1974.

–. *ספרות המוסר והדרוש [Hebrew Ethical and Homiletical Literature]*. Jerusalem: Keter, 1975.

–, ed. *ספר הישר [Sefer haYashar]*. Jerusalem: Bialik Institute, 1986.

Davenport, Tony. *Medieval Narrative: An Introduction*. Oxford: Oxford University Press, 2004.

Davies, Gwyn. *Roman Siege Works*. Stroud, Gloucestershire: Tempus, 2006.

Dawood, N. J., translator. *Tales from the Thousand and One Nights*. London: Penguin, 1954. Repr., 1973.

De Lange, Nicholas. "Hebrew Scholarship in Byzantium." Pages 23–37 in *Hebrew Scholarship and the Medieval World*. Edited by Nicholas De Lange. New York: Cambridge University Press, 2001.

Denis, Albert-Marie. *Introduction aux pseudépigraphes grecs d'ancien testament*. Leiden: Brill, 1970.

Eco, Umberto. *A Theory of Semiotics*. Bloomington: Indiana University Press, 1976.

Eisenstein, Judah David, ed. *אוצר מדרשים [Otzar midrashim]*. 2 vols. NY: 1915. Repr., Benei Berak: Sifrei Kodesh Mishor, 1990.

Elbaum, Jacob. "From Sermon to Story: The Transformation of the Akeidah." *Prooftexts* 6 (1986): 97–116.

–. "*Yalqut Shim'oni* and the Medieval Midrashic Anthology." *Prooftexts* 17:2 (1997): 133–51.

–. "בין עריכה לשיכתוב–לאופיה של הספרות המדרשית המאוחרת [Between Editing and Composition: On the Nature of Late Midrashic Literature]." Pages 3:57–62 in *Proceedings of the Ninth World Congress of Jewish Studies*. Edited by Moshe Goshen-Gottstein. Jerusalem: Magnes Press, 1988.

–. "המליצה, המוטיב והעניין: לדרך עיצובו של הסיפור בפרקי דרבי אליעזר [Style, Theme and Subject: On the Fashioning of Story in Pirkei d'Rabbi Eliezer." Pages 99–126 in *מחקרי ירושלים בפולקלור יהודי לכבוד דב נוי [Jerusalem Studies in Jewish Folklore in Honor of Dov Noy]*. Edited by Tamar Alexander and Galit Hasan-Rokem. Jerusalem: Magnes Press, 1992.

–, ed. *להבין דברי חכמים: מבחר דברי מבוא לאגדה ולמדרש [Understanding the Words of the Sages: A Selection of Introductions to Aggadah and Midrash]*. Jerusalem: Bialik Institute, 2000.

Eleazar b. Yehudah of Worms. *פרושי סדור התפילה לרוקח [Rokeah's Explications of the Prayerbook]*. Edited by Moshe and Yehudah Alter Hershler. Jerusalem: Wagshal, 1992.

Elitzur, S. "מפיוט למדרש [From Piyyut to Midrash]." Pages 2:383–97 in ספר היובל לרב מרדכי ברויאר *[Jubilee Volume for Rabbi Mordechai Brauer]*. Edited by M. Bar-Asher. Jerusalem: Adademon, 1992.

Elman, Yaakov, and Israel Gershoni, eds. *Transmitting Jewish Traditions: Orality, Textuality, and Cultural Diffusion*. New Haven: Yale University Press, 2000.

Emden, Jacob. *סדור בית יעקב מעמדין [Siddur Beit Yaakov of Emden]*. Vol. 1. Lemburg: David Balaban, 1904. Repr., 2003.

Ephraem. *The Book of the Cave of Treasures*. Translated by E. A. Wallis Budge. New York: Cosimo Classics, 1886. Repr., 2005.

Epstein, A. "Tosefta du Targoum Yerouschalmi." *Revue des Études Juives* 30 (1895): 44–51.

Epstein, Morris, ed. *Tales of Sendebar*. Philadelphia: Jewish Publication Society of America, 1967.

Even-Shemuel, Yehuda. *מדרשי גאולה [Midrashim on Redemption]*. Jerusalem: Bialik Institute, 1953.

Firestone, Reuven. *Journeys in Holy Lands: The Evolution of the Abraham-Ishmael Legends in Islamic Exegesis*. Albany: State University of New York Press, 1990.

Fishbane, Michael A. *Biblical Interpretation in Ancient Israel*. Oxford: Oxford University Press, 1985.

–. "Inner-Biblical Exegesis." Pages 1:33–48 in *Hebrew Bible/Old Testament: The History of its Interpretation*. Edited by Magne Sæbø. Göttingen: Vandenhoeck & Ruprecht, 1996.

–. "Inner Biblical Exegesis: Types and Strategies of Interpretation in Ancient Israel." Pages 19–37 in *Midrash and Literature*. Edited by Geoffrey H. Hartman and Sanford Budick. Binghamton, N.Y.: Vail-Ballou Press, 1986.

Fishman, Talya. *Becoming the People of the Talmud: Oral Torah as Written Tradition in Medieval Jewish Cultures*. Philadelphia: University of Pennsylvania Press, 2011.

Flusser, David. "*Palaea Historica:* An Unknown Source of Biblical Legends." *Scripta Hierosolymitana* 22 (1971): 48–79.

Foley, John Miles. *The Singer of Tales in Performance*. Bloomington: Indiana University Press, 1995.

Fonrobert, Charlotte. "The Handmaid, the Trickster, and the Birth of the Messiah." Pages 245–75 in *Current Trends in the Study of Midrash*. Edited by Carol Bakhos. Leiden: Brill, 2006.

–. "When the Rabbi Weeps: On Reading Gender in Talmudic Aggadah." *Nashim* 4 (2001): 56–83.

Fraade, Steven. "Literary Composition and Oral Performance in Early Midrashim." *Oral Tradition* 14:1 (1999): 33–51.
Online: http://journal.oraltradition.org/issues/14i/fraade.

–. "Locating Targum in the Textual Polysystem of Rabbinic Pedagogy." *Bulletin of the International Organization for Septuagint and Cognate Studies* 39 (2006): 69–91.

–. "Rabbinic Views on the Practice of Targum, and Multilingualism in the Jewish Galilee of the Third-Sixth Centuries." Pages 253–86 in *The Galilee in Late Antiquity*. Edited by Lee I. Levine. New York: Jewish Theological Seminary of America, 1992.

–. "Rewritten Bible and Rabbinic Midrash as Commentary." Pages 59–77 in *Current Trends in the Study of Midrash*. Edited by Carol Bakhos. Leiden: Brill, 2006.

–. "Sifre Deuteronomy 26 (*ad* Deut 3:23): How Conscious the Composition?" *Hebrew Union College Annual* 54 (1983): 245–301.

Fraenkel, Yonah. *דרכי האגדה והמדרש [Methods of Aggadah and Midrash]*. Givatayim: Masada, 1991.

–. *עיונים בעולמו הרוחני של סיפור האגדה [Studies in the Spiritual World of the Aggadic Story]*. Tel Aviv: Hakibbutz Hameuchad, 1981.

–. "קווים בולטים בתולדות מסורת הטקסט של סיפורי האגדה [Notable Trends in the History of Textual Tradition in Aggadic Narratives]." Pages 3:45–69 in *Proceedings of the Seventh World Congress of Jewish Studies*. Jerusalem: Magnes Press, 1977.

Friedlander, Gerald, ed. *Pirke de Rabbi Eliezer (according to the text of the manuscript belonging to Abraham Epstein of Vienna)*. London, 1916. Repr., Hermon Press: New York, 1965.

Friedmann, Meir. *מדרש פסיקתא רבתי [Midrash Pesiqta Rabbati]* Vienna: Joseph Kaiser, 1880.

Funkenstein, Amos. *סגנונות בפרשנות המקרא בימי הביניים [Styles in Medieval Biblical Exegesis]*. Tel Aviv: Israel Ministry of Defense, 1990.

Gager, John G. *Moses in Greco-Roman Paganism*. Nashville: Abingdon Press, 1972.

Garcia, Michael. "Medieval Medicine, Magic and Water," in *Peregrinations 1:3*. Cited 13 November, 2007. Online: http://peregrinations.kenyon.edu/vol1-3.pdf.

Gardiner, Harold C. *Mysteries' End: An Investigation of the Last Days of the Medieval Religious Stage*. New Haven: Yale University Press, 1946.

Gaspary, Adolf. *The History of Early Italian Literature to the Death of Dante*. Translated by Herman Oelsner. London: George Bell and Sons, 1901.

Gaster, Moses. *Jewish Sources of Parallels to the Early English Metrical Romances of King Arthur and Merlin*. London: Anglo-Jewish Historical Exhibition, 1887.

–. *Studies and Texts in Folklore, Magic, Mediaeval Romance, Hebrew Apocrypha, and Samaritan Archaeology*. New York: Ktav, 1971.

Gaster, Theodor H. "Myth and Story." Pages 110–36 in *Sacred Narrative*. Edited by Alan Dundes. Berkeley: University of California Press, 1954. Repr., 1984.

Gautier, Léon. *Histoire de la poésie liturgique au moyen âge*. Paris, 1886. Repr., Ridgewood, N.J.: Gregg Press, 1966.

Gerritsen, William P. *A Dictionary of Medieval Heroes*. Translated by Tanis Guest. Woodbridge: Boydell Press, 1998.

Geula, Amos. "מדרשי אגדה אבודים הידועים מאשכנז בלבד: אבכיר, אספה ודברים זוטא [Lost Aggadic Works Known Only From Ashkenaz: Midrash Abkir, Midrash Esfa and Devarim Zuta]." Doctoral dissertation, Hebrew University, 2006.

Ginsberg, Harold. "Daniel, Book of." Pages 5:1277–86 in *Encyclopaedia Judaica*. Jerusalem: Keter, 1972.

Ginsburger, Moses. "Aramäische Introductionen zum Thargumvortrag an Festtagen." *Zeitschrift der deutschen morgenländischen Gesellschaft* 54 (1900): 113–24.

–. "Die Thargumim zur Thoralection am 7. Pesach- und 1. Shabuoth-Tage." *Monatsschrift für Geschichte und Wissenschaft des Judentums* 39 (1895): 97–105, 67–75, 93–206.

Ginzberg, Louis. *Legends of the Bible*. New York: Simon and Schuster, 1956.

–. *Legends of the Jews*. 2 vols. Philadelphia: Jewish Publication Society, 1909. Repr., 2003.

–. *על הלכה ואגדה [On Jewish Law and Lore]*. Tel Aviv, 1960.

Girón Blanc, Luis Fernardo. "La Crónica de Moisés [The Chronicle of Moses]." *Sefarad* 48:2 (1988): 390–425.

Glick, Leonard B. *Abraham's Heirs: Jews and Christians in Medieval Europe*. Syracuse: Syracuse University Press, 1999.

Goitein, S. D. *A Mediterranean Society: The Jewish Communities of the Arab World as Portrayed in the Documents of the Cairo Geniza*. Berkeley: University of California Press, 1967.

Goitein, S. D., Shelomo Morag, Issachar Ben-Ami, and Norman A. Stillman, eds. *Studies in Judaism and Islam*. Jerusalem: Magnes Press, 1981.

Goldschmidt, Aryeh, ed. *מחזור ויטרי [Maḥzor Vitry: A Critical Edition]*. Jerusalem: Otzar haPoskim, 2004.

Goldziher, Ignaz. *Muslim Studies*. Translated by C.R. Barber and S.M. Stern. Vol. 2. London: Allen and Unwin, 1971.

Graham, William A. *Beyond the Written Word: Oral Aspects of Scripture in the History of Religion*. Cambridge: Cambridge University Press, 1987.

Green, Arthur. "The Children in Egypt and the Theophany at the Sea." *Judaism* 24 (1975): 446–56.

Grossman, Avraham. "Social Structure and Intellectual Creativity in Medieval Jewish Communities (Eighth to Twelfth Centuries)." Pages 3:1–19 in *Studies in Medieval Jewish History and Literature*. Edited by Isadore Twersky and Jay M. Harris. Cambridge: Harvard University Press, 2000.

–. "The School of Literal Jewish Exegesis in Northern France." Pages 2:321–71 in *Hebrew Bible/Old Testament: The History of its Interpretation*. Edited by Magne Sæbø. Göttingen: Vandenhoeck & Ruprecht, 1996.

Grunwald, Max. *סיפורי עם: רומנסות ואורחות חיים של יהודי ספרד [Folk Stories: Romances and Daily Life of Sephardic Jewry]*. Jerusalem: Magnes Press, 1982.

Gunzberg, Aryeh. *שאגת אריה [Sha'agat Aryeh: Questions and Responsa]*. Vilna, 1874. Repr., Jerusalem: Hatam Sofer Institute, 1974.

haKohen, Mordechai. *שפתי כהן על התורה [Siftei Kohen al haTorah]* Jerusalem: Makor haSefarim, 2004.

haNagid, David. *מדרש רבי דוד הנגיד [Midrash of Rabbi David haNagid]*. Translated by Abraham Katsch. Jerusalem: Mosad haRav Kook, 1964.

haNagid, David. *מדרש רבי דוד הנגיד על הגדה של פסח [Midrash Rabbi David haNagid al Haggadah shel Pesah]*. Translated by Shmuel Yerushalmi. Jerusalem: Wagshel, 1981.

Hartman, Geoffrey H., and Sanford Budick, eds. *Midrash and Literature*. New Haven: Yale University Press, 1986.

Hasan-Rokem, Galit. *Tales of the Neighborhood: Jewish Narrative Dialogues in Late Antiquity*. Berkeley: University of California Press, 2003.

–. *Web of Life: Folklore and Midrash in Rabbinic Literature*. Translated by Batya Stein. Stanford: Stanford University Press, 2000.

Haynes, Stephen R. *Noah's Curse*. Oxford: Oxford University Press, 2002.

Hayward, Robert. "Pirqe de Rabbi Eliezer and Targum Pseudo-Jonathan." *Journal of Jewish Studies* 42 (1991): 215–46.

Heinemann, Joseph. "The Proem in the Aggadic Midrashim." *Scripta Hierosolymitana* 22 (1971): 100–22.

–. *אגדות ותולדותיהן [Aggadah and its Development]*. Jerusalem: Keter, 1974.

–. "שרידים מיצירתם הפיוטית של המתורגמנים הקדומים [Fragments of Poetic Composition of the Early Meturgemans]." *HaSifrut* 4 (1973): 362–75.

Heinemann, Joseph, and Dov Noy, eds. *Studies in Aggadah and Folk-literature. Scripta Hierosolymitana, v. 22*. Jerusalem: Magnes Press, 1971.

Heinemann, Yitzhak. *דרכי האגדה [The Methods of Aggadah]*. Jerusalem: Magnes Press, 1954.

Heller, B. "Das hebraische und arabische Märchen [The Hebrew and Arabic Fairytale]." Pages 4:350–2 in *Anmerkungen zu den Kinder: u. Hausmärchen der Brüder Grimm*. Edited by Johannes Bolte and Jirí Polívka. Leipzig: Dieterichsche Verlagsbuchhandlung, 1930.

Herman, David, ed. *The Cambridge Companion to Narrative*. Cambridge: Cambridge University Press, 2007.

–, ed. *Narratologies: New Perspectives on Narrative Analysis*. Columbus: Ohio State University Press, 1999.

Herr, Moshe. "Midrashim, Smaller." Pages 16:1515–18 in *Encyclopaedia Judaica*. Jerusalem: Keter, 1972.

Himmelfarb, Martha. *Ascent to Heaven in Jewish and Christian Apocalypses*. New York: Oxford University Press, 1993.

–. "R. Moses the Preacher and the Testaments of the Twelve Patriarchs." *AJS Review* 9:1 (1984): 55–78.

–. "Sefer Zerubbabel." Pages 67–90 in *Rabbinic Fantasies: Imaginative Narratives from Classical Hebrew Literature*. Edited by David Stern and Mark Mirsky. Philadelphia: Jewish Publication Society, 1990.

–. "Some Echoes of *Jubilees*." Pages 115–41 in *Tracing the Threads: Studies in the Vitality of Jewish Pseudepigrapha*. Edited by John C. Reeves. Atlanta: Scholars Press, 1994.

Hitzig, Ferdinand. *Das Buch Daniel*. Leipzig: Weidmann, 1850.

Hollender, Elisabeth. "Narrative Exegesis in Ashkenas and Zarfat: The Case of 'Piyyut' Commentary." Pages 429–35 in *Jewish Studies at the Turn of the Twentieth Century: Proceedings of EAJS Congress*. Edited by Judit Borras and Angel Saenz-Badillos. Leiden: Brill, 1999.

Horowitz, Carmi. *The Jewish Sermon in 14th-century Spain: The Derashot of R. Joshua ibn Shu'eib*. Cambridge, Mass.: Harvard University Press, 1989.

Hugh, of St. Victor. *Didascalicon: A Medieval Guide to the Arts*. Translated by Jerome Taylor. New York: Columbia University Press, 1961.

Hyman, Arthur B., Isaac Lerer, and Isaac Shiloni, eds. *ילקוט שמעוני על הנביאים [Yalqut Shimoni on the Prophets]*. Jerusalem: Mosad haRav Kook, 1972.

ibn Shueib, Joshua. *דרשות ר"י אבן שועיב [Sermons of R. Joshua ibn Shueib]*. Edited by R. Zeev Metzger. Jerusalem: Wagshel, 1992.

Idel, Moshe. "Enoch is Metatron." *Immanuel* 24/25 (1990): 220–40.

Irshai, Oded. "Confronting a Christian Empire: Jewish Culture in the World of Byzantium." Pages 181–222 in *Cultures of the Jews: A New History*. Edited by David Biale. New York: Schocken Books, 2002.

Iser, Wolfgang. *Prospecting: From Reader Response to Literary Anthropology*. Baltimore: Johns Hopkins University Press, 1989.

Issaverdens, P. J. *Collection of Uncanonical Writings of the Old Testament Found in the Armenian Mss. of the Library of St. Lazarus*. Venice: Armenian Monastery of St. Lazarus, 1901.

Jaffee, Martin S. "Literary Composition and Oral Performance in Early Midrashim." *Oral Tradition* 14:1 (1999): 3–32.
Online: http://journal.oraltradition.org/issues/14i/jaffee.

–. "The Oral-Cultural Context of the Talmud Yerushalmi: Graeco-Roman Rhetorical Paideia, Discipleship and the Concept of Oral Torah." Pages 27–61 in *The Talmud Yerushalmi and Graeco-Roman Culture I*. Edited by Peter Schäfer and Catherine Hezser. Tübingen: Mohr Siebeck, 1998.

–. "Oral Tradition and Rabbinic Studies." *Oral Tradition* 18:1 (2003): 37–39. Online: http://journal.oraltradition.org/issues/18i/jaffee.

–. *Torah in the Mouth: Writing and Oral Tradition in Palestinian Judaism, 200 BCE–400 CE*. New York: Oxford University Press, 2001.

Jellinek, Adolph, ed. *בית המדרש [Bet ha-midrasch]*. Leipzig: 1853–57, Wien 1873–77. Repr., Jerusalem: Wahrmann Books, 1967 in 2 vols.

Jonssen, Jakob. *Humor and Irony in the New Testament*. Reykjavík: Bókaútgáfa Menningarsjóôs, 1965. Repr. Leiden: Brill, 1985.

Jung, Leo. *Fallen Angels in Jewish, Christian, and Mohammedan Literature*. New York: Ktav, 1974.

Kaegi, Walter Emil. *Byzantium and the Early Islamic Conquests*. Cambridge: Cambridge University Press, 1992.

–. *Some Thoughts on Byzantine Military Strategy*. Brookline, Mass.: Hellenic College Press, 1983.

Kahle, Paul. *Masoreten des Westens 2*. Stuttgart, 1930. Repr., Hildesheim: G. Olms, 1967.

Kamesar, Adam. "The Evaluation of the Narrative Aggada in Greek and Latin Patristic Literature." *Journal of Theological Studies* 45 (1994): 37–71.

Kasher, Rimon. "שתי תוספתות תרגום על מות משה [Two Targumic Toseftot on the Death of Moses]." *Tarbiz* 54 (1985): 217–24.

Kaufmann, Yehezkel. *The Religion of Israel, From its Beginnings to the Babylonian Exile*. Chicago: University of Chicago Press, 1960.

Kelber, Werner H. "Orality and Biblical Studies: A Review Essay." *Review of Biblical Literature* (Dec. 2007). Cited 3 December 2007. Online: www.bookreviews.org/pdf/2107_6748.pdf.

Kessler, Gwynn. *Conceiving Israel: The Fetus in Rabbinic Narratives*. Philadelphia: University of Pennsylvania Press, 2009.

Klapholtz, Yisroel Yaakov. *Tales of the Heavenly Court*. Tranlsated by Sheindel Weinbach. Bene Brak: Peer haSefer, 1982.

Klatzkin, Joseph. "Armilus." Pages 3:476–77 in *Encyclopaedia Judaica*. Jerusalem: Keter, 1972.

Klausner, Yehudah. *הנובלה בספרות העברית [The Novella in Hebrew Literature]*. Tel Aviv: J. Chachik, 1947.

Klein, Ernest, and Baruch Sarel. *A Comprehensive Etymological Dictionary of the Hebrew Language for Readers of English*. Jerusalem: Carta, 1987.

Klein, Michael. *The Fragment-Targums of the Pentateuch According to their Extant Sources*. 2 vols. Rome: Biblical Institute Press, 1980.

–. "The Targumic Tosefta to Exodus 15:2." *Journal of Jewish Studies* 26 (1975): 61–67.

Klein, Samuel. *תולדות הישוב היהודי בארץ-ישראל [History of Jewish Settlement in the Land of Israel]*. Tel Aviv: Tel Aviv University, 1935.

Knox, Norman. "Irony." Pages 626–34 in *Dictionary of the History of Ideas: Studies of Selected Pivotal Ideas*. Edited by Philip P. Wiener. New York: Charles Scribner's Sons, 1973.

Kogman-Appel, Katrin. "The Sephardic Picture Cycles and the Rabbinic Tradition: Continuity and Innovation in Jewish Iconography." *Zeitschrift für Kunstgeschichte* 60:4 (1997): 451–81.

Kohler, Kaufmann. "Armilus." Pages 1:296–7 in *Jewish Encyclopedia*. New York: Funk and Wagnalls, 1906.

Komlosh, Yehudah. "נוסח התרגום על קריעת ים סוף [Targum on the Splitting of the Sea]." *Sinai* 45 (1959): 223–28.

–. "קטע של תרגום ירושלמי ל'ואז ישיר משה' [A Fragment of Targum Yerushalmi on 'Then Moses sang']." Pages 7–11 in *ספר זיידל [Sefer Zeidel]*. Edited by Eliezer Eliner. Jerusalem: Israel Society for Biblical Research, 1962.

Kraeling, Carl. *The Excavations at Dura-Europos: The Synagogue*. New Haven: Yale University Press, 1956.

Kraemer, David. *The Mind of the Talmud*. New York: Oxford University Press, 1990.

Krauss, Samuel. *Griechische und lateinische Lehnwörter im Talmud, Midrasch und Targum [Greek and Latin Loanwords in Talmud, Midrash and Targum]*, 2 vols. Berlin: S. Calvary, 1898.

–. *פרס ורומי בתלמוד ובמדרשים [Persia and Rome in Talmud and Midrash]*. Jerusalem: Mosad haRav Kook, 1948.

Krueger, Roberta L., ed. *The Cambridge Companion to Medieval Romance*. Cambridge: Cambridge University Press, 2000.

Kugel, James L. *The Bible as it Was*. Cambridge, Mass.: Belknap Press, 1997.

–. *In Potiphar's house: The Interpretive Life of Biblical Texts*. San Francisco: Harper, 1990.

–. "Two Introductions to Midrash." *Prooftexts* 3:2 (1983): 131–55.

Kushelevsky, Rella. *Moses and the Angel of Death*. New York: P. Lang, 1995.

Lane, Edward William. *Arabian Society in the Middle Ages: Studies from the Thousand and One Nights*. New York: Barnes & Noble, 1971.

Lehman, Marjorie. "The Ein Ya'aqov, a Collection of Aggadah in Transition." *Prooftexts* 19:1 (1999): 21–40.

Lesley, Arthur M. "A Survey of Medieval Hebrew Rhetoric." Pages 107–27 in *Approaches to Judaism in Medieval Times*. Edited by David R. Blumenthal. Chico, CA: Scholars Press, 1984.

Lévi, Israel. "L'apocalypse de Zorobabel et le roi de Perse Siroès." *Revue des études juives*: 68 (1914):129–60, 69 (1919):108–21, 71 (1920): 57–65.

–. "Un recueil de contes juifs unédits." *Revue des études juives* 47 (1903): 202–13.

Leviant, Curt. "Jewish Influence upon Arthurian Legends." Pages 639–56 in *Salo Wittmayer Baron Jubilee Volume*. Edited by Saul Lieberman. New York: Columbia University Press, 1974.

–. *King Artus: A Hebrew Arthurian Romance of 1279* New York: Ktav, 1969.

Levine, Etan. "The Targums: Their Interpretive Character and Their Place in Jewish Text Tradition." Pages 1:323–31 in *Hebrew Bible/Old Testament*. Edited by Magne Sæbø. Göttingen: Vandenhoeck and Ruprecht, 1996.

Levinson, Joshua. "Dialogical Reading in the Rabbinic Exegetical Narrative." *Poetics Today* 25:3 (2004): 497–528.

–. *הסיפור שלא סופר: אמנות הסיפור המקראי המורחב במדרשי חז"ל [The Twice Told Tale: A Poetics of the Exegetical Narrative in Rabbinic Midrash]*. Jerusalem: Magnes Press, 2005.

Lewin, Benjamin M., ed. *אוצר הגאונים: תשובות גאוני בבל ופירושיהם, ברכות [Otzar haGeonim: Responsa of the Babylonian Geonim and their Explication, Tractate Berakhot]*. Haifa, 1928.

Lewis, C. S. *The Discarded Image*. Cambridge: Cambridge University Press, 1964.

Lieberman, Saul. *Greek in Jewish Palestine; Hellenism in Jewish Palestine*. New York: Jewish Theological Seminary of America, 1994.

–. *Texts and Studies*. New York: Ktav, 1974.

–, ed. *מדרש דברים רבה [Midrash devarim rabbah]*. Jerusalem: Bamberger, 1940.

Lindahl, Carl, John McNamara, and John Lindow, eds. *Medieval Folklore: An Encyclopedia of Myths, Legends, Tales, Beliefs, and Customs*. 2 vols. Santa Barbara, Calif.: ABC-CLIO, 2000.

Lindbeck, Kristen. *Elijah and the Rabbis: Story and Theology*. Columbia University Press, 2010.

Lord, Albert Bates. *The Singer of Tales*. Cambridge, Mass.: Harvard University Press, 1960.

Macdonald, John, ed. *Memar Marqah: The Teaching of Marqah*. Berlin: A. Töpelmann, 1963.

Maier, H. et. al. "The Oak Processionary Caterpillar as the Cause of an Epidemic Airborne Disease: Survey and Analysis." *British Journal of Dermatology* 149:5 (2003): 990–7.

Mandel, Paul. “Midrashic Exegesis and its Precedents in the Dead Sea Scrolls.” *Dead Sea Discoveries* 8:2 (2001): 149–68.
Mann, Jacob. *The Bible as Read and Preached in the Old Synagogue*. Cincinnati: Hebrew Union College, 1940.
Marcus, Jacob Rader, ed. *The Jew in the Medieval World: A Source Book, 315–1791*. Cincinnati: Hebrew Union College Press, 1983.
Margulies, Reuben. *מלאכי עליון [Heavenly Angels]*. Jerusalem: Mosad haRav Kook, 1945.
Marx, Alexander. “Studies in Gaonic History and Literature.” *Jewish Quarterly Review* 1 (1910): 61–104.
Mayor, Adrienne. *Greek Fire, Poison Arrows, and Scorpion Bombs: Biological and Chemical Warfare in the Ancient World.* Woodstock: Overlook, 2003.
McAuliffe, Jane Dammen, Barry Walfish, and Joseph Ward Goering, eds. *With Reverence for the Word: Medieval Scriptural Exegesis in Judaism, Christianity, and Islam*. Oxford: Oxford University Press, 2003.
McNamara, Martin. “The New Testament and the Palestinian Targum to the Pentateuch.” Thesis, Pontifical Biblical Institute, 1966.
Meier, John P. “The Historical Jesus and the Historical Law: Some Problems within the Problem.” *Catholic Biblical Quarterly* 65:1 (2003): 52–79.
Meir, Ofra. “The Story as a Hermeneutic Device.” *AJS Review* 7 (1982): 231–62.
–. “הסיפור ה"דרשני" במדרש קדום ומאוחר [The Darshanic Story in Early and Late Midrash].” *Sinai* 86 (1980): 246–66.
–. *הסיפור הדרשני בבראשית רבה [The Darshanic Story in Genesis Rabbah]*. Tel Aviv: HaKibbutz HaMeuchad, 1987.
–. *סוגיות בפואטיקה של סיפורי חז"ל [The Poetics of Rabbinic Stories]*. Tel Aviv: Sifriat haPoalim, 1993.
Meyendorff, John. *Imperial Unity and Christian Divisions: The Church, 450–680 AD*. Crestwood, N.Y.: St. Vladimir's Seminary Press, 1989.
Mikva, Rachel S. “Midrash in the Synagogue and the Attenuation of Targum.” *Jewish Studies Quarterly* 18:4 (2011): 319–42.
–. “*Midrash vaYosha* and the Development of Narrative in Medieval Jewish Exegesis.” Doctoral Dissertation, Jewish Theological Seminary, 2008.
–. “Talking Back to God: An Examination of *Hutzpa K'lapei Shamaya* in the Babylonian Talmud.” Rabbinic Thesis, Hebrew Union College, 1990.
–. “Weeping as Discourse Between Heaven and Earth: The Transformative Power of Tears in a Medieval Jewish Exegesis.” Pages 156–72 in *Aqua roris: Crying in the Middle Ages*. Edited by Elina Gertsman (Routledge: London, 2011).
Milikowsky, Chaim. “Trajectories of Return, Restoration and Redemption in Rabbinic Judaism: Elijah, the Messiah, the War of Gog and the World to Come.” Pages 265–80 in *Restoration: Old Testament, Jewish, and Christian Perspectives*. Edited by James M. Scott. Leiden: Brill, 2001.
Minnis, A. J., A. Brian Scott, and David Wallace, eds. *Medieval Literary Theory and Criticism, c. 1100–c. 1375: The Commentary-Tradition*. Oxford: Oxford University Press, 1988.
Mintz, Alan. *Hurban: Responses to Catastrophe in Jewish Literature*. Syracuse: Syracuse University Press, 1996.
Mirsky, Aaron. *יסודי צורות הפיוט [The Origin of Forms of Early Hebrew Poetry]*. Jerusalem: Magnes, 1985.
Moran, W.L. “The Ancient Near Eastern Background of the Love of God in Deuteronomy.” *The Catholic Biblical Quarterly* 25 (1963): 77–87.

Morris, Colin. *The Discovery of the Individual, 1050-1200*. Toronto: University of Toronto Press, 1987.
Muffs, Yochanan. *Love and Joy: Law, Language, and Religion in Ancient Israel*. New York.: Jewish Theological Seminary, 1992.
Müller, Joel. *מפתח לתשובות הגאונים [Index of Geonic Responsa]*. Berlin, 1891. Repr., New York: Menorah, 1956.
Neubauer, Adolf. *Catalogue of the Hebrew Manuscripts in the Bodleian Library*. Oxford: 1886.
Neusner, Jacob. *Introduction to Rabbinic Literature*. New York: Doubleday, 1994.
Nickelsburg, George W.E. "The Bible Rewritten and Expanded." Pages 89–156 in *Jewish Writings of the Second Temple Period: Apocrypha, Pseudepigrapha, Qumran, Sectarian Writings, Philo, Josephus*. Edited by Michael E. Stone. Assen, Netherlands: Van Gorcum, 1984.
Niedermeier, Hans. "Der altjiddische Midrasch Wojoschah." *Judaica* 21 (1965): 25–55.
Noy, Dov. "Motif-index of Talmudic-Midrashic literature." Doctoral dissertation, Indiana University, 1954.
–. *הסיפור העממי בתלמוד ובמדרש [The Folktale in Talmud and Midrash]*. Jerusalem: Mifal HaShikhpul, 1960.
Origen. *Origen: Homilies on Genesis and Exodus*. Translated by R. E. Heine. Fathers of the Church 71. Washington, D.C.: Catholic University of America Press, 1982.
Orlov, Andrei A. *The Enoch-Metatron Tradition*. Tübingen: Mohr Siebeck, 2005.
Pagels, Elaine H. *The Gnostic Gospels*. New York: Random House, 1979.
Pardes-Feinstein, Zahara. "מדרש ויושע: מבוא, מהדורת טקסט ודיון [Midrash vaYosha: Introduction, Textual Edition and Discussion]." Master's thesis, Hebrew University, 1993.
Patai, Raphael, ed. *The Messiah Texts*. Detroit: Wayne State University Press, 1979.
Patai, Raphael, Francis Lee Utley, and Dov Noy, eds. *Studies in Biblical and Jewish Folklore*. Bloomington: Indiana University Press, 1960.
Paul, Robert. *Moses and Civilization*. New Haven: Yale University Press, 1996.
Pederson, Johs. "The Criticism of the Islamic Preacher." *Die Welt des Islams* (new series) 2 (1952): 215–31.
–. "The Islamic Preacher." Pages 226–51 in *Ignace Goldziher Memorial Volume*. Edited by Samuel Lowinger and Joseph Somogyi. Budapest, 1948.
Pérez Fernández, Miguel. *Los capítulos de Rabbí Eliezer*. Biblioteca Midrásica 1. Valencia: Institución S. Jerónimo para la Investigación Bíblica, 1984.
Phelan, James. *Reading People, Reading Plots: Character, Progression, and the Interpretation of Narrative*. Chicago: University of Chicago Press, 1989.
Philo. *Philo*. Translated by F. H. Colson and G. H. Whitaker. London: Heinemann, 1929.
Pietersma, Albert, ed. *The Apocryphon of Jannes and Jambres the Magicians*. Leiden: E.J. Brill, 1994.
Polliack, Meira. *Genres in Judaeo-Arabic Literature*: off-print, 1998.
Posner, Raphael, and Israel M. Ta-Shma, eds. *The Hebrew Book: An Historical Survey*. Jerusalem: Keter, 1975.
Pratt, Karen, Elspeth Kennedy, and Penny Eley, eds. *Shifts and Transpositions in Medieval Narrative*. Cambridge: D.S. Brewer, 1994.
Pritchard, James. *Ancient Near Eastern Texts*, Vol. 1. Princeton: Princeton University Press, 1973.
Rabinowitz, Haim. *דיוקנאות של דרשנים [Portraits of Jewish Preachers]*. Jerusalem: Rubin Mass, 1967.

Rabinowitz, Louis and Stephen Wald. "Right and Left." Pages 17:301–2 in *Encyclopaedia Judaica*. 2d ed. Macmillan Reference USA, 2006.

Rawnitzki, Yehoshua, and Hayyim Nahman Bialik. *מדרשים קטנים [Midrashim Ketanim]*. Odessa: Moriah, 1919.

Reed, Annette Yoshiko. *Fallen Angels and the History of Judaism and Christianity: The Reception of Enochic Literature*. Cambridge: Cambridge University Press, 2005.

Reed, Annette Yoshiko, and Adam Becker, eds. *The Ways that Never Parted: Jews and Christians in Late Antiquity and the Early Middle Ages*. Tubingen: Mohr-Siebeck, 2003.

Reeves, John C. "The Flowing Stream: Qur'anic Interpretations and the Bible." *Religious Studies News: SBL Edition* 2:9 (December 2001).

–. *Trajectories in Near Eastern Apocalyptic: A Postrabbinic Jewish Apocalypse Reader*. Atlanta: Society of Biblical Literature, 2005.

–, ed. *Tracing the Threads: Studies in the Vitality of Jewish Pseudepigrapha*. Atlanta: Scholars Press, 1994.

Rodrigues Pereira, Alphons S. *Studies in Aramaic Poetry (c. 100 B.C.E.–c. 600 C.E.): Selected Jewish, Christian, and Samaritan Poems*. Assen: Van Gorcum, 1997.

Rosen, Tova, and Eli Yassif. "The Study of Hebrew Literature of the Middle Ages: Major Trends and Goals." Pages 241–94 in *The Oxford Handbook of Jewish Studies*. Edited by Martin Goodman. Oxford: Oxford University Press, 2002.

Rosen-Zvi, Ishay. "Measure for Measure as a Hermeneutical Tool in Early Rabbinic Literature." *Journal of Jewish Studies* 57:2 (2006): 269–86.

Rosenberg, Bruce A. *Folklore and Literature: Rival Siblings*. Knoxville: University of Tennessee Press, 1991.

Roth, Cecil. *The Intellectual Activities of Medieval English Jewry*. London: Oxford University Press, 1949.

Rubenstein, Jeffrey L. "From Mythic Motifs to Sustained Myth: The Revision of Rabbinic Traditions in Medieval Midrashim." *Harvard Theological Review* 89 (1996): 131–59.

–. *Talmudic Stories: Narrative Art, Composition, and Culture*. Baltimore: Johns Hopkins University Press, 1999.

Ryding, William W. *Structure in Medieval Narrative*. The Hague: Mouton, 1971.

Sabar, Yona. "Kurdistani Realia and Attitudes as Reflected in the Midrashic-Aggadic Literature of the Kurdish Jews." Pages 287–96 in *Studies in Jewish Folklore: Proceedings of a Regional Conference of the Association for Jewish Studies, Chicago, May 1–3, 1977*. Edited by Frank Talmage. Cambridge, Mass.: Association for Jewish Studies, 1980.

–. "תפסיר להפטרה של שמיני דפסח (ישעיה י,לב–יב,ו) בארמית חדשה של יהודי כורדיסטאן [A Commentary on Haftarah of the Eighth Day of Passover (Isa 10:32–12:6) in Neo-Aramaic of the Jews of Kurdistan]." Pages 317–32 in *מחקרים באגדה ובפולקלור יהודי [Studies in Aggadah and Jewish Folklore]*. Edited by Issachar Ben-Ami, Joseph Dan and Dov Noy. Jerusalem: Magnes Press, 1983.

–. "תפסיר למקרא ופיוטים בלשונם הארמית של יהודי כורדיסתאן [Paraphrases of Bible and Piyyutim in the Aramaic of the Jews of Kurdistan]." *Sefunot* 10 (1966): 335–412.

Sabar, Yona, translator. *Peshat Vayehi Beshallah: A Neo-Aramaic Midrash on Beshallah*. Wiesbaden: Otto Harrassowitz, 1976.

Salzer, Anselm. "Passion Plays," in *The Catholic Encyclopedia*. 1911. Cited 14 March 2008. Online: http://www.newadvent.org/cathen/11531a.htm.

Saperstein, Marc. "Jewish Preachers and Their Literary Remains." *Jewish Quarterly Review* 87:1–2 (1996): 147–55.

–. *Jewish Preaching, 1200–1800 : An Anthology*. New Haven: Yale University Press, 1989.

Sarason, Richard. "The Petihot in Leviticus Rabba: 'Oral Homilies' or Redactional Constructions?" *Journal for Jewish Studies* 33 (1982): 557–65.

Sarna, Nahum. "Hebrew and Bible Studies in Medieval Spain." Pages 323–66 in *The Sephardi Heritage*. Edited by Richard David Barnett. London: Valentine, Mitchell, 1971.

Sautman, Francesca, Diana Conchado, and Giuseppe C. Di Scipio, eds. *Telling Tales: Medieval Narratives and the Folk Tradition*. New York: St. Martin's Press, 1998.

Schäfer, Peter. *The Hidden and Manifest God: Some Major Themes in Early Jewish Mysticism*. Albany: State University of New York Press, 1992.

–. *Mirror of His Beauty: Feminine Images of God from the Bible to the Early Kabbalah*. Princeton: Princeton University Press, 2002.

Schäfer, Peter, and Hans G. Kippenberg, eds. *Envisioning Magic: A Princeton Seminar and Symposium*. Leiden: Brill, 1997.

Schechter, Solomon. "Fragments of a Zadokite Work." *Documents of Jewish Sectaries edited from Hebrew MSS. in the Cairo Genizah Collection, now in the possession of the University Library, Cambridge, Volume I*. Cambridge: Cambridge University Press, 1910. Repr., New York: Ktav, 1970.

Scheindlin, Raymond. "Medieval Jewish Literature." Pages 127–66 in *From Mesopotamia to Modernity*. Edited by Burton L. Visotzky and David Fishman. Boulder CO: Westview Press, 1999.

Schmelzer, Menahem. " פירוש אלפביטין, פירוש על י"ג פיוטים ארמיים לר' בנימין בן אברהם מן הענוים [*Perush Alfabeitin*: An Explication of Thirteen Aramaic *Piyyutim* by R. Benjamin ben Abraham min haAnavim]." Pages 1:167–274 in *מחקרים ומקורות [Texts and Studies]*. Edited by H. Z. Dimitrovsky. New York: Jewish Theological Seminary, 1977.

Scholem, Gershom. *Jewish Gnosticism, Merkabah Mysticism, and Talmudic Tradition*. New York: Jewish Theological Seminary, 1960.

–. *Major Trends in Jewish Mysticism*. New York: Schocken Books, 1961.

–. "Metatron." Pages 11:1445 in *Encyclopaedia Judaica*. Jerusalem: Keter, 1972.

Schor, Naomi. *Reading in Detail: Aesthetics and the Feminine*. New York: Methuen, 1987.

Schwarzbaum, Haim, and Eli Yassif, eds. *Jewish Folklore between East and West*. Beer-Sheva: Ben-Gurion University of the Negev Press, 1989.

Segal, Alan F. *Two Powers in Heaven: Early Rabbinic Reports about Christianity and Gnosticism*. Boston: Brill, 2002.

Sermoneta, Giuseppe. *Alfabetin. Traduzione giudeo-siciliana in caratteri ebraici del servizio della Pentecoste*. Palermo: Centro di Studi Filologici e Linguistici, 1994.

Shah, Idries. *Oriental Magic*. London: Octagon Press, 1968.

Shapira, Anat. *מדרש עשרת הדברות [Midrash on the Ten Commandments: Text, Sources and Interpretation]*. Jerusalem: Bialik Institute, 2005.

Sharot, Stephen. "Jewish Millennial-Messianic Movements: A Comparison of Medieval Communities." Pages 61-87 in *Comparative Studies in Society and History*. Edited by Todd Endelman. Ann Arbor: University of Michigan, 1997.

Shaw, George Bernard. *Plays Pleasant*. London: Penguin Classics, 2003.

Shemesh, Yael. "Measure for Measure in the David Stories." *Scandinavian Journal of the Old Testament* 17:1 (2003): 89–109.

Shiloni, Isaac, and Arthur B. Hyman, eds. *ילקוט שמעוני [Yalkut Shimoni: A Critical Edition]*. Jerusalem: Mosad haRav Kook, 1973.

Shinan, Avigdor. "Echoes from Ancient Synagogues: Vocatives and 'Emendations' in the Aramaic Targums to the Pentateuch." *Jewish Quarterly Review* 81:3–4 (1991): 353–64.

–. "Live Translation: On the Nature of the Aramaic Targums to the Pentateuch." *Prooftexts* 3:1 (1983): 41–9.

–. "Sermons, Targums, and the Reading from Scriptures in the Ancient Synagogue." Pages 97–110 in *The Synagogue in Late Antiquity*. Edited by Lee I. Levine. Philadelphia: American Schools of Oriental Research, 1987.

–. "Targumic Additions in Targum Pseudo Jonathan." *Textus* 16 (1991): 139–55.

–. "דברי הימים של משה רבנו [Chronicles of Moses]." *HaSifrut* 24 (1977): 110–16.

–. "האגדה בתרגומים הארמיים ה"ארץ-ישראליים" לתורה: עיצובה, תכניה ומקומה בספרות חז"ל [The Form and Content of the Aggadah in the 'Palestinian' Targumim on the Pentateuch and its Place within Rabbinic Literature." Doctoral dissertation, Hebrew University, 1977.

–. "מדרשת הפסוק אל האגדה החופשית: פרק בתולדות הסיפור המקראי המורחב [From Exegesis of a Verse to Free-standing Aggadah: A Chapter in the History of the Expanded Biblical Narrative]." *Mech'k'rei Yerushalayim b'sifrut ivrit* 5 (1984): 203–20.

–. *מקרא אחד ותרגומים הרבה [Biblical Story as Reflected in its Aramaic Translations]*. Tel Aviv: Hakibbutz Hameuhad, 1993.

–. *תרגום ואגדה בו [The Embroidered Targum: The Aggadah in Targum Pseudo-Jonathan of the Pentateuch]*. Jerusalem: Magnes Press, 1992.

Sirat, Colette. *Hebrew Manuscripts of the Middle Ages*. Cambridge: Cambridge University Press, 2002.

Sivan, Daniel. *A Grammar of the Ugaritic Language*. Leiden: Brill, 1997.

Smalley, Beryl. *The Study of the Bible in the Middle Ages*. Oxford: Basil Blackwell and Mott, 1940. Repr., Notre Dame, Ind.: University of Notre Dame Press, 1964).

Sokoloff, Michael, and Joseph Yahalom. "Aramaic Piyyutim from the Byzantine Period." *Jewish Quarterly Review* 85:3 (1985): 309–21.

Solomon, Bishop of Basra. *The Book of the Bee*. Translated by Ernest A. Wallis Budge. Oxford: Clarendon Press, 1886.

Sperber, Daniel. *Magic and Folklore in Rabbinic Literature*. Ramat-Gan: Bar-Ilan University Press, 1994.

Spiegel, Shalom. *The Last Trial: On the Legends and Lore of the Command to Abraham to Offer Isaac as a Sacrifice*. Translated by Judah Goldin. New York: Behrman House, 1979.

Steinmetz, Devorah. "Beyond the Verse: Midrash Aggadah as Interpretation of Biblical Narrative." *AJS Review* 30:2 (2006): 325–45.

–. "A Portrait of Miriam in Rabbinic Midrash." *Prooftexts* 8 (1988): 35–65.

Stemberger, Günter. "Midráš Wa-yoša'. Fuentes y tendencias de una narración medieval." *'Ilu: revista de ciencias de las religiones* 3 (2000): 11–27.

–. "Midrasch Wa-yosha–Quellen und Tendenzen einer mittelalterlichen Erzählung." Pages 587–601 in *Judaica Minora II* (Texts and Studies in Ancient Judaism, 138). Tübingen: Mohr Siebeck, 2010.

–. "Samael und Uzza: zur Rolle der Dämonen im späten Midrasch." Pages 636–61 in *Die Dämonen: die Dämonologie der israelitisch-jüdischen und frühchristlichen Literatur im Kontext ihrer Umwelt*. Edited by Armin Lange. Tübingen: Mohr Siebeck, 2003.

Stern, David. *Parables in Midrash: Narrative and Exegesis in Rabbinic Literature*. Cambridge, Mass.: Harvard University Press, 1991.

–, ed. *The Anthology in Jewish Literature*. New York: Oxford University Press, 2004.

Sternberg, Meir. *Expositional Modes and Temporal Ordering in Fiction*. Bloomington: Indiana University Press, 1993.

–. "How Narrativity Makes a Difference." *Narrative* 9 (2001): 115–22.

–. *The Poetics of Biblical Narrative: Ideological Literature and the Drama of Reading*. Bloomington: Indiana University Press, 1985.

Stillman, Norman A. *The Jews of Arab Lands: A History and Source Book*. Philadelphia: Jewish Publication Society, 1979.

Stock, Brian. *Listening for the Text: On the Uses of the Past*. Philadelphia: University of Pennsylvania Press, 1996.

Strack, Hermann Leberecht, and Paul Billerbeck. *Kommentar zum neuen Testament aus Talmud und Midrasch*. 6 vols. Munich: Beck, 1965 (orig. 1922).

Strack, Hermann Leberecht, and Günter Stemberger. *Introduction to the Talmud and Midrash*. Minneapolis: Fortress Press, 1992.

Strohm, Paul. *Theory and the Premodern Text*. Minneapolis: University of Minnesota Press, 2000.

Talmage, Frank, and Barry Walfish. *Apples of Gold in Settings of Silver: Studies in Medieval Jewish Exegesis and Polemics*. Toronto: Pontifical Institute of Mediaeval Studies, 1999.

Talmon, Shemaryahu. "Biblical Concept of Jerusalem," *The Journal of Ecumenical Studies* 8 (1971): 300–16.

Tannus, Jarays. *עימות נעים: מילון המילים הזהות והדומות בשתי השפות: העברית והערבית [Apt Parallels: A Dictionary of Hebrew and Arabic Cognates]*. Akko: Abu Rahamun, 2006.

Ta-Shma, Israel M. *Creativity and Tradition: Studies in Medieval Rabbinic Scholarship, Literature and Thought*. Cambridge, Mass.: Harvard University Center for Jewish Studies, 2006.

–. "The 'Open' Book in Medieval Hebrew Literature: The Problem of Authorized Editions." *Bulletin of the John Rylands University Library* 75:3 (1993): 7–24.

–. "Rabbinic Literature in the Middle Ages: 1000–1492." Pages 219–40 in *The Oxford Handbook of Jewish Studies*. Edited by Martin Goodman. Oxford: Oxford University Press, 2002.

–. *כנסת מחקרים: עיונים בהסטוריה היהודית ובספרותה [A Collection of Studies: Explorations in Jewish History and its Literature]*. 3 vols. Jerusalem: Bialik Institute, 2004.

–. "לתולדות הקשרים התרבותיים בין יהודי ביזנטיון ואשכנז [Toward a History of Cultural Contacts between the Jews of Byzantium and Ashkenaz]." Pages 61–70 in *מאה שערים: עיונים בעולמם הרוחני של ישראל בימי הביניים [One Hundred Gates: Studies of the Spiritual World of Israel in the Middle Ages]*. Edited by Ezra Fleischer, et al. Jerusalem: Magnes Press, 2001.

Teugels, Lieve M., and Rivka Ulmer. *Recent Developments in Midrash Research: Proceedings of the 2002 and 2003 SBL Consultation on Midrash*. Piscataway, N.J.: Gorgias Press, 2005.

Theodor, Julius. “Zur Composition der agadischen Homilien.” *MGJW*, Vol. 28 (1879) 3:97–113, 4:164–175, 6:271–78, 8:337–50, 9:408–18, 10:455–462; Vol. 29 (1880) 1:19–23; Vol. 30 (1881) 11:500–10.

Thompson, Reginald Campbell. *Semitic Magic: Its Origins and Development*. New York: Ktav, 1971.

Thompson, Stith. *Motif-index of Folk-literature: A Classification of Narrative Elements in Folktales, Ballads, Myths, Fables, Mediaeval Romances, Exempla, Fabliaux, Jest-books, and Local Legends*. Bloomington: Indiana University Press, 1955.

Touitou, Elazar. *הפשטות המתחדשים בכל יום: עיונים בפירושו של רשב"ם לתורה [The Contextual Meanings that are Discovered Anew Each Day: Studies in the Torah Commentary of Rashbam]*. Ramat-Gan: Bar Ilan University, 2003.

Towner, W. Sibley. “Form Criticism of Rabbinic Literature: Laws of Transmission Governing Oral Literature.” *Journal of Jewish Studies* 24:2 (1973): 101–18.

Tudor, Adrian P. “Preaching, Storytelling, and the Performance of Short Pious Narratives.” Pages 141–53 in *Performing Medieval Narrative*. Edited by Evelyn Birge Vitz, Nancy Freeman Regalado and Marilyn Lawrence. Cambridge: D.S. Brewer, 2005.

Urowitz-Freudenstein, Anna. “Hammer, Rock, Sword: Exegesis and Folklore in Midrashic Narrative.” Paper presented to the Society of Biblical Literature, 2000.

van Bekkum, Wout Jac. “Jewish Messianic Expectations in the Age of Heraclius.” Pages 95-112 in *The Reign of Heraclius (610–641): Crisis and Confrontation*. Edited by G. J. Reinink and Bernard H. Stolte. Leuven, Belgium: Peeters, 2002.

Venice Haggadah. Venice: Giovanni da Gara, 1609.

Verbeke, Werner, Ludovicus Milis, and Jean Goossens. *Medieval Narrative Sources: A Gateway into the Medieval Mind*. Leuven, Belgium: Leuven University Press, 2005.

Vermès, Géza. *Scripture and Tradition in Judaism: Haggadic Studies*. Leiden: E. J. Brill, 1961.

Vinokur, Roman. “Acoustic Noise as a Non-lethal Weapon.” *Sound and Vibration* (2004): 19–23.

Visotzky, Burton L. *Golden Bells and Pomegranates*. Tübingen: Mohr Siebeck, 2003.

–. “The Literature of the Rabbis.” Pages 71–102 in *From Mesopotamia to Modernity*. Edited by Burton L. Visotzky and David E. Fishman. Boulder, Col.: Westview Press, 1999.

–. *The Midrash on Proverbs*. New Haven: Yale University Press, 1992.

–. “The Misnomers '*Petihah*' and 'Homiletic Midrash' as Descriptions for Leviticus Rabbah and Pesikta de-Rav Kahana,” *Jewish Studies Quarterly* (2011): 19–31.

–. “Most Tender and Fairest of Women: A Study in the Transmission of Aggada.” *Harvard Theological Review* 76:4 (1983): 403–18.

–. “On Critical Editions of Midrash.” Pages 59–77 in *Recent Developments in Midrash Research: Proceedings of the 2002 and 2003 SBL Consultation on Midrash*. Edited by Carol Bakhos and Rivka Ulmer. Piscataway, N.J.: Gorgias Press, 2005.

–. *מדרש משלי [Midrash on Proverbs]*. New York: Jewish Theological Seminary of America, 1990.

Vitz, Evelyn Birge. *Medieval Narrative and Modern Narratology: Subjects and Objects of Desire*. New York: New York University Press, 1989.

Wasserstrom, Steven. “Jewish Pseudepigrapha in Muslim Literature: A Bibliographical and Methodological Sketch.” Pages 87–114 in *Tracing the Threads: Studies in the Vitality of Jewish Pseudepigrapha*. Edited by John C. Reeves. Atlanta: Scholars Press, 1994.

Wies-Campagner, Elisabeth. "Midrasch Wajoscha." Doctoral dissertation, University of Vienna, 2007.

–. *Midrasch Wajoscha: Edition-Tradition-Interpretation*. Berlin: de Gruyter, 2009.

Wertheimer, Solomon Aaron, and Abraham Joseph Wertheimer. *בתי - במדרשי הגניזה מדרשות [Midrashim from the Genizah - Batei midrashot]*. 2nd ed. 2 vols. Jerusalem: Ktav v'Sefer, 1968.

Wheeler, Brannon M. *Moses in the Quran and Islamic Exegesis*. London: Routledge Curzon, 2002.

Wünsche, August. *Aus Israels Lehrhallen*. Leipzig: Eduard Pfeiffer, 1907.

Yaeri, Abraham. *תולדות חג שמחת תורה [History of the Festival of Simhat Torah]*. Jerusalem: Mosad haRav Kook, 1964.

Yahalom, Joseph. "The Aramaic *Alfabetin*: From Eretz-Israel to Italy." *Materia Giudaica* 3 (1997): 56–60.

–. "*Piyyut* as Poetry." Pages 111–26 in *The Synagogue in Late Antiquity*. Edited by Lee I. Levine. Philadelphia: American Schools of Oriental Research, 1987.

–. "The Temple and the City in Liturgical Hebrew Poetry." Pages 270–94 in *The History of Jerusalem: The Early Muslim Period, 638–1099*. Edited by Joshua Prawer and Haggai Ben-Shammai. Jerusalem: Yad Izhak Ben-Zvi, 1996.

–. "אזל משה בפפירוס [Ezel Moshe according to a Papyrus]." *Tarbiz* 47 (1978): 173–82.

–. "על תוקפן של יצירות ספרות כמקור לבירור שאלות היסטוריות [On the Strength of Literary Works as a Source for Clarification of Historical Questions]." *Cathedra* 11 (1979): 125–33.

Yahalom, Joseph, and Michael Sokoloff. *שירת בני מערבא [Jewish Palestinian Aramaic Poetry from Late Antiquity]*. Jerusalem: Israel Academy of Sciences and Humanities, 1999.

Yamauchi, Edwin. "Aramaic Magic Bowls." *Journal of American Oriental Society* 85:4 (1965): 511–23.

Yassif, Eli. *The Hebrew Folktale: History, Genre, Meaning*. Translated by Jacqueline Teitelbaum. Bloomington: Indiana University Press, 1999.

–. *Jewish Folklore: An Annotated Bibliography*. New York: Garland, 1986.

–. "הסיפורת העברית בארצות המזרח: התגבשותה בימי הביניים ומערבה לעת החדשה [Hebrew Narrative in the East: Its Crystallization in the Middle Ages and it Western Movement Prior to the Modern Period]." *P'amim* 26 (1986): 53–70.

–. *סיפור העם העברי: תולדותיו, סוגותיו ומשמעותו [The Hebrew Folktale: Its History, Types and Significance]*. Jerusalem: Bialik Institute, 1994.

–. *ספר הזכרונות הוא דברי הימים לירחמיאל [Book of Remembrances: Chronicles of Yerahmiel]*. Ramat Aviv: Tel Aviv University, 2001.

–. "ספר המעשים: לאופיו, מקורותיו, והפשעתו של קובץ סיפורים מזמנם של בעלי התוספות [Sefer haMaasim: Its Characteristics, Sources and the Influence of a Story Collection from the Time of the Tosafot]." *Tarbiz* 53 (1983–4): 409–29.

–. *עקידת יצחק: מחקרים בהתפתחותה של מסורת ספרותית [The Binding of Isaac: Research on the Development of a Literary Tradition]*. Jerusalem: Makor, 1977.

Yehiel, Nathan ben, and updated by Benjamin Musafiyah. *ספר ערוך השלם [Sefer Arukh haShalem - A Medieval Lexicon]*. Vienna: Menorah, 1926.

Ziegler, Ignaz. *Die Königsgleichnisse des Midrasch*. Breslau: S. Schottlaender, 1903.

Zornberg, Avivah. *The Particulars of Rapture: Reflections on Exodus*. New York: Doubleday, 2001.

Zunz, Leopold. *Die gottesdienstlichen Vorträge der Juden historisch entwickelt*. Berlin, 1832.

–. *Literaturgeschichte der synagogalen Poesie*. Berlin: L. Gerschel Verlagsbuchhandlung, 1865.
–. *הדרשות בישראל [Derashot in Israel]*. Translated by Chanoch Albeck. Jerusalem: Bialik Institute, 1946.

Index of Textual References

Hebrew Bible

Philo and Josephus

Apocrypha, Pseudepigrapha and Texts from Qumran

Graeco Roman Authors

Early Christian Literature

Targum

Mishnah, Tosefta and the Talmudim

Midrash

Medieval Jewish Commentary, Prayerbooks, Halakha and Varia

Non-Jewish Varia

Index of Subjects

Texts and Studies in Medieval and Early Modern Judaism

Alphabetical Index